SCHOOLS, VIOLENCE, AND SOCIETY

SCHOOLS, VIOLENCE, AND SOCIETY

Edited by Allan M. Hoffman

PRAEGER

Westport, Connecticut
London

Library of Congress Cataloging-in-Publication Data

Schools, violence, and society / [edited] by Allan M. Hoffman.
    p. cm.
   Includes bibliographical references and index.
   ISBN 0–275–94978–8 (hardcover : alk. paper).—ISBN 0–275–95506–0
(pbk. : alk. paper)
    1. School violence—United States. I. Hoffman, Allan M. (Allan
Michael)
   LB3013.3.S377   1996
   371.7′8—dc20   95–40089

British Library Cataloguing in Publication Data is available.

Library of Congress Catalog Card Number: 95–40089
ISBN: 0–275–94978–8
    0–275–95506–0 (pbk.)

First published in 1996

Praeger Publishers, 88 Post Road West, Westport, CT 06881
An imprint of Greenwood Publishing Group, Inc.

Printed in the United States of America

The paper used in this book complies with the
Permanent Paper Standard issued by the National
Information Standards Organization (Z39.48–1984).
P

This book is dedicated to the children in our schools. It is my hope and prayer that in some small way this book will help bring about a peaceful and tranquil environment where learning can take place and flourish.

Contents

Acknowledgments

I owe a debt of gratitude and thanks to many people who helped make this book a reality. I would like to thank Yvonne Thayer of the Gloucester County Schools (Virginia) for the time she spent with me on the telephone discussing the topic of violence and its impact on our nation's schools. Richard Verdugo of the National Education Association (Washington, D.C.) deserves a special thanks for providing insights to the scope of the problem of violence from a national perspective. S. D. Vestermark read the entire manuscript in draft form and provided invaluable suggestions regarding the format of the book. Nancy Campbell is deserving of special thanks for her editorial efforts and for efforts in helping produce this volume. She responded to all "cries for help" with lightening speed. Sher Quaday of the Harvard School of Public Health; Kami Amirheshmat of California State University, Dominguez Hills; Ariel Zhuang, New York City Public Schools; Christie Bourgeois, former member of Texas Governor Ann Richards' staff; Loretta Stock, Gaithersburg, Maryland; Mary Hatwood Futrell of George Washington University; Randal Summers of Laguna Niguel, California; and each of the contributing authors deserve a special note of thanks.

Allan A. Foster deserves special mention for his computer and desktop publishing efforts. Without his hard work and untiring efforts, the book you now hold in your hands could never have become a reality. My very good friend and neighbor, Melinda Schaffner, is to be thanked for her sound legal advice which has clearly contributed to this volume. I also wish to thank the staff of the Greenwood Publishing Group.

Of very special note is my family. I owe them more than mere words can adequately say. To DeeDee for her untiring hard work and motivation. She is both an inspiration and critic. Her attention to detail was instrumental in the creation of a quality product. Emily helped research areas of this book and without her efforts,

I might still be in the library or out in the field conducting research and interviews. Andrew has been extremely tolerant and helpful. He deserves thanks for understanding when I couldn't wrestle or play ball because the manuscript was due. To each member of my family, you are special, and thanks for putting up with deadlines, revisions, and having to listen to new developments in the "violence book."

A.M.H.
Santa Ana, California

Introduction

On a bright, sunny day with wispy clouds and a gentle breeze, the faint laughter of children can be heard. The school yard, a place where children play with friends, jump rope, throw and kick balls, trade cards, laugh, and just hang out in this peaceful—albeit temporary—sanctuary. Inside the school, a warm welcome smile from the teacher, grateful for the apple from a kind student. The school, a place to read and write and create and learn. In the decades to come the sounds of laughter fade, and the once hospitable sanctuary is transformed into a place of fear. Instead of apples, the children bring guns to school. Instead of games or laughter, there are profanity, assaults, drugs, and alcohol.

What happened? We have seemingly awakened from a peaceful, idyllic slumber to find a world gone mad. Violence has taken center stage. It is a prime concern of our society and has become the focus of investigative journalism on television and in our newspapers. It has struck the workplace, with workers taking the lives of others. It has become a major issue in political elections, resulting in the enactment of various crime legislation and a "get tough on crime" attitude among politicians. And it has crept into our schools.

It has been suggested that our education system mirrors the dynamics of our society. But just how prevalent is violence in our schools? What form does it take? What are its root causes? What effect has violence had on students, teachers, administrators, and the learning process in general? What can be done to combat this menace and once again provide a safe and secure place of learning—an intellectual sanctuary—for our children? Finally, who is responsible for dealing with violence in schools? These are the questions addressed by this book.

This overview refers to specific chapters in this book as they relate to these topical questions. For the sake of brevity, we do not mention some of the chapters here; however, the editor and publishers gratefully acknowledge all of the authors for their significant contribution to this work.

HOW PREVALENT IS VIOLENCE IN OUR SCHOOLS?

Mary Hatwood Futrell in "Violence in the Classroom: A Teacher's Perspective" states that disagreements between students are more likely to be settled with some type of weapon than with an "old-fashioned fistfight." Nor is the prevalence of school violence restricted to public or urban schools: "public, private, and nonsectarian schools have all experienced an increase in school violence." Victims of school violence cover the spectrum: "over two thousand students and forty teachers are physically attacked on school grounds every hour of every school day each year."

WHAT FORM DOES IT TAKE?

Jennifer C. Friday in "Weapon-Carrying in Schools" reports that 20 to 26 percent of students have carried a weapon of some type to school. In 1990, 4 percent carried a gun; in 1991, 6 percent; and in 1993, the number increased to 8 percent of students. In addition, approximately 2 percent of teachers have carried guns to school.

In "Gangs and School Safety" Kenneth S. Trump suggests that our awareness and response to gang behavior vary on a continuum from lack of awareness (not knowing what to look for or how to respond) to overreaction. Offering insights into gang development and how to recognize gang behavior, he suggests strategies for managing gangs in the school.

WHAT ARE ITS ROOT CAUSES?

In "Media and Television Violence: Effects on Violence, Aggression, and Antisocial Behaviors in Children," Daniel John Derksen and Victor S. Strasburger point out that the media-portrayed violence continues to have "powerful negative effects on American children"—specifically, as a contributing factor to real-life violence.

Jeffrey J. Haugaard and Margaret M. Feerick, in "The Influence of Child Abuse and Family Violence on Violence in the Schools," discuss whether being abused at home or witnessing violence in the home increases the likelihood of a child's aggressiveness in school. They maintain that there is a correlational, not causal, link between abuse and later school violence, although "there is a fairly robust association between physical abuse and subsequent aggression in children."

WHAT HAS BEEN ITS EFFECT?

In "Victims of Violence: Helping Kids Cope," Melba F. Coleman cites sobering figures from the Children's Defense Fund. Every day in America:

—13 children die from guns.
—7,945 children are reported abused or neglected.
—3 children die from abuse.
—2,255 students drop out of school.
—100,000 children are homeless.

Coleman points out that "[d]espite the staggering statistics, most of these children are left to navigate the stages of grief on their own."

Nel Noddings suggests in "Learning to Care and to Be Cared For" that "the widespread violence and alienation so characteristic of life in the United States" results at least in part from the lack of a caring climate in the schools. Whereas "violence-prevention programs may add the skills and knowledge needed to resist particular forms of violence…students must believe that the adults in their schools and communities care about them, that their well-being and growth matter."

WHAT CAN BE DONE?

S. D. Vestermark, Jr., in "Critical Decisions, Critical Elements in an Effective School Security Program," discusses the need for professionally developed school security programs—whether police-based or school-based—as a long-term solution to increasing school violence. He stresses, however, that practical security measures (such as police officers and metal detectors) must "become part of the total blend of activities supporting educational objectives."

In "From Fight or Flight to Collaboration: A Framework for Understanding Individual and Institutional Development in the School," Steven Brion-Meisels and Robert L. Selman discuss how "developmental changes in children's social awareness" enable them to deal with an ever–broadening range of social problems—and how this, in turn, can affect how schools as institutions deal with problems such as violence.

Several chapters—"Waging Peace in Our Schools: The Resolving Conflict Creatively Program" (Linda Lantieri, William DeJong, and Janet Dutrey) and "Strategies to Reduce School Violence: The New Mexico Center for Dispute Resolution" (Melinda Smith)—discuss specific programs used by various school districts to prevent or deal with violence. Others—"Violence in Schools: The Texas Initiative" (former Governor Ann W. Richards and Christie Bourgeois) and "NEA's Perspective and Policies on Violence in Schools" (Keith Geiger)—offer ideas on how state and local government as well as education organizations have dealt with issues of school violence.

WHO IS RESPONSIBLE?

Gwendolyn J. Cooke in "Safe School for All" perhaps answers this question most directly: "The responsibility for change rests with every facet of our society. Gun manufacturers, filmmakers, educators, parents, police, health providers, legislators, and the media—none is exempt from the challenge." We are, all of us, responsible for saving the children.

—Allan M. Hoffman

Part I

THE PROBLEM OF SCHOOL VIOLENCE

1

Violence in the Classroom: A Teacher's Perspective

Mary Hatwood Futrell

> If we can put a man on the moon, why can't we stop violence in our schools?
>
> –Student asking a question
of President Clinton[1]

The public's concern about violence in schools has been manifested in media stories, congressional testimony, and numerous studies and reports that vividly underscore the pervasiveness of the problem. Nowhere, however, is the magnitude of the nation's concern about school violence reflected more urgently than in Goal 6 of the Goals 2000: Educate America Act adopted by Congress and signed into law by President Clinton in March 1994. Goal 6 states that "by the year 2000, every school in America will be free of drugs and violence and will offer a disciplined environment conducive to learning." The supporting narrative for this goal states that "no child or youth should be fearful on the way to school, be afraid while there, or have to cope with pressures to make unhealthy choices."[2]

Students in school environments where violence occurs will not or cannot concentrate on the achievement of rigorous standards, stay in school, perform at high academic levels, and excel intellectually. When teachers and students are more concerned about being victimized than about education, they cannot concentrate on teaching and learning.

This chapter focuses on how teachers and students perceive the problem of violence in schools. First, it addresses school violence as a strong impediment to education reform. Second, it focuses on teachers' and students' perceptions about the problem of violence in our schools. The chapter synthesizes three major reports on violence in our schools: *The National Education Goals Report for 1993: Building a Nation of Learners;* The Metropolitan Life Survey of the American

Teacher 1993, *Violence in America's Public Schools;* and the U.S. Department of Justice report, *School Crime: A National Crime Victimization Survey Report.*[3] It also includes anecdotes about school violence gleaned from my seventeen years as a middle and high school teacher. Third, the chapter outlines some recommendations about what schools and communities can do to stem the tide of violence in our schools.

A VIGNETTE

The best way to illustrate teachers' perceptions of school violence is through a vignette: The tardy bell has just rung, signaling that students should be in their homeroom or first-period class. It is also the signal for Mrs. Johnson and the other teachers standing near their classroom doors to prepare for another day with the approximately one thousand students who attend North Lakes Middle School. The school is located in a bedroom community called North Lakes, which is just outside a large urban center in one of the nation's midwestern states.

Mrs. Johnson has taught in the North Lakes community for her entire twenty-year teaching career, first in one of the elementary schools and then in the middle school. Her husband teaches at the high school and coaches football and track. They have watched as the community changed from a small town to part of a huge metropolitan area connected by superhighways, beltways, and subways. North Lakes has always prided itself on its economic stability, pluralism, and "progressive" politics. In addition, it has always taken great pride in its education system.

Most students are from middle-income families; however, about 25 percent of the students' families are in the low-income bracket. The student body reflects a rich ethnic, cultural, racial, and religious diversity. The school district has been recognized nationally for its innovative programs, especially in areas such as technology, science, mathematics, music, and foreign languages. It also has a long record of successes in extracurricular activities, including its award-winning debate program and school newspaper production. Moreover, its athletic teams are recognized as powerhouses in crew, track, and basketball.

The faculty is considered to be exceptionally well qualified and committed. As a matter of fact, the district has a reputation for attracting and retaining one of the best teaching and administrative staffs in the state. The Johnsons and the vast majority of their colleagues have enjoyed long-term relationships with the school district and the community.

The North Lakes community does not believe it has a serious school violence problem like those described by teachers in other school districts throughout the state. For the most part, discipline problems have been minor infractions such as being tardy, failing to complete assignments, talking in class, or smoking in undesignated areas. Although a few instances of verbal abuse toward faculty and students have been reported, major incidents of physical violence at North Lakes Middle School are few. Incidents are handled quickly and firmly by the teachers and administrators, usually with complete cooperation from parents. The message has always been strong and clear: the school district of North Lakes will maintain safe environments in all of its schools in order to maximize learning and teaching.

The Johnsons have noticed that the issue of violence in schools is raised everywhere. It dominates conversations at professional meetings and constantly appears in newspaper and magazine articles and in television exposes. Media reports underscore the fact that violence in schools is no longer viewed as an urban problem, but one that affects rural and suburban communities as well.

Over the past decade, however, although the emphasis on cultivating academic excellence remains strong, the ethos within some of the North Lakes schools has changed gradually, but steadily. Within North Lakes Middle School, for instance, teachers have expressed frustration at students' lack of willingness to assume responsibility for their class work, often reflecting an attitude of "Why do I have to do this?" or "I'm too busy to do homework" or "If this will not help me get a job or into college, I'm not going to do it." More and more students also exhibit hostility if teachers insist that the work be completed. Some students have even suggested that they should get a grade simply for showing up in class and not causing trouble.

In most classrooms, when the teacher signals that the class is about to start, the students settle down to work. Increasing numbers of teachers, however, indicate that it takes longer for students to settle down, and that they interrupt class frequently by talking, teasing, loitering, playing cassette tapes, or kidding around. Teachers have also noted that students seem to become angry much more quickly than in the past; they are less willing to control their tempers or discuss problems in a calm manner.

The other day, a fight almost started in one class when a student became angry because another took a pair of sunglasses from her. When the second student failed to return the glasses, the two started arguing loudly and threatening each other. The teacher quickly intervened, retrieved the glasses, and requested that the students report to her at the end of the school day. Unfortunately, this incident created tension in the class, and it took a while before the situation calmed down and the students resumed their work. At the end of the day, the student to whom the glasses belonged returned, but the other student did not.

Last week a group of boys were disciplined for fighting in the cafeteria. The fight started because some of the boys felt they were being deliberately bumped by other boys as they walked through the hallway on their way to and from class. Even though the boys who bumped them apologized, the others did not believe their apology was sincere. When one of the boys was bumped in the cafeteria, he shoved back, and the fight started and quickly became a melee. The teachers and monitors in the cafeteria were able to stop the fight, but not before chairs and tables were overturned, food and drinks were spilled all over the floor, and utter chaos prevailed. Those involved in the fight were taken to the principal's office. Parents of all the students were contacted. Some of the parents were surprised that their child was involved in the incident; a few seemed to resent being asked to come to the school to confer on the matter.

The boys who initiated the fight were suspended for three days and informed that their parents would have to return with them in order for the students to be reinstated in school. Others were given a warning and assigned to two days of in-school suspension, which meant they were not allowed to go to their regular classes. Instead, they were assigned to a special classroom for the duration of their punishment.

Mrs. Johnson and her husband often compare notes about what is happening in the school district, especially at the schools where they work. Mr. Johnson has expressed increasing frustration and concern about students' behavior at the high school. Frequently, they hear colleagues counting the days until the end of the school year or until their retirement.

Earlier this year the administration heard rumors that some students were bringing weapons to school. A faculty meeting was held, and all staff members were asked to be vigilant in monitoring the school and campus. Because the rumors persisted over the next couple of days, it was decided that a surprise search of students' lockers would be conducted. The decision to conduct the search was authorized because the district did not want to take any risks. During the past couple of years, several students were caught on or near school property with guns, knives, and other weapons. Working cooperatively with law enforcement officers, the search was conducted, and it yielded several knives and a couple of bully sticks.

Searches for weapons are a new phenomenon in the North Lakes schools. However, the administration and faculty believe that they are a necessary precaution. They do not want to experience an incident like the one that took place in the neighboring county when rumors about students bringing weapons into the school went unchecked. A teacher was shot when he inadvertently walked in on a gun sale occurring in the boys' restroom. The teacher survived but was unable to return to school for the remainder of that year. The boy who shot the teacher said it was an accident. He was arrested, however, and is still awaiting sentencing. As a result of the incident, the relationship between the faculty and the students in the school will never be the same. Fear, distrust, and suspicion have prevailed.

An increasing number of teachers in North Lakes have expressed concern and anger because they feel that the administration and the school board are not doing enough to stem the problem. Teachers often believe they are not told about problems, or state that they hear of them only from students. They are particularly upset that the district's public relations staff has succeeded in playing down most of the incidents. Many believe that protecting the image of the school district is of more concern to the administration than school safety. Others believe that there is a strong denial by the administration and the school board of the North Lakes School District's problem with violence in its schools.

School district officials believe they have been successful in addressing the problem. Nevertheless, in recent months community pressure has escalated to force the school district to develop concrete strategies to respond more quickly and responsibly to acts of violence in school. A special commission consisting of teachers, administrators, parents, students, school board members, and representatives from the community was established by the North Lakes City Council to study the problem and to develop short- and long-term strategies to address the issue of violence in school. The commission had six months to complete its work, including holding public hearings, before reporting to the city council on its findings and recommendations.

As part of its report, the commission is recommending a revised discipline code, at least one guidance counselor in every school, and conflict-resolution programs for all students. The commission is also recommending that the school district develop a mission statement and specify the goals it will use to fulfill that mission. Furthermore, the school district will be required to establish professional development programs for all school personnel on effective strategies for dealing with youth violence. Each school is required to design and implement by the beginning of the new school year a plan to increase parental and community involvement programs.

In addition, the commission is recommending that the school district consider implementing a dress code for all students. The proposal for the dress code is in response to concerns that certain clothing items can be used as weapons (that is, camping boots with metal toes, heavy jewelry, or belts with heavy metal buckles). Furthermore, the commission recommended hiring additional security staff to monitor the halls, cafeteria, and campus grounds. No recommendation has been proposed to install metal detectors in the middle and high schools. Generally, the commission believes that installing metal detectors gives the impression that students are attending a facility for juvenile delinquents rather than a school. The commission believes that the situation in North Lakes does not warrant taking such drastic measures.

VIOLENCE IN SCHOOL TODAY

The situation described in this vignette is being faced by an increasing number of schools today. The issue of school violence, however, is not a new phenomenon. "Discipline in the Public Schools: A Problem of Perception?," an article that appeared in the January 1979 edition of *Phi Delta Kappan* traces the problem back to the 1950s, when the problem was not discipline but juvenile delinquency. John W. Williams, author of the article, wrote that in the 1950s "there seemed to be a marked increase in both the serious and less serious antisocial behavior on the part of our youth."[4]

In 1955, according to Williams, a national study conducted by the National Education Association's Research Division entitled "Discipline in the Public Schools" documented two particularly startling problems: violence committed against teachers and the increased use of narcotics by students. More than twenty years later, the *Phi Delta Kappan* report bore a striking resemblance to that of the 1950s, except that the problem was worse.[5]

Today the possibility that a disagreement among students will be settled with some type of weapon rather than an old-fashioned fistfight has increased significantly. A major difference between violence in the schools in the 1950s and the

1990s is the presence and use of weapons, especially guns. Also, students seem to hold a grudge much longer. Some students wait until the last day of school to settle an incident that occurred weeks or even months earlier.

School violence is not unique either to the public schools or to the nation's urban centers. According to the U.S. Department of Justice, public, private, and nonsectarian schools have all experienced an increase in school violence. Nine percent of public, 7 percent of private, and 6 percent of nonsectarian school students reported being victims of violent acts or property crimes in 1989.[6] Furthermore, media reports indicate that the issue of violence in school is a national problem that has seeped into the very heartland of America. No geographic region is excluded anymore. The findings of a National School Boards Association survey, "Violence in the Schools," of 1,216 administrators indicated that 54 percent of suburban and 64 percent of urban school officials reported more violent acts in their school in 1993 than five years earlier.[7] Newspaper articles report that communities large and small, urban, suburban, and rural—from Chicago, Illinois, to Little Rock, Arkansas, to Walton, New York, to Lorain, Ohio, to Lindhurst, California, to Butte, Montana, to Washington, D.C.—are struggling with the issue of school violence.

Almost forty years after the NEA study on discipline was conducted, the public's attention is once again focused on the issue of discipline and violence in the schools. And that concern is justifiable and accurate. Problems of violence caused by our school age children (in and out of schools) are worse now than they have ever been. Youth violence is on the rise and permeates every segment of our society. That is not to say, however, that all of today's youths are discipline problems or perpetrators of violent acts. To the contrary, the vast majority of our youth are *not* violent and have not committed acts of violence.

Generally speaking, there are three groups of students in a school. Eighty percent of the students rarely break the rules or violate principles. Fifteen percent break the rules on a somewhat regular basis by refusing to accept classroom principles and resisting restrictions. If not given clear expectations and consequences regarding their behavior, these students can disrupt learning for all the other students. The last 5 percent of the students are chronic rule breakers and are generally out of control most of the time. These students are more likely to commit acts of violence in school and in the community.[8]

Before discussing teachers' and students' perceptions about violence in schools, it is necessary to emphasize that lack of discipline, inappropriate and disruptive behavior, and violence are often used interchangeably. Within this chapter, discipline is used to refer to self-control or positive behavior. Inappropriate classroom behavior refers to unacceptable eating or drinking, refusing to cooperate, and talking back to the teacher. Disruptive classroom or in-school behavior includes listening to cassette tapes, taking something from others without their permission, walking around the classroom, talking about non-class-related issues (especially while the lesson is being taught), playing or shoving, arguing, arriving late, or leaving class without the teacher's permission. Violence refers to verbal or physical abuse (including the threat of or the actual use of guns, knives, and other weapons) perpetrated against school staff, students, or others. It also includes vandalism and property crimes (that is, taking someone's belongings without their permission or by force, destruction of property).

Where Does Violence Occur in Schools?

Most teachers believe that violence occurs in hallways or under staircases, in the lunchroom or cafeteria, or in unattended classrooms. Students concur that most acts of violence erupt in these places, but add the gym and locker rooms as prime sites. Students are also victimized in restrooms.[9] Most acts of violence occur where adult supervision is minimal, or where there are large crowds of people moving to and fro. Students, especially those who have been victims, learn quickly to avoid certain areas of the school.

According to the Metropolitan Life Survey of the American Teacher 1993, violence is more likely to occur in schools where the quality of education is poor.[10] Teachers and students agree that a major factor contributing to increased violence in the schools is the perception that the quality of education is not up to par. Thirty-three percent of the teachers who feel their school provides only a fair or poor education have been victims of property crime, while 11 percent have been victims of acts of violence.[11]

Factors That Contribute to Violence in Schools

Factors contributing to school violence are numerous, complex, and, for the most part, community related. For example, teachers perceive that the major factors contributing to student violence are lack of parental supervision at home (71 percent), lack of family involvement with the school (66 percent), and exposure to violence in the mass media (55 percent).[12] Teachers also believe that certain types of parenting produce children who contribute to school violence. On numerous occasions, teachers have shared anecdotes about students, even very young students, who state that their parents have told them (the children) that they do not have to do what the teacher says or that if anyone tries to take something from them, insults them, or hits them, they should fight back. Unfortunately, many parents admit that they have so instructed their child and are offended that teachers question such directions.

Children often receive mixed messages from parents and other adults about what is right and what is wrong. The use of material goods to persuade children to behave in one way or dissuade them from behaving in another is one example of sending a mixed message. In such situations, children are bribed by promises of expensive clothing or toys. In addition, today's youth seem surprised when asked if they are required to perform chores in and around their homes.[13] Many indicate that they do not do chores unless they are paid to do them. These attitudes and actions relay strong lessons about roles, responsibilities, and rights all of us must learn to assume. How we learn what these lessons are is as important as what we learn.

With more and more parents working outside the home, students are very aware that it is difficult for school officials to contact their parents, and that even if they do their parents often refuse to respond. Exacerbating this problem further are parents who refuse to come to the school when asked to do so, because the child has been in trouble repeatedly and they are tired of dealing with the child's problems, they believe the school is at fault, or they believe nothing they can do will control the child.

Students (36 percent) concur that lack of parental supervision at home is the major factor contributing to violence in schools. However, they (34 percent) cite as a second major factor the presence of gang or group membership or peer group pressure.[14] The Metropolitan Life and Department of Justice studies, as well as an article by Jackson Toby, concluded that peer group pressure is perhaps the fastest growing and most disturbing cause of acts of violence among youth, whether in school or out.[15]

Why do children and youth join gangs or negative peer groups? Some of their responses to this question are interesting and troublesome. Students who were queried as to their membership in these groups or gangs often responded that they join because they want to be accepted by their peers and need to belong. Others join to feel empowered and to be respected. When there is group violence, whether against one person or many, those involved deny being personally responsible by claiming they were caught up in the frenzy of the crowd, or that they were afraid that failure to participate would result in their becoming a victim or being excluded by the group. These young people fail to realize that more often than not these memberships prove to be destructive, not constructive.

Students cited involvement with drugs and alcohol as the third major factor contributing to school violence. Although reports indicate that the use of drugs such as heroin, cocaine, marijuana, and crack is down among students in grades 6 through 12, the consumption of alcohol is not. Alcohol is the number one drug used by teenagers and young adults. Students who reported the availability of drugs in school did not vary significantly by ethnicity, level of family income, or geographic location.[16]

It is also interesting to note the reaction of parents to their children's use of drugs. In one school district a student entered his typing class well after the tardy bell had sounded. He then proceeded to talk loudly to the students around him. When the teacher reprimanded him, the student became angry and began knocking over tables, chairs, and typewriters. The police were called; they subdued the student and then took him to jail. Before leaving the school, the police informed the teacher and the principal that the student was intoxicated. Later, when the parents were informed about what had happened, their response was, "Oh, is that all? I thought it was something more serious." All too often, alcohol abuse among our youth is not considered a serious drug abuse problem and, therefore, does not receive the attention it deserves.

Another emerging trend is the number of acts of violence related to race or religion. The 1993 Lou Harris Study on Racism and Violence in American High

Schools reported that racism and violence are rising significantly in America's high schools. Seventy-five percent of all students surveyed reported seeing or hearing about racially or religiously motivated confrontations on a regular basis, up from 57 percent in the 1990 Lou Harris survey.[17] This trend is particularly disturbing in light of the fact that America is becoming more, not less, pluralistic.

Perpetrators of School Violence

It is important to examine, within the context of the school, who the victims and the perpetrators are. For example, according to Jackson Toby, two kinds of violence should be distinguished when we are discussing violence in schools. One is violence perpetuated by trespassers who enter school buildings to steal, rob, or assault someone. The other type of violence is committed against teachers, administrators, other staff members, or fellow classmates by students enrolled in the school.[18] Students' acts of violence may include stealing or extorting valuables or money, verbal abuse, intimidation, and physical assaults.

Victims and perpetrators of school violence represent all racial, ethnic, and economic groups. Although males are more likely to be involved in acts of violence in schools, in recent years an alarming trend indicates that girls are engaging more frequently in such acts.

The perpetrators often do not have or need a serious reason for lashing out. It could be something as simple as a look or stare or an accidental bump into someone that triggers a violent reaction. An act of violence could result from idle gossip, courtship jealousies, extortion, feeling slighted or disrespected, or an attempt to impress friends. It could result from the perpetrator's dislike for a person or their perception that the person is weak or is a "nerd" (makes good grades). In other words, a logical reason for the incident is not necessary. The tempers of many students today are triggered quickly, and the results are often disastrous.

When a fight occurs, for example, especially if it is outside the classroom, other students are not likely to try to stop it. To the contrary, students are more likely to "egg on" their colleagues. I remember a rather vicious fight erupting between two girls in the hallway of the school where I taught. The girls were quickly surrounded by other students who happened to be walking through that section of the hall. Many of the students in the crowd were shoving the girls at each other and encouraging them to continue fighting. Several members of the faculty, including me, tried to get through the crowd. It took us several minutes to force our way to the girls to break up the fight. A faculty member took the girls to the principal's office while the rest of us tried to clear the hallway.

One of the girls who had been fighting was a student in my class. She was very intelligent, and her teachers, including me, considered her to be a hard worker and a model student. She was suspended from school for three days for fighting; the other girl was suspended for a week because she started the fight. On her way home, my student stopped by to get her assignment. She was still very upset and very embarrassed. After she explained what caused the fight, I asked her why she did not walk away from the other girl or simply refuse to fight her. She responded,

"If I had refused to fight the other girl or tried to walk away, it would have been worse. I would have been viewed as being afraid or weak, and others would attack me here or outside school. I could not afford to walk away!"

It is disturbing that most high school students today would probably stand by and watch a fight without doing anything to stop it, or without reporting the incident to school authorities. There appears to be a code of silence among the students. Interestingly, similar reactions have developed with honor-code violations at the university level. Even if other students observe their colleagues victimizing someone or cheating, unless the perpetrators are caught in the act by a school official or the victim happens to be a personal friend, observers are very reluctant to tell school officials who committed the act. Reluctance to report such incidents may be motivated by fear of possible retaliation or may be a result of apathy. It may also be a way of opposing or hampering school authorities' efforts to enforce rules and regulations.

This behavior reflects attitudes we often see in our adult society: "It's not my problem," or "I don't want to get involved." It also reflects our society's reverence for aggressiveness and violence as part of our culture, whether at a sports event or in the movies. Our children spend thousands of hours each year absorbing scenes of violence in the media, in our homes, and in the community. They are the products of the culture and the society we have created. It is little wonder they exhibit violent behavior in school.

Likely Victims of School Violence

Victims of violence in schools cover the spectrum. For example, nine hundred teachers are threatened, and over two thousand students and nearly forty teachers are physically attacked on school grounds every hour of every school day each year. According to the Department of Justice, every day in the United States one hundred thousand youngsters carry guns to school and forty youngsters are injured or killed by guns.[19]

Students. According to the three reports referenced at the beginning of this chapter, younger students in (grades 6 through 10) are much more likely to be victims of violence than are senior high school students.[20] The Department of Justice also reports that students whose families move more frequently and students from racial or ethnic groups that are minorities within the school are more likely to be victims of physical assaults. Students who wear expensive or fashionable clothing or jewelry or bring cameras, cassette players, beepers, and other electronic devices to school, however, are more likely to be victims of property crime.

Teachers. Although the majority of teachers believe that they are unlikely to be victims of violence in and around school, studies state just the opposite. Most teachers feel safe in their schools during the day, but after school hours many teachers, especially those in urban areas, do not. Women and younger, less experienced teachers are often targets, but they are not the primary victims of violence among school staff. Teachers who are considered to be strict and who insist that students adhere to rigorous academic and behavioral standards are most at risk of being victimized. Thirty-eight percent of teachers and 57 percent of students rank strict teachers as more at risk of becoming a victim than any other members of the teaching staff.[21] This could have a chilling effect on school districts that are attempting to reform education and restructure their schools.

If teachers fear they will be targets of students' physical or verbal abuse, they will be less willing to insist that all students meet new, more rigorous standards. This is particularly so if teachers do not believe school administrators can or will provide a safe environment in which the standards can be achieved.

Also, teachers will be unwilling to intervene in situations, especially altercations between students, if they do not believe the parents, school officials, or community will back them up. Teachers are concerned not only about being victimized, but also about being sued if they intervene in student altercations or acts of violence. They also may not intervene aggressively because of fear of being accused of child abuse.

The increasingly disruptive and often violent behavior in schools is reflected in part in the increasing number of teachers who are leaving the profession. One in five teachers who decide to leave teaching leave because they are tired of the hassle of trying to teach in environments that are not conducive to learning.[22] They are also demoralized by the lack of respect, appreciation, and support. These teachers are described as "burned out."

The Impact of Student Violence on the Classroom

Violence or the threat of violence has a direct impact on the quality of education provided and on the way teachers and students work together in the classroom. Students are very perceptive. They may not be able to articulate their perceptions, but most of them know whether they are receiving a good education, an education that will prepare them to compete in the job market, college, or anywhere else. When students perceive that their education is inadequate or inferior, when the expectations for them are less than for others in the class, they often develop a sense of helplessness and frustration. This sense of frustration often turns to anger and violence when there appears to be no viable solution to the problem.

Students frequently act out their hostility by being disruptive. This, in turn, creates an atmosphere in the classroom and the school that militates against constructive teaching and learning. For example, teachers are less apt to teach at their full potential, the class assignments are less creative and challenging, and the ethos in the school is less motivating if tension constantly permeates the environment. In addition, teachers, like students, are less eager to go to school every day. Thus, students in these schools are much more likely, according to Arthur Wise and Jonathan Kozol, to be taught by a "revolving door" of substitutes.[23]

WHAT IS BEING DONE TO ENSURE SAFETY IN OUR SCHOOLS

The most common school security measure used to prevent violence or other disruptive acts in school is to require school staff—in particular, teachers and security staff—to monitor students' movements in and around the school. This means staff monitoring hallways, doorways, restrooms, the cafeteria or lunch rooms, and the areas of the campus where students tend to congregate.

The institutionalization of discipline and dress codes is another strategy used to curb violence. Schools are also establishing counseling programs for students and inviting high-profile leaders in the community (that is, police officers, athletes, media representatives, and parents) to visit schools and talk with students about crime and violence. Many schools are moving to physical means of control—fences, blocked access roads, and locked and chained doors. Such means are costly and reflect the real and unpleasant image of being locked up.

Because of students' increased access to weapons, especially guns, and the fact that more and more of these weapons are showing up in schools, schools are resorting to random checks of students' book bags, backpacks, or lockers. Schools are also increasing their use of metal detectors to identify students carrying weapons. In addition, to support school administrators' efforts to reduce violence, more and more schools' funds are used to hire retired police officers or security guards to patrol buildings.

Students who violate school rules by threatening or committing acts of violence face a variety of punishments, including suspension from classes with detention in the school building or an alternative special school, or confinement to their home for a designated period of time; expulsion from the school; or, if the act is a violation of the community's laws, incarceration.

The issue of youth violence in our schools and communities has reached pandemic proportions. Since schools are part of our communities, we cannot separate what happens in schools from what happens in our communities. In some communities the situation is so bad young offenders are being sent to boot camps, "shock incarceration programs," or are required to perform supervised community service. These programs are generally for young men and women who are repeat offenders and whose actions are becoming increasingly violent (that is, committing sexual assaults or using weapons).

The magnitude of youth violence is reflected in U.S. House Resolution 4092, the Violent Crime Control and Law Enforcement Act, which contains a variety of provisions for dealing with juvenile offenders. One provision would allow for the prosecution of a thirteen-year-old as an adult in federal court for certain violent offenses, such as using a gun to commit a crime. The act would also make it a federal crime for anyone "to sell or transfer a handgun, or ammunition for a handgun to a person under 18 years of age..."[24]

WHAT ELSE CAN BE DONE?

All of the strategies described herein are important and, perhaps, necessary. However, these strategies are too little and, perhaps, too late. Most strategies to curb violence in schools and in society are designed to respond to violence after it has occurred rather than to prevent its occurrence in the first place.

Forty years ago, when violence in schools caused enough concern to result in national studies being conducted, most people probably thought the issue of violence was being blown out of proportion. Sixteen years ago, when the issue once again garnered national attention, people responded by saying that it was an inner-city problem. Today, according to headlines in the media and several high-profile reports on the topic, the prominent coverage this issue has received reflects the pervasiveness of violence, not only in schools but throughout society.

The Department of Justice reports that the number of incidents of violence in the United States is down, but it is the viciousness of the incidents that alarms citizens. In the last decade, the Department's most alarming statistic is the significant increase in the number of incidents of violence and crime committed by youths.[25] This finding is corroborated by the National School Boards Association study, "Violence in the Schools," referenced earlier, which states that 82 percent of the school officials surveyed believe school violence has increased in the past five years, especially student-on-student violence.[26]

The problems we face in our schools, however, manifest themselves long before students explode in uncontrollable anger and violence. The culprits and causes are many. America's children are exposed to a steady diet of verbal and physical violence that begins early and continuously throughout their lives. Numerous reports, for example, have cited the fact that children in the United States spend more time watching television than attending school. Most of what children watch, including cartoons, is unsupervised, and much of it is filled with scene after scene of unadulterated sex and violence. All too often children who exhibit violent behavior are themselves victims of an overdose of violence.

In too many communities, children feel isolated from and maligned by our society. Again, these feelings know no geographic, social, or economic boundaries. Many youths increasingly come from communities where the vast majority of the experiences to which they have been exposed have been hostile. They have had to fight simply to survive. These young men and women are filled with rage and a sense of rejection and, as a result, do not believe they owe society anything.

At the same time, other violent youth have not grown up in hostile environments. It is more difficult to understand their rebellion against society. In 1994, for instance, in a suburban community, a large number of youth were arrested after being caught vandalizing cars and property, shoplifting, beating people, and engaging in drunken brawls. Those involved were from upper-middle-class homes. When asked why they engaged in such deviant behavior, their responses included to overcome boredom and to experience a sense of control and power.[27]

Some Possible Long-Term Solutions

Recognizing and accepting the need for change are critical steps toward any efforts to reduce violence in schools. Change is a process that requires a sustained commitment from those desiring change—individuals, families, schools, and communities. Increased discipline, order, and safety in schools require all parties to examine the attitudes, behaviors, and values that define them.

It is at the formative level of a child's life (until approximately nine years of age) that families and communities must begin to inculcate positive attitudes and modes of behavior. At this formative level, school districts should implement counseling programs, role-modeling and mentoring, and antiviolence or safety programs for students (pre-kindergarten through fourth-grade level). Part of this agenda must also include developing respect for oneself as well as for others. Forums should be provided, for example, where students can discuss sensitive issues related to racism, poverty, sexism, religion, and violence. These programs should be introduced early, and resources should be committed to sustain them at all levels of the school system. Such programs should also be accessible to parents who may wish to participate in them.

Furthermore, every school district should have a clearly defined discipline code that is shared with students and their parents each year. A major focus of such a code should be the understanding of discipline as a positive rather than a negative sense of being. Equally important, the discipline code should be enforced consistently, firmly, and fairly.

Prevention to Avoid Intervention

Teachers see the negative and positive sides of student behavior and attitudes long before school boards or central administrators or the community become alarmed and decide to act. Teachers know the symptoms long before the metal detectors, security guards, or random searches become part of the school environment. Teachers see signs of disruptive, even violent, behavior as early as preschool and elementary school. Whatever the reason, preventive measures must be taken to intervene before acts of violence occur.

Yet, teachers are often unprepared to address the needs of these disruptive, often violent youth. It is imperative that schools of education include, as part of teacher and administrator preparation programs, methodologies that can be used in schools to address the types of problems described in this chapter. Teachers and building-level administrators must receive intensive training and sustained staff development in dealing with violence in order to make schools safe, orderly places in which to teach and learn. At the same time, teachers and their professional organizations, school district officials, and community leaders must work together to develop programs to reduce and prevent violence in schools. These methodologies must include strategies for working with families and community groups; schools cannot do the job alone.

Students must also have experiences in their communities that reinforce positive attitudes and behaviors. Religious groups, the media, civic organizations, and student groups, such as Girls' and Boys' Clubs, should constantly provide opportunities and experiences that help students develop attitudes and behaviors that enable them to resolve differences or conflicts in nonviolent ways. Central to these efforts must be the parents or guardians of youth. They, in particular, must assume a greater responsibility for their sons' and daughters' behavior within the home, the school, and the community. Finally, but most important, youths themselves must learn that they are responsible for their behavior and actions, and that they are personally accountable for what they do.

We can hope that communities will urge all these groups to work with schools to ensure that comprehensive and long-term strategies are in place to support children and youth as they struggle toward maturity. Communities, for example, spend thousands of dollars on metal detectors and security guards each year. What would happen if some of those dollars were used to create jobs for youths, build recreation facilities for children, and establish year-round counseling and tutoring programs for students who need them? What would happen if child care programs were established in schools so that children could receive supervised attention, rather than stay at home alone and unsupervised for hours? What would happen if instead of sending adolescents to boot camp we sent them to residential academies where they could learn about math, science, computers, and have fun at the same time? What would happen if more of these children were in programs such as Outward Bound? These types of investments would yield far more for our tax dollars and be more beneficial to society than installing metal detectors in school or hiring more hall monitors.

CONCLUSION

School violence has reached an untenable level in many communities. Much of what is being acted out in the classrooms and corridors of schools are symptoms of what is occurring in society, and it does not bode well for the future if we do not respond now. School violence was ignored in the 1950s, 1970s, and again in the 1980s. Today, what is happening to youth, not only in school but throughout society, can no longer be ignored.

The get-tough strategies being implemented in many communities are deemed necessary but are woefully insufficient. First, efforts that address students' developmental needs and the problems should be introduced early in their educational experience. Second, children and youth need to understand that ultimately they are responsible for their behavior and actions. Third, schools cannot do the job alone. The entire community, particularly parents, must work with school officials if there is to be success in keeping this generation and future generations of young people from self-destructing. Many students are filled with rage and resentment. The self-destructive behaviors and negative attitudes seen in growing numbers of young men and women reflect, in part, the pandemic nature of the violence bankrupting our schools and corrupting our society.

Americans cannot afford to ignore or minimize the magnitude of violence in schools and the implications it has for the larger society. Nor can we simply build more prisons and chant slogans like "Three strikes and you're out!" This is not a game. In five to ten years these young men and women will become part of the adult population. They are the people who will be expected to safeguard and enhance the civil, human, political, and economic rights of the citizens of our country. It is the future of this nation and the kind of society we want that is at stake.

NOTES

1. S. Goodwillie, ed., *Voices from the Future: Our Children Tell Us about Violence in America* (New York: Crown Publishers, 1993).

2. U.S. Department of Education, *Goals 2000: Educate America Act* (Washington, D.C.: Government Printing Office, 1993), 8–9; U.S. Department of Education, Office of Educational Research and Improvement, *Reaching the Goals, Goal 6: Safe, Disciplined, and Drug-Free Schools* (Washington, D.C.: Government Printing Office, 1993).

3. U.S. Department of Education, *The National Education Goals Report for 1993: Building a Nation of Learners* (Washington, D.C.: Government Printing Office, 1993); Metropolitan Life Insurance Company, *Violence in America's Public Schools* (New York: Metropolitan Life Survey of the American Teacher, 1993); U.S. Department of Justice, Bureau of Justice Statistics, Office of Justice Programs, *School Crime: A National Crime Victimization Survey Report* (Washington, D.C.: Government Printing Office, 1991).

4. J. W. Williams, "Discipline in the Public Schools: A Problem of Perception?," *Phi Delta Kappan 60,* No. 5 (January 1979): 385–87.

5. Ibid., 385.

6. U.S. Department of Justice, *School Crime: A National Crime Victimization Survey Report,* 2.

7. National School Boards Association, "Violence in the Schools" (Alexandria, Va.: National School Boards Association, 1994).

8. R. L. Curwin and A. N. Mendler, *Discipline with Dignity* (Alexandria, Va.: Association of Supervision and Curriculum Development, 1988), 27–28.

9. Metropolitan Life Insurance Company, *Violence in America's Public Schools,* 35–41.

10. Ibid., 73.

11. U.S. Department of Education, *Reaching the Goals, Goal 6: Safe, Disciplined, and Drug-Free Schools,* 8.

12. Metropolitan Life Insurance Company, *Violence in America's Public Schools,* 35–38.

13. L. Franks, "Little BIG People," *New York Times* (October 1993), section E.

14. Metropolitan Life Insurance Company, *Violence in America's Public Schools,* 39–41.

15. Ibid.; U.S. Department of Justice, *School Crime: A National Crime Victimization Survey Report,* 8; J. Toby, "Violence in Schools" in *School Discipline: Order and Autonomy* (New York: Praeger, 1994), 1–47.

16. U.S. Department of Justice, *School Crime: A National Crime Victimization Survey Report,* 4.

17. National Consortium for Academics and Sports, "The 1993 Lou Harris Study on Racism and Violence in American High Schools: Project Teamwork Reports," in *Sports in Society,* Northeastern University Center for the Study of Sports in Society (November 10, 1993).

18. Toby, "Violence in Schools," 19–20.

19. A. Stone, "Kids, Guns: 'It's Shoot or Be Shot'," *USA Today* (June 3, 1993), A1, A4.

20. U.S. Department of Justice, *School Crime: A National Crime Victimization Survey Report,* 2, 10; Metropolitan Life Insurance Company, *Violence in America's Public Schools,* 43–44; U.S. Department of Education, *The National Education Goals Report: Building a Nation of Learners 1993,* 51.

21. Metropolitan Life Insurance Company, *Violence in America's Public Schools,* 45–47.

22. U.S. Department of Education, National Center for Education Statistics, Office of Educational Research and Information, "Characteristics of Stayers, Movers, and Leavers: Results from the Teacher Follow-up Survey 1991–92" (Washington, D.C.: Government Printing Office, 1994).

23. J. Kozol, *Savage Inequalities: Children in America's Schools* (New York: Crown Publishers, 1991); A. E. Wise, "Equal Opportunity for All?," *Quality Teaching* 3, No. 1 (Fall 1993): 4.

24. U.S. House of Representatives, "The Crime Bill," Democratic Study Group Fact Sheet (March 21, 1994): 19–20.

25. U.S. Department of Justice, *Violence in America's Public Schools.*

26. National School Boards Association, "Violence in the Schools."

27. K. Kennedy Manzo, "Working to Curb, Prevent Youth Crime: Community Panel Urges More Recreation, Counseling, Parental Involvement," *Washington Post* (date unknown).

2

Weapon-Carrying in Schools

Jennifer C. Friday

Violence among young people is a growing problem in communities across America, taking a substantial toll in loss of life, physical and mental injury, and economic costs. The problem of violence in society is being brought into the school rooms around the country.[1]

Young people are disproportionately represented both as victims and as perpetrators of interpersonal violence in the United States. Teenagers are more likely to be victims of violence than are persons in any other age group.[2] The Bureau of Justice reports that 37 percent of the violent crime victimizations of youths ages twelve to fifteen years occur on school property.[3]

Weapon-carrying in schools reflects easy access to weapons in the community, their presence in many homes, and the apparently widespread attitude in American society that violence is an effective way to solve problems.[4] Violence and weapon-carrying in schools also reflect the personal attitudes of students and their families. About one-half of the students in a New York City school survey reported that their families supported hitting back when hit and defending themselves if they have to, even if it means using a weapon.[5] In another study of attitudes, nearly 40 percent of parents said they would tell their children "if someone attacked them, they should defend themselves, even if this means using a weapon."[6]

Although weapons in schools is probably not a new phenomenon, few data are available to provide information about the magnitude of the problem and how it has changed over the years. It is perceived that more weapons are being brought to school, that they are increasingly lethal, and that more young people are being injured or killed because of them. On the basis of anecdotal evidence, opinion surveys, and news reports, gun-related incidents in schools appear to have risen over the last few years.[7] Reports of weapons use appeared as early as 1978, in the first studies about victimization in schools. In 1986 about 20 percent of the personal victimizations in schools involved a weapon.[8] Another trend is toward younger victims and perpetrators.[9]

This chapter discusses the prevalence of weapon-carrying in and around schools and among school age youth. It also provides a brief review of efforts around the country to prevent students from bringing weapons to school, or at the very least to limit the number of weapons on campus.

PREVALENCE OF FIGHTING AND WEAPON-CARRYING

Estimates of fighting and weapon-carrying in schools vary. The available studies have used a variety of methods, with varying student populations. Some are national studies, and some are limited to individual states or individual school districts. A number of studies have used questions from the Youth Risk Behavior Survey (YRBS) conducted by the Centers for Disease Control and Prevention (CDC). Those cited in this chapter represent the core of studies that have looked systematically at fighting and weapon-carrying in schools.

Fighting among students appears to be fairly common. Studies suggest that about one-half of all high school students have been involved in a physical fight, with a much smaller proportion reporting fighting on school property. In New York City, during the 1991–1992 school year, 21 percent of all physical fights involving public high school students occurred in school, 31 percent occurred while traveling to or from school, and 48 percent were unrelated to school.[10]

CDC's 1993 Youth Risk Behavior Survey of 16,296 students in grades 9 through 12 nationwide indicated that 42 percent of the students were involved in a fight, somewhere, during the previous twelve months, and 16 percent of the students reported fighting at school. DeJong reported that 53 percent of students in a 1987 study said they had been in a fight with someone their own age in the past six months.[11] The Joyce Foundation study conducted by LH Research reported that 20 percent of its respondents had been in a physical fight at school during the school year.[12] During the 1991–1992 school year, 25 percent of New York City public school students in grades 9 through 12 reported having been involved in a physical fight.[13]

Fighting behavior may be a contributing factor in weapon-carrying behavior. Students appear to view weapons as a means of protecting themselves if they get into a fight or of warding off possible attacks. According to a 1991 U.S. Justice Department report, 2 percent of students during a six-month period had at least once taken a weapon to school to protect themselves from attack or harm.[14] These weapons are often used to threaten, injure, or kill someone or oneself. According to Sampson and Lauritsen, individuals who use weapons to threaten other people are more likely to be the victims of property and violent offenses than those who do not use weapons.[15]

Five studies conducted from 1990 to 1993 reported that an estimated 20 to 26 percent of students had carried weapons (anywhere),[16] whereas five surveys conducted from 1989 to 1993 reported estimates of students carrying a weapon to school ranging from 2 to 13 percent.[17] Another survey, which asked about the past year rather than the past thirty days, estimated that 22 percent of students had carried a weapon to school.[18]

Weapon-carrying by teenagers appears to be a frequent occurrence, according to studies. The CDC's YRBS reported that in 1990 about 20 percent of all students in grades 9 through 12 reported having carried a weapon such as a gun, knife, or club anywhere on one or more days during the thirty days preceding the survey. Of these students, more than one-third (36 percent) reported carrying a weapon six or more times during the previous thirty days. Subsequent surveys showed increases in weapon-carrying among this population. In 1991 reports of weapon-carrying increased dramatically to 26 percent, although this rise may be due to a change in the structure of the question. There were slight declines in 1993, when 22 percent reported carrying a weapon. Also in 1993, nearly 12 percent of students reported having carried any weapon onto school property at least once in the thirty days prior to the survey.[19]

The National Educational Goals Report found that in 1992, 9 percent of eighth-graders, 10 percent of tenth-graders, and 6 percent of twelfth-graders reported having brought a weapon to school at least once during the previous month. Of this group, 2, 4, and 3 percent, respectively, reported carrying a weapon on ten or more days in the previous month.[20]

There is more variation reported in gun-carrying, specifically, than in weapon-carrying. In studies published between 1991 and 1993, from 5 to 35 percent of different student groups reported having carried a gun sometime at any location in the previous six months. The 5 percent is from a survey of students in grades 11 and 12 in South Carolina, and the 35 percent is from a survey of high school age males living near a juvenile correctional facility.[21]

Sheley and Wright, in their survey of male inmates of juvenile correctional facilities and males from a public high school near the facilities, looked primarily at gun acquisition and possession. Both groups of males reported a significantly higher prevalence of weapon-carrying both in and away from school. While the study is not generalizable to the male population, it provides some information about youth who live in high-risk settings.[22]

The 1990 CDC YRBS showed that 4 percent, or one in twenty-four, students carried a firearm for fighting or self-defense during the thirty days preceding the survey. In 1991 this figure increased to 6 percent; in 1993 it rose to 8 percent, or roughly one in thirteen students.

Across the studies, carrying a gun *to school* seemed to show the smallest variation. In the seven studies that asked about carrying guns to school, between 4 and 9 percent of students reported having carried a gun to school during the past thirty days.[23] These figures are similar to ones found in other studies. The 1987 National Adolescent School Health Survey reported that 6 percent of eighth- and tenth-grade male students had carried a handgun to school during the year, and 2 percent had carried a handgun to school every day.[24] An Illinois survey of thirty-one schools in 1990 disclosed that one in twenty students had carried a gun to school sometime during that year.[25] In the LH Research study done for the Joyce Foundation, 15 percent of students reported carrying a handgun in the last thirty days, and 4 percent said they had taken a handgun to school that year.[26]

In a study done in ten inner-city high schools in four states, Sheley and associates found that 22 percent of the students said they had carried a gun outside of school, and 6 percent had carried a gun to school "now and then."[27]

DEMOGRAPHICS OF WEAPON-CARRYING

In general, weapons (including guns) are more likely to be carried by younger than older students, by males more than by females, by blacks more than by Hispanics, by Hispanics more than by whites, and by those in urban more than in suburban or rural geographic locations.

Age

Most studies about weapon-carrying in schools have looked at students in grades 9 through 12, and all show the same basic trend: younger students are more likely than older students to be in fights, to carry weapons, and to be victimized.[28] Current data suggest that both physical fighting and weapon-carrying decrease as grade level and age increase. Ninth-graders are much more likely than twelfth-graders to be in a fight or to carry weapons in and around school.[29] The 1991 YRBS reported that 9.1 percent of ninth-graders, 8.6 percent of tenth-graders, 7.4 percent of eleventh-graders, and 6.6 percent of twelfth-graders carried a gun during the thirty days preceding the survey.[30]

Gender

In all surveys, male students are much more likely than female students to carry weapons. The 1993 YRBS suggests that males are three times more likely than females to carry weapons,[31] and the MetLife survey reports males are five times more likely than females to have carried a weapon.[32] The proportion is even higher for males when gun-carrying behavior is considered. CDC reports that males are nearly eight times more likely than females to carry guns anywhere.[33]

Race and Ethnicity

Black students are more likely than Hispanic or white students to be involved in a violent incident and are also more likely to carry a weapon. Black and Hispanic students are more likely than white students to be victims of violent acts involving weapons at school.[34] Black and Hispanic students are also more likely than white students to carry a gun.[35]

Geographic Location

Despite the perception that nonurban schools are free of violence, communities of all sizes, ethnic makeup, and socioeconomic status have experienced violence in schools. Bastian and Taylor found equal percentages of central city (2 percent) and suburban (2 percent) students report violent victimization at school, compared with 1 percent of rural students.[36] (Violent victimizations are largely composed of simple assaults and involve attacks without weapons.) Other studies show similar proportions of students involved in fights and carrying weapons among students in urban centers and suburban areas. LH Research reported that 19 percent of central city school students have been in a fight in the past year, compared with 20 percent of suburban school students. In the same study, 62 percent of central city young people reported that they could get a gun, compared with 58 percent of suburban and 56 percent of small-town and rural students. Seventeen percent of students in the central city schools carried a handgun in the past thirty days, compared with 15 percent of suburban students.[37]

TYPES OF WEAPONS CARRIED TO SCHOOL

Weapons confiscated from students across the country include firearms, such as guns, starter guns, and toy pistols; knives; brass knuckles; box cutters; mace; pipes; smoke bombs; slapsticks; ax handles; tire irons; a sock with a pool ball inside; scissors; hatchets; hammers; razor blades; and bullets.[38]

Students are more likely to carry knives than any other weapon.[39] In 1990 about one-half (55 percent) of all high school students who reported carrying weapons to school indicated that they had carried a knife or razor.[40] In the New York City Public School Survey, 16 percent of the students reported they had carried a knife or razor anywhere, and 7 percent reported they had carried a handgun.[41] Nationwide, 11 percent of students reported carrying a knife or razor, and 4 percent reported carrying a firearm in the previous thirty days.[42] Among eighth- and tenth-graders, almost 7 percent of boys and 2 percent of girls reported carrying knives to school nearly every day.[43]

Weapons in schools are brought in by teachers as well as by students. A small portion of public school teachers (2 percent) has indicated that they have carried a weapon to school. This percentage is consistent for teachers in all regions of the country and all (urban, suburban, or rural) locations. Among teachers who took a weapon to school, mace was the reported weapon of choice; 44 percent of the school teachers in the MetLife sample reported bringing it to school to protect themselves. Twenty-six percent of the teachers brought knives to school, and about 5 percent, or one in one thousand, teachers brought handguns.[44]

REASONS FOR WEAPON-CARRYING

When students were asked why they carried weapons, the primary response was to protect themselves against possible aggressors. Other reasons cited were showing off to impress friends; to make themselves feel important; and to emulate their friends.[45] Teachers, students, and law enforcement officials believe that students carry weapons for four main reasons: (1) for protection while going to school; (2) for impressing their friends; (3) for self-esteem; or (4) for protection in school.[46] Lou Harris found similar reasons. When asked, "What is the single most important reason some students carry a weapon?" 41 percent of the students answered "for protection against possible attacks by other people," 34 percent said to "show off and impress their friends," 10 percent "because it makes them feel important," 8 percent "because they are angry and want to hurt someone," and 4 percent "because their friends carry weapons."[47]

A survey of New York City public high school students found that 85 percent of students who carried a weapon said they did so to protect themselves against attack by others. Students who carried a weapon in school were also more likely than other students to believe that threatening to use a weapon and carrying a weapon were effective ways to avoid a physical fight. They were more likely to say they would feel safer during a physical fight if they had a knife or a handgun.[48]

In the National Crime Survey, less than 20 percent of students reported fear of being victimized. Victims of violent crimes were three times more likely to be afraid than those who were not. Younger students were more likely to fear an attack than were older students.[49]

METHODS FOR REDUCING WEAPON-CARRYING

Preventing violence and weapon-carrying in schools is complicated by numerous variables that play into the root causes of such behavior. Nonetheless, many efforts are underway to try and address some of the causes. Efforts to reduce weapon-carrying focus on three broad prevention and intervention categories: (1) education; (2) legal and regulatory change; and (3) environmental modifications.

Education

Education activities generally serve to provide information and teach skills. Most of the educational efforts are focused on the general area of violence prevention. These efforts are geared toward reducing the incidence of violence in schools, which would in turn reduce the need for students to bring weapons to school. Many schools are starting an assortment of violence-prevention programs, including conflict-resolution curricula; mentoring programs; and general education about violence and its impact on the lives of students, their families, and their communities. Neither their effect on weapon-carrying nor their effect on violence reduction has been established.

Legal and Regulatory Change

Legal and regulatory activities focus on the laws or rules that may lower the risk of violent behavior and of students' carrying weapons. These include regulations that focus on the use of and access to weapons by students, such as enforcement of current weapons laws, the Drug Free Act, and the Gun Free School Zones Act.

Schools and their jurisdictions are making a better effort to enforce existing weapon laws. The Brady Bill, for example, is designed to help limit who has access to guns. The Gun Free School Zone Act of 1990 prohibits the possession of a firearm in a school zone (within one thousand feet from the grounds of any school). Legal and regulatory activities also include instituting dress codes—something many schools have done. Dress codes have been instituted in some schools not only as a way of preventing weapons coming onto school property, but also as a means of reducing violent behavior. Some schools have banned baggy clothing, overcoats, sweatpants with elastic around the ankles, metal jewelry, leather, and special brand-name garments. In addition, some schools are introducing uniforms as means of reducing the threat of and actual violent behavior that has occurred because of clothing and the wearing of gang colors in school. The Baltimore City School District instituted a dress code, backed up by penalties, and was able to lower the incidence of firearm- and weapon-related incidents in its jurisdiction. They reported 55 firearm-related incidents in 1987, 35 in 1988, and 28 in 1989.[50]

Environmental Modifications

Environmental changes include metal detector programs, security patrols, and school surveillance methods. In the MetLife study, 31 percent of teachers reported their schools had made random checks of book bags, backpacks, and lockers as a means of reducing weapon-carrying in their schools. Twenty-eight percent of the teachers in the study also said that their schools had hired security guards or police to patrol in and around the school. Five percent said that their schools used hand-held metal detectors, and 2 percent indicated that their schools made students walk through metal detectors to enter the buildings.[51]

About one-fourth of large urban school districts in the United States use metal detectors to help reduce weapon-carrying in schools.[52] Metal-detector systems in schools vary. Walk-through or portal metal detectors that require each person who enters the building to pass through are expensive and can be time-consuming.[53] Most schools use either hand-held metal detectors or walk-through lanes that randomly select entering students. Metal detectors may provide a false sense of security; at the same time, they may have the opposite effect. The mere presence of metal detectors in a school may imply to some that the environment is unsafe and therefore that some protection may be necessary.

Some schools use security personnel, teachers, other students, and volunteer parents to patrol hallways and playgrounds. Others have used school surveillance methods, including closed-circuit televisions, random searches, and see-through bags as ways to ensure that students do not bring contraband items on campus.

Closed-circuit television is used more often in very large schools, especially in urban centers, than in smaller school settings. The television monitors are strategically placed in and around school buildings and on school property, especially buses, and they are usually monitored from the principal's office or in the school security office if there is one.

Instead of regular backpacks and book bags, some schools require students to bring bags that are made of clear materials such as plastic or mesh that will allow easy viewing of their contents. Schools are also allowing random searches of book bags and lockers as a means of controlling weapons in schools; others have removed lockers completely.

EFFECTIVENESS OF METHODS

Very few of the prevention methods have been evaluated. Because those that have been evaluated at some level have produced mixed results, it is difficult to say which methods have been effective. According to student reports, there is some indication that violent crimes have occurred about as frequently in schools using security measures as in schools without these measures.[54] Sheley and associates report a similar finding.[55]

Metal detector programs are fairly new and have undergone some limited evaluation. Early results indicate that students who attended high schools with metal detector programs were as likely as students who attended schools without such programs to have carried a weapon anywhere, but were less likely to have carried a weapon inside a school building or while going to or from school.[56] Although metal detectors may reduce the number of weapons that come onto school grounds, they do not appear to reduce either weapon-carrying off of school property or violent behavior such as threats or physical fighting at or away from school. New York City schools have reported some successes with their metal detector program. Weapon-related incidents have decreased, school attendance has increased, and students anecdotally reported an increased sense of security as a result of the metal detector program.[57]

Despite the fact that many large urban school districts currently employ elaborate physical security measures (including the use of metal detectors, often at a cost of millions of dollars), there have been no rigorous, controlled evaluations of their effectiveness in reducing violence-related injuries and deaths. Moreover, many of these security measures have been challenged through the courts. Some, such as the Gun Free School Zones Act, have been upheld while others are still being debated.

CONCLUSION

Few data exist to document long-term trends or to accurately assess the incidence and prevalence of violence and weapon-carrying behavior in schools across the country. It is difficult to identify trends because there is no standardized reporting system for school violence. Data on weapon-carrying in schools are fairly limited. Systematic data collection is recent, and trends for periods longer than five years are virtually nonexistent. The YRBS has been done three times in the past four years and provides some trend data, but most of the other surveys are one-time studies. Data limitations include the sizes and representativeness of the samples and survey response rates.

More work needs to be done to assess the reliability and validity of data collected by self-report methodology. One way to verify the self-report data is to collect other objective data from secondary sources. Some examples of this are to match hospital/clinic records with students' reports of being treated for an injury, or to use qualitative methods such as focus groups to assess some of the reported information. Still, many of the programs to reduce violence and weapon-carrying behavior in schools simply have not been in place long enough to permit thorough evaluation of their effectiveness.

Violence and weapon-carrying are not simply school problems. The root causes of these behaviors involve issues whose solutions require cooperation among the school, community, and public and private agencies that serve the community. Schools need to build alliances with their communities. Safe schools require safe communities. School children who fear for their lives are more likely to want to carry weapons, and the biggest threat to effective education is an armed student body.

NOTES

1. J. F. Sheley, Z. T. McGee, and J. D. Wright, "Gun-Related Violence in and around Inner-City Schools," *American Journal of Diseases of Children* 146 (1992): 677–82; D. Smith, *Caught in the Crossfire: A Report on the Gun Violence in Our Nation's Schools* (Washington, D.C.: Center to Prevent Handgun Violence, 1990).

2. C. J. Whitaker and J. D. Bastian, *Teenage Victims* (Washington, D.C.: U.S. Department of Justice, 1991).

3. B. Allen-Hagen and M. Sickmund, *Juveniles and Violence: Juvenile Offending and Victimization* (Washington, D.C.: U.S. Department of Justice, 1993).

4. G. Butterfield and B. Turner, *Weapons in Schools: NSSC Resource Paper* (Malibu, Calif.: National School Safety Center, 1989).

5. Centers for Disease Control, "Violence-Related Attitudes and Behaviors of High School Students—New York City, 1992," *Morbidity and Mortality Weekly Reviews* 42 (1993): 773–77.

6. L. Harris, *A Survey of the American People on Guns as a Children's Health Issue* (Boston: Harvard School of Public Health, 1993).

7. Harris, *A Survey of the American People;* Smith, *Caught in the Crossfire.*

8. National School Safety Center, *Student and Staff Victimization* (Malibu, Calif.: National School Safety Center, 1993).

9. L. Rosen, "Violence Prevention: School's Newest Challenge," *School Safety* (Spring 1993).

10. Centers for Disease Control, "Violence-Related Attitudes and Behaviors."

11. W. DeJong, *Preventing Interpersonal Violence among Youth* (Washington, D.C.: National Institute of Justice, 1994).

12. L. Harris, *A Survey of Experience, Perceptions, and Apprehensions about Guns among Young People in America* (Chicago: LH Research for the Joyce Foundation, 1993).

13. Centers for Disease Control, "Violence-Related Attitudes and Behaviors."

14. L. D. Bastian and M. Taylor, *School Crime: A National Crime Victimization Survey Report* (Washington, D.C.: U.S. Department of Justice, 1991).

15. R. J. Sampson and J. L. Lauritsen, "Deviant Lifestyles," *Journal of Research in Crime and Delinquency* 27 (1990): 110–39.

16. Centers for Disease Control, *Violence-Related Attitudes and Behaviors;* Centers for Disease Control, "Youth Risk Behavior Survey—1993," *Morbidity and Mortality Weekly Reports* (1995); R. F. Valois, M. L. Vincent, R. E. McKeown, C. Z. Garrison, and S. D. Kirby, "Adolescent Risk Behaviors and the Potential for Violence: A Look at What's Coming to Campus," *Journal of American College Health* 41, No. 4 (1993): 141–47; D. Evans and E. Z. Taylor, *Interim Report, Select Committee on Violence* (Harrisburg: Pennsylvania

House of Representatives, 1994); Centers for Disease Control, "Behaviors Related to Unintentional and Intentional Injuries among High School Students–United States, 1991," *Morbidity and Mortality Weekly Reports* 41 (1992): 760–65, 771–72.

17. Centers for Disease Control, *Violence-Related Attitudes and Behaviors;* University of Michigan, *National Education Goals Report,* Volume 1 (Ann Arbor: University of Michigan, 1993); Bastian and Taylor, *School Crime;* Centers for Disease Control and Prevention, *Youth Risk Behavior Study—1993;* Metropolitan Life Insurance Company, *The Metropolitan Life Survey of the American Teacher 1993: Violence in America's Public Schools* (New York: L. Harris and Associates, 1993).

18. Harris, *A Survey of Experience, Perceptions, and Apprehensions.*

19. Centers for Disease Control, *Violence-Related Attitudes and Behaviors.*

20. University of Michigan, *National Education Goals Report,* Volume 1.

21. Valois et al., "Adolescent Risk Behaviors"; J. F. Sheley and J. D. Wright, *Gun Acquisition and Possession in Selected Juvenile Samples* (Washington, D.C.: National Institute of Justice, 1993).

22. Sheley and Wright, *Gun Acquisition and Possession.*

23. Sheley et al., *Gun-Related Violence in and around Inner-City Schools;* Centers for Disease Control, *Violence-Related Attitudes and Behaviors;* Harris, *A Survey of Experience, Perceptions, and Apprehensions;* DeJong, *Preventing Interpersonal Violence among Youth;* Sheley and Wright, *Gun Acquisition and Possession;* American School Health Association, Association for the Advancement of Health Education and Society for Public Health Education, *The National Adolescent Student Health Survey: A Report on the Health of America's Youth* (Oakland, Calif.: Third Party Press, 1989); C. M. Callahan and F. P. Rivara, "Urban High School Youth and Handguns: A School-Based Survey," *Journal of the American Medical Association* 267, No. 22 (1992): 3038–42.

24. American School Health Association, *The National Adolescent Student Health Survey.*

25. L. McCart, ed., *Kids and Violence* (Washington, D.C.: National Governor's Association, 1994).

26. Harris, *A Survey of Experience, Perceptions, and Apprehensions.*

27. Sheley et al., *Gun-Related Violence in and around Inner-City Schools.*

28. Bastian and Taylor, *School Crime.*

29. Centers for Disease Control and Prevention, *Youth Risk Behavior Survey—1993.*

30. CDC, *Youth Risk Behavior Survey—1991.*

31. CDC, *Youth Risk Behavior Survey—1993.*

32. Metropolitan Life Insurance Company, *The Metropolitan Life Survey of the American Teacher 1993.*

33. CDC, *Youth Risk Behavior Survey—1993.*

34. University of Michigan, *National Education Goals Report,* Volume 1.

35. CDC, *Youth Risk Behavior Survey—1993.*

36. Bastian and Taylor, *School Crime.*

37. Harris, *A Survey of Experience, Perceptions, and Apprehensions.*

38. Bastian and Taylor, *School Crime;* D. Northrop and K. Hamrick, *Weapons and Minority Youth Violence* (Boston: Education Development Center, 1990); Georgia Department of Education, *Report of the Violence and Schools Task Force* (Atlanta: Department of Education, 1993); National School Safety Center, *Weapons and Schools* (Malibu, Calif.: National School Safety Center, 1993).

39. National School Safety Center, *Student and Staff Victimization;* Metropolitan Life Insurance Company, *The Metropolitan Life Survey of the American Teacher 1993;* Northrop

and Hamrick, *Weapons and Minority Youth Violence;* CDC, "Weapon-Carrying among High School Students—United States, 1990," *Morbidity and Mortality Weekly Reports* 40 (1991): 681–84.

40. CDC, "Weapon-Carrying among High School Students."

41. CDC, "Violence-Related Attitudes and Behaviors."

42. CDC, "Weapon-Carrying among High School Students."

43. American School Health Association, *The National Adolescent Student Health Survey.*

44. Metropolitan Life Insurance Company, *The Metropolitan Life Survey of the American Teacher 1993.*

45. Harris, *A Survey of Experience, Perceptions, and Apprehensions.*

46. Metropolitan Life Insurance Company, *The Metropolitan Life Survey of the American Teacher 1993.*

47. Harris, *A Survey of Experience, Perceptions, and Apprehensions.*

48. CDC, "Violence-Related Attitudes and Behaviors."

49. Bastian and Taylor, *School Crime.*

50. Northrop and Hamrick, *Weapons and Minority Youth Violence.*

51. Metropolitan Life Insurance Company, *The Metropolitan Life Survey of the American Teacher 1993.*

52. Rosen, *"Violence Prevention."*

53. Northrop and Hamrick, *Weapons and Minority Youth Violence;* T. Toch, T. Gest, and M. Guttman, "Violence in Schools," *U.S. News and World Report* (November 8, 1993).

54. Bastian and Taylor, *School Crime.*

55. Sheley et al., "Gun-Related Violence in and around Inner-City Schools."

56. CDC, "Violence-Related Attitudes and Behaviors."

57. Northrop and Hamrick, *Weapons and Minority Youth Violence.*

3

The Anatomy of Gangs

Allan M. Hoffman and Randal W. Summers

Gangs and gang activity are not new phenomena. Criminal gangs were reported in the United States as early as 1760.[1] And although categorically different, crime syndicates such as the Mafia can be historically traced to the Gabelloti and Sicilian feudalism from 1812 to 1833.[2] There were also the Budhuk or robber gangs of India in the nineteenth century. However, street gangs seem to be in many ways a uniquely American institution. Klein states that "our gangs are like no others in the world—ours are far more prevalent, more permanent in their communities, larger and more complex, and more criminally involved by far."[3]

What is new is the proliferation and increasingly violent activity of gangs across the country. Once thought to be solely a problem of big cities like New York, Chicago, or Los Angeles, gang activity is now being reported in every state and in many different communities, ranging from urban to suburban to rural. In addition, the nature of gang violence is changing. Gangs have acquired more sophisticated weapons, and the intensity of gang violence appears to be escalating. For example, in Los Angeles in 1991 it was estimated that 40 percent of the homicides were gang-related. In the five-year period from 1986 to 1991, this represented 2,400 gang-related homicides.[4]

WHAT DO WE MEAN BY A GANG?

Is a social group that is not involved in crime considered a gang? Law enforcement agencies typically define a gang as an organization that is based on criminal activity. Huff defines a gang as "a collectivity whose members range in age from their early teens to their mid-twenties, who are frequently and deliberately involved in criminal acts, who have a group identification (typically a name and perhaps a territory or turf), for which leadership is better defined than an informal group."[5] Klein describes a gang as "a denotable group composed primarily of males who are committed to delinquent (including criminal) behavior or values and call forth a consistent negative response from the community such that the community comes to see them as qualitatively different from other groups."[6] Conly refers to gangs as "groups of youths and young adults who have engaged in a sufficient amount of antisocial activity to warrant attention by the criminal justice system."[7] Although there is little agreement on the exact definition of a gang, there is considerable agreement that they exist and that they disrupt the life of their local community.

ARE GANGS INCREASING IN NUMBERS?

Gangs *are* increasing in numbers. It is conservatively estimated that there are at least one hundred thousand gang members in Los Angeles County alone. In the city of Los Angeles, the number of gangs increased from 450 in 1988 to 750 in 1991 and 1,000 in 1993; in Orange County, California, the increase for the same years was from 83 to 140 to 206.[8] Los Angeles has been a chronic gang site, along with New York and Chicago. But in the last ten years, cities like Miami, Boston, Portland, Hartford, Dallas, Milwaukee, and Columbus all have experienced a significant increase in gang problems.

Gangs continually recruit new members, and most jailed gang members eventually are released back into their communities with more sophisticated contacts and knowledge. There are no nationally reported statistics on what percentage of the juvenile institution population comprises gang members, however, and surveys conducted by Knox indicate a wide range of estimates: One-half of the institutions surveyed reported that at least 10 percent of their male juvenile inmates were gang members, with 30 percent reporting a rate of approximately 25 percent and 10 percent a rate of 50 percent or higher. For females, gang membership ranges from zero to 40 percent of the total population. One out of every five institutions surveyed claimed that at least 10 percent of its juvenile female inmates were gang members.[9]

Statistics on the number of adult gang members in correctional facilities are equally sketchy. Camp and Camp conducted a national survey in which they reported that prison gangs exist, at a minimum, in thirty-three states.[10] Lane reported that 80 to 90 percent of inmates in the Illinois correctional system are affiliated with gangs.[11]

WHY DO PEOPLE JOIN GANGS?

A number of theories have been proposed to explain why gangs emerge. Macroanalytic theories look at issues of social organization that affect gang membership, whereas microanalytic theories focus on the individual needs, character traits, and personalities of typical gang members. Any theory attempting to account for the emergence of gangs, however, must contain explanations that encompass the individual, community, and society.[12]

It is commonly believed that gangs are part of lower-class communities in urban settings; however, they also exist in suburban and rural areas.[13] Because gangs represent a cohort of people from the local area, the community's attitude often comes close to denial. This, in turn, furthers gang activity since gangs tend to flourish in climates of tolerance or ambivalence. Whether causes or symptoms, poverty, racism, and rapid demographic changes all are associated with the presence of gangs and often indicate that the community is in trouble or crisis.

Gangs often emerge when businesses have migrated out of the community, or where the job market has shifted from an industrial to a more service-oriented focus. Frederick Thrasher, one of the often-cited and early gang researchers, has noted that gang communities are characterized by "deteriorating neighborhoods, shifting populations, and the mobility and disorganization of the slum."[14] Many gang members eventually "mature-out" of the gang by getting a job or going back to school. However, continuing economic hardship and social isolation prolong the life span of gang affiliation. As Conly indicates, "the lack of opportunities for jobs in a community doesn't allow a gang member to mature-out, so there is re-emergence."[15]

Gangs also emerge where there has been disorganization caused by rapid shifts in the ethnic or racial makeup of an area. The racial oppression hypothesis considers ethnic rivalry and racial discrimination to be at the heart of the gang problem.[16] For example, in Reno, Nevada—an area with ample jobs in the gaming and hospitality industries—the city's changing ethnic composition has caused gang activity to increase. Reno is estimated to have approximately twenty gangs, thus raising the potential for racial conflict.

In respect to microanalytic theories, Hagedorn analyzes gang crime in terms of "life chances"—a version of "underclass theory," that sees poverty and social decay as giving rise to criminality.[17] Vigil uses the term *multiple marginality*, meaning that people who experience prejudice and discrimination experience alienation.[18] Quinney, Young, and Knox use the term *surplus population* to identify groups that cannot obtain economic livelihood because they are not absorbed into a productive capacity in the economy.[19] Therefore, in a society that emphasizes material success, this surplus population becomes a causal link for gang affiliation and criminality. Still within the microanalytic view, people are said to join gangs because they have little "opportunity structure"—employment opportunities, family support, educational achievement, or access to services.[20]

Knox suggests that the "H-factor"—a cluster of human development traits or "human capital"—overlaps both the underclass and surplus population concepts. The H-factor includes such important variables as education, employment history, job training, and socialization. As Knox relates, "This 'H-factor' can be conceived of as either a factor at the individual level of analysis facilitating the onset of deviance, delinquency, crime, or gang activity or a factor that compounds the ability of society to reintegrate these persons into a legitimate career trajectory."[21]

Klein notes that the individual's need for identity, status, or belonging is responsible for gang activity.[22] Conly adds to this list the need for acceptance, recognition, protection, love, understanding, money, opportunity, power discipline (consistency), structure, shelter, food, clothing, nurturing, respect, self-esteem, social support or friendship, entertainment or fun, and to accomplish goals that are difficult to achieve without gang affiliation. She also cites as factors circumstances such as hopelessness, violence in youths' lives, growing up with values counter to the mainstream, dysfunctional families, dropout/school failure, and previous involvement in crime.[23]

Spergel indicates that peer groups can be a significant factor in gang affiliation.[24] Gang members are frequently recruited from schools. Students who are doing poorly and struggling with the language as well as students who need and want to be accepted by their peers are often vulnerable to gang recruitment. In many ways, the gang provides support that is not found in traditional institutions such as the family or school. The recruitment strategy is utilitarian: gangs will recruit those whose interests and skills match the group's needs.

The family unit has been referred to as the last line of defense against the origin of crime. However, the family scenario too often is one of living in public housing or poverty, witnessing violence, drug abuse, predominantly single parenting, a lack of positive male role models, few people working, and everyone struggling to survive. Still, family breakdown or disorganization is only one of the many factors that give rise to gangs.

WHAT ARE SOME CHARACTERISTICS OF GANGS?

The characteristics of gangs vary depending on their demographics, structure, degree of organization, and the social milieux in which they exist. Gangs can be at various stages of development and risk to the community, ranging from loosely knit organizations to established criminal syndicates. Some gangs, such as the Aryan Brotherhood, form around a philosophical perspective and engage in a variety of "hate crimes." Others, such the Tongs, are more profit-oriented and prey on businesses more regularly than do street gangs. The more well-organized gangs may affiliate with adult community organizations and have national or international networks and secret societies.

Fagan studied gangs in Chicago, Los Angeles, and New York and found four general types: (1) social gangs (28 percent) with little delinquency or drug use; (2) party gangs (7 percent) of drug users involved in drug dealing to support their own habit; (3) serious delinquents (37 percent) involved in violence, vandalism, and property offenses but with little or no drug dealing activity; and (4) heavy drug users (28 percent) involved in large-scale drug dealing—usually with one of the cliques rather than the whole gang specializing in drug dealing.[25]

Jankowski describes gang members as "defiant individualists"—self-reliant, with a strong sense of competitiveness and mistrust of others.[26] Klein suggests that 50 percent of a gang is composed of hard-core members who are quite violent and spend a significant portion of their lives in gang activities.[27] Yablonski also describes gang members as either "core" or "marginal."[28] In addition to these gang members, there are "wannabes" who are not yet committed to the gang but nevertheless are intrigued by it.

The organizational structure of gangs can be complex and subject to change over its lifetime. Jankowski notes that New York, Boston, and Los Angeles gangs assume one of three structures: (1) the vertical/hierarchical, in which the leadership is divided hierarchically into three or four offices or categories; (2) the horizontal/commission, in which officers have equal responsibility over gang members; and (3) the influential, which have two to four informal leaders.[29]

The typical gang is divided into five or so cliques or smaller groups, each of which may have about thirty or forty members. Each clique has its own leader and primary activities, depending on its interests or area of criminal specialization. In some gang organizations, cliques have little interaction, and it is rare for members to change cliques; in others, there may be more such interaction.

Spergel indicates that gangs comprise mostly males varying in age from adolescence (as young as twelve) to young adulthood (early to mid-twenties).[30] Klein states that the average age for a gang member, once estimated to be sixteen, is now closer to twenty.[31] Some gangs are age-graded, and they can be single-sex, whereas others have no such restrictions. Some gangs—like those in Miami, for example—might have a racial mix, but typically gangs are ethnically homogeneous.[32] Cliques usually pattern their ethnicity after the whole gang—whether a single ethnic/racial group or mixed.

There is often an intergenerational nature to gang involvement: Some law enforcement officers have reported witnessing two and three generations of gang involvement in a family. Moore reported that one-half of Chicano gang members have at least one relative in a gang; more than one-third have three or more relatives in a gang.[33] Such gang recruitment is traditionally through courtship rather than force, with older members often bringing their younger siblings into the gang.

HOW MUCH DO GANGS CONTRIBUTE TO CRIME?

It is difficult to answer this question from a statistical point of view. There are three commonly used sources of crime statistics: (1) the FBI Uniform Crime Report, (2) the victimization survey, and (3) self-report surveys. Offense reports are not "double-tagged" (to indicate whether a gang was most likely responsible for a specific crime) by local enforcement agencies, so it is difficult to get a national perspective on gang-related crime. The victimization survey fails to ask victims whether they thought the crime was gang related.[34] Moreover, all statistics on gangs require careful interpretation, because the definition of a gang varies depending on who is collecting the data and what methods are used. The political climate also can be a significant factor: When there is a desire to present an image that gang activity is under control, statistics tend to be underreported. Conversely, when law enforcement activity related to gangs is stepped up or prosecution patterns are changed, gang statistics increase (arrests and incarcerations).

Despite our lack of precision, there is enough information to conclude that gangs are overwhelmingly destructive in the communities where they operate. Their impact is aptly described as follows: "they do not strike back at the cause of their frustration and oppression, they strike back at themselves more conveniently."[35] Thrasher describes how white gangs took advantage of the race riots in Chicago in the 1960s.[36] The recent LA riots are another example of how gangs prey on their own neighborhoods. Gangs reportedly were responsible for a considerable amount of arson and theft during the riots, causing many businesses to close and, in turn, magnifying economic hardships in inner-city Los Angeles. Many members of the community lost their jobs and, some, their life savings as well. Criminal gang activity includes assault, murder, trafficking in illicit drugs, prostitution, extortion, theft, arson, gambling, loan-sharking, and even the well-organized chop shop (in which stolen vehicles are dismantled and sold for their parts). Hollywood movies have portrayed gangs as fighting over "turf." In reality, many gangs care more about money-making opportunities than they do about territory.[37] Although gang fights in school settings are often motivated by territorial disputes, such fighting is more characteristic of younger (early teenage) gang members; eventually, economic survival becomes paramount.

Indeed, although gangs are responsible for significant criminal activity, researchers indicate that their purpose is not solely crime.[38] Drug trafficking, for example, is one of the primary sources of income for gang members; it is estimated that 50 percent of gang members deal drugs at some time. It is unusual for a gang to be organized solely around drug dealing, however. When an individual gang member becomes successful at and exclusively engaged in drug dealing, he or she tends to leave or lose affiliation with the gang and become a private entrepreneur.

Conly reports that Los Angeles law enforcement officials have set the maximum penalty of law for gang members committing crimes, on the basis of the following guidelines:

- With regard to delinquency, a gang member delinquent is "worse" than a non-gang member delinquent.

- There are more non-gang delinquents, but gangs are associated with more violent and nonviolent crime, truancy, and alcohol and drug abuse.

- Female gang members have higher rates of delinquency and drug abuse than male non-gang members.[39]

With respect to lethal crime, studies indicate that gangs are associated with approximately 40 percent of all homicides. Some estimates indicate that 50 percent of juvenile crime and one-third of violent crime in urban areas are gang related.[40] It is generally easy for gang members to obtain weapons—primarily guns— which are frequently stolen and then sold on the street for under $100 (or a little more for automatic weapons). Automatic weapons are usually used in drive-by shootings, as opposed to hand-to-hand fighting with another gang. Gang violence tends to escalate when younger gang members try to outdo their predecessors or rival gang members. Moore suggests that violence itself can become a value or a gang subculture (subgroup or clique).[41] For example, when gang members refer to themselves as "wild" or "crazy," they tend to become focused on violent activity.

WHAT IS THE RELATIONSHIP BETWEEN GANG ACTIVITY AND SCHOOL VIOLENCE?

Often, gang activity and school violence are related; however, it is very difficult to determine the exact relationship. There is often a lack of awareness or outright denial by many school officials that gangs are a problem in the school setting. This leads to underreporting of violence that might be gang related. Conversely, once there is heightened awareness among school officials of the existence of gangs, the tendency is to overreport or attribute every incident to gang-related activity. Therefore, data on school violence and gangs are somewhat speculative. For example, surveys suggest that assaults constitute most of school violence. Assault is also a common gang activity. But to say that the two are related may be more correlational than causal.

Marginal gang members and younger "wannabes" may engage in school violence, particularly vandalism and fighting. There is evidence to suggest that before gang members eventually drop out of school, they attend infrequently and are often suspended or expelled for fighting or disruptive behaviors.[42] Eventually, these gang members may harass the school from the outside; data on school violence suggest that many assaults on students occur on the way to or from school. Moreover, if the gang is involved in drug dealing, schools are one of the primary marketplaces for this activity.

Surveys indicate that from 3 to 7 percent of students have carried a gun to school at least once.[43] Gang members indicate that they have easy access to guns and that 50 percent of them own a gun as either a status item or for their own protection.[44]

WHAT DOES THE FUTURE HOLD WITH RESPECT TO GANGS?

The gang phenomenon is not a temporary phase, nor will it disappear on its own. As American society becomes more complex, more violent, and more narcissistic, gangs will continue to excite and flourish. According to Klein, "[t]he American street gang is not a temporary aberration: it is a permanent by-product of our cities' enclaves and many of their suburban surroundings."[45] The question is: Will the current trends—increasing gang membership, increasing gang violence, and increasing school violence—continue?

Society's Role

Judging by the extent of recidivism, it appears that current efforts to suppress gang activity and rehabilitate criminal gang members have not only been merely reactive, but also often too late to effectively arrest the development and evolution of delinquent behavior. Yet, the "get tough on crime" policies currently popular throughout the country rely heavily on traditional suppression strategies such as law enforcement, prosecution, and incarceration.

Many believe that strategies such as community and neighborhood mobilization and other social intervention techniques and opportunities must be employed to deal with the gang problem.[46] Huff claims that there are "ecological areas that generate the highest crime rates, delinquency incarceration, mental illness, public assistance and other indicators of social pathology. So it is wise to invest in communitywide coordination to address the broad range of social ills in those communities."[47]

Authors such as Walter Miller suggest, however, that strategies that attempt to change the characteristics of lower socioeconomic classes are simply not effective.[48] This reasoning points to the obvious existence of other causal links to gang activity: some poor socioeconomic areas do not have gangs, while, on the other hand, gangs sometimes exist in areas where most households have at least one person employed.

A possible solution is a coordinated approach—involving prevention, intervention, and suppression strategies—to control gang behavior, and also improve the quality of life in many communities where gangs exist.

The School's Role

The school plays an important role in dealing with students at risk for gang involvement. School personnel, if properly educated and trained, can play a key role in intervening in gang activities. However, the role of schools in preventing and controlling gang activity must be expanded.

Schools should attempt to meet a wider range of student needs and improve their relationship with the community by assisting with parent training, crisis intervention, and employment and skills training.[49] Many more schools need to provide self-esteem-building programs, drug abuse prevention education, peer counseling, conflict resolution, tutoring, nutritional supplements, and testing for learning disabilities. Schools also should provide more after-school programs that offer students positive alternatives to gang activity.

In short, educators must *intervene* and offer programs for children at all levels, from preschool to high school—as well as the education provided in youth correctional institutions. For example, we have noted that rapid changes in the racial or ethnic composition in a community can result in the formation of gangs. Thus the school could address this issue directly by providing family counseling, tutoring, and socialization training for new immigrants. Moreover, strategies for educating teachers should emphasize the whole child and not just the child's educational needs.[50] The following programs serve as viable models for our schools:

The Paramount School. Paramount, California is a multiethnic community in transition whose schools have developed a program focused on preventing student gang involvement. The program—which involves second-, fifth-, and seventh-graders— raises students' knowledge about the negative consequences of gang membership (for example, the potential for loss of one's individual freedom, and for arrest or other trouble with police). Guest speakers from local colleges and private industry talk to the seventh-graders about future opportunities, jobs, careers, and so forth. There is also a program to heighten parents' awareness of gang activity and to suggest strategies for helping their children avoid or get out of gangs. A family counselor is also available, and everyone in the program is encouraged to get involved in recreation activities as alternatives to gang involvement.

Cities in Schools. Cities in Schools, and similar programs, strive to keep students in school. The program, which was founded in 1977 and operates in approximately twenty-two states, targets "high-risk" students who need help coping with issues such as drug abuse, teen pregnancy, and family relations. Each student is assigned to a professional worker and a "family" (other students in the program), while a counseling team works with the relevant people in the student's life (teachers, family members, medical professionals, probation officers, and so forth).

CONCLUSION

The United States seems to have adopted a renewed emphasis on values, ethics, and parenting skills—and schools can play a pivotal role in this trend. Our societal approach to dealing with gangs and reversing the increasing trend toward violence requires a coordinated allocation of resources and efforts by the law enforcement and criminal justice systems, communities, and schools.

NOTES

1. R. L. Bonn, *Criminology* (New York: McGraw-Hill Book Co., 1984), 33.

2. J. L. Albini, *The American Mafia: Genesis of a Legend* (New York: Appleton-Century-Crofts, 1971).

3. M. W. Klein, "Foreword," in *An Introduction to Gangs,* ed. G. W. Knox (Berrien Springs, Mich.: Vande Vere Publishing, 1991).

4. Ibid.

5. R. C. Huff, "Denial, Overreaction, and Misidentification: A Public Policy," in *Gangs in America*, ed. R. C. Huff (Newbury Park, N.J.: Sage, 1990), 280–81.

6. Interview with M. W. Klein conducted by C. Conly on February 28, 1991, as cited in *Street Gangs: Current Knowledge and Strategies, Issues and Practices in Criminal Justice* (Washington, D.C.: National Institute of Justice, 1993). Also see M. W. Klein, *Street Gangs and Street Workers* (Englewood Cliffs, N.J.: Prentice-Hall, 1971), 13.

7. C. Conly et al., *Street Gangs: Current Knowledge and Strategies, Issues and Practices in Criminal Justice* (Washington, D.C.: National Institute of Justice, 1993).

8. *Sword and Shield* 9, No. 22 (November 1993).

9. G. W. Knox, *An Introduction to Gangs* (Berrien Springs, Mich.: Vande Vere Publishing, 1991).

10. G. and C. G. Camp, *Prison Gangs: Their Extent, Nature, and Impact on Prisons* (Washington, D.C.: U.S. Department of Justice, 1985).

11. M. Lane, "Inmate Gangs," *Corrections Today* 51, No. 4 (July 1989): 98–99, 126–28.

12. Knox, *An Introduction to Gangs.*

13. J. M. Hagedorn and P. Macon, *People and Folks: Gangs, Crime and the Underclass in a Rustbelt City* (Chicago: Lakeview Press, 1988); D. J. Vigil, *Barrio Gangs: Street Life and Identity in Southern California* (Austin: University of Texas Press, 1988).

14. F. M. Thrasher, *The Gang: A Study of 1,313 Gangs in Chicago* (abridged) (Chicago: University of Chicago Press, 1968).

15. Conly et al., *Street Gangs*, 7–8.

16. J. Moore, *Homeboys: Gangs, Drugs, and Prison in the Barrios of Los Angeles* (Philadelphia: Temple University Press, 1978); R. K. Jackson and W. D. McBride, *Understanding Street Gangs* (Sacramento, Calif.: Custom Publishing, 1985).

17. Hagedorn and Macon, *People and Folks.*

18. Vigil, *Barrio Gangs.*

19. R. Quinney, *Class State and Crime* (New York: David McKay Co., 1977); T. R. Young, "Crime and Capitalism," a paper prepared for the Western Social Science Association, Denver, Colo. 1978; Knox, *An Introduction to Gangs.*

20. R. A. Cloward and L. E. Ohlin, *Delinquency and Opportunity* (New York: Free Press, 1960); G. W. Knox, "Perceived Closure and Respect for the Law Among Delinquent and Nondelinquent Youths," *Youth and Society* 9, No. 4 (June 1978): 385–406.

21. Knox, *An Introduction to Gangs.*

22. Conly interview with Klein as cited in *Street Gangs.*

23. Conly et al., *Street Gangs.*

24. I. Spergel, "Youth Gangs: Continuity and Change," in *Crime and Justice: A Review of Research,* eds. N. Morris and M. Tonry (Chicago: University of Chicago Press, 1990).

25. J. Fagan, "The Social Organization of Drug Use and Drug Dealing among Urban Gangs," *Criminology* 27, No. 4 (1989): 633–64.

26. M. S. Jankowski, *Islands in the Street and American Urban Society* (Berkeley, Calif.: University of California Press, 1991).

27. Klein, *Street Gangs and Street Workers.*

28. L. Yablonski, *The Violent Gang* (New York: Macmillan Publishers, 1962).

29. Jankowski, *Islands in the Street.*

30. Spergel, "Youth Gangs: Continuity and Change."

31. M. W. Klein, C. Maxon, and L. Cunningham, *"Crack," Street Gangs and Violence* (Center for Research on Crime and Social Control, University of Southern California, 1990).

32. Knox, *An Introduction to Gangs.*

33. J. Moore, "Changing Chicano Gangs: Acculturation, Generational Change, Evolution of Deviance or Emerging Underclass?," in *Proceedings of the Conference on Comparative Ethnicity,* eds. J. H. Johnson, Jr. and M. L. Oliver (Los Angeles: UCLA, Institute for Social Science Research, 1988).

34. Knox, *An Introduction to Gangs.*

35. C. S. Taylor, *Dangerous Society* (East Lansing: Michigan State University Press, 1990).

36. F. M. Thrasher, *The Gang: A Study of 1,313 Gangs, Third Impression* (abridged) (Chicago: University of Chicago Press, 1968).

37. D. G. Hardman, "Small Town Gangs," *Journal of Criminal Law, Criminology and Police Studies* 60, No. 2 (1969): 173–81.

38. Klein, *Street Gangs and Street Workers*; C. H. Conly, *Hearing Summary of the National Field Study on Gangs and Gang Violence in Dallas, Texas* (Washington, D.C.: National Institute of Justice, 1991).

39. Conly, *Street Gangs.*

40. W. B. Miller, *Violence by Youth Gangs and Youth Groups as a Crime Problem in Major American Cities* (Washington, D.C.: Government Printing Office, 1976); W. B. Miller, "Gangs, Groups and Serious Youth Crime," in *Critical Issues in Juvenile Delinquency,* eds. D. Schichdor and D. Kelly (Lexington, Mass.: Lexington Books, 1980).

41. Moore, "Changing Chicano Gangs."

42. A. Campbell and S. Muncer, "Them and Us: A Comparison of the Cultural Context of American Gangs and British Subcultures*," Deviant Behavior* 10, No. 3 (1989); 271–88.

43. Conly et al., *Street Gangs*; L. D. Bastian and B. M. Taylor, *A National Crime Victimization Survey Report* (Washington, D.C.: U.S. Department of Justice, 1991); L. Harris and Associates, *Violence in America's Public Schools*, Metlife Survey of the American Teacher, 1993.

44. C. M. Callahan and F. P. Rivara, "Urban High School Youth and Handguns, A School-Based Survey," *Journal of the American Medical Association* 267, No. 22 (June 10, 1992).

45. Klein, "Foreword" in *An Introduction to Gangs.*

46. Spergel, "Youth Gangs: Continuity and Change."

47. Huff, *Gangs in America.*

48. Miller, "Gangs, Groups and Serious Youth Crime."

49. Conly et al., *Street Gangs.*

50. Ibid.

4

Gangs and School Safety

Kenneth S. Trump

> Gangs infiltrate area middle schools.
> Gang members rob student of jacket.
> Gang member arrested with gun in school.

Headlines such as these top the list of nightmares of many school administrators. Teachers in schools across the country are expressing increased fear for their safety and the safety of their students. Parents are pressuring school administrators and boards to take swift action to prevent gang and other violence in their schools.

Should school officials and parents worry about a gang presence in school? Should they acknowledge that they cannot eliminate such a presence and simply pack their bags and close shop? Or is the presence of gang members, like many of the other social ills crossing the school entrance, something that is manageable when proper steps are taken to deal with the issue?

This chapter presents a practical perspective for recognizing that in the worst scenarios, steps can be taken to improve school safety and security. The success of these efforts depends largely on a rational awareness and response by teachers and staff, principals, top administrators, board members, parents, and the overall school community. By understanding gang growth and development, assessing the awareness and response styles, and quickly recognizing the identifiers, school officials, parents, and others will be better prepared to apply balanced strategies for minimizing gang behavior in and around schools.

The mystery is not why we have youth violence and gangs in schools but why we cannot better manage our response to these issues.

GANG GROWTH AND DEVELOPMENT

Simply put, gang development is a process, not an event. School officials do not go home on Friday evening and return on Monday morning to find that over the weekend gang troubles popped out of the woodwork, and now they have an unmanageable problem that will not go away.   Recognition and acceptance that there is a gang presence in and around a school in the early stages of the process is one key factor to successfully managing gang concerns.

What is the definition of a gang? Are there "good gangs?" We have always had gang members in schools, right? These questions surface frequently in educational circles when discussing gangs in schools. Although the questions sound simple, the answers are more complex.

There is no universal definition of a gang in the United States. Dr. C. Ronald Huff offers the following definitions, distinguishing the youth gang from an organized crime group:

Youth gang: A collectivity consisting primarily of adolescents and young adults who (a) interact frequently with one another; (b) are frequently and deliberately involved in illegal activities; (c) share a common collective identity that is usually, but not always, expressed through a gang name; and (d) typically express that identity by adopting certain symbols or claiming control over certain "turf" (persons, places, things, or economic markets).

Organized crime group: A collectivity consisting primarily of adults who (a) interact frequently with one another; (b) are frequently and deliberately involved in illegal activities directed toward economic gain, primarily through the provision of illegal goods and services; and (c) generally have better defined leadership and organizational structure than does the youth gang.[1]

While the two terms may at times be interrelated and the distinction somewhat unclear, Huff's definitions provide an important explanation for the failure of school officials to recognize and acknowledge a gang presence in their school. Most school administrators, and even many community leaders, conceptualize the gang in terms of the organized crime group definition based on their limited exposure to the gang phenomenon, which often stems only from media sources. Thus, when confronted with the idea that there is a growing gang presence in their school, the average administrator denies that this is taking place since, in most cases, there is not a highly sophisticated network of youth engaged in providing illegal goods and services in the school—that is, no organized crime group. Therefore, there is no significant gang threat to the school, and, at best, the school may have some students who are "just wannabes."

Unfortunately, this line of thinking contains many flaws. First and most important, the administrator fails to recognize the youth gang and its members who, although involved individually and at times collectively in illegal activities, are more turf and locally oriented than the organized crime group. Although there most likely will not be the organized structure and leadership associated with the organized crime group in a school setting, the administrator has completely dismissed the other gang—the youth gang—and in doing so allows the youth gang to continue its process of growth and development in the school.

In addition, by viewing students affiliated with youth gangs as "just wannabes," the school administrator fails to recognize that a wannabe may be more of a safety threat to staff and students than the real gang member. Wannabes, those perceived to be mimicking the appearance and behavior of actual gang members, may perform more blatant acts of disruption and criminal activity than the confirmed gang member, simply for the purpose of establishing their credibility in the gang and school communities. Furthermore, by appropriately focusing on the *behavior* of youth, administrators will quickly recognize that there really is no difference between a "wannabe" and a "real" gang member. What is the difference between a "wannabe" gang of Rollin' Twenty Crips in Cleveland, Ohio, who are breaking into gun shops, dealing drugs, and assaulting youth, and a "real" gang of Rollin' Twenty Crips in Long Beach, California, who are also breaking into gun shops, dealing drugs, and assaulting youth? The answer is simple: There is no difference. The behavior is identical. And *behavior* is the key factor for school officials to assess.

This is not to completely dismiss the impact of the "megagangs" of major urban areas such as Los Angeles and Chicago on mid-sized and smaller communities across the nation. Most school gang violence stems from local gangs that fit the Huff definition of a youth gang rather than an organized crime group similar to the megagangs. Still, many youth gangs pattern their names, signs, symbols, appearance, and behavior after the organized crime groups, most notably the Crips and Bloods of Los Angeles and the Folk and People nations of Chicago. Again, the focus should be not on whether the youth are affiliated with the "real" gangs from these cities, but rather on their behavior. Many communities will see the development of gangs whose names and identities are defined by a particular local neighborhood, school, or other factor, with no resemblance to gangs in other cities. School officials must concentrate on the disruption of rules and criminal behavior in and around the school. The names of the gangs, the nicknames of their members, and related identifiers are critical knowledge for school staff, but are critical as an investigative tool, not as the final point of focus.

School officials, parents, and others in the school community must exercise caution to avoid falling into the stereotypes and misperceptions fostered by the media and broader society as they relate to gang members. Typically, gang members are portrayed as inner-city minority males. In reality, gang membership crosses all boundaries of age, sex, race, academic achievement, and economic status. Gangs, like drugs and other crime, are a symptom of broader social and economic conditions, and are present in urban, suburban, and even rural areas of the country.

It is therefore not unthinkable to find a white male straight-A student from a two-parent family who holds gang meetings in the basement of a $180,000-suburban-home basement. Police and school employees are also recognizing that female students sometimes carry weapons and drugs for male students; enforcement officials often rely on past stereotypes of females, leading them to become lax in their search and pursuit of these items. There is also an increased awareness of the potential for adverse behavior in even very young children. It is not uncommon for second- and third-graders to be aware of the gangs and gang members in their community; unfortunately, it is also not uncommon to see the early signs of gang behavior in the fifth and sixth grades.

Although there is no universal definition for gangs, Dr. Huff's distinction between youth gangs and organized crime groups is a good tool for helping school officials better conceptualize "gang" as it applies to their setting. It also abolishes the notion that "good gangs" exist; gangs are involved in illegal or antisocial behavior, and this definitely is not good. Finally, while gangs existed several decades ago, today's gang members are generally younger, better armed, and more violent than their counterparts in the past.

THE AWARENESS/RESPONSE CONTINUUM

Understanding the gang growth and development process and recognizing the impact of stereotypes related to gang composition are only two important aspects of better addressing the issue of gangs in the school environment. Recognizing where other individuals, organizations, and communities stand in terms of awareness and response provides insight into formulating appropriate strategies for better managing and minimizing gang and other school violence. The continuum along which individuals, organizations, and communities may lie in terms of awareness and response to gangs ranges from lack of awareness to overreaction.

Lack of awareness is not knowing what to look for and not knowing how to respond when a problem is detected. This characterizes the status of many educators in terms of violence-related issues, particularly gangs. Few, if any, colleges and universities require courses on school safety for undergraduate or graduate-level programs for school personnel. Because of contractual and time limitations, and the unavailability of quality trainers, many schools are unable to provide adequate in-service training to faculty and staff. Therefore, what many educators know about gangs and youth violence comes only from the media and personal experience, neither of which adequately prepares them to prevent, minimize, or manage those incidents that do occur.

Denial occurs when there is an awareness of the problem but instead of acknowledging it, the individual, organization, or community refuses to admit that it exists. There may also be knowledge of the appropriate response needed to address the problem. In his 1988 study on Ohio gangs, Huff identified denial as a major obstacle to effectively managing the youth gang problem. Huff particularly noted the impact on schools:

It is probable that the official denial of gang problems actually facilitates victimization by gangs, especially in the public schools. School principals in several Ohio cities are reluctant to acknowledge "gang-related" assaults for fear that such "problems" may be interpreted as negative reflections of their management ability. This "paralysis" may actually encourage gang-related assaults and may send the wrong signals to gang members, implying that they can operate within the vacuum created by this "political paralysis."[2]

Concerns about image may further exacerbate denial when districts are seeking public support for additional funding during difficult financial times.

Wayne C. Torok, a veteran Cleveland (Ohio) Police Department lieutenant who designed and serves as the officer in charge of the city's youth/gang unit, describes the next stage on the continuum as a *qualified admittance*. According to Lieutenant Torok, a qualified admittance exists when visible steps are undertaken to make it appear that the problem is being recognized and handled, or to actually recognize and respond to the problem but only in a limited manner and not to the actual degree in which it needs to be addressed.[3] A school-specific example of a qualified admittance would be:

> School principal: We recognize the presence of gangs as a community issue that could spill over into the schools. We maintain regular communication with the police.

> Translation: Gangs start in the community, but now they are in my school. We call the police to report crimes that take place in the school because we have to do so.

By making the first statement, the school administrator attempts to convince the audience (staff, parents, the media, and so forth) that the problem is outside of the school and implies that the administrators maintain regular contact with the police to be proactive in minimizing the problem. In reality, the translation is what is actually happening. While this example—of an administrator's partial picture of the problem and the minimal official response to address it—may seem harsh, it is not unrealistic.

A *balanced and rational* perspective recognizes that there is neither a single cause for gang formation nor a single strategy to eliminate gangs. While this may appear to be common-sense thinking, experienced gang specialists find it to be the least common position held by most individuals, organizations, or communities. Police blame parents. Parents blame school officials. School officials blame societal influences. Politicians blame the media and each other. After pointing the finger of blame, each offers a solution: hold parents accountable, make teachers teach better, unplug television, and so forth. The finger-pointing and single-strategy solution offerings continue, with few recognizing that not only are a combination of the "blame factors" responsible for the problem, but also a combination of the single strategies necessary for an effective response to better manage and minimize gang behavior.

Finally, the potential for *overreaction* exists when dealing with high-profile issues such as gang violence and school safety. Overreaction occurs when a gang presence is overdramatized and responses are drastic or inappropriately focused. The classic example of overreaction followed a community awareness presentation by a gang specialist who received a call the next day from a citizen who said, "After your presentation last night, I realized that there is gang graffiti all over my sidewalk. The gangs must be all around me. Something needs to be done immediately." On inspection, the specialist found the "gang graffiti" to be markings by local utility workers repairing a nearby sewer. Similar overreaction exists in schools, such as when untrained or misinformed staff believe that every student wearing a particular brand of sports apparel belongs to a gang.

These categories—lack of awareness, denial, qualified admittance, balanced and rational, and overreaction—can help assess the awareness and response levels of individuals, organizations, and communities. While individuals generally fall into one category, it is possible for an organization to hold one position while individuals within the organization hold a different position. For example, a school board may have a lack of awareness, while the superintendent is in denial, and, at the same time, teachers and administrators hold a balanced and rational perspective of what is taking place and what needs to be done to address the problem.

While all of these different positions are held just in the school system, the overall community could be in a state of overreaction owing to one or more high-profile incidents, increased or distorted media coverage, or for other similar reasons. Meanwhile, the city government response to the entire situation may be a qualified admittance; for example, "We have had several isolated incidents take place recently. We have stepped up police patrol in the areas where these have taken place and increased our communication with the different agencies involved." At the same time, entities of other city subdivisions, such as the police department, may hold multiple perspectives similar to the school example.

This model illustrates how officials think and act, or in many cases do not think and act, to manage gang behavior in schools and communities. Considering all of the differences in awareness and response, both within and among organizations in the same communities, it is not difficult to understand why the gang situation is not better managed. Until everyone pulls together, schools and communities will never experience a balanced, rational, efficient, and effective method of managing gang violence.

GANG IDENTIFIERS IN SCHOOLS

Although there is no checklist of criteria that will guarantee easy recognition of a gang presence in schools, certain identifiers may alert school staff to recognize and investigate suspected gang membership in its early stages. These identifiers include graffiti, colors, tattoos, handsigns and handshakes, initiations, language, and behavior.

Graffiti

Gang members love to advertise their gang affiliation. One of the most common ways of doing so is to write their gang signs and symbols on desks, walls, clothing, books, and other locations throughout the school. Teachers should look closely at all notebooks and textbooks for unusual signs or symbols, as well as inside notebooks for gang literature or "lit," as the gang members call it. Gang "lit" books contain the signs, symbols, poems, prayers, initiation procedures, rank and structure, members' nicknames, and even members' real names and telephone numbers. It is not unusual for school officials to find lit books as large as sixty to one hundred pages. Gang graffiti has also been found on desktops, chalkboards, bulletin boards, cafeteria tables, chairs, restroom walls, the outside of the school building, and inside lockers, to name just a few places. In fact, gang graffiti has even been found in the principal's office, put there by gang members awaiting disciplinary hearings.

Colors

Typically, the term *colors* refers to a particular color of clothing associated with a specific gang. Areas with chronic gang problems may even see bandannas or clothing worn, with gang names and symbols openly displayed. In other areas, it may be more subtle, such as a particular brand of clothing, possibly a specific line of sports or athletic wear, or even lower profile, such as the same type of jewelry item, haircuts, one finger nail painted a certain color, and so forth.

Tattoos

Another gang identifier is the tattoo. Gang tattoos are usually found on the arms or chest of male gang members; however, it is not unusual to find them on female gang members, too. Some tattoos have also been found on hands, fingers, and ankles. Teardrop tattoos near the eye, a symbol of respect to fallen fellow gang members or a reference to individuals killed by the gang member wearing it (depending who you talk to), is yet another identifier. Many tattoos are put on by the gang members themselves rather than a professional tattoo artist. Generally, tattoos are worn by more hard-core and high-ranking gang members.

Handsigns and Handshakes

Members use handsigns to acknowledge membership in a particular gang. These signs are usually a version of the symbols associated with the gang. They are often hard to decipher, particularly because they are "thrown up" in rapid fashion. Some gang members are particularly skilled in "stacking"—throwing up multiple signs in an ongoing, rapid fashion. Alert observers recognize this as suspicious activity. However, most observers are not able to identify the specific symbols being used, particularly during stacking. Two or more gang members may perform handshakes representative of the gang signs and unique to their respective gang.

Initiations

Gang members often have to pass an initiation ritual to obtain membership in a gang. The exact initiation procedure varies by gang. Some unusual initiations have included females having to have sex with multiple male gang members and self-infliction of injuries such as ankle-shooting, and so forth. By far the most common method, however, involves taking beatings or fighting multiple gang members at the same time. Although initiations often take place at gang meetings in parks or playgrounds after school hours and on weekends, it is not unusual to have initiations take place on school grounds and inside school buildings. Gang initiations have been detected as students go to and from school; on school grounds during school hours by students cutting class; during gym classes, disguised as part of a physical training class exercise; in school restrooms; and even in hallways between and during classes. School personnel should be alert for suspicious bruises, wounds, and injuries, particularly those where officials suspect gang involvement and those accompanied by student accounts that simply do not add up to a believable story.

Language

Uncommon terms or phrases associated with gangs are more difficult for the school official to detect, since pop culture and the language of youth change so frequently. Still, gangs have their own unique language to some extent, particularly words and phrases to show disrespect for opposing gang members. For example, Crips show disrespect for Bloods by calling them "Slobs," Bloods show disrespect for Crips by calling them "Crabs," and the list goes on. To help better understand the student population in general, teachers and administrators should attempt to keep up with pop culture, including the meanings of words and phrases frequently used by youth. The same concept applies to gang members. When in doubt, go right to the source—ask the students.

Behavior

Too often, attention to gangs focuses strictly on the identifiers, particularly graffiti interpretation, recognition of colors, handsigns, and so forth. These identifiers are important because they serve as a tool for school officials to recognize gang presence more quickly and as a lead to further investigate the involvement of specific students for early intervention and prevention purposes. The critical element is student behavior. Gangs differ from youth social clubs and student activity groups in that gangs are involved in criminal or antisocial behavior. Thus the inquiry should not stop at interpreting graffiti symbols or prohibiting students from wearing a particular color bandanna. School officials must go one step beyond to assess changes in student behavior.

What behavior do school officials need to examine? Typically, gang-related activity is perceived to center on guns and drugs. However, the majority of school gang-related incidents involve assaults, fights, threats, and related offenses. For example, 1992 statistics from the Youth Gang Unit of the Cleveland (Ohio) Public Schools revealed that approximately 75 percent of their school gang-related incidents involved assaults, threats, fights, menacing, disruptive behavior, and trespassing.[4] Many of the incidents that take place in school start as "he-said, she-said" rumors, boyfriend and girlfriend trouble, and other interpersonal conflicts that escalate into group and gang altercations. The difference, however, between gang and non-gang offenses is that gang offenses tend to escalate more quickly, involve a larger number of people than one-on-one conflicts, and pose a significant threat for more intense violence in the schools and outside in the community. While an administrator may be able to resolve a one-on-one altercation between two male students over a girl, it is much more difficult to resolve what starts as a one-on-one altercation between two male gang member students over a girl but escalates to involve the dozen associates of each participant in a short period of time.

STRATEGIES FOR MANAGING GANGS IN SCHOOL

The balanced and rational perspective presented earlier noted that many individuals focus on one single strategy as the key to better managing and minimizing gang behavior. Beyond the realm of academic research, common sense alone should suggest that if there is a single solution to the gang problem, there would be no need for further discussion. Since it is obvious that there is no single solution, school officials, in an effort to reach a balanced and rational perspective, should design a program of combined strategies based on strict enforcement of disciplinary regulations and criminal codes; provision of services to intervene with children displaying current involvement or interest in gangs; and the use of education and training for preventing gang growth in the schools and overall school community. Program components may include schools as neutral grounds; order, structure and discipline; dress standards; training school personnel; student intervention and prevention programs; school security assessments; parental involvement; and community collaboration.

Schools as Neutral Grounds

Administrators should identify schools as neutral grounds and communicate that gang, drug, and weapon activities in and around schools will receive a priority response. School board policies and district procedures must reflect the communicated priority. Most important, follow-through by administrators and staff must reflect that the policies and procedures are not simply communication alone, but that they are enforced in a firm, fair, and consistent manner.

Unfortunately, too many educational administrators are more concerned that their suspensions, expulsions, and incident reports will be viewed as a negative reflection of their management abilities. So they make every effort to reduce these figures by partially dealing with the problems, underreporting the problems, or ignoring the problems altogether. The result is that educators communicate one message in their written policies and procedures and public communications, but in reality they send the message to the students, including the gang members, that they can operate with few or no consequences for their criminal or disruptive behavior in and around schools. In the end, when incidents take place that they can no longer hide or distort in their reporting, school administrators are accurately perceived as inefficient managers—the very label they tried so hard to avoid.

Order, Structure, and Discipline

Schools must provide the same offerings as gangs—order, structure, and discipline. Believe it or not, gangs want structure and respect the discipline provided by teachers and administrators, as long as it is applied in a firm, fair, and consistent manner. The gang provides order by establishing rules and regulations to be followed by the member; structure by having specific ranks with identified roles and responsibilities; and discipline by administering punishments, most notably in the form of severe beatings by fellow gang members, for those members who violate the rules of the gang. It is therefore understandable that if youth do not receive order, structure, and discipline at home, in school, and in the community, they will turn to another source—the gang. Thus, while the student, gang member or not, will most likely not thank the teacher or principal each day for imposing order, structure, and discipline, he or she will, in the long run, respect the officials for providing such an environment. If this environment is not provided, school officials can expect increased gang activity and increased gang victimization of students and staff.

Dress Standards

As part of the effort to provide an orderly educational setting, schools should adopt standards as to the appearance of students during school hours. Many schools are moving toward dress codes that establish a uniform appearance for all students. This not only reduces the wearing of gang-related apparel, but also minimizes the competition and status challenges that occupy far too much of the students' attention. When the issue of uniforms is brought up, however, red flags appear regarding the concern of infringement on students' freedom of expression, parental concerns about buying new clothing, infringement on parents' choice of clothing, and so forth. Contrary to the rhetoric associated with the initial opposition to such a proposal, many school officials, parents, and even students who proceed with school dress codes report few problems and, believe it or not, an actual acceptance of the program once it is initiated and in place for a period of time. Parents quickly find that the uniform method of dress is actually cheaper, not more expensive, than popular brands of clothing that forever change in popularity among youth. Parents also find that it reduces the morning hassle of figuring out what the youth will wear to school each day. For their part, school officials find that it helps in a variety of ways, ranging from reducing competition among students to helping school officials identify nonstudents who trespass in school buildings.

A few basic points regarding uniform dress are as follows:

- Uniform should be interpreted to mean a uniform or standard method of dress. Input from school staff, parents, and students should be obtained in the process of determining what the standards will be and in implementing a specific policy.
- Uniform dress will not totally eliminate gang identifiers or student conflicts.
- Uniform dress is one part of an overall program. This component alone will not solve gang and other school violence problems.

School officials who choose not to proceed with a uniform standard of dress still must enforce basic rules regarding student appearance that is disruptive to the educational process. Some fashion trends in the broader community simply are not appropriate for schools. For example, regardless of whether baggy pants represent pop culture style or gang affiliation, the bottom line (no pun intended) is that an exposed derriere is inappropriate for and disruptive to the school environment. To allow such disruptive behavior only signals to the students that their behavior is acceptable, leaving them open to progress to even more disruptive behavior in school.

Training School Personnel

School administrators, teachers, and support staff need a great deal more training than they currently receive on gangs, drugs, and related crime topics. Most colleges and many school districts fail to adequately train school personnel in these areas since they have not been part of the traditional educational preparation curriculum. As a result, too many people working with kids in schools are unable to recognize the mere presence of gangs, drugs, and other ills, much less understand the reasons for their presence or methods to create appropriate strategies for early intervention and prevention.

While no finger is pointed at the educator per se, fingers are starting to point at colleges and school districts for failing to better prepare school personnel to deal with these issues. Colleges and school districts are slowly beginning to address these needs. However, the question then arises: What is appropriate training for school personnel?

This question may be answered in several ways. First, what is *not* appropriate is the scare-tactic approach of showing educators slides or video of graffiti and weapons, and then sending them out to deal with the issue once they can merely recognize it. It is also inappropriate to conduct extensive lectures on the sociological causes of gang formation without telling educators more than simply why the problem exists. In short, it is inappropriate to discuss why the problem exists and how to recognize it without giving the educators suggestions on what they can do about the problem in their school.

Training for school personnel on gangs (and other related issues) should address a minimum of three questions:

1. *What is the problem?* This segment should include discussions of the sociological perspective of why kids join gangs, how gangs grow and develop, how gangs are organized and structured, and so forth.
2. *How do you recognize it?* This segment should concentrate on practical identifiers of gangs and gang members. It should also describe the behaviors associated with gang membership. It is here that the graffiti and weapon slides are appropriate.
3. *What do you do?* Once educators understand why the problem exists and how to recognize it, the next step is to determine what should be done to address it. Too often trainers forget that the average educator has not received any training in gangs, or even crime in general. Trainers should inform educators of the basic steps to be taken to minimize school gang activity, and of the resources available

in the neighborhoods to help school personnel deal with the broader community issue of gangs.

School officials must also determine who should be conducting the staff training. Typically, administrators turn to local police officials for training. While the police are one potential source of information, school officials should realize that the police department may have provided limited training or no training to its own staff because of budgetary constraints, denial, or other factors.

On the other end of spectrum, school officials should recognize that former gang members may also not be the answer to educating school officials, students, or anyone else on the subject. While this seems like a novel idea, school personnel should give this option close consideration, particularly in light of the increasing organization, sophistication, and political manipulation of former gang members. Though reformed individuals have a legitimate role to play in education, caution should be taken and further investigation made into the background of the so-called experts who appear to have the answers to all of the schools' problems.

Many cities will have individuals within schools, police departments, probation offices, or youth service agencies who have undergone training or self-initiated study on the subject long before their own agencies officially recognize the gang problem. A little bit of searching may ensure quality information and avoid headaches in the long term.

Student Intervention and Prevention Programs

Although many schools have initiated education programs and intervention services for students on the subject of drugs, gangs, and other street crime, knowledge possessed by the average elementary school student often is not openly addressed in schools. There are many curriculum-based programs to educate students about the underlying issues of gang involvement, but only recently have these programs been implemented in local schools. Beyond traditional programs, schools should consider having local professionals knowledgeable about gangs talk with students about the negative aspects of gang involvement and the practical alternatives available to students. Depending on the intensity of gang problems in a given district, the school system may need to consider hiring its own internal staff to conduct gang training, education, and intervention efforts.

Schools also need to create conflict-resolution mechanisms for students so that they can avoid attempting to solve problems themselves, or by using their gang. Such strategies have included peer mediation programs or teen courts actually operated by specially trained students. Students, including gang members, appear to respect the punishment, consequences, and intervention strategies applied by their peers better than those applied by adults. Of course, these programs still require adult involvement and supervision.

Too often officials attempt to identify the problems and appropriate solutions without consulting the main population affected—the youth. It is important to acquire student input when identifying school safety concerns and, most important, identifying strategies that can be implemented to minimize violence in schools. This may be accomplished in numerous ways, including use of formal written student surveys or class time to solicit input from students. Some schools have even held public hearing sessions to identify student concerns and strategies. Adults are often surprised to learn that the problems they identify are different from those identified by the students, as are the solutions for minimizing youth violence.

School Security Assessments

School leaders need to take a close look at the security posture of their facilities. Typically, security assessments focus on physical security issues such as locks, lighting, and equipment. Too often, responses to the entire school security issue focus on fences, locks, cameras, and even metal detectors. While these issues are important and in some schools may be unquestionably necessary, they are not the total solution to improving school safety and security.

Administrators need to examine in detail a much broader scope of issues when conducting school security assessments. These issues include special event management, crisis planning, transportation safety, discipline policies and procedures, intervention services, physical security, and much more. By broadening their perspective of school security, educational leaders will be better able to assess their current safety posture and implement corrective actions to minimize future risks.

Parental Involvement

Most teachers and principals quickly acknowledge that there is a clear need for increased parental involvement with their children and the school. While it is easy to point fingers and assign blame, it is not as easy to secure parental involvement. There are no magical solutions for doing so. However, it is important that school officials be persistent in informing parents of suspected gang involvement and in offering, in a nonthreatening manner, assistance in securing resources for addressing the child's needs that may otherwise be fulfilled by the gang. The school should also serve as a facilitator, if not provider, of gang awareness training for parents and others in the broader school community.

Community Collaboration

Schools alone cannot expect to successfully have an impact on gangs and other violence issues generated by the broader social and economic ills of the larger society. Gangs are not solely a school problem, nor are they solely a community problem. School officials must establish formal cooperative relationships and communication networks with parents, criminal justice service agencies, social services, and other community entities to coordinate limited resources and to share information that affects all of these different agencies and individuals who serve the same children. These efforts, whether in the form of a committee, task force, or other formal body, should be ongoing, regardless of whether there are specific incidents causing alarm in the school community.

A WORD OF CAUTION

As school districts are increasingly faced with addressing violence in schools, and as funding to do so is also increased, a potential for abuse quickly surfaces. School officials should be very cautious of "overnight experts" offering packaged programs, training, and curriculum materials for large fees. Schools, like society as a whole, have been alarmed by the growing youth violence, and so, in many areas appear willing to try any approach, traditional or nontraditional, that might work to minimize youth violence.

It is recommended that administrators closely examine the qualifications, background, and experience of individuals offering to bring such services into schools. They should also look closely at the goals and objectives of the programs these individuals propose, as well as at the evaluation methods used to substantiate the program's effectiveness.

CONCLUSION

School officials cannot politicize the safety and security of students and staff. Educators must learn about gang growth and development, understand the awareness and response methods to the problem, come to recognize a gang presence, and respond in a balanced and rational manner. In short, educators need only remember their ABCs:

Assess the problem or problem potential, acknowledge and act with a

Balanced and rational approach that is undertaken as a part of a broader

Community collaboration.

Remember, the mystery is not why we have youth violence and gangs in schools, but why we cannot better manage our response to these issues.

NOTES

1. C. R. Huff, "Gangs in the United States," in *The Gang Intervention Handbook*, eds. A. P. Goldstein and C. R. Huff (Champaign, Ill.: Research Press, 1993), 4–5.

2. C. R. Huff, "Youth Gangs and Public Policy in Ohio: Findings and Recommendations," a report to the Ohio Conference on Youth Gangs and the Urban Underclass (Columbus: Ohio State University, 1988), 9.

3. W. C. Torok, personal interview, November 17, 1994.

4. Cleveland Public Schools, "Youth Gang Unit Statistics" (Cleveland: Cleveland Public Schools, 1992).

Part II

THE CAUSES OF SCHOOL VIOLENCE

5

Media and Television Violence: Effects on Violence, Aggression, and Antisocial Behaviors in Children

Daniel John Derksen and Victor C. Strasburger

> Nothing takes the sorry measure of the television industry's supposed sense of responsibility more than the state of children's programming. Periodic apologies for too much violence are followed by still another spate of cartoons featuring ferocious warriors or karate killers. Promises to improve schedules end up with news reports that some broadcasters list "GI Joe" as educational programming. Content quality is obviously not as important as product tie-ins.[1]

Violent and other antisocial behaviors involving children and adolescents are being blamed on the media. In the United States, controversy over the influence of the media on children remains intense. Yet more violent acts are depicted on television, sales of video games depicting death and destruction are skyrocketing, and many rock videos show violence as a viable means of conflict resolution. Efforts to limit the acts of violence shown in the media are met with the industry's considerable financial resources to resist responsible programming. Although media violence is not the leading cause of real-life violence, it is a significant cause, and one that is easily remediable. The major components of the media affecting children—television (videos, movies), print (comic books, magazines, and newspapers), and radio—continue to have powerful negative effects on American children.

Television has a dominant role. American children view two hundred thousand violent acts on television by the age of eighteen.[2] While parents have a central role in influencing the lives of their children, television has a powerful effect on the development of unhealthy activities, negative attitudes, and antisocial behaviors. American children and adolescents spend twenty-three to twenty-eight hours per week viewing television.[3] This three to four hours per day displaces healthy activities, including exercise, play, reading, and homework. By high school graduation, twelve thousand hours will have been spent in formal classroom instruction, yet fifteen thousand hours will have been spent in front of the television.[4]

The United States ranks first among industrialized nations in violent death rates,[5] and over one thousand studies and reviews suggest media-portrayed violence as a cause of or contributing factor to real-life violence.[6] Current television programming exposes children to twelve thousand violent acts per year.[7] This media violence may facilitate the learning of aggressive and antisocial behavior and desensitize viewers to violence. Although the entertainment industry claims that images portrayed in movies and television are not real, children believe them to be real.[8] Furthermore, the effect is subtle and ingrained over time by repetition of images and stereotypes that offer children distorted information about gender roles and violence as an acceptable means of conflict resolution. Much of the research showing that exposure to media violence increases aggressive behavior in young people is now ten to twenty years old.[9] Experts believe that the basic connection has been proven beyond a reasonable doubt.[10]

THE EXTENT OF VIOLENCE ON TELEVISION AND IN OTHER MEDIA

American television, music videos, movies, and video games are the most violent in the world.[11] According to learning theory, exposure to media violence influences children's violent or aggressive behavior by demonstration (modeling), reward (reinforcement), and practice (rehearsal). Studies link television violence with aggressive behaviors in children. This negative effect is particularly evident in children from single-parent households and from low socioeconomic groups.[12] Until the age of four, many children cannot differentiate fact from fantasy, even with adult coaching.[13] As they get older, children are better at it, but early impressions lay the foundations of the belief that the world is violent, threatening, and dangerous.[14]

Television

The average child is exposed through television to twelve thousand murders, rapes, and assaults per year.[15] In addition to the violent scenarios in television programming, children are inundated with commercials that encourage the purchase of war toys and weapons. Toy guns are a $100 million per year industry in the United States, and prime-time network programs show weapons an average of nine times per hour.[16] Unable to differentiate play from real weapons, children are vulnerable to injury when they come across a weapon in the home. As a result, children are more likely to be shot in the United States than in any other country.[17]

Rock Videos

Rock videos, such as those shown on Music Television (MTV), are viewed by preteens and teens up to one to two hours per day.[18] Over half of the music videos on MTV contain violence.[19] In addition to the violent content, rock videos often use sexual imagery, sexism, and stereotypical images of women as objects. Seventy-five percent of concept videos (videos that tell a story) contain sexually suggestive material.[20]

Movies

Movies are often more violent than television, but the average American child watches only one or two movies per week. Eventually, movies shown in theaters make their way into the home via rented movies, television, or pay-cable channels. Ratings of movies are affected more by sexual content than by the frequency and intensity of the violence portrayed—unlike the ratings systems of every other Western country in the world.[21] Ratings do not appear to discourage viewing by children: the graphically violent, R-rated *Friday the 13th* was viewed by 20 percent of five- to seven-year-olds in one community.[22]

Video Games

An explosion in the video game market has pushed sales above $7 billion.[23] Data suggest that video game playing is not an entirely harmless activity. Over half of the most popular video games have violent content.[24] Data extrapolated from the general media violence research suggest that violent interactive video games may cause aggressive behaviors.[25] Seventh- and eighth-grade boys spend over four hours per week playing video games; girls play about half that amount.[26]

Video game violence runs the gamut from martial arts opponents punching, kicking, decapitating, and ripping out hearts ("Mortal Kombat I" and "II") to vampires victimizing scantily clad coeds, drilling them through the neck with a power tool ("Night Trap"). In fact, violence is the major theme of forty of forty-seven of the most popular video games.[27]

Commercialism

Hidden in media messages directed toward children is an intense effort to get children to convince parents to buy products advertised in the media. Until 1984 the Federal Communications Commission (FCC) limited commercial time during children's programming. Prior to that time, the FCC opposed "practices in the body of the program itself which promote products in such a way that they may constitute advertising."[28] The intent was to make programming distinct from selling products. As early as 1969, Mattel tested the limits of such rulings with a program called "Hot Wheels," which coincided with the introduction of a toy line by the same name. Again in 1982, Mattel tested the waters of the new political environment of deregulation with the toy line and Saturday morning program "He-Man and the Masters of the Universe." The FCC ban was eliminated, opening the flood gates for the current fare of Saturday morning children's television featuring program-length toy commercials.[29] Often the content of such program-length toy commercials emphasizes "action" toys with fighting heroes, soldiers, weapon-clad mutants, and alien beings.

THE EFFECTS OF MEDIA VIOLENCE ON SCHOOL VIOLENCE

What would happen to a community newly introduced to media violence? A lag time might be predicted from the introduction of media violence to the time of aggressive behavior changes, increased violent activity, and an effect on crime rate parameters such as assault, rape, and homicide. Short-term media violence exposure could be measured, especially in younger children. Longer-term effects would be more difficult to measure since variables such as socioeconomic factors, community growth rates, and changing demographics would challenge the statistical significance of the effect of media violence alone. As television, movies, music videos, and video games were more widely used by children, effects on the displacement of other activities could be measured. If the effects of media violence were limited to impressionable youth, the lag time of violence observed in the community would mirror that of the emergence of the youth into the community as young adults.

Hypotheses—Studies Supporting the Predicted Effects

Several such scenarios are described in the literature.[30] In locations where television was first being introduced, decreased participation in outdoor activities, community events, and sports resulted. Leisure-time activities were replaced by television, with decreased creativity.[31] In a Canadian town in which television was introduced for the first time, an increase in aggressive behaviors was observed.[32] In both Canada and the United States, there was a lag of ten to fifteen years between the introduction of television and the doubling of the homicide and larceny rates.[33]

Studies demonstrated that urban homicides rose before rural, as would be expected since television was available in urban areas before rural areas. Homicide rates rose earlier in locations where television was first introduced and among more affluent whites who presumably could afford the initial TV sets. Students in communities without television scored lower in aggressiveness than those in areas with television, but quickly caught up to their peers within two years of the introduction of television.[34] In addition to the observed displacement of normal childhood activities by television and the increased violence after introduction of television into communities, studies that eliminate or reduce exposure to television result in better classroom performance, less aggressive playground behavior, and increased family activities.[35]

Basic Research into the Media Effects of Social Learning

Early research into the effects of the media on children's behavior involved social learning theory. These studies fall into the following categories: field experiments and laboratory studies, correlational studies, longitudinal studies, and meta-analyses. When collated from various surveys, the size of the effect of media violence to real-life violence is estimated to surpass 5 to 15 percent.[36] Perhaps ten thousand homicides per year could be prevented if television were less violent.[37]

Field Experiments and Laboratory Studies—Beating up on Bobo. An early study placed a Bobo doll (a punching bag with a sand base and a red nose that squeaked) in a playroom filled with toys.[38] Nursery school children were studied to investigate the circumstances necessary for children to learn and imitate aggressive actions. Children were randomly assigned to either experimental or control groups. Both groups were allowed to enter a room full of attractive toys and were then taken away from the room. Each child from the control group returned individually, and his or her behavior was observed through a one-way mirror. The experimental group was divided into three smaller groups and was first brought into a room to view a film on a television set that:

[b]egan with a scene in which an adult male walked up to an adult-sized plastic Bobo doll and ordered him to clear the way. After glaring for a moment at the noncompliant antagonist the model exhibited four novel aggressive responses, each accompanied by a distinctive verbalization. First, the model laid the Bobo doll on its side, sat on it, and punched it in the nose while remarking, "Pow, right in the nose, boom, boom." The model then raised the doll and pommeled it on the head with a mallet. Each response was accompanied by the verbalization, "Sockeroo...stay down." Following the mallet aggression, the model kicked the doll about the room, and these responses were interspersed with the comment, "Fly away." Finally, the model threw rubber balls at the Bobo doll, each strike punctuated with "Bang." This sequence of physically and verbally aggressive behavior was repeated twice.[39]

Two of the three subgroups were then exposed to an additional segment of film: the model-rewarded group was shown the bully being rewarded with candy, and the model-punished group was shown the bully being reprimanded for his behavior. No further film was viewed by the neutral group.

Each child from these three subgroups was then brought into a playroom containing Bobo, three balls, a mallet, a doll house, and other toys and was observed through a one-way mirror. The observer did not know which group the children belonged to. Play behaviors were observed and documented in the categories of:

- Modeling—imitative, aggressive behavior; or
- Generalization or disinhibition—nonimitative but aggressive behavior.

Children who had watched the film in which the aggressive model had been rewarded or treated neutrally demonstrated a considerable number of imitative behaviors. Children observing the film in which the aggressive model was punished showed little imitation. Control children displayed few or none of the behaviors. If children were rewarded for demonstrating aggressive behaviors observed in the film, even the group exposed to the segment where the aggressor was punished would show an increase in aggressive behaviors. Such learned aggressive responses could be reproduced when the behavior was modeled by a cartoon character.[40] Thus cartoon-related violence and aggressive behaviors demonstrated during Saturday morning programming may teach children inappropriate behaviors.[41]

Similar experiments using other characters and different aggressive scenarios suggest that children's real-life play and other activities in school are influenced by media displays of violent, aggressive, and hostile behaviors.[42]

Experiments looking into the consequences of aggression are important. For example, a study of children who saw a character rewarded for socially unacceptable behavior showed that they were more likely to model such behavior as long as it was "successful."[43] Younger children can learn modeled behavior, with serious implications for subsequent behaviors during adolescence. Such settings include circumstances that:

- Reward or fail to punish the aggressor.
- Portray the violence as justified.
- Portray the victim as similar to real-life models that the child dislikes.
- Depict violent activities without showing consequences to such actions.
- Fail to criticize violent acts.
- Show male sexual aggression or conquest over females.
- Stimulate arousal, whether the action is violent or not.
- Are shown to angry or provoked individuals.[44]

Field studies in a natural environment are more difficult to manipulate than experiments because of extraneous introduction of uncontrolled variables. Such studies can result in mixed results and fail to support laboratory data.[45]

Correlational Studies. Correlational studies strongly link the quantity of television viewed with the presence of aggressive behaviors. A study of high school students demonstrated that the greater the aggressiveness or deviancy of behavior (measured by scales regarding fighting, problems with the law, and other activities), the higher the violent content of their favorite shows.[46] Fourth- to sixth-graders were found to have a positive correlation between high television exposure to violence and willingness to use violence and approval of the use of violence as a means of conflict resolution.[47] Males between the ages of twelve and seventeen were measured for TV violence exposure and aggressive behaviors. In this study, the violence portrayed in cartoons, science fiction, sports, and slapstick programs and violence in other media (newspapers, comic books, and films) produced less serious as well as more serious forms of aggression.[48]

Longitudinal Studies. Studies carried out in the field or in the laboratory, as well as correlational studies, are often unable to measure the cumulative effects of media violence exposure.[49] Longitudinal study designs emphasize correlations and speak to causality. One of the most extensive such studies looked into the relationship between viewing television violence in third grade and aggressive behavior ten and twenty years later.[50] The studies demonstrated that aggressive habits were learned early on in life, were resistant to change, and were predictive of adult violent and antisocial behavior. The studies concluded that children's observation of media violence promotes learning of aggressive habits, with harmful and lifelong consequences.[51]

Meta-Analyses. Meta-analyses use previous studies wherein each study becomes a data point in a newly combined "super-study."[52] Assessments of a body of scientific studies are performed whereby the individual study is analogous to a single respondent in a survey. The three studies in existence using meta-analysis all convincingly support the thesis that exposure to TV violence increases the likelihood of future aggressive or antisocial behavior.[53]

MORBIDITY AND MORTALITY OF MEDIA VIOLENCE AND ANTISOCIAL BEHAVIOR

Children are particularly susceptible to misleading advertising and promotion of commercial products in the media. Adolescents are pressured by peers to gain acceptance and engage in risk-taking behaviors. Such vulnerabilities are not lost on the commercial media industry. Elaborate advertising campaigns are designed to appeal to youth, with stunning financial windfalls to successful business interests. Sexuality, alcohol, and tobacco are insidiously pitched to children and adolescents, resulting in considerable mobidity and mortality in American youth.

The central issues of development for adolescents include movement toward independence, development of a sexual identity, and establishment of a core of ideals and a sense of self-direction. While children do model behavior provided by their parents, adolescents also seek information externally and are particularly vulnerable to seductively produced mass media identities and values.

Firearms

Firearms play a central role in the morbidity and mortality of American children. At the same time, prime-time television is replete with weapons and shoot-'em-up gunfights. The United States leads the Western world in handgun availability and handgun deaths.[54] Half of all households have at least one gun,[55] and guns kept at home are more likely to kill or injure a family member than an intruder.[56] More than four thousand teenagers are killed by firearms per year.[57] Eighty adult deaths per day as well as nine children and adolescent deaths are attributable to firearms.[58] Moreover, for each firearm fatality there are at least five nonfatal injuries.[59] Children see guns on cartoon shows such as "He-Man and the Masters of the Universe," "Power Rangers," and "G.I. Joe," and in prime-time action adventures and cop shows. Such demonstrations appear to have real-life consequences. For example, one seven-year-old boy found his parents' unloaded handgun, loaded it with ammunition, and accidentally killed his three-year-old sister.[60] Firearm use is portrayed in the media as an acceptable means of resolving conflict. Small wonder that firearms and other weapons are increasingly found in the schools.

Suicide

Kurt Cobain, the troubled and rebellious lead singer of the rock group Nirvana, took his own life in 1994 with a shotgun blast to the head. In the media frenzy in the weeks that followed, several imitative attempts and at least one death occurred.[61] The suicide rate among teens has quadrupled during the last three decades.[62] Several studies link television programming or news reports and teenage suicide.[63] The more networks that carried a story about suicide, the greater the increase in imitative suicides.[64] News accounts and television reports of a suicide, especially someone who is seen as "attractive," may significantly increase the number of suicide attempts in a region. Imitative suicides are consistent with learning theory that postulates behavior as learned through modeling. The attractiveness of the role model, as well as the attention and rewards associated with the suicide, influence whether the behavior is acquired and implemented. Easy access to weapons is highly associated with suicide.[65] Since suicide gestures outnumber "successful" attempts by one hundred to two hundred to one, firearm attractiveness as portrayed on television and access to firearms cannot be ignored when dealing with solutions to teenage suicide.

Tobacco

If 434,000 Americans were to die in the Persian Gulf war, governments would topple. World War III would be under way. The world and the world order as we know it would be shaken to its foundations. Yet, last week, the Centers for Disease Control announced that 434,000 Americans died in 1988 from tobacco-related causes. The body count drew only a shrug and a few paragraphs of newspaper ink.[66]

Banned from television in 1969, tobacco advertising has emerged with renewed vigor in film, print, and other venues (that is, sporting events). Tobacco kills 434,000 Americans per year,[67] and the tobacco industry spends $3.27 billion per year to find new clients to keep market share.[68] As a result, as one study shows, Joe Camel has become as recognizable to six-year-olds as the Disney Channel logo.[69]

The Joe Camel campaign has resulted in a jump from 0.5 to 32.8 percent of smokers under eighteen years of age choosing Camel cigarettes, with illegal sales to smokers younger than eighteen jumping from $6 million before the campaign to $476 million with the campaign in full swing.[70] Tobacco campaigns often target areas where youth congregate, including sporting events, shopping malls, and state fairs. Typically, the company gives away samples, articles, candy cigarettes, and other items appealing to youth. Over 3 million adolescents smoke cigarettes, and more than 1 million male adolescents use smokeless tobacco.[71] Tobacco use in young people is associated with several disconcerting facts:

- Almost all adult tobacco users began their habit in adolescence.

- Tobacco is often the first drug used by young people who subsequently go on to abuse alcohol, marijuana, and other drugs (serves as a "gateway drug").

- Young people with poor grades and low self-esteem are more likely to use tobacco.

- Cigarette advertising increases young people's risk of smoking by conveying inaccurate images that tobacco use has positive social and physical benefits.[72]

As producers of the leading cause of preventable death, cigarette manufacturers have escaped the legal responsibility of the morbidity and mortality caused by their product, and have also evaded efforts to force adherence to truth-in-advertising principles. The industry could be forced to make more honest disclosures in media advertising, reduce misleading advertising, and compensate injured parties through the tort system.[73] Meanwhile, schools are struggling with ways to reduce on-campus tobacco use.

Alcohol

Over $900 million per year is spent on beer and wine advertising in the media.[74] Images of happy, well-adjusted, attractive, fun-loving models with a beer in hand are powerful and effective, as demonstrated by sales. In one Maryland suburb, children were able to identify fewer American presidents than brands of beer.[75] For every responsible drinking public service announcement, youth are subjected to twenty to fifty regular alcohol advertisements.[76] The leading killers of young Americans—accidents (half of which are alcohol-related and usually involve motor vehicles), homicides, and suicides—are closely linked to the use of alcohol and other drugs.[77] Alcohol advertising often appears in the context of risk-taking behaviors such as the racing of high-performance cars, implying that drinking and driving mix.

Sexuality

Television exposes children to more than fourteen thousand sexual situations and innuendoes per year, while less than 175 of the episodes depicted make any reference to one of the following: birth control, self-control, or abstinence.[78] Like the media's treatment of violence, the consequences of sexual activity are rarely addressed. The morbidity of sexual activity in adolescents is shocking: the United States leads all Western countries in teen pregnancy rates, with 1 million teenage pregnancies per year.[79] Television, especially daytime soap operas, provides inappropriate portrayals of sexuality—frequent affairs, underestimation of the consequences of sexual activity (such as HIV infection and pregnancy), and the infrequent use of contraception and condoms. Women in television shows are often stereotyped as more passive than males, more concerned with shopping and grooming, and more obsessed with dating, while intelligent girls are sometimes depicted as social misfits.[80]

CONCLUSION

The major effects of violence, antisocial behavior, and aggression in the media can be placed into the following categories:

1. *Displacement of Healthy Activities:* The three to four hours per day of watching television displaces healthy activities including exercise, play, reading, and homework.
2. *Modeling of Inappropriate Behavior:* Over one thousand studies and reviews suggest that media violence is a cause of or contributing factor to real-life violence.[81]

Behavior is modeled by attractive role models and is assimilated by vulnerable and impressionable children.

3. *Disinhibition*: Violent programming results in aggressive, but nonimitative, behavior. Such media presentation results in antisocial behaviors that have been generalized into novel, aggressive activities.
4. *Desensitization*: The daily repetition of the violent television shows, video games, and music videos viewed by children results in indifference to the suffering of the victims of aggression. Negative effects include blaming the victim and accepting the current high levels of violence in the media.
5. *Aggressive Arousal*: Media violence and antisocial behaviors arouse aggressive responses in individuals or groups that are exposed.
6. *Association with Risk-Taking Behavior*: Frequent commercial advertising of unhealthy products increases the use of tobacco and alcohol. Other risk-taking behaviors, including unprotected sexual intercourse and the use of recreational drugs, are also portrayed in the media.[82]

Factors influencing violent and antisocial behaviors in schools include:

- *How aggression is depicted*—"Justified" aggression, especially when directed toward women. Justified retribution is one of the most strongly reinforcing elements of learned aggression.[83]
- *Rewarded aggression*—Depiction of an immediate reward for the aggressive or antisocial behavior, with both the characters and the viewer feeling gratified.[84]

Aggression, antisocial behaviors, and violent activities are *learned* behaviors. Young children are particularly vulnerable; even though behaviors may not become problematic until adolescence or adulthood, they are often first manifested in school. While media violence is not the only cause of such behavior in the schools, it is one significant factor that will respond to modification. Whether financial concerns govern the immediate response to the violence crisis is unclear. What is clear is that, as a society, Americans are already paying dearly with lives lost, educational opportunities squandered, and employment choices severely curtailed.

All developed Western countries, except the United States, require that the commercial networks produce one hour per day of educational programming for youth.[85] Shows such as "Sesame Street" measurably increase children's abilities with the alphabet and mathematics. Such shows also emphasize the prosocial concepts of racial harmony, cooperation, and kindness. Television, videos, books, and other media can act as a highly interactive experience for young children, especially when parents participate.[86] Yet television has a deleterious effect on reading scores if it is watched in excess of two to three hours per day.[87] Fewer adults read newspapers and more young adults depend on network news to obtain information, which contain less, on average, than a single newspaper page.[88] Since the effects of television and other media are dose-dependent, the focus should be on reduction of the exposure time. It is easier to shape viewing habits than to break bad habits once they are established.

The influence of the media on children does not *have* to be negative. Parents who read to their children promote literacy. Creative prosocial application of the media includes interactive, nonviolent video games; educational television; and programs and movies with positive nonviolent social contexts. The negative effects of television on children can be prevented in several ways.

- Limit television viewing to one to two hours per day. Do *not* allow a pattern of three to four hours per day of television viewing to become established. Set strict limits of television viewing from the beginning.
- Control which programs children watch.
- Watch programs with your children.
- Discuss objectionable scenes with your children.
- Do not use television as an electronic babysitter; however, it can be used for limited periods of time to keep children engaged and occupied. Videocassettes with acceptable programs can be used in this regard.
- Ensure that physicians take a detailed television viewing history of every child.
- Take an active role in providing feedback—both negative and positive—to the networks. The networks estimate that each letter represents ten thousand viewers.
- Limit after-school television and encourage and plan for other after-school activities.

Parents and teachers should collaborate to ensure positive effects of the media on children in schools. The appendix to this chapter lists resources available to parents and teachers regarding educational media for children. Efforts to reduce the potential negative impact of the media on children should stress policy changes to reduce the number of scenes with gratuitous violence on television, news reports, film, and video.

Promotion of more responsible depictions of sexual activity is also important. Reduction of children's media exposure to alcohol, tobacco, and aggressive and antisocial behaviors is critical. Ratings of violent content in television, music videos, video games, and other media would help parents and educators choose appropriate materials for children, families, and students. Parents, educators, and community leaders must advocate for responsible and educational television programming in order to create a more positive and nurturing media environment for their children.[89]

APPENDIX: RESOURCE LIST OF EDUCATIONAL MEDIA FOR CHILDREN

Networks

ABC/Entertainment President, 2040 Avenue of the Stars, Fifth Floor, Los Angeles, Calif. 90067

CBS/Entertainment President, 7800 Beverly Blvd., Los Angeles, Calif. 90036

NBC/Entertainment President, 3000 West Alameda, Burbank, Calif. 91523

FOX/President, Fox Broadcasting, P.O. Box 900, Los Angeles, Calif. 90213

Federal Communications Commission FCC/Mass Media Bureau, Enforcement Division, Room 8210, 2025 M St., Washington, D.C. 20554

Groups

Action for Children's Television, 20 University Rd., Cambridge, Mass. 02138, (617) 876-6620. Available kits on Choices for Children include *An Action Kit to Implement the Children's Television Act.*

American Academy of Pediatrics, Committee on Communications, 141 Northwest Point Blvd., P.O. Box 927, Elk Grove Village, Ill. 60009-0927, (708) 228-5005. "Television and the Family" is a free brochure produced by the AAP.

American Academy of Family Physicians, 8880 Ward Parkway, Kansas City, Mo. 64114-2797, (800) 274-2237.

Other Resources

Listening Library, One Park Avenue, Old Greenwich, Conn. 06870–1727, (800) 243-4504, produces the Rabbit Ears series of classic childhood stories narrated by Hollywood stars, accompanied by music from well-known performers.

Parents' Choice, Box 185, Waban, Mass. 02168, (617) 965-5913, produces a newsletter for parents that reviews children's videos, magazines, and books.

Coalition for Quality Children's Videos, 535 Cordova Rd., Suite 456, Santa Fe, N.M. 97501, (505) 989-8076, produces a quarterly newsletter on children's videos.

Entertainment Weekly and *TV Guide* publish regular children's video columns. The Sunday *New York Times* rates the appropriateness of current movies for children and adolescents.

Center for Media Values, 1962 South Shenandoah, Los Angeles, Calif. 90034, (310) 559-2994, produces several publications to help parents develop their children's critical reviewing skills.

The Yale Television Research Center, 405 Temple St., New Haven, Conn. 06511, (203) 432-4565, produces the "Degrassi Junior High" series adaptation, provides an excellent health series for older children, and also has an excellent curriculum for younger children.

The Learning Company, 6493 Kaiser Drive, Fremont, Calif. 94555, (800) 852-2255, produces interactive, educational, and nonviolent video games for children based on age, including Reader Rabbit's Ready for Letters, Reader Rabbit 1, New! Math Rabbit, Reader Rabbit 2, Treasure MathStorm!, Super Solvers Midnight Rescue, Super Solvers OutNumbered, Super Solvers Spellbound, The Writing Center.

Broderbund Software, Inc, 500 Redwood Blvd., Novato, Calif. 94948-6121, produces interactive, educational, and nonviolent video games for children, including The Treehouse, The Playroom, and The Backyard.

NOTES

1. J. O'Connor, "Children's Viewing: Brighter Side of a Bleak Picture," *New York Times* (September 22, 1994), B1.

2. American Psychological Association, *Summary Report of the American Psychological Association Commission on Violence and Youth,* Vol. 1 (Washington, D.C.: American Psychological Association, 1993).

3. Nielson Media Research, *AC Nielson Company: 1992–1993 Report on Television* (New York: Nielson Media Research, 1993).

4. W. H. Dietz and V. C. Strasburger, "Children, Adolescents, and Television," *Current Problems in Pediatrics* 21 (1991): 8–31.

5. U.S. Department of Health and Human Services, *Healthy People 2000: National Health Promotion and Disease Prevention Objectives* (Washington, D.C.: U.S. Department of Health and Human Services, 1990).

6. V. C. Strasburger, "Children, Adolescents, and the Media: Five Crucial Issues," *Adolescent Medicine* 4 (1993): 479–93.

7. Dietz and Strasburger, "Children, Adolescents, and Television."

8. Strasburger, "Children, Adolescents, and the Media."

9. Ibid.; D. Pearl, *Television and Behavior: Ten Years of Scientific Progress and Implications for the Eighties,* Vol. 1, U.S. Department of Health and Human Services, publication no. ADM 82–1195 (Washington, D.C.: Government Printing Office, 1982).

10. L. R. Eron, *The Problem of Media Violence and Children's Behavior* (New York: Henry Frank Guggenheim Foundation, 1993).

11. Dietz and Strasburger, "Children, Adolescents, and Television."

12. F. S. Andison, "TV Violence and Viewer Aggressiveness: A Cumulation of Study Results," *Public Opinion Quarterly* 41 (1977): 314–31; G. Comstock and V. C. Strasburger, "Media Violence: Q & A," *Adolescent Medicine: State of the Art Reviews* 4 (1993): 495–501; S. Hearold, "A Synthesis of 1,045 Effects of Television on Social Behavior," in *Public Communication and Behavior,* ed. G. Comstock (New York: Academic Press, 1986).

13. J. H. Flavell, "The Development of Children's Knowledge about the Appearance–Reality Distinction," *American Psychologist* 41 (1986): 418–25.

14. Hearold, "A Synthesis of 1,045 Effects of Television."

15. A. C. Huston, E. Donnerstein, H. Fairchild et al., *Big World, Small Screen: The Role of Television in American Society* (Lincoln: University of Nebraska Press, 1992).

16. K. K. and T. Cristoffel, "Handguns as a Pediatric Problem," *Pediatric Emergency Care* 2 (1986): 343; D. Schetky, "Children and Handguns: A Public Health Concern," *American Journal of Diseases of Children* 139 (1985): 229.

17. L. A. Fingerhut and J. C. Kleinman, *Firearm Mortality among Children and Youth,* National Center for Health Statistics Advance Data No. 178 (1989).

18. S. W. Sun and J. Lull, "The Adolescent Audience for Music Videos and Why They Watch," *Journal of Communication* 36 (1986): 79–93.

19. R. L. Baxter, C. DeRiemer, A. Landini et al., "A Content Analysis of Music Videos," *Journal of Broadcasting and Electronic Media* 29 (1985): 333–40; B. L. Sherman and J. R. Dominick, "Violence and Sex in Music Videos: TV and Rock 'n' Roll," *Journal of Communication* 36 (1986): 115–25.

20. Sherman and Dominick, "Violence and Sex in Music Videos."

21. F. Federman, *Film and Television Ratings: An International Assessment* (Studio City, Calif.: Mediascope, 1993).

22. A. David, "Screen Stats," *Entertainment Weekly* (May 2, 1993).

23. J. B. Funk, "Video Games," *Adolescent Medicine: State of the Art Reviews* 4 (1993): 589–98; J. Horn, "Al Gore, Cyberpunks Mingle in TV Summit," *Associated Press* (January 7, 1994).

24. Funk, "Video Games."

25. S. B. Silvern and P. A. Williamson, "The Effect of Video Game Playing on Young Children's Aggression, Fantasy, and Prosocial Behavior," *Journal of Applied Social Psychology* 8 (1987): 453.

26. J. Funk, "Reevaluating the Impact of Video Games," *Clinical Pediatrics* 32 (1993): 86–90.

27. E. F. Provenzo, *Video Kids: Making Sense of Nintendo* (Cambridge, Mass.: Harvard University Press, 1991).

28. B. Watkins, "Improving Educational and Informational Television for Children When the Marketplace Fails," *Yale Law Policy Review* 5 (1987): 345–81.

29. B. DeSilva, "Public Taste, Business Demands Guide TV Programs for Children," *Hartford Courant* (October 11, 1987).

30. T. M. Williams, ed., *The Impact of Television. A Natural Experiment in Three Communities* (New York: Academic Press, 1985), 143–213; J. P. Murray and S. Kippox, "Children's Social Behavior in Three Towns with Differing Television Experiences," *Journal of Communication* 30 (1978): 19–29.

31. Williams, *The Impact of Television.*

32. Ibid.

33. B. S. Centerwall, "Children, Television and Violence," in *Children and Violence,* D. F. Schwarz, ed. (Columbus, Ohio: Ross Laboratories, 1992), 87–97; B. S. Centerwall, "Television and Violence: The Scale of the Problem and Where to Go from Here," *Journal of the American Medical Association* 267 (1992): 3059–63.

34. Williams, *The Impact of Television.*

35. Farmington Library Council, *Farmington TV Turnoff: A Review of the Farmington Experience* (Farmington, Conn.: Farmington Library Council, 1984).

36. G. Comstock and V. C. Strasburger, "Deceptive Appearances: Television Violence and Aggressive Behavior—An Introduction," *Journal of Adolescent Health* 11 (1990): 31–44.

37. Centerwall, "Children, Television and Violence"; Centerwall, "Television and Violence."

38. A. Bandura, D. Ross, and S. A. Ross, "Imitation of Film-Mediated Aggressive Models," *Journal of Abnormal and Social Psychology* 66 (1963): 3–11.

39. Ibid.

40. Ibid.

41. D. G. Singer, "Does Violent Television Produce Aggressive Children?," *Pediatric Annals* 14 (1985): 804–10.

42. D. J. Hicks, "Imitation and Retention of Film-Mediated Aggressive Peer and Adult Models," *Journal of Personality and Social Psychology* 2 (1965): 97–100; M. A. Hanratty, E. O'Neal, and J. L. Sulzer, "The Effect of Frustration upon Imitation of Aggression," *Journal of Personality and Social Psychology* 21 (1972): 30–34; F. B. Steuer, J. M. Applefield, and R. Smith, "Televised Aggression and Interpersonal Aggression of Preschool Children,"*Journal of Experimental Child Psychology* 11 (1971): 442–47; E. Joe and L. Berkowitz, "A Priming Effect Analysis of Media Influences: An Update," in *Media Effects: Advances in Theory and Research*, eds. J. Bryant and D. Zillmann (Hillsdale, N.J.: Lawrence Erlbaum, 1994), 43–60.

43. Bandura, Ross, and Ross, "Imitation of Film-Mediated Aggressive Models."

44. Comstock and Strasburger, "Deceptive Appearances."

45. K. D. Gadow and J. Sprafkin, "Field Experiments of Television Violence with Children: Evidence for an Experimental Toxin?," *Pediatrics* 83 (1989): 399–405; D. G. Singer, "Children, Adolescents, and Television 1989. I. Television Violence: A Critique," *Pediatrics* 83 (1989): 445–46.

46. J. J. McIntyre and J. J. Teevan, "Television Violence and Deviant Behavior," in *Television and Adolescent Aggressiveness*, eds. G. A. Comstock and E. A. Rubenstein (Washington, D.C.: Government Printing Office, 1972): 383–485.

47. J. R. Dominick and B. S. Greenberg, "Attitudes Toward Violence: The Interaction of Television Exposure, Family Attitudes and Social Class," in *Television and Adolescent Aggressiveness*, eds. G. A. Comstock and E. A. Rubenstein (Washington, D.C.: Government Printing Office, 1972): 314–35.

48. W. A. Belson, *Television Violence and the Adolescent Boy* (Westmead, England: Saxon House, Teakfield Ltd., 1978).

49. Singer, "Children, Adolescents, and Television 1989."

50. L. R. Heusmann, "Television Violence and Aggressive Behavior," in *Television and Behavior: Ten Years of Scientific Progress and Implications for the Eighties*, eds. D. Pearl, L. Bouthilet, and J. Lazar (Rockville, Md.: National Institute of Mental Health II, 1982), 126–37; L. R. Heusmann, "Psychological Processes Promoting the Reaction Between Exposure to Media Violence and Aggressive Behavior by the Viewer," *Journal of Social Issues* 42 (1986): 125–39; L. R. Heusmann and L. D. Eron, eds., *Television and the Aggressive Child: A Cross-National Comparison* (Hillsdale, N.J.: Lawrence Erlbaum, 1986); L. R. Heusmann, L. D. Eron, and M. M. Lefkowitz et al., "Stability of Aggression over Time and Generations," *Developmental Psychology* 20 (1984): 1120–34.

51. Heusmann and Eron, *Television and the Aggressive Child.*

52. B. Mullen, *Advanced Basic Meta-Analysis* (Hillsdale, N.J.: Lawrence Erlbaum, 1989).

53. Hearold, "A Synthesis of 1,045 Effects of Television"; H. J. Paik, "The Effects of Television Violence on Aggressive Behavior," unpublished doctoral dissertation (Syracuse, N.Y.: Syracuse University, 1991); F. S. Andison, "TV Violence and Viewer Aggressiveness: A Cumulation of Study Results," *Public Opinion Quarterly* 41 (1977): 324–31.

54. Fingerhut and Kleinman, *Firearm Mortality among Children and Youth.*

55. K. K. Cristoffel, "Toward Reducing Pediatric Injuries from Firearms: Charting a Legislative and Regulatory Course," *Pediatrics* 88 (1991): 294–305.

56. Centers for Disease Control, "Deaths Resulting from Firearm and Motor Vehicle Related Injuries—United States, 1968–1991," *Morbidity and Mortality Weekly Reports* 43 (1994): 27–42.

57. Associated Press, "Teen Deaths from Guns on the Rise," *Albuquerque Journal* (March 24, 1993).

58. American Academy of Pediatrics, Committee on Adolescence, "Policy Statement: Firearms and Adolescents," *Pediatrics* 89 (1992): 784–87.

59. Ibid.

60. J. R. Martin, D. P. Sklar, and P. McFeeley, "Accidental Firearm Fatalities among New Mexico Children," *Annals of Emergency Medicine* 20 (1991): 58–61.

61. N. Strauss, "The Downward Spiral," *Rolling Stone* 683 (1994): 43.

62. C. Scanlan, "Teen Suicides Rise in Homes with Guns," *Albuquerque Journal* (June 27, 1993); D. Shaffer and P. Fisher, "The Epidemiology of Suicide in Children and Young Adolescents," *Journal of the American Academy of Child Psychiatry* 20 (1981): 545–65.

63. M. S. Gould and L. Davidson, "Suicide Contagion among Adolescents," *Advances in Adolescent Mental Health* 3 (1988): 29–59; D. P. Phillips and L. L. Carstensen, "Clustering of Teenage Suicides after Television News Stories about Suicide," *New England Journal of Medicine* 314 (1986): 685–89; D. Shaffer, A. Garland, M. Gould et al., "Preventing Teenage Suicide: A Critical Review," *Journal of the American Academy of Child Psychiatry* 27 (1988): 675–87.

64. Phillips and Carstensen, "Clustering of Teenage Suicide."

65. D. A. Brent, J. A. Perper, G. Moritz et al., "Firearms and Adolescent Suicide: A Community Case-Control Study," *American Journal of Diseases of Children* 147 (1993): 1066–71; A. L. Kellerman, F. P. Rivara, G. Somes et al., "Suicides in the Home in Relation to Gun Ownership," *New England Journal of Medicine* 327 (1992): 467–72.

66. J. Beck, *The Associated Press* (February 8, 1991).

67. U.S. Department of Health and Human Services, *Reducing the Health Consequences of Smoking: 25 Years of Progress, A Report of the Surgeon General*, CDC Publication No. 89–8411 (Washington, D.C.: U.S. Department of Health and Human Services, 1989).

68. Centers for Disease Control, "Cigarette Advertising—United States, 1988," *Morbidity and Mortality Weekly Reports* 39 (1990): 261–65.

69. P. M. Fischer, M. P. Schwartz, J. W. Richards, Jr., et al., "Brand Logo Recognition by 3- to 6-Year Old Children," *Journal of the American Medical Association* 266 (1991): 3145–48.

70. J. R. DiFranza, J .W. Richards, Jr., P. M. Paulman et al., "RJR Nabisco's Cartoon Camel Promotes Camel Cigarettes to Children," *Journal of the American Medical Association* 266 (1991): 3149–53.

71. U. S. Department of Health and Human Services, *Preventing Tobacco Use among Young People. Smoking and Health Information. A Report of the Surgeon General*, CDC Publication No. 460017 (Washington, D.C.: U.S. Department of Health and Human Services, 1994).

72. Ibid.

73. L. O. Gostin, A. M. Brandt, and P. D. Cleary, "Tobacco Liability and Public Health Policy," *Journal of the American Medical Association* 266 (1991): 3178–82.

74. C. Atkin, "Effects of Media Alcohol Messages on Adolescent Audiences," *Adolescent Medicine: State of the Art Reviews* 4 (1993): 527–42; D. Singer, "Alcohol, Television, and Teenagers," *Pediatrics* 76 (1985): 668–74.

75. Center for Science in the Public Interest, *Kids Are as Aware of Booze as President, Survey Finds* (Washington, D.C.: Center for Science in the Public Interest, 1994).

76. V. C. Strasburger, "Why Just Say No Just Won't Work," *Journal of Pediatrics* 114 (1989): 676–81.

77. U.S. Department of Health and Human Services, *Vital Statistics of the United States,* Publication No. (PHS) 85–1101 (Washington, D.C.: U.S. Department of Health and Human Services, 1985).

78. L. Harris et al., *Sexual Material on American Network Television During the 1987–88 Season* (New York: Planned Parenthood Federation of America, 1988).

79. R. Blum, "Contemporary Threats to Adolescent Health in the United States," *Journal of the American Medical Association* 257 (1987): 3390–95; E. F. Jones, J. D. Forrest, S. K. Henshaw et al., "Unintended Pregnancy, Contraceptive Practice and Family Planning Services in Developed Countries," *Family Planning Perspectives* 20 (1988): 53–67.

80. S. Steenland, *Growing Up in Prime Time: An Analysis of Adolescent Girls on Television* (Washington, D.C.: National Commission on Working Women of Wider Opportunities for Women, 1988).

81. Strasburger, "Children, Adolescents and the Media."

82. J. D. Klein, J. D. Brown, K. W. Childers et al., "Adolescents' Risky Behavior and Mass Media Use," *Pediatrics* 92 (1993): 24–31.

83. L. Berkowitz and E. Rawlings, "Effects of Film Violence on Inhibitions Against Subsequent Aggression," *Journal of Abnormal and Social Psychology* 66 (1963): 405–12.

84. Bandura, Ross, and Ross, "Imitation of Film Mediated Aggressive Models."

85. Strasburger, "Children, Adolescents and the Media."

86. D. Lemish and M. L. Rice, "Television as a Talking Picture Book," *Journal of Child Language* 13 (1986): 251–74.

87. Strasburger, "Children, Adolescents and the Media."

88. P. Charren and M. W. Sandler, *Changing Channels* (Reading, Mass.: Addison-Wesley Publishing, 1983).

89. M. Feingold and G. T. Johnson, "Television Violence—Reactions from Physicians, Advertisers and the Networks," *New England Journal of Medicine* 296 (1977): 424–27.

6

The Influence of Child Abuse and Family Violence on Violence in the Schools

Jeffrey J. Haugaard and Margaret M. Feerick

Over the past two decades, reports of both violence in schools and violence in homes have increased dramatically. The extent to which these increases reflect actual increases in school and family violence versus increases in only the reporting of violence is unclear. Nonetheless, the increases in both forms of violence have led to questions about their association, which is the focus of this chapter. Of particular interest is whether being abused at home, or witnessing violence in the home, increases the likelihood that a child will be aggressive at school.

BASIC ISSUES IN ABUSE AND VIOLENCE RESEARCH

This chapter begins with a discussion of several issues that are of importance when considering research regarding the association between home and school violence: the difficulty of defining child abuse and school violence unambiguously; problems with making causal links between child abuse and subsequent school violence; limitations imposed by the samples available to researchers on child abuse; and the difficulty of isolating the effects of child abuse from other family characteristics when examining children's aggressive behavior. Research is then reviewed regarding the connections between school violence and (1) child physical abuse, (2) child sexual abuse, and (3) witnessing violence in the home. Finally, there is a discussion of some psychological mechanisms that may explain connections between home and school violence.

Defining Child Abuse and School Violence

The definitions used by child abuse researchers have differed, and a generally accepted definition of physical or sexual abuse remains elusive.[1] Communication about child abuse is complicated by this lack of a common definition, and miscommunication can occur if the definitions employed are not specified clearly.

There is relatively little disagreement when classifying some acts as abusive; classifying other acts results in greater disagreement. For example, a father's sexual intercourse with his nine-year-old daughter is considered sexual abuse by almost everyone, but significant disagreement occurs when classifying a mother who regularly bathes her nine-year-old son.[2] Most people would agree that a mother's holding her daughter's hand over a flame to punish her is physical abuse, but there would be greater disagreement about a father spanking a son on the buttocks. Similar problems exist when trying to determine what behaviors constitute aggression in school settings—for example, whether pushing another child in a line would be considered aggression.

Research definitions of aggression or child abuse that are very inclusive may reinforce conclusions about the widespread nature of abuse and aggression. However, considering the wide range of behaviors as a group may be problematic because of their diverse nature. For example, the negative consequences to children experiencing certain types of abuse may be offset by the minimal consequences experienced by children who have endured less traumatic types of abuse, when they are considered together. On the other hand, if the definitions are more circumscribed, the negative consequences of abuse may be more evident, but meaningful abusive or violent behaviors may not be considered. On one side there is the risk of including so many children that the terms become relatively meaningless; on the other side is the risk of excluding children who may be at risk for the development of emotional or mental disorders because of their experiences.

The problems in determining a shared definition of child abuse and violence reflect our societal confusion about what are appropriate ways for parents to interact with and discipline their children and what are acceptable ways for children to interact with each other. Expecting exact and shared definitions at this point is probably unreasonable. As a result, researchers must carefully describe the definition of child abuse or violence that they employ, and readers of the research must note the characteristics of the subjects of the research and, consequently, to whom the research can be generalized.

Causal Links Between Home and School Violence

The social science research examining the links between child abuse and subsequent aggression is correlational. That is, researchers try to determine whether there is a greater incidence of aggressive behavior among children who have been abused than among nonabused children. If there is a greater incidence among abused children, then it can be said that there is an association between child abuse and subsequent aggressive behavior. The fact that there is an association, however, does not indicate that child abuse directly influences aggression, even though the abuse may have occurred prior to the aggression.

Finding an association between two variables does not preclude the possibility that a third variable is affecting both of them. In such a case, it is their common relationship to the third variable that causes the association between the first two variables, not a direct relationship between them. For example, consider a young child who, for whatever combination of genetic and environmental influences, has an aggressive temperament or interpersonal style. The child's aggression may influence the development of harsh disciplinary practices in his or her parents and also may lead to aggressive behavior in school. In this situation it might appear that the harsh disciplinary practices caused the child's later aggression in school. In actuality, it was the combination of genetic and environmental influences on the child's early aggressive behavior that caused both the harsh parenting and the aggression in school. As an example from a more social-environmental perspective, it may be that certain combinations of social-environmental factors increase the likelihood of violence in homes in certain neighborhoods and also increase the likelihood of violence in the schools fed by those neighborhoods. Again, it would be these social-environmental factors, not simply child abuse or the occurrence of home violence, that were influencing the level of school violence.

Because it is impossible to confidently assign cause and effect in correlational research, we must proceed cautiously when interpreting research examining the relationship between child abuse and later school violence. It is easy to forget the problems associated with correlational research and to let cause-and-effect thinking influence the conclusions we draw from the research. We should guard against this and keep our minds open to alternative hypotheses that may explain both child abuse and school violence.

Influences of Sample Selection

Whenever possible, social science researchers strive to get a random sample of the population they are studying. Gathering a random sample and an appropriate comparison group is often difficult, however, and it is even more difficult when the issue being examined is one in which the participants are asked to reveal behavior that is illegal or socially unacceptable. For a potential subject in child abuse research to give informed consent to participate, he or she would have to be told of the researcher's obligation to contact law enforcement officials if the researcher suspected that unreported abuse was occurring or had occurred in the past. Potential subjects who are engaging in behavior that they fear is abusive might decline to participate or may not be honest about their behaviors. Consequently, the more serious forms of abusive behavior may not be included, and children who have experienced abuse may be unlikely to be sampled in community surveys.

Some researchers deal with the problem of gathering a community sample of abused children or abusive families by gathering subjects from those reported for abuse to departments of social services (DSS) or from mental health clinics where abused children are in treatment. Although this method allows for the gathering of relatively large samples of subjects, the children and families included may not represent all abusive families. Children who show little outward signs of disability owing to abusive behavior may never appear at mental health clinics. Consequently, clinic samples may overrepresent those who have been more seriously damaged by their abuse experiences. Some research suggests that abuse cases reported to law enforcement authorities are not representative of all abuse cases and are more likely to come from minority and low-income families.[3] It is unclear, however, whether the abuse experiences of reported children are different from those of unreported children. Because it is probably impossible to gather a sample of children and families that represents the spectrum of child abuse and family violence, we must keep in mind how the subjects included in both the abused and comparison groups may bias the results of a study in one way or another.

Difficulty of Isolating the Influence of Child Abuse

Research on the influence of child abuse on later aggression has typically contrasted the aggression of children who are known abuse victims with that of a comparison group of children who have not been abused. Even matching the comparison children to the abused children on demographic variables, however, cannot control completely other differences in the families of the abused and nonabused children that may have an influence on the children's aggression. For example, Straus and Smith found that families that reported child abuse also reported higher levels of spousal conflict and aggression.[4] In addition, they found that the parents of abusive families had been physically punished more often by their parents and had witnessed higher levels of violence between their parents than had parents from nonabusive families. These experiences of the abusive parents may have influenced their parenting behavior in many ways other than the extent to which they hit their own children and may have had an influence on their children's aggression. Because of the potential influence of these unknown family characteristics, it is important not to assume that differences in aggression in the children from abusive families are due solely to their abuse experiences.

PHYSICALLY ABUSED CHILDREN AND AGGRESSION IN SCHOOLS

With a few exceptions, strong links have been found between physical abuse and aggression in children. Studies using a variety of methodologies and focusing on children at different developmental stages have often reported such links.[5]

Analogue Studies

A few analogue studies have examined presumed indicators of children's aggression through psychological tests. For example, Kinard gave thirty physically abused and thirty nonabused five- to twelve-year-old children the Rosenzweig Picture-Frustration Scale, which consists of twenty-four drawings of frustrating scenes.[6] All the abused children had been reported to a DSS, and the nonabused children had been matched on several demographic characteristics. Although no statistically significant levels of overall aggression appeared, the abused children described more aggression in pictures involving peers than did the nonabused children. Using the same procedure, however, Straker and Jacobson found no differences between abused and nonabused children in levels of aggression in their stories.[7] It is not clear why the two studies had conflicting results. It should be noted that these studies did not examine behaviors, and thus they do not address whether the abused children actually behaved more aggressively than the nonabused children. Furthermore, the conflicting results may point to the difficulty associated with using responses to a subjective test as an analogue for behaviors.

Harsh Discipline and Aggression

Other studies have examined the connection between harsh parental discipline and aggression in children. These studies have typically found an association between harsh discipline and children's aggression, particularly at higher levels of harsh discipline (which would be considered physical abuse by some observers). For example, Weiss, Dodge, Bates, and Pettit used teacher and peer ratings of aggression for a group of kindergarten children and also made behavioral observations of the children.[8] Harsh discipline had a unique influence on the children's aggression after controlling for family socioeconomic status (SES) and child temperament. Children whose parents used the highest levels of harshness were significantly more aggressive than those whose parents used moderate levels.

Fry reported on the types of discipline given children in two rural communities in Mexico.[9] One of the communities had a high level of overall aggression, and the other had a low level. There was no difference between the two communities in the number of less severe physical punishments (that is, slaps, pulls, knuckle-raps). However, the more aggressive community had a much higher level of child beatings. Although this study cannot directly link the child beatings to overall levels of community aggression, the authors suggest that the intergenerational transmission of aggression may be influenced by the child beatings.

Abuse and Reports of Aggressive Behavior

Several studies have examined the abuse/aggression association using teacher and parent ratings of children's aggressive behaviors and behavioral observations of children at school or in playgroups. In a study of very young children, George and Main observed physically abused and demographically matched nonabused one- to three-year-old children in a daycare setting.[10] The abused children exhibited more aggressive behavior toward both peers and caregivers than did the nonabused children. Hoffman-Plotkin and Twentyman examined teacher and parent ratings of aggression for, and observed the classroom behavior of, physically abused, neglected, and nonabused/nonneglected three- to six-year-olds.[11] Behavioral observations indicated that the physically abused children were more aggressive with peers than were the neglected or nonabused/nonneglected children. Teacher and parent ratings of the children's behavior showed that the abused children were rated as more aggressive than the nonabused/nonneglected children. There were no differences in the rated aggression between the abused and the neglected children. Rosenthal and Doherty also found higher levels of observed aggression in ten abused preschool children than in nonabused preschool children.[12]

Research with school age children also has shown higher levels of aggression in abused children. Downey and Walker and Walker, Downey, and Bergman studied nine- to ten-year-old children referred by child protective services or psychiatric facilities, using parent reports of aggressive behavior on the Child Behavior Checklist.[13] After matching subjects on a variety of demographic characteristics, they found that physically abused children received higher ratings on aggressive behavior than did the nonabused comparison children. Kurtz, Gaudin, Howing, and Wodarski found that both parent and teacher ratings for aggression were higher for a group of eight- to sixteen-year-old abused children referred by child protective services than for a matched comparison group.[14]

Williamson, Borduin, and Howe obtained parent reports of a variety of behaviors for physically abused, neglected, and a matched comparison group of twelve- to seventeen-year-olds.[15] The physically abused adolescents had higher levels of aggression than did the comparison adolescents. However, the neglected adolescents were reported as more aggressive than the physically abused adolescents.

Not all researchers have found evidence of increased aggression in abused children. Camras and Rappaport had nine dyads of abused and nonabused children ages three to seven engage in an activity that required them to take turns playing with a gerbil, away from adult supervision. Abused children showed no more aggressive behavior to gain access to the gerbil or to deny access to the other child than did the nonabused children. The researchers suggested that the context of their experiment—play with one other child in an unfamiliar setting—may have resulted in lower levels of aggression. They hypothesized that abused children may be no more aggressive than nonabused children in certain environments.[16]

Summary

Although there are some exceptions, studies using a variety of methods and examining children in different age groups generally report greater aggression in physically abused than in nonabused children. As noted above, specific methodological limitations exist for each of the studies. Taken together, however, they provide relatively convincing evidence that physically abused children are more likely to be aggressive than are nonabused children.

Sample selection is a problem in most of the research since the children are typically those identified by a DSS. It is not clear whether the same abuse/aggression association would occur for children whose abuse is less likely to result in a DSS referral (that is, infrequent or relatively mild abuse) or children from families that are less likely to be reported (that is, upper-middle class). Weiss et al. did find a connection between harsh discipline and childhood aggression in a sample that was not referred to DSS, which may reduce somewhat the concerns about the sample selection.[17]

Finally, it should be noted that the research is not able to isolate the specific influence of physical abuse on aggression. Families reported to DSS for physical abuse may be different from nonreported families on many factors (for example, parenting behaviors, parental substance abuse, chaotic home conditions). These other factors may have an influence on the development of aggression in children that is independent of the influence of abuse, or they may work in concert with the physical abuse to raise the risk that a child will become aggressive.

SEXUALLY ABUSED CHILDREN AND AGGRESSION IN SCHOOLS

Although the research on physical abuse and aggression has involved studies using a variety of methodologies, much of the research on sexual abuse and aggression comes from studies using parental ratings of child behavior or from clinically oriented studies using medical charts or clinical interviews. Such studies have generally found strong links between sexual abuse and aggression, with sexually abused children of different ages reported as more aggressive than nondistressed comparison groups and somewhat less aggressive than some clinical groups or other groups of abused children.[18]

Behavioral Reports Comparing Sexually Abused Children with Nonabused Children

Several studies have examined the relationship between sexual abuse and aggression by comparing children who were referred to sexual abuse treatment programs with nonclinical, nonabused community samples of children. Conte and Schuerman compared 369 sexually abused children between the ages of four and seventeen with 318 children recruited from daycare centers, church groups, and private schools.[19] Inderbitzen-Pisaruk, Shawchuck, and Hoier compared seventeen sexually abused children between the ages of five and fifteen with seventeen children matched on sex, age, SES, and child's current living situation (whether the child was living with one or both parents).[20] Einbender and Friedrich compared forty-six sexually abused girls with a group of forty-six nonabused girls who were matched on age, race, family income, and family constellation (if the child was living with both birth parents or siblings).[21] All three studies found the sexually abused children to be significantly more aggressive than nonabused children, based on parental ratings of the aggression items from the Child Behavior Checklist.

In a similar study, Tong, Oates, and McDowell compared forty-nine sexually abused children between the ages of five and nineteen with a comparison group from the same school area, matched on age, sex, SES, and ethnicity.[22] Parents of the children were given a structured interview that asked about the effects of sexual abuse on behavior at home and school, including several items about aggressive behavior. In addition, parents of thirty-eight children in each group and teachers of twenty-eight children in each group completed the aggression items of the Child Behavior Checklist. Thirty older children in each group completed the Youth Self Report of the Child Behavior Checklist. Teacher and parent ratings showed that the sexually abused children were significantly more aggressive than the nonabused children. There were no differences in self-reported aggression between the sexually abused and nonabused children. Results of the structured interview showed that following the disclosure of the abuse, 20 percent of the children were more aggressive at home and 15 percent were more aggressive at school than they were prior to the disclosure.

Behavioral Reports Comparing Sexually Abused Children to Clinical Comparison Groups or Other Abused Children

Several other studies have examined the link between sexual abuse and aggression by comparing sexually abused children with both nondistressed and clinical groups of nonabused children. Gomes-Schwartz, Horowitz, and Sauzier compared parental ratings of 112 sexually abused preschool, school age, and adolescent children to the norms of the Louisville Behavior Checklist (LBC).[23] (The LBC has norms for both general population and clinical samples.) Sexually abused children were more aggressive than the general population norms, although they were significantly less aggressive than the clinical norms. A similar pattern of results was reported by Cohen and Mannarino for a sample of twenty-four sexually abused girls between the ages of six and twelve, using standardized behavioral norms for the Child Behavior Checklist.[24]

Two studies using similar methodology presented conflicting results. Each used three groups: sexually abused children referred to treatment; nonclinical, nonabused children; and clinical, nonabused children. Parents rated their children on the aggression items of the Child Behavior Checklist. Friedrich, Beilke, and Urquiza found the sexually abused group to be significantly more aggressive than the nonclinical, nonabused group, and significantly less aggressive than the clinical, nonabused group.[25] Mannarino, Cohen, and Gregor found the sexually abused children to be significantly more aggressive than the nonclinical, nonabused group, but not significantly different from the clinical, nonabused group.[26] Although it is unclear why the results of these studies differ, they may be due to the different ages of the subjects. Whereas Friedrich et al. included children ages three to twelve, with a mean age of approximately seven years, Mannarino et al. included children between the ages of six and twelve, with a mean age of approximately nine years. It may be that older abused children are more aggressive than younger abused children and, consequently, that the older children more closely resemble the clinical samples.

Other research has compared sexually abused children to physically abused and neglected children and to nonabused children. These studies have generally reported inconsistent results. White, Halpin, Strom, and Santilli compared seventeen sexually abused preschool children with eighteen neglected and twenty-three nonreferred children.[27] Using maternal ratings of aggression, the authors found sexually abused children to be significantly more aggressive than the neglected children and the nonreferred children. In contrast, Williamson, Borduin, and Howe, using parent reports on the Revised Behavior Problem Checklist, found that sexually abused adolescents were not more aggressive than nonmaltreated adolescents, and they were significantly less aggressive than neglected adolescents.[28] It is not possible to reconcile the inconsistencies of these studies since they involved children of different ages and used different measures of aggression.

Clinical Studies

Several clinically oriented studies have also examined the sexual abuse/aggression relationship by comparing sexually abused children with nonabused, clinical children in terms of symptoms and behaviors recorded in medical charts or behavior problems recorded in diagnostic interviews. Gale, Thompson, Moran, and Sack reviewed the charts and intake information of thirty-five physically abused, thirty-seven sexually abused, and 130 nonabused children under the age of seven who were seen at a child and family community mental health clinic.[29] They found no differences in aggression between the groups, although sexually abused children demonstrated higher levels of sexually inappropriate behaviors than did the other two groups. Similar results were reported by Kolko, Moser, and Weldy, who evaluated the charts and symptoms of twenty-nine sexually abused, fifty-two physically abused, and forty-four nonabused children between the ages of five and fourteen who were on an inpatient psychiatric unit.[30]

Using a similar methodology, Deblinger, McLeer, Atkins, Ralphe, and Foa compared twenty-nine sexually abused and twenty-nine physically abused children between the ages of three and thirteen with twenty-nine nonabused clinical children.[31] They found that sexually abused children were significantly more sexually abusive toward younger children than were nonabused inpatients, and marginally more sexually abusive than were physically abused children. Other types of aggressive behavior were not recorded; therefore, the overall aggression of the three groups is not known.

Summary

Although there are some exceptions, studies comparing sexually abused children to nonabused, nondistressed children generally report greater aggression among sexually abused children. In contrast, studies comparing sexually abused children with nonabused, clinical children, or with other types of abused children, have generally reported lower aggression among sexually abused children. These results, however, are somewhat inconsistent across different samples and methodologies. As with the research on physical abuse, sample selection is a problem in these studies since they all used sexually abused children who had been referred to treatment. It is not clear whether the same relationships would be observed for sexually abused children who are less likely to be referred to treatment or whose abuse is never reported. In addition, although some researchers have been careful to separate sexually abused children from physically abused children in some studies, there may be an overlap between these two groups in other studies, making it difficult to isolate the unique influences of sexual abuse. A related complication is that some of the sexual abuse may have involved considerable physical abuse, and it may be this physical abuse, rather than the sexual abuse, that influenced the child's aggression.

AGGRESSION IN CHILDREN WHO WITNESS DOMESTIC VIOLENCE

A variety of psychological theories predict that witnessing violence between their parents may increase children's aggressiveness.   Being raised in a violent home has been linked to a variety of interpersonal, emotional, and cognitive deficits.[32] The specific association between witnessing abuse and subsequent aggression in children has been explored in only a few studies, however, and these studies have yielded conflicting results.

Most of these studies have assessed the behaviors of children and mothers in shelters for battered women. This method of subject selection is problematic since it is not clear how representative the women and children in shelters are of all families in which there is spousal violence. It could be that extreme levels of violence have occurred in these families and that is why shelter has been sought. This could result in an overestimation of the consequences of witnessing abuse across all violent families. On the other hand, the mothers who leave violent homes and turn to shelters may have greater internal or external resources, and examining children who are being raised by these mothers may underestimate the consequences that are experienced by children with less capable mothers. At this point, it is impossible to know whether or in what direction study results are skewed by examining children in shelters. One study, however, does provide some information in this regard. Fantuzzo, DePaola, Lambert, Martino, Anderson, and Sutton found that children who had witnessed parental violence, been abused themselves, and whose families had lived in a shelter showed higher levels of behavioral and social disturbance than children who had witnessed abuse and been abused but whose family had not lived in a shelter.[33]

Research Results

Jaffe, Wolfe, Wilson, and Zak studied fifty mother/child pairs from shelters and fifty mother/child pairs from nonviolent homes.[34] The mothers completed the Child Behavior Profile (from the Child Behavior Checklist), which included a rating of the children's aggression. Boys from violent homes exhibited more aggression than did boys from nonviolent homes. There was no significant difference in the aggression of the girls from either type of home, suggesting that spousal violence could have different influences on boys and girls. Jouriles, Murphy, and O'Leary divided a group of families requesting psychotherapy for marital discord into those in which marital aggression occurred and those in which it did not.[35] They found that, after controlling for child gender and age and level of marital adjustment in the family, the level of marital aggression was positively correlated with a variety of conduct disorder and acting-out behaviors. In addition, Fantuzzo et al. found that children who had witnessed physical violence between their parents exhibited more externalizing behaviors on the Child Behavior Checklist than did children who witnessed only verbal violence between parents or children who came from nonviolent homes.[36]

Two studies using similar methodology presented conflicting results. Each used three groups of mothers: victims of spousal abuse, those in discordant but nonviolent marriages, and those in satisfactory marriages. The mothers rated their children's behaviors on the Peterson-Quay Behavior Problem Checklist. Rosenbaum and O'Leary found no differences in aggression between the three groups of children.[37] Hershorn and Rosenbaum found that the children in both the violent and discordant marriages differed from children in satisfactory marriages on overall ratings of problem behavior, including aggression.[38] However, the children from the violent and discordant marriages did not differ from each other on aggression.

One important issue in studies of the influence of marital aggression on child behaviors is the extent to which the children have experienced physical abuse themselves, in addition to witnessing physical abuse between their parents. Since, as discussed above, it appears that there is an association between being physically abused and subsequent aggression in children, it is important to differentiate the influence of physical abuse from the influence of witnessing violence. Several studies have attempted to do this.

Hughes studied ninety-seven three- to twelve-year-old children residing in shelters for battered women and eighty-three children from nonviolent, low-income homes.[39] Children who had witnessed abuse and who had not been abused did not differ significantly from the children in the comparison families. Children who had witnessed parental abuse and who had also been abused exhibited higher levels of problem behaviors than did children in the other families. Salzinger, Feldman, Hammer, and Rosario conducted research with eighty-seven children residing in shelters and a group of comparison children from nonabusive homes.[40] They found that the children from violent homes who had been abused themselves were rated by peers as being more aggressive, and by teachers and mothers as having more behavior problems than the comparison children. Furthermore, they found that after the presence of child abuse had been entered into a multiple regression analysis, the presence of physical violence between parents did not add to the predictive value of the regression equation. This suggested that marital violence had little additional influence on the children's behavior once the influence of the children's abuse had been accounted for.

Summary

The extent to which witnessing parental violence influences children's aggression is unclear. Some studies have reported significant differences between the conduct-disordered and aggressive behaviors of children who witness parental violence and those who do not. Other studies find no differences between these groups of children. One possible explanation for this can be found in the studies showing that witnessing parental violence has little additional influence on the behavior of a child who also has been the victim of physical abuse. It may be that there were varying numbers of physically abused children in the samples of the various studies examining the influence of witnessing violence and that these sample differences caused the differences in results. It is clear that additional research needs to be done in this area before we can begin to understand whether there are unique associations between witnessing parental violence and children's subsequent aggression, or whether the apparent connection is due to the physical abuse perpetrated on many of the children who witness interspousal violence.

CONCLUSIONS ON THE LINK BETWEEN ABUSE AND AGGRESSION

Taken together, the research reviewed in this section suggests that there is a fairly robust association between physical abuse and subsequent aggression in children. The research on the connections between witnessing family violence and later aggression and between child sexual abuse and later aggression is inconsistent. Both lines of research show higher aggression when the comparison groups consist of nonclinical, nonabused children. However, they are inconsistent when the comparison groups are other abused children or children experiencing other emotional problems. One important consideration in evaluating these inconsistencies is that the experience of physical abuse among the sexually abused children and the children who witness violence is not usually assessed. Thus, it is unclear whether the higher levels of aggression seen in some sexually abused or witnessing-abuse groups are due to concomitant physical abuse.

As noted earlier, correlational connections between abuse and school violence do not preclude the possibility that other factors are influencing or causing both. If these other possibilities (that is, community violence, hopelessness) are not considered, we run the risk of making simplistic assumptions (that is, if we reduce child abuse we will reduce school violence) and missing the opportunity to focus on actual causes of school violence.

Although the research has shown that some groups of abused children have higher levels of aggression, it is important to note that the range of behaviors among abused children is great. Many abused children are no more aggressive than nonabused children, and some of these abused children are withdrawn, depressed, anxious, or hyperactive. Since this chapter focused on the association between abuse and aggression, research examining these other responses was not discussed. Because of their varying reactions, abused children must be considered on an individual basis, and conclusions about an abused child's likelihood of being aggressive cannot be made based on his or her abuse status alone.

EXPLANATIONS FOR THE ASSOCIATION BETWEEN CHILD ABUSE AND AGGRESSION

A variety of biological and psychological explanations can be used to hypothesize about the connection between abuse and school aggression, and some of these explanations are reviewed in this section. Explanations appropriate for use with a small number of children are not reviewed because of space limitations. (For example, Multiple Personality Disorder found in some traumatically abused children may increase aggression, but this appears rarely.)

Neurological Explanations

A variety of neurological and hormonal abnormalities have been associated with human aggression. However, the exact nature of these abnormalities and the mechanism by which they influence aggression are still controversial.[41] Children who have been physically abused may have experienced some sort of neurological damage during their abuse, particularly if they were abused or severely neglected during their early years. Research has implicated physical abuse as causes of brain damage,[42] cerebral palsy,[43] and pinpoint hemorrhages in brain tissue.[44] Although these types of neurological damage have not been tied directly to aggression in children, the existence of such a link remains possible. Research also has shown, however, that neurological damage can place a child at greater risk for subsequent abuse.[45] Consequently, it cannot be assumed that physical abuse leads to neurological damage and, in turn, to heightened aggression in all cases where neurological damage is present. It may be that the neurological damage led to the abuse and that the abuse was associated with the subsequent aggression through some other mechanism.

Learning and Social Learning Explanations

Perhaps the most widely recognized explanations for the connection between home violence and aggression in schools come from the learning and social learning perspectives. From the operant learning perspective, it is argued that children learn to be aggressive through reinforcement of their aggressive behaviors. Patterson has developed and tested one clear model for the way this can occur.[46] Patterson suggests that aggression develops initially through poor parenting practices. When a young child is verbally or physically aggressive in response to parental demands and the parent withdraws, the parent is providing negative reinforcement for the child's behavior. (That is, the aggression is reinforced through the withdrawal of demands that the child considers noxious.) This reinforcement increases the likelihood that the child will act aggressively in other situations in which people put demands on the child. In school, for example, the child may act aggressively toward teachers and peers if they act in ways that the child does not like. If the child develops a pattern of aggression, the child may be ostracized by peers and adults. This may lead the child to enter a peer network with other aggressive children where the child's aggression is positively reinforced. At this point, the child is in a situation where he or she receives little reinforcement except when being aggressive.

The social learning perspective, initially formulated by Bandura,[47] combines modeling and observational learning with operant conditioning. Behaviors can be learned by observing the reinforcement or punishment received by others in response to their behaviors. For example, a young child could observe an older sibling receiving punishment or reinforcement for aggressive behavior, and the observation of this behavior may have an influence on the younger child's aggressive behavior.

There are a variety of ways in which the learning perspectives help to understand the influence of child abuse on aggression in schools. Some abusive families are quite chaotic. A child may learn (either through observation or direct experience) that the reinforcement of obtaining the limited resources of the family (for example, food, space) can be obtained through verbal or physical aggression. This aggressive behavior is then used later when the child tries to obtain things in school (for example, a place in line for a game, attention from the teacher). In these situations, however, the chaos associated with abusive families, not the abuse itself, is influencing the development of aggression.

The development of aggression in both physically and sexually abused children also can be understood using Patterson's model. The abused child may learn that the abuse directed at the child can be reduced or stopped when the child acts aggressively toward the abuser. The cessation of the abuse would be a strong negative reinforcer for the child's aggressive behavior. This reinforced aggressive response would be more likely to occur in subsequent situations where the child is confronted by adults or peers. Some abusers, of course, may react to the child's aggression by becoming even more abusive. These children may develop much more compliant behavior. Thus, parental reactions to the child's attempt to stop the abuse through aggression may be an important factor in the development of the two child behavioral styles that are often associated with physical or sexual abuse: extreme compliance and heightened aggression.

Finally, a child can observe a physically abusive parent or sibling getting what he or she wants through aggression. As noted above, spousal abuse is more likely to occur in families with child abuse problems than in families without child abuse. Thus, abused children may also experience seeing a parent give in to the demands of another parent or older sibling in the face of physical violence or the threat of violence. Children who are sexually abused may observe their own abusive situation as one in which the abuser engages in sex with the child through the use of violence or threats. Thus, the child is able to see how aggression helps the abuser achieve sexual dominance over the child, and the child may then use aggression when trying to achieve dominance over others.

Attachment Perspective Explanations

Bowlby described attachment as a biologically based bond with a caregiver.[48] The child's biologically driven behaviors (for example, crying, calling) are designed to maintain proximity to an attachment figure (usually the mother) and thus maintain the child's safety. The child's behaviors are met by the caretaker with either consistently supportive and responsive interactions, consistently unresponsive and rebuffing interactions, or inconsistent interactions. Responsive interactions lead to secure attachments and a pattern of behavior including proximity-seeking, pleasure during close contact, and developmentally appropriate willingness to explore away from the caretaker. Unresponsive or inconsistent interactions lead to anxious attachment that results in either avoidance of contact with the caregiver or a combination of contact-seeking and angry, aggressive behavior toward the caretaker. Through the early attachment experiences, the child develops an internal working model of relationships that influences the child's behaviors with others. The attachment history leads the child to expect that he or she is either worthy and capable of getting needed attention, or unworthy and incapable of getting needed attention. In addition, the child forms a model of others as either trustworthy, accessible, and responsive, or untrustworthy, inaccessible, and unresponsive.[49]

Crittenden's observation of maltreated infants and toddlers showed two patterns of attachment: (1) avoidant and openly resistant, and (2) avoidant and overwhelmingly passive.[50] She theorized that these patterns developed in response to the children's need for proximity with their parents and their expectations of their mother's angry and aggressive reactions to their proximity-seeking behavior. The internal working models of these maltreated children lead them to expect aggression and neglect from others. In response, they become overly vigilant and misinterpret the actions of others as being aggressive. Abused children who remain resistant to their parents (rather than overly passive) will experience ongoing, and perhaps increased, parental anger and abuse. The internal working model of these children may include a negative appraisal of others and a justification of their own angry/aggressive behavior. A combination of vigilance and misinterpretation of other's behavior as aggressive, and a sense of justification for their own aggression/anger, could lead these children to be overly aggressive with peers and adults across a variety of situations.[51]

Social Development Explanations

Several studies have found that abused children have deficits in their social development or are different from nonabused children in their perceptions of social situations. It is hypothesized that these deficits or perceptual differences increase the likelihood that abused children will interact aggressively in social situations. For example, some research has shown that maltreated children are less able to recognize a range of emotions in audiotaped scenarios[52] or in photographs.[53] Maltreated children have been found to be overly attentive to peripheral aggressive stimuli[54] and in the extent to which they misinterpret neutral behavioral cues as being aggressive.[55] These results suggest that maltreated children tend to see aggression across all contexts more often than do nonmaltreated children and that they are less adept at identifying other behaviors and emotions. Although these findings do not specify how these differences developed, they do help us understand how maltreated children's aggressive behaviors may come about as a response to their view of their world. Most of the studies done in this area focused on maltreated children, without specifying differences due to type of abuse or to neglect. Therefore, it is not possible to determine the relative value of these explanations for understanding the behaviors of physically or sexually abused children, or of children who only observe violence.

Combining Explanations for a Fuller Understanding of Abuse and School Violence

Being able to draw on several explanations for the apparent connection between some types of abuse and school violence enhances one's ability to understand the connection. In some cases, one particular explanation by itself may provide an understanding of one child's behavior while another explanation by itself provides an understanding for another child's behavior. It is more likely, however, that using a combination of explanations will prove most advantageous when attempting to understand most individual children's behavior. The combination of explanations may be different depending on the type of abuse that a child has suffered or the type of school violence in which the child engages. In addition, even within each type of abuse, different combinations are likely to be of different levels of utility when thinking about certain children. For example, consider a child whose early abuse led to an avoidant attachment style and a working model of relationships that includes aggression and the need for self-protection (the attachment model). This is likely to influence the child's expectation of aggression in interpersonal interactions and perception of aggression in them (social development model) and thus lead the child to act in a manner that protects against the aggression. If the initiation of early aggression has been useful in reducing aggression from others (the learning model), then an aggressive style of interpersonal interaction is likely to develop.

The apparent connection between abuse and school violence is a complicated one, both when considering individual cases and when considering abused children as a group. Recognizing this complexity will result in a better understanding of any link between abuse and school violence and will subsequently result in better efforts to prevent or reduce the amount of school violence that has been influenced by children's abuse experiences.

NOTES

1. J. J. Haugaard and R. E. Emery, "Methodological Issues in Child Sexual Abuse Research," *Child Abuse and Neglect* 13 (1989): 89–100; G. E. Wyatt and S. D. Peters, "Issues in the Definition of Child Sexual Abuse Research," *Child Abuse and Neglect* 10 (1986): 231–40.

2. J. J. Haugaard and N. D. Reppucci, *The Sexual Abuse of Children* (San Francisco: Jossey-Bass, 1988).

3. R. J. Gelles, "Violence in the Family: A Review of Research in the Seventies," *Journal of Marriage and the Family* 42 (1980): 873–84; R. L. Hampton, "Race, Class, and Child Maltreatment," *Journal of Comparative Family Studies* 18 (1987): 113–26; K. J. Lindholm and R. Wiley, "Ethnic Differences in Child Abuse and Sexual Abuse," *Hispanic Journal of Behavioral Sciences* 8 (1986): 111–25.

4. M. A. Straus and C. Smith, "Family Patterns and Child Abuse," in *Physical Violence in American Families,* eds. M. A. Straus and R. Gelles (New Brunswick, N. J.: Transaction Publishers, 1990), 245–61.

5. R. T. Ammerman, J. E. Cassisi, M. Hersen, and V. B. Van Hasselt, "Consequences of Physical Abuse and Neglect in Children," *Clinical Psychology Review* 6 (1986): 291–

310; L. P. Conaway and D. J. Hansen, "Social Behavior of Physically Abused and Neglected Children: A Critical Review," *Clinical Psychology Review* 9 (1989): 627–52; E. Mueller and N. Silverman, "Peer Relations in Maltreated Children," in *Child Maltreatment: Theory and Research on the Causes and Consequences of Child Abuse and Neglect,* eds. D. Cicchetti and V. Carlson (Cambridge: Cambridge University Press, 1989), 529–78.

6. E. M. Kinard, "Emotional Development in Physically Abused Children," *American Journal of Orthopsychiatry* 50 (1980): 686–98.

7. G. Straker and R. S. Jacobson, "Aggression, Emotional Maladjustment, and Empathy in the Abused Child," *Developmental Psychology* 17 (1981): 762–65.

8. B. Weiss, K. A. Dodge, J. E. Bates, and G. S. Pettit, "Some Consequences of Early Harsh Discipline: Child Aggression and a Maladaptive Social Information Processing Style," *Child Development* 63 (1992): 1321–35.

9. D. P. Fry, "The Intergenerational Transmission of Disciplinary Practices and Approaches to Conflict," *Human Organization* 52 (1993): 176–85.

10. C. George and M. Main, "Social Interactions of Young Abused Children: Approach, Avoidance, and Aggression," *Child Development* 50 (1979): 306–318.

11. D. Hoffman-Plotkin and C. Twentyman, "A Multimodal Assessment of Behavioral and Cognitive Deficits in Abused and Neglected Children," *Child Development* 55 (1984): 794–802.

12. P. A. Rosenthal and M. B. Doherty, "Serious Sibling Abuse by Preschool Children," *Journal of the American Academy of Child Psychiatry* 23 (1984): 186–90.

13. G. Downey and E. Walker, "Social Cognition and Adjustment in Children at Risk for Psychopathology," *Developmental Psychology* 25 (1989): 835–45; E. Walker, G. Downey, and A. Bergman, "The Effects of Parental Psychopathology and Maltreatment on Child Behavior," *Child Development* 60 (1989): 15–24.

14. P. D. Kurtz, J. M. Gaudin, P. T. Howing, and J. S. Wodarski, "The Consequences of Physical Abuse and Neglect on the School-Age Child," *Child Abuse and Neglect* 17 (1993): 85–104.

15. J. M. Williamson, C. M. Borduin, and B. A. Howe, "The Ecology of Adolescent Maltreatment: A Multilevel Examination of Adolescent Physical Abuse, Sexual Abuse, and Neglect," *Journal of Counseling and Clinical Psychology* 59 (1991): 449–57.

16. L. A. Camras and S. Rappaport, "Conflict Behaviors of Maltreated and Nonmaltreated Children," *Child Abuse and Neglect* 17 (1993): 455–64.

17. Weiss et al., "Some Consequences of Early Harsh Discipline."

18. A. Browne and D. Finkelhor, "Impact of Child Sexual Abuse: A Review of the Research," *Psychological Bulletin* 99 (1986): 66–77; R. K. Hanson, "The Psychological Impact of Sexual Assault on Women and Children: A Review," *Annals of Sex Research* 3 (1990): 187–232; K. A. Kendall-Tackett, L. M. Williams, and D. Finkelhor, "Impact of Sexual Abuse on Children: A Review and Synthesis of Recent Empirical Studies," *Psychological Bulletin* 113 (1993): 164–80.

19. J. R. Conte and J .R. Schuerman, "Factors Associated with an Increased Impact of Child Sexual Abuse," *Child Abuse and Neglect* 11 (1987): 201–11.

20. H. Inderbitzen-Pisaruk, C. R. Shawchuck, and T. S. Hoier, "Behavioral Characteristics of Child Victims of Sexual Abuse: A Comparison Study," *Journal of Clinical Child Psychology* 21 (1992): 14–19.

21. A. J. Einbender and W. N. Friedrich, "Psychological Functioning and Behavior of Sexually Abused Girls," *Journal of Consulting and Clinical Psychology* 57 (1989): 155–57.

22. L. Tong, K. Oates, and M. McDowell, "Personality Development Following Sexual Abuse," *Child Abuse and Neglect* 11 (1987): 371– 83.

23. B. Gomes-Schwartz, J. M. Horowitz, and M. Sauzier, "Severity of Emotional Distress among Sexually Abused Preschool, School-Age, and Adolescent Children," *Hospital and Community Psychiatry* 36 (1985): 503–08.

24. J. A. Cohen and A. P. Mannarino, "Psychological Symptoms in Sexually Abused Girls," *Child Abuse and Neglect* 12 (1988): 571– 77.

25. W. N. Friedrich, R. L. Beilke, and A. J. Urquiza, "Children from Sexually Abusive Families," *Journal of Interpersonal Violence* 2 (1987): 391–402.

26. A. P. Mannarino, J. A. Cohen, and M. Gregor, "Emotional and Behavioral Difficulties in Sexually Abused Girls, " *Journal of Interpersonal Violence* 4 (1989): 437–51.

27. S. White, B. M. Halpin, G. A. Strom, and G. Santilli, "Behavioral Comparisons of Young Sexually Abused, Neglected, and Nonreferred Children," *Journal of Clinical Child Psychology* 17 (1988): 53–61.

28. Williamson, Borduin, and Howe, "The Ecology of Adolescent Maltreatment."

29. J. Gale, R. J. Thompson, T. Moran, and W. H. Sack, "Sexual Abuse in Young Children: Its Clinical Presentation and Characteristic Patterns" *Child Abuse and Neglect* 12 (1988): 163–70.

30. D. J. Kolko, J. T. Moser, and S. R. Weldy, "Behavioral/Emotional Indicators of Sexual Abuse in Child Psychiatric Inpatients: A Controlled Comparison with Physical Abuse," *Child Abuse and Neglect* 12 (1988): 529–41.

31. E. Deblinger, S. V. McLeer, M. S. Atkins, D. Ralphe, and E. Foa, "Post-Traumatic Stress in Sexually Abused, Physically Abused, and Nonabused Children," *Child Abuse and Neglect* 13 (1989): 403–408.

32. P. G. Jaffe, M. Sudermann, and D. Reitzel, "Child Witness of Marital Violence," in *Assessment of Family Violence: A Clinical and Legal Sourcebook,* eds. R. Ammerman and M. Hersen (1992), 313–331; C. Widom, "Does Violence Beget Violence? A Critical Examination of the Literature," *Psychological Bulletin* 106 (1989): 3–28.

33. J. W. Fantuzzo, L. M. DePaola, L. Lambert, T. Martino, G. Anderson, and S. Sutton in *Journal of Consulting and Clinical Psychology* 59 (1991): 258–65.

34. P. G. Jaffe, D. Wolfe, S. Wilson, and L. Zak, "Critical Issues in the Assessment of Children's Adjustment to Witnessing Family Violence," *Canada's Mental Health* 33 (1985): 27–42.

35. E. N. Jouriles, C. M. Murphy, and D. O'Leary, "Interspousal Aggression, Marital Discord, and Child Problems," *Journal of Consulting and Clinical Psychology* 57 (1989): 453–55.

36. Fantuzzo et al., in *Journal of Consulting and Clinical Psychology.*

37. A. Rosenbaum and D. O'Leary, "Children: The Unintended Victims of Marital Violence," *American Journal of Orthopsychiatry* 51 (1981): 692–99.

38. M. Hershorn and A. Rosenbaum, "Children of Marital Violence: A Closer Look at the Unintended Victims," *American Journal of Orthopsychiatry* 55 (1985): 260–66.

39. H. M. Hughes, "Psychological and Behavioral Correlates of Family Violence in Child Witnesses and Victims," *American Journal of Orthopsychiatry* 58 (1988): 77–90.

40. S. Salzinger, R. Feldman, M. Hammer, and M. Rosario, "The Effects of Physical Abuse of Children's Social Relationships," *Child Development* 64 (1993): 169–87.

41. N. R. Carlson, *Physiology of Behavior,* 4th ed. (Boston: Allyn and Bacon, 1991).

42. A. Buchanan and J. E. Oliver, "Abuse and Neglect as a Cause of Mental Retardation," *British Journal of Psychiatry* 131 (1977): 458–67.

43. L. J. Diamond and P. K. Jaudes, "Child Abuse in a Cerebral-Palsied Population," *Developmental Medicine and Child Neurology* 25 (1983):169–74.

44. J. Caffey, "On the Theory and Practice of Shaking Infants," *American Journal of Diseases in Children* 124 (1972): 161–69.

45. Diamond and Jaudes, "Child Abuse in a Cerebral-Palsied Population"; K. B. Sherrod, S. O'Connor, P. Vietze, and W. A. Altemeir, "Child Health and Maltreatment," *Child Development* 55 (1984): 1174–83.

46. G. R. Patterson, B. D. DeBaryshe, and E. Ramsey, "A Developmental Perspective on Antisocial Behavior," *American Psychologist* 44 (1989): 329–35.

47. A. Bandura, *Social Learning Theory* (Englewood Cliffs, N.J.: John Wiley, 1977).

48. J. Bowlby, *Attachment and Loss*, Vol. I: *Attachment* (New York: Basic Books, 1969).

49. P. C. Alexander, "Application of Attachment Theory to the Study of Sexual Abuse," *Journal of Consulting and Clinical Psychology* 60 (1992): 185–95.

50. P. M. Crittenden, "Social Networks, Quality of Child-Rearing, and Child Development," *Child Development* 56 (1985): 1299–1313.

51. P. M. Crittenden and M. D. S. Ainsworth, "Child Maltreatment and Attachment Theory," in *Child Maltreatment* , eds. D. Cicchetti and V. Carlson (Cambridge: Cambridge University Press, 1989), 432–63.

52. R. M. Barahal, J. Waterman, and H. Martin, "The Social Cognitive Development of Abused Children," *Journal of Consulting and Clinical Psychology* 49 (1981): 508–16.

53. L. Camras, S. Ribordy, J. Hill, S. Martino, S. Spaccarelli, and R. Stefani, "Recognition and Posing Emotional Expressions by Abused Children and Their Mothers," *Developmental Psychology* 24 (1988): 776–81.

54. C. Reider and D. Cicchetti, "An Organizational Perspective on Cognitive Control Functioning and Cognitive Affective Balance in Maltreated Children," *Developmental Psychology* 25 (1989): 382–93.

55. K. Dodge, G. Pettit, C. McClaskey, and M. Brown, *Social Competence in Children. Monographs of the Society for Research in Child Development*, Serial No. 213, vol. 51 (1986), 1–85.

Part III

SCHOOL SECURITY AND RELATED LEGAL ISSUES

7

Critical Decisions, Critical Elements in an Effective School Security Program

S. D. Vestermark, Jr.

Two major, continuing shifts in the relationship between American schools and the social worlds just outside them now shape all the efforts of those charged with developing and administering effective school security programs. Always a potential source of pressure on the distinctive missions of the American public school, these trends seem to have intensified over the past several generations, with important contemporary consequences.

First, *the school has been increasingly losing its status as a sanctuary,* a place set apart from larger societal concerns and traumas. Many now perceive the school as no longer "off limits" to secular conflicts of the moment, whether they be as broad as ideological conflicts over issues such as sex education, school prayer, or creationism, or as sharply focused as criminal acts— including assault, robbery, and attempted murder—by one individual against another. The school security administrator can no longer comfortably assume that the school provides both the moral standing and physical apartness necessary to insulate it, at least relatively, from the intrusive social pressures and problems that now directly influence student behavior in school.

Americans have tended to view their public schools as agencies of social improvement. In earlier years it was assumed that the public schools would socialize and educate children of diverse backgrounds in common values and institutional practices, and that these children would later emerge from school as autonomous but responsible citizens. In today's school setting, however, it is becoming more widely assumed that the school will be directly involved in achieving present-time solutions to social problems.

In some areas, the school today is a locus for programs intended to reduce family and gang violence outside the school. The public school also has become a vehicle to provide greater equality of opportunity through such programs as school busing or magnet schools, intended to foster racial desegregation. In some places the school has become a locus for both sex education and postnatal as well as prenatal child care. Moreover, in a reversal of its traditional assimilationist, so-cializing role, today's public school must often recognize and encourage multiculturalism and ethnic diversity—which not only can reinforce resentments by those who have felt the need to suppress their own distinctive cultural values, but can also trigger sometimes violent counterassertions by students who have been in the traditionally dominant majority. In short, instead of being relatively set apart, some schools have now become explicitly defined arenas for conflict.

The injection of interpersonal violent conflict as well as debate over societal problems intruding into the school setting underscores a second change in the sta-tus of the school: *many schools have declined as, or even ceased to be, communi-ties,* and in the worst cases have become barely controlled aggregations of warring factions. A community is, in general, a defined group of individuals who share certain integrative values and commitments with each other, and who organize at least part of their individual behaviors in terms of the larger group's values.[1] A community is not necessarily a legal or governmental entity, even though such communities as schools may be initially organized around legally mandated as-semblages of people. More important, a community is a group of people who feel at least a minimum sense of responsibility for each other, and who view their own personal safety as well as self-fulfillment as dependent in some measure on how community members discharge their perceived responsibilities to each other.

Evoking the values of the school community—common school traditions, what it is to be a "good citizen," how the good school citizen behaves toward outsid-ers—has always been a powerful control available to principals and teachers. Amitai Etzioni, who is concerned with reinforcing the role of the school as a setting for experiences that contribute to the moral education of the young, lists a number of conditions that, in fact, define the existence or absence of a sense of school com-munity. Although his model appears to be the large suburban high school, his list nonetheless has more general interest:

[S]chools should be seen not as a collection of teachers, pupils, classrooms, and curricula. Instead, examine the parking lots: Are they places in which wild driving takes place and school authorities are not to be seen, or are they places where one learns respect for others' safety, regulated either by faculty or fellow students? Are the cafeterias places where stu-dents belt each other with food and the noise is overwhelming, or are they civilized places where students can conduct meaningful conversations over lunch? Are the corridors areas where muscles and stature are required to avoid being pushed aside by bullies, or are they safe conduits patrolled by faculty or students? Does vandalism go unpunished, are drugs sold openly, and are pupils rewarded or punished according to criteria other than achieve-ment (perhaps because they avoid confrontation, obey without question, or come from af-fluent or otherwise socially preferred backgrounds)? Or is vandalism held in check and the damage, when vandalism does occur, corrected by the offending students? Are drug sales dealt with swiftly and severely? Are students treated according to reasonable and under-standable criteria?[2]

The sense of school community breaks down, however, when members of what had been the school community themselves become outsiders, and when the immediate groups through which they define themselves (friends, neighborhood acquaintances, racial or cultural groups, gangs, or other peer associations) emerge as contenders among the competing factions that try to define and control the school climate or, failing that, establish "turfs" in the school and its immediate surroundings. As the sense of the school as a unified place, held in common, declines, conflict— between students, between students and teachers or administrators— can be expected to increase.

Conflict-resolution then becomes a priority of those charged with school security. To be successful in the long run, conflict resolution must be seen as part of the process of enhancing or restoring a sense of school community. Conflict-resolution tactics—ranging from short-term conflict *suppression* through use of law enforcement and security personnel, to longer term community-building efforts, which may include adult counseling or peer mediation techniques—will be only palliatives unless the school in conflict has a strategy for restoring at least a minimal sense of school community. At the secondary school level—usually the center of a school system's security concerns—absence of a controlling sense of school community creates a vacuum in which adolescents can individually or collectively act out aggressive impulses, secure in the imagined support provided by immediate peers. Even the solitary deviant individual may imagine that his or her acts of assault, robbery, or vandalism will be condoned by "friends."

EMERGENCE OF THE SCHOOL SECURITY PROFESSIONAL

In the early 1970s, a new type of full-time professional specialist committed to designing and administering school security programs began to emerge in a variety of school systems across the United States.[3] They began to emerge into public view just when such phenomena as violence spawned by the decline of the urban family structure and anxieties over federally mandated school desegregation programs combined to emphasize that the public schools were becoming arenas in which to act out society's larger and unresolved social and political concerns.[4]

Police-Based Professionals

Sometimes these professionals came from successful uniformed police-community relations programs that used specially qualified and trained school-based officers to project a benign, supportive presence in daily school life.[5] The purpose of these officers, beyond projecting a positive image of the police, was to deter school crime incidents and, when an incident occurred, to deal with it in ways that would as nearly as possible meet the developmental and educational needs of the young people involved.

School-Based Professionals

Of perhaps greater long-term impact on school security policies, school systems themselves began to develop their own distinctive school security programs.

These programs were located inside the school system, under the control of the board of education and the superintendent of schools. Under the operational control of a director or chief of security, these programs used a combination of school-focused professional field personnel and hardware systems (for example, intrusion detection systems, perimeter controls) to achieve desired levels of security in the system's schools. Advocates of the school system-based security program contended—and contend—that only a program *inside* the school system, steeped in the values and methods of the schools' educational mission and devoted to the rights as well as the needs of developing young people, can create a supportive, yet nonoppressive, security presence in school buildings.[6]

An Inherent Tension

As the school security profession has evolved, a tension remains between those who believe in a law enforcement orientation and those who desire a primarily educational orientation. These emphases may reflect the distinctive histories and preoccupations of particular school systems. Large, diverse urban systems that perceive themselves to have mounting levels of interpersonal crime in schools may style their officers as "school police" and emphasize their law enforcement powers. Systems that feel able to maintain an emphasis on security as part of the community support and civic educational mission of particular schools—still the case in many suburban school systems—tend to view their security officers as directly supportive of the educational process, and style their officers as "investigators," "aides," "counselors," or even "investigator/counselors."

The tensions between varying approaches to school crime control certainly ensure that in the near term, at least, there will be no one totally accepted body of "school security doctrine" agreed to by all professionals. Indeed, the name of today's leading professional association of school security personnel—the National Association of School Safety and Law Enforcement Officers (NASSLEO)—exactly reflects the basic tension as well as dynamic in today's emergent school security profession.[7]

WHAT IS THE APPROPRIATE SCHOOL SECURITY PROGRAM? A CASE STUDY

The following case study illustrates some present difficulties in maintaining or redefining the specific school security program emphases that have been deemed appropriate by a school system:

> On Friday morning, April 8, 1994, a seventeen-year-old male student at Largo High School in Prince Georges County, Maryland, brought a 9mm handgun into the school. He went to a boys' lavatory, where he displayed it to another male student. While this was occurring, both students were discovered by a male teacher on hallway monitoring duty.
> The teacher asked the student who brought the gun into the school to give it to him. While accounts then and during the subsequent trial differ, it appears

that the teenager said words to the effect, "No way." The gun discharged, and the teacher was shot once in the right chest. The shooter fled, but later turned himself in to police, at which time he was charged as an adult with assault with intent to murder, possession of a firearm on school property, and use of a firearm in the commission of a felony.

This shooting immediately created an uproar, both in the school and among its parents, who streamed to the school to retrieve their children, as well as in the regional news media, who also flocked to the site. This shooting of a teacher *in school* was the first that could be remembered in the sprawling Washington–Baltimore area of which the Prince Georges County school system is a part. Located a relatively short distance from the media center of downtown Washington, D.C., Largo High School became the focus of intense electronic and print coverage which emphasized that a teacher had actually been attacked in a school. No less a figure than Madeline M. Kunin, deputy secretary of the U.S. Department of Education, found herself asked to make immediate comments about this shooting from a local call-in radio talk show, where she happened to be a guest on the midmorning segment.

Parents, as well as some school board members and teachers, said this demonstrated the need for metal detectors at the entrances to all schools. There was a proposal to require all students and teachers to wear identification badges. Conversations overheard on the street suggested that there was even some support for surrounding selected schools with high chain-link fences topped with razor wire. Local media reported that the school system's force of security officers, now totaling forty, would increase by eighteen during the next budget cycle.

All this, plus more extreme reactions, took place in spite of the facts that Largo High School had been relatively incident-free, was a stable, multicultural school, is located in a system that had been nationally recognized for its innovative and effective school security program, and is itself physically located literally next door to that system's security headquarters.[8]

This incident struck raw communal sensibilities, which quick disclosure of key facts did not fully alleviate. Within a few hours it developed that the perpetrator was a black male; had stolen the personal weapon of his father, a respected police officer; and had brought it to school to attempt to sell it to another black male. In the process, he shot a black male teacher. Thus, a shooting that had initially aroused some racial fears—did a black student shoot a white teacher?—in a metropolitan area where racial anxieties lie just below the surface, came to be seen as a classic case of adolescent resistance to adult authority. If anything, this made the incident even more threatening, because racial variables offered no easy avoidance of the basic issues. A teacher had been shot in school, by a student.[9] The basic, necessary relationship between teacher and student, *a deference to each other* based on authority, respect, and trust, had been breached in the most fundamental way: by a life-threatening act of one against the other.

Questions began to fly among those who had to deal with the event. Implicitly, they covered the whole range of issues central to setting school security policy for today. For example:

- What image of the school do we want to project to young people and parents? If we retrofit today's often sprawling school building—which was designed to be "open" and to offer multiple points of access—with fewer entrances, perimeter fences with closed-circuit (CCTV) surveillance, and metal detectors at all entrances, have we not-so-subtly converted it into a custodial facility with many of the attributes of a prison?

- How can security programs have an impact on and compensate for prior failures to socialize young people, in order to deter violent conflicts and limit their consequences?

- If they can have such impact, how then do these security program elements relate to established counseling and social adjustment programs under the traditional control of formally certified educators?

- What is the proper ratio of security personnel—both school system-based and from outside law enforcement agencies—to the overall staff of a school? What are the criteria for establishing this ratio?

- Do school security personnel have new, evolving background and training requirements as schools are perceived to be becoming settings for increased interpersonal violence?

- What kinds of support can, and should, today's public schools offer to the kinds of communities from which it draws, or to the community immediately around it?

- What are the primary missions of today's public schools that must be supported by school security programs in an atmosphere where many schools are under pressures to become residual repositories of larger, unsolved societal problems?

Highly visible, media-intensive incidents such as that at Largo force everyone to face just what it is that schools can and cannot do in today's society. What is a school to be? Schools *sometimes* can be very dangerous places. Yet this is quite different from asserting that *all* or most schools are dangerous *much* or *most* of the time.

FIVE CRITICAL POLICY QUESTIONS

Given the often highly charged atmosphere in which many school systems will be deciding what school security programs are appropriate to their needs, experience suggests that security planners need to consider at least five basic questions before they attempt to develop a program specific to a system.[10]

1. *Does the system have—or can it establish—a valid, reliable method and administrative structure for tracking security incidents as well as important supplemental indicators? In short, does it have an "incident reporting system?"* An "incident" is any category of event that is of importance to the school security

program.[11] *Crimes against persons* in the school setting include assaults (student on student, student on teacher, outsider on student or teacher), robbery (including attempts), extortion (including attempts), drug violations, sex offenses, carrying of weapons, and trespassing. *Crimes against property* include arson, bombings and bomb threats, burglary, theft of school property, theft of student or teacher property, and vandalism.

In addition to these standard incident categories, the school system needs to monitor certain *indicators of process*, which can help identify developing security problems systemwide or in certain schools. These indicators include unusual absentee rates, class-cutting, dramatic changes in the suspension or expulsion rate, presence and quantity of "hate literature" on school premises, racial unrest, student demonstrations, and evidence of "turf wars" through patterns of gang activity—including fighting.

The school system's most critical step in readying an effective school security program is to establish a comprehensive incident and indicator reporting system. Using stable, valid definitions of important categories, over time, this system will reliably report what is happening throughout the system. There may be strong political resistance to keeping such records, especially when the system perceives itself to be under stress, as when new ethnic minorities are establishing a presence and may, in fact, be becoming the majority. Monitoring such trends requires a degree of detachment that is at least equivalent to that exercised by the professional school guidance staff, which tracks disciplinary and dropout problems, or the local police force, which monitors overall local area crime rates.

These considerations reflect two more general problems that must often be overcome in establishing an incident reporting system. First, regardless of the local crises of the moment, those who cherish a traditional, sentimentalized view of schools will find it difficult to acknowledge the existence of any school security problems. These problems threaten them, but they will deny them. A 1994 National League of Cities survey produced this statement from a local official:

"I live in a city that is in a state of denial," wrote a municipal official from a medium-sized suburban city in the Northwest who said schools there are not always reporting incidents. "We have no idea how much is occurring in schools. It is surely underreported and a rapidly growing problem."[12]

In addition, those who establish an effective school incident reporting system are likely to experience at least a short-term upsurge in incident rates.[13] This will probably be an artifact of more effective reporting and not indicative of a real increase in incidents. Even so, such data trends can be deeply upsetting to school boards and superintendents, even when their meanings are explained.

But a good incident and indicator reporting system does more than reactively report events after the fact. It should allow the school security program to be *proactive*—to target in advance those schools or areas where unacceptable incidents appear likely to occur, and to suggest specific preemptive possibilities.

2. *Given the meanings of "safety" and "security" in the school setting, what is the acceptable level of risk against which to measure the effectiveness of the school security program?* As the recently announced national zero tolerance policy for guns in schools suggests, there is certainly some support for making schools "no-risk" places. As a widespread state, however, no-risk is probably an unattainable goal, given the contrasting demands many school security programs face.

For example, the security program officers in a large, multicultural, urban high school, where many students come from broken families and gangs provide an alternative peer group structure, may view a "safe" condition as one where murders have been avoided through metal detectors, security sweeps, and intensive group interventions, and where two-person or group fights are now substantially fewer. Such a notion of "safety" would probably seem appalling to the average suburban PTA officer or parent. Moreover, it would seem simply exotic to security officials in a vast rural district, where the big seasonal problem may be to ensure that the bus fleet delivers kids safely on snowy days.

Conceptually, there is an important difference between "safety" and "security" as applied to the school setting:

Traditionally, the terms "safety" and "security" have been interchangeable. They both equally implied a freedom from harm. In our view, however, safety is...*an acceptable level of risk*.... In the school setting, security is *the process of achieving acceptable levels of risk* from crimes against persons and property in the school community.... *Safety, then, is the continuing outcome of a well-managed security program.*[14]

In the school setting where acceptable levels of incident and indicator rates have been achieved (and "acceptable" here means not only to the board of education, superintendent, and local police, but also to administrators, teachers, students, and parents), a state of relative security exists. Yet it must always be remembered that safety is a condition measured at a *point in time.* To achieve a desired state of safety, the schools must support a *security process*, with its requisite resources, over time. For school security planners the basic question becomes: What resources—including in-place policies, personnel, and hardware—are required to achieve and sustain desired and acceptable incident rates?

3. *Is the school system prepared to make a stable, long-term commitment to a distinct, separately defined security program?* This question follows from the previous two. An effective school security program must be founded on accurate, continuing intelligence data, and to achieve continuing results it must support a continuing security process. Any approach that focuses on immediate reduction of those incidents that most alarm the public, without follow-through, will end up as little more than a quick fix.

Some may argue that, in a time of limited budgets, the school security program will have been successful if it reduces immediate threats. Once that happens, the argument then goes, it is possible to reduce the amount of resources committed to the program. This view fails to recognize a hard-to-measure but nevertheless real outcome of any successful security program: that it becomes a *deterrent* to further undesired events. A hard fact in today's society is that once a security program is in place it tends to become self-perpetuating, because those who must be deterred from further criminal or violent acts are now consciously or semiconsciously "scanning" their environments to see whether opportunities exist for new acts. Media publicity of past acts certainly encourages this scanning process.[15]

A decline in incident rates will not, therefore, be an indicator that any security effort is successful in permanently eliminating all undesired events—only that it may be having a crucial and ongoing deterrent effect. As measured by declines in incident rates and additional indicators of instability in the school climate, effective school security can be justified as fully by its deterrent possibilities as by more dramatic, more visible cuts in rates on key indicators.

An established school security program that both cuts rates of critical incidents and acts as a continuing deterrent will require clear definition as a visible, freestanding program under its own internal direction—even if it uses resources from outside the school system, such as local police officers. This implies that it will be a distinct item or set of items in the school system's budget, or in whatever budgets contribute to its funding. For many school systems, security costs are becoming essentially permanent costs.

4. *What is the appropriate "mix" of resources required in a particular district's school security program?* As school security costs become a substantial item in budgets, a number of decisions will be required about appropriate program emphases. Apart from fine-tuned decisions about the specific numbers that should go on specific line items, there will be questions of what general emphases best reflect the needs as well as the traditions of the system.

Perhaps the most basic question of emphasis is choosing the desired mix of personnel versus physical resources in the security program. This is not just a question of the "people budget" versus the "hardware budget." In a system where parents and teachers are demanding such hardware as metal detectors and intrusion detection (alarm) systems, the question quickly becomes: Assuming that the hardware functions as its seller claims, what personnel will staff it? Mechanical screening of people entering schools or intrusion alarm monitoring will sometimes be performed, in order to save money, by marginally trained, hourly contract personnel.[16] Such persons may miss just those situations or incidents that it is most important they detect. Furthermore, those in contact with students and parents may behave in ways that unnecessarily alienate them.

So, costly hardware implies that competent personnel be able to use it. But there is really a larger question here: Are resources available to create a security program that can, operating essentially *within* a school system, present a level of professionalism comparable to and consistent with that of the professionals already in the system? Teachers and administrators will be quick to judge the school security operative by his or her behavior as measured not only by general educational standards, but also according to the subtle blend of security professionalism and human sensitivity he or she brings to actual incidents.

Such requirements suggest that the people budget will always be of more significance than the hardware budget in achieving school security goals. For the financially most strapped and criminally most stressed systems, with high interpersonal incident rates, this may indicate the need for a greater uniformed police presence in schools, simply because there are no resources to provide comparable training to school personnel or fund independent school security positions. Yet people working daily in schools with students and teachers will be judged, like it or not, by whether they are contributing to educational goals—which include maintenance of a supportive and humane as well as relatively stress-free environment. While crucial as last-resort support and enforcement personnel, police will be seen by many educators and students essentially as outsiders. (Indeed, for some potentially disruptive young people, the fact that police are not educational personnel makes them fascinating and at least marginally acceptable.)

When a system finds that personnel costs are more critical than hardware costs, then what are the standards by which personnel will be recruited, trained, and deployed in the school? In the educational as well as larger American cultural setting, this raises the issue of professionalism. How can professional standards be applied to emergent school security programs?

5. *What is the role of professional standards in defining and conducting the school security program?* A school security program founded on accurate, continuing intelligence data, with clear risk-reduction goals, a stable and separately defined and budgeted status, and an appropriate mix of resources, will necessarily become a major actor in its jurisdiction. This guarantees that the performance of its individual staff and administrative personnel, as well as overall program performance, will be judged closely, critically, and sometimes even with hostility. Embedded in the school system, with the task of increasing safety and security, the program will be evaluated, at least in part, by the standards that govern its two principal reference groups, educators and law enforcement professionals.[17]

It is therefore inevitable that the program and its personnel will be judged by "professional standards." The question is not *whether* this will happen, but rather whose or what professional standards will be applied, when, and in what ways?

In developing the security program, responsible school officials, including the one in direct charge of security, must be able to meld educational with security professionalism, beginning with the recruitment and training of a school security operative, in order to achieve an acceptable definition and solution of school security problems. From the professional standards and knowledge of educators, school security personnel must draw techniques of working with a student and teacher population. These include methods of providing acceptable intervention, helping build a sense of school community, and offering pertinent counseling. However, intervening and counseling may quickly become part of an ongoing security investigation. Here law enforcement professionalism must be a source of expertise in how to conduct a lawful investigation, how to enhance personal and physical security, how to interdict criminal behavior, and how to maintain the rights of those who become involved with school security personnel. The resultant body of emergent professional knowledge is complex and subtle, and often straddles the traditionally accepted boundaries between education and law enforcement. Indeed, some school districts require their school-based security personnel to undergo training at the local police academy, and one pioneering program has styled its line security officers as "school investigator/counselors."[18]

How the school security program draws on and tailors to its own needs sometimes seemingly conflicting professional standards can crucially affect its acceptance and effectiveness among the various constituencies it must serve. These constituents include not only students and their families and others in the outside community, but also educators and uniformed law enforcement personnel. In the minds of these two latter groups—and particularly where the addition of school security personnel triggers institutional jealousies—this question always lies just below the surface: How competent are these people? Understanding and applying professionally based knowledge are among the school security person's indispensable answers.

THE EFFECTIVE SCHOOL SECURITY PROGRAM: THE NECESSARY AND POSSIBLE VERSUS THE OPTIMAL

This analysis has assumed that the most effective general approach to solving school security problems will place the school security program in a very close relationship with the traditional educational activities of the schools. From this perspective, school security personnel are part of the educational team that works with students every day. Thus, the *optimal* school security program is one that tries to preserve the school as a place somewhat set apart from outside pressures, where young people can focus on learning in a safe environment, and where security activities remain, as far as possible, nonintrusive in the overall atmosphere that teachers and educational administrators try to set for a school.

Immediate Requirements Versus Educational Objectives

In many of today's schools, there are strong pressures to address what are seen as the practical necessities inherent in dealing with serious security threats. Where weapons are being brought into school, there will be immediate and understandable demands for metal detectors at entrances. Where there is a high rate of interpersonal violence in school, particularly from intruders, there will be demands for a clear, continuing uniformed police presence, as both deterrent and suppressor. Incidents such as drive-by shootings or attacks by armed intruders in the school, who assault or take hostages, will amplify these demands. Where school athletic contests now provide opportunities for violence *off* as well as on the field or court, police officers reinforced by highly visible hardware deterrents such as metal detectors and industrial-strength perimeter fencing may become routine.[19]

While uniformed police patrols and supporting hardware may be viewed as intrusive by some well-meaning critics—because they subject students to individual body searches as well as seemingly reinforce a "siege atmosphere" in the school—the hard fact remains that in some youth subcultures there can be no effective "educational intervention" without first stopping violent behavior.

Use of Police and Metal Detectors in Schools

Deployment of police and use of student search devices— metal detectors— are perhaps the two most visible and controversial "noneducational" options used today to deter and suppress school crime and violence. Their use reflects many pressures of necessity, ranging from the need to control violent youth who are not otherwise deterred, to the need to reinforce limited school-based security budgets with outside, traditional security capabilities.

A 1994 survey of its members by the National League of Cities (NLC) provides useful data on how police and metal detectors are, in fact, being deployed in schools today. For 345 of the 700 cities reporting, police patrol schools throughout the day. In the majority of cities where police patrol the schools, these patrols have been in effect for five years or more; in a little less than one-half of all cities and central cities, only uniformed police patrol. It is noteworthy that when asked to report whether a city's schools had police patrols only in high schools, a majority of schools that responded reported police patrolling "lower grades also." Despite its limitations, this survey suggests that there is now a substantial police presence in the schools of the nation's largest urban subdivisions.[20]

The NLC survey also reported on whether a city's schools "regularly use" metal detectors. Here, the size and location/density of a city appear to be positively correlated with use of these devices. While only 19 percent (127) of the seven hundred respondents reported such use, 34 percent of the largest cities and 35 percent of central cities reported it. In contrast, only 17 percent of medium-sized and 16 percent of smaller cities reported regular use of metal detectors, as did only 13 percent of suburban cities and 20 percent of both nonmetro and rural cities.[21]

Clearly, police presence has become a significant element in the school security posture of American cities. It is also clear that a significant minority of cities now use metal detectors in school security. Local needs, reinforced by local customs and traditions, have permitted the emergence of these measures, which, though obviously intended to support the schools' educational efforts, do not spring from conventional educational practice. Some hard-pressed building administrators and teachers may find this fact to be of only philosophical interest, given the harsh realities of today's large urban schools.

Elementary Versus Secondary School Needs

The NLC finding—that substantially more cities include elementary schools with high schools in police patrols, when compared with the number of cities that place police patrols only in high schools—is clear evidence that elementary schools have become major locations for security concerns. This does not necessarily mean that these younger children are susceptible to the full range of criminal and violent behavior manifested by older children. Nevertheless, elementary schools are especially vulnerable to:

- The child who naively brings a weapon or drugs to school.
- The outsider who enters to rob, burglarize, take hostages, or exact revenge.
- Secondary school students who extend turf battles or rivalries to elementary buildings and playgrounds through physical confrontations or drive-by shootings.
- Older and more mature elementary students who may extort and intimidate younger children, or who may act out aggression against them.[22]

As is true of all security efforts, the presence of police or school security personnel and hardware can only reduce the probability that these and similar categories of incidents will occur in the elementary school. As in other settings, a determined, focused person intent on committing a criminal or violent act will often find an elementary school to be a relatively easy place to exercise his or her will in the very short term. The quality of the security response determines whether this person's will prevails.

General Guidelines Versus Highly Specific Structures

A high school principal was once heard to exclaim, "Cut all this school security crap! What I want is for you to loan me a platoon of the 82nd Airborne Division."[23] Among the more sympathetic things that could be said about this remark is that the school administrator needed a flexible, cross-trained, onsite capability that could both deter and respond to all contingencies. This capability would automatically include many of the basic requirements of an effective security program: planning, budgetary approval, training, an intelligence system, proper personnel-to-hardware mix, precise deployability, flexibility, tactical advantage, high visibility, and accountability through a tight chain of command.

Unfortunately, among the key things lacking in this plan *is acceptability.* Perhaps the most important challenge facing school security planning today is to comprehend and support what schools have meant and should mean generically as educational institutions in American society. How school security is defined and implemented at the local district level can have a disproportionate effect—for the better as well as for the worse—on how local schools carry out the missions set out by their public.

Given the diversity of American society, and given the fact that school security activities both reflect and affect local values, it would be simplistic to propose here one or even several "model" program structures. Americans pragmatically improvise and blend experiences to meet perceived needs. What will be offered here are, rather, some suggested general elements that experience indicates are essential to the success of any school security program. These suggested elements will sometimes be given prescriptively, sometimes descriptively. When it is useful, these elements will be followed by questions that security planners and administrators will need to explore as they develop programs suitable to their own districts.

1. The foundation of the school security program will be a *clearly defined and accepted security policy* for the system's schools, including measurable goals, adopted by the top policy authorities (board of education, school commissioners, school committee, and the superintendent). When nonschool agencies such as the local police are part of the school system's security resources, there may be a need for mutually ratified interjurisdictional agreements regarding the roles of the various participants. Will the local political climate allow for such agreements? Will it allow, in fact, for a clearly defined security policy enunciated by the school system that may require open debates before the school board? If the answer to either question is "no," then the school district may not be ready to pass from a stage of problem denial to a stage of implementing effective security practices.

2. School security policies, goals, procedures, and operations should be based on a *comprehensive, continuing incident reporting system* for all schools and personnel, which will generate a data base sufficient to determine not only immediate security needs, but also longer term trends that require proactive measures. This system will avoid the problems created by overaggregation of data; it will target conditions and problems at particular schools.[24] The specific categories and indicators for this system have been suggested in this chapter. The first but not the only challenge provided by such a system will be for the school district to learn how to deal with incident data and data trends that may be emotionally and politically threatening to those who must respond to them. Where the incident and indicator reporting system suggests the need for proactive measures—as, for example, when the interpersonal assault rate indicates mounting interracial gang tensions in a school—will these data be suppressed?

3. At the overall district level, the school security program should be a *clearly defined administrative entity, with stable, separately demarcated line-item budgetary status*; on the school building level, the program must have an *accepted, visible role in support of the ongoing educational process*. If security problems are urgent problems for the district, then everyone involved with the schools will demand results, which can best be measured when there is a visible, accountable administrative entity in charge of achieving specific goals. At the very least, even when the security program cannot influence all the conditions that create school crime and violence—and when it therefore cannot be held accountable for some of the basic social changes needed in and around the school system—it can clearly define problems from a security and safety point of view. Part of this definitional task will be forcing the larger community to confront and determine just what kind of atmosphere it wishes to have in its schools. Does it want, in fact, barbed wire, covert surveillance, and body searches of students? Forcing this self-examination was one vital function performed by security leadership in the Largo High School incident cited in this chapter.

When uniformed and nonuniformed police are a major part of the school security program, there will be a need for accountability to both the police department and the school district. Ultimate accountability implies that resources have an impact. Do given deployments of police appear to achieve desired results?

How is the deterrent role of police to be measured in the school setting? Does a simple drop in incident rates measure it?

At the building level, security measures—personnel and hardware—become part of the total blend of activities supporting educational objectives. The school is the actual location where the attainment of most educational objectives—including those of security—is measured. Attainment of school security objectives at a particular school assumes that the security program there is sufficiently defined and visible to have measurable outcomes.

Development and support of a stable, definable security program at all levels of the school system—regardless of the particular mix of components—is one of the clearest available signals that the school district has accepted a mandate to deal with problems of school crime and violence.

4. The effective school security program will require a *professionally qualified, experienced lead administrator*—titled "director," "chief," or another title consistent with local custom—who has full operational control over the program and who reports to the highest levels of the school administration (superintendent or major department or division head). Security programs, regardless of whether they are school-based, law enforcement-based, military-based, corporate-based, or with any of the other obvious bases require some kind of chain-of-command model under the control of a demonstrably qualified security professional. This is because any security program necessarily touches directly the safety and well-being of individual humans, and it must often deal with matters of utmost sensitivity and confidentiality. Its leader sets the tone for the operation. That leader must have a secure, confidential relationship with the general policy leaders of the organization he or she serves, and they must be able, in turn, to hold him or her fully accountable.

5. *Professional standards*—including but not limited to those derived from educational as well as law enforcement and security practice—should govern recruitment, training, deployment, and operations of all school security personnel. Accepted standards of professionalism are a crucial safeguard not only for the clients of the program—students, educators, parents, and community leaders and activists—but also for security personnel themselves when they must intervene in ugly, confusing, controversial real-life situations that may have no one "correct" outcome. If for no other reason, the role of and need for professional standards in volatile daily encounters place continuing pressures on school security people to see themselves as an emerging profession.

6. The program must have a *locally acceptable mix of operational capabilities* that combine in ways appropriate to the school system's required law enforcement, educational, and additional youth counseling needs. Local policy and politics as well as custom, will influence the relative emphases given to the major components of this mix. They will not, however, eliminate the need for in some way including each of these major capabilities.

7. The program must have *a central role in directing or controlling short-term crisis management within a school population*, with coordinated phaseout of

these actions, toward line counseling services and normal routines established by the school administration. Security personnel will be central managers of major disruptive incidents, including the aftereffects of a major crime such as a shooting, or a collective disturbance such as fighting triggered by hate propaganda or gang activity. They will need to know how to return the school as quickly as possible to the control of regular educators and counselors. In the case of the school's collective shock at occurrences such as the nonschool death of a student (for example, from a car accident), the role of security will be minimal, and the role of psychologically trained professional counselors maximal. Here the primary role of security will be to keep outsiders, including media, from meddling inside the school.

8. Security program planners must have a *role in developing and applying proactive measures* before security incidents occur. Security personnel will have critical insights to offer as well as roles to play in developing proactive security measures. For example, school security leadership has a clear place in programs to develop student peer-counseling activities that aim to resolve interpersonal conflicts before they become violent altercations. For teachers and others in contact every day with those who come to school, the school security program may provide experience-based workshops on how they can address and defuse potentially dangerous encounters with or among students, parents, and outsiders.

9. Qualified security personnel should be in *control of using and evaluating supporting hardware* adopted by the school district. This hardware will include intrusion detection systems (perhaps the single most expensive as well as the potentially most fallible capital item), metal detectors, closed-circuit television, and installation of special perimeter control fencing. Certain hardware items may be subject to short-term bursts of enthusiasm by their proponents. For example, disruptive behavior on school buses has led some school districts to install on-board surveillance cameras, pointed at riders with red lights to indicate that they are "on." The theory is that these will deter dangerous distractions. Unfortunately, local media sometimes report that because of budgetary constraints, only a few of these cameras are functional—most are dummies.[25] Question: Who will be the first student to test whether the surveillance camera aboard his or her bus is "real"?

10. The school security *budget should provide for in-service training* for its own and other designated personnel. Such training may include not only the use of recent research knowledge on how to intervene proactively in human behavior, and thus may involve nonsecurity personnel as both facilitators and trainees, but also knowledge and techniques that will upgrade traditional professional qualifications of security personnel. This applies a basic axiom of professional practice—that professional skills decay without renewal.

11. The program should *actively involve students wherever possible*, in student-centered as well as school-based security activities. Properly enlisted and involved older students will have many ideas about specific actions they can take to make their schools safer and, in the process, help restore a sense of school community.[26] Some students will want to participate in overall security planning and management. A school security committee formed around a school-based

security officer, and working with the principal or other faculty adviser, is an obvious starting point. Others will want to develop and extend peer-counseling skills to larger security issues—and it is not unthinkable to have these students as members of school crisis management teams.

Even in an era when students may say they do not want to enforce rules on other students, the fact is that there are acceptable roles in which students can provide direct security functions. As always, these depend on local history and custom. Examples in some areas of the United States are patrol and traffic direction at high school athletic events by uniformed Junior ROTC cadets.

Even inside the classroom, school security topics may be of academic interest to some students when developments in school law and student rights can be debated as part of the civics curriculum. Discussion of court decisions can be a vehicle for raising such issues as student responsibilities for the school community and the proper roles of security personnel who have both educational and law enforcement demands placed on them.[27]

If effective school security practice depends on maintaining and enhancing a sense of school community, then the largest constituency of this community—the students—needs active roles in its support.

12. The program must have *certain procedural guarantees and safeguards*:

- The ability to *conduct secure, confidential activities,* including investigations.
- When needed, *direct access* to students and parents.
- The ability to *initiate necessary prosecution* of criminal acts in school, implying a defined law enforcement status for field personnel.
- *Independence* from outside, political command and pressure.
- *Review authority* over outside initiatives, such as "drug-free" or "zero-tolerance" schools, automatic expulsion policies for weapons violations, and the possible structure of alternative schools, with their consequent security requirements.
- *Accepted relationships with key educators*, especially building principals.

CONCLUSION

The scope of these elements judged to be critical to any school security program reflects the two governing assumptions of this chapter: (1) that security problems have become an essentially permanent concern for a significant number of American public schools, and (2) that school-based security programs appear to offer the only effective long-term solutions. In the jargon of the social scientist, criminal and violent behavior is rapidly becoming "institutionalized" in some school systems. The best hope of reversing this process does not lie in throwing piles of money, high-tech hardware, a massive police presence, or a variety of ad hoc quick fixes at the schools. The future appears to lie, instead, in nurturing, guiding, and controlling the emerging school security subprofession within education and law enforcement, so that it can be a key support in maintaining the kinds of schools Americans have wanted.

But this comes at a paradoxical time within American public opinion. Many authorities claim that general levels of crime are declining in American society, yet public anxieties about crime appear to be rising.[28] Part of this anxiety reflects public concern over violent crimes among young people, and it is fueled by the almost obsessive contemporary mass media interest in reporting crime and violence among the young, within as well as outside of school. Certainly, President Clinton's gun-free schools initiative of October 1994 was stimulated by this climate.

Nearly a generation ago, the social critic Martin Mayer made this observation about the causes of what was then perceived as the rising amount of violent conflict in schools:

The American school has been through a "sea change" in its relation to the community. What was once a sanctuary is now a focus of community involvement. And the community comes in across what was once an impermeable barrier.

One of the things that has been happening to us in the schools is a move away from a collegial solidarity in which people take responsibility for each other and into an ethnic solidarity in which they stand together against the rest of the world.[29]

Today many would probably argue that in many school buildings and districts, the sense of community has declined even further, with ethnicity being only one factor in a worsening situation.

In today's society, the ultimate task of an effective school security program must be understood as nothing less than reinforcing or restoring the sense of community that makes a school a relatively *safe* place, because it is a *self-protecting* place based on the positive commitment of its members to each other. In this light, an effective school security program must do far more than try to achieve acceptable reductions, however permanent, in crime rates that are of momentary importance to citizens or the media. It must be seen as part of a long-term community-building effort in the schools—an effort that goes far beyond the often misrepresented crises of the moment.

Without a sense of community, the school is fated to become a static fortress frozen in time, a garrison that looks inward because the enemy is inside, draining resources from the future into fighting battles in a perpetual present. With a sense of community, the school becomes a place where young people can safely both cooperate and compete in using the educational process as the opening to futures they want, for themselves and for each other.

NOTES

1. While this definition is sociological, it emphasizes that the school community is a link in that larger community system that is the fundamental resource assumed by the philosophy underlying Anglo-Saxon police work. The basic philosophical assumption of the U.S. policing system is that the citizens of the community bear a large responsibility for policing themselves and for supporting a relatively small number of police officers, who are their agents. This is how a responsible, self-governing community avoids the overwhelming presence of police and security officers typical of authoritarian political systems.

"A school is, in short, not a unitary repository or target in a narrow, physical sense, but a system of life of its own, where people who live together must assume a primary responsibility for their own safety." (S. D. Vestermark, Jr. and P. D. Blauvelt, *Controlling Crime in the School: A Complete Security Handbook for Administrators*, West Nyack, N.Y.: Parker Publishing Co., a subsidiary of Prentice-Hall, 1978), 60, see also 49–58.

2. A. Etzioni, *The Spirit of Community: The Reinvention of American Society* (New York: Simon and Schuster, 1993), 104.

3. Vestermark and Blauvelt, *Controlling Crime in the School*, 73– 90.

4. Ibid.

5. Such police activities are often known as "Officer Friendly" programs and have a long tradition in American police-community relations. Among many articles that accompanied a resurgence of interest in this issue two decades ago, see J. E. Surratt and W. C. Katzenmayer, "Police Services for Public Schools: What School Superintendents and Police Chiefs Think about This Growing Responsibility," *The Police Chief,* No. 6 (June 1975): 59–60. For an early study of the positive effects of putting police in counseling relationships with students in school, see D. H. Bouma, *Kids and Cops: A Study in Mutual Hostility* (Grand Rapids, Mich.: William B. Eerdmans Co., 1969). See also D. H. Bouma, D. G. Williams, and D. J. Dingman, *An Evaluation of a Police-School Liaison Program as a Factor in Changing Student Attitudes Toward Police and Law Enforcement* (East Lansing: Michigan Department of State Police, 1970).

6. See, for example, Vestermark and Blauvelt, *Controlling Crime in the School,* 73–90, 239–83.

7. NASSLEO's current logo is a silhouette of a classic teacher's apple within which is superimposed a five-pointed marshal's or sheriff's star badge. NASSLEO's journal, *The Quarterly*, carries this motto on its masthead: "Dedicated to ensuring safe learning environments where rules are fairly enforced for all." The address for inquiries about the journal and association is:

NASSLEO
8803 Prudence Drive, Suite 500
Annandale, Va. 22003

8. As reported by R. Abramowitz and V. Jennings, "P. G. Teacher Is Shot: Officer's Son Charged," *Washington Post (*April 9, 1994), A1, 10–11.

9. See S. Twomey, "The Right Man in the Right Place for These Wrong Times," *Washington Post* (April 14, 1994), B1, 4, which profiles the teacher, Barrington Miles.

10. These five questions are a matter of judgment, based on the author's experience in a number of school districts. But see Vestermark and Blauvelt, *Controlling Crime in the School*, 93.

11. On the definition of "incident" and "indicator" in school security planning, see Vestermark and Blauvelt, *Controlling Crime in the School,* 34–43.

12. National League of Cities, "School Violence in America's Cities: NLC Survey Overview" (Washington, D.C.: NLC, 1994).

13. Where there has been no effective incident reporting system, establishing even a relatively comprehensive system must inevitably lead to an artifactual "increase" in incidents. This can sometimes be highly threatening in the short term to school and community leaders. See, for example, Vestermark and Blauvelt, *Controlling Crime in the School*, 33–35.

14. Vestermark and Blauvelt, *Controlling Crime in the School*, 33–34 (some emphasis

added).

15. This is certainly one reason why it will be difficult to dismantle such new, seemingly permanent security measures as those in place today at airports for passenger and cargo screening.

16. On possible problems with hourly contract personnel, see Vestermark and Blauvelt, *Controlling Crime in the School*, 67–71.

17. The term *reference group* as used here derives ultimately from modern sociological research, as formulated by R. K. Morton and A. S. Kitt, "Reference Group Theory and Social Mobility," in *Class, Status and Power: A Reader in Social Stratification*, eds. R. Bendix and S. M. Lipset (Glencoe, Ill.: Free Press, 1953), 403–10.

18. This was the designation used in the formative phases of the school security program in the Prince Georges County, Maryland system, to which the author was a consultant.

19. A topic for research on the behavioral dynamics that create school security problems: Does violence on the school athletic field or court, or as reported about senior athletes in the media, help legitimize violence at and around school athletic contests? Fighting and shooting became so common at certain high schools in a prosperous suburban district (Fairfax County, Virginia) that the superintendent considered canceling nighttime sporting events. (R. O'Harrow, "School Chief May Cancel Night Events," *Washington Post* [September 27, 1994], B1.)

20. NLC, "School Violence in America's Cities." Although "cities" are the units reported in this survey, the questionnaires were completed by individual officials such as mayors, city managers, and—overwhelmingly (75 percent)—police chiefs or other public safety officials. Does this survey therefore overreport police presence in schools, as compared with a more diverse sample of officials or cities? Since only 700 of the 1,850 cities queried responded, were police officials predisposed to respond when a city responded at all, and thus to give their data a disproportionate emphasis in the final tallies, as compared to what other officials might have reported?

The findings of the NLC survey suggest a marked increase over the past twenty-five years in the police presence in schools, when compared with a 1970 study by the International City Management Association. In this study, which went only to police departments, 1,409—or 68 percent—of the 2,072 surveyed city departments responded in whole or in part. Of the 1,409, only 94—or 7 percent—reported "stationing police coverage of all or selected city schools" (J. Gansel and D. Harmon, *Police and the Schools* [Washington, D.C.: International City Management Association, Urban Data Service II, 1970], 23).

21. NLC, "School Violence in America's Cities."

22. An effective sense of community in the elementary school can counter at least some of these threats. See Vestermark and Blauvelt, *Controlling Crime in the School*.

23. Personal communication from a principal of a large high school.

24. Many of the best-known—and most sensational—surveys of school crime and violence produce highly aggregative data, which are of limited use in precise planning to meet the security needs of specific schools and districts. For example, when Gallup, Lou Harris, and the CDC survey "nationwide samples" of "students" or "teenagers" and issue such findings as "X percent of the nationwide student sample said guns were easily available in school," they have charted a broad trend in response to a highly generalized question, among a broadly defined respondent category—a "nationwide student sample." While useful in tracking the general development of a major category of concern about school crime and violence, by their nature these data do little to inform planners about what is happening in those specific schools where there may be specific security needs. For this, the school system must have, at a minimum, *reactively generated reports* of actual inci-

dents of crime and violence as they occur at these schools. Ideally, a complete incident monitoring system would also include *proactive surveys* of student perceptions of problems at these schools, as well as data on the school climate, such as reports of attendance rates, suspension rates, and tensions apparently resulting from changes in the school's demographics (which may be socioeconomic as well as ethno-cultural).

25. K. Plum, "Smile, They're Watching You: More School Buses Carrying Camera Boxes," *Dominion Post* (Morgantown, W. Va.) (August 9, 1994), 1A–2A.

26. Vestermark and Blauvelt, *Controlling Crime in the School*, 287–315.

27. Ibid., 317–44.

28. See C. Krauss, "Urban Crime Rates Falling This Year," *New York Times* (November 8, 1994), A14; R. Dvorchak, "Crime Control Joins Learning as a Priority of Schools," *Associated Press* article as reprinted in *Montgomery Journal* (Montgomery County, Md.) (September 12, 1994): A10; and M. Kokianaris, "Area Schools Get Set to Open Amid Big Increase in Security." *Washington Times* (August 28, 1994), A1, A12.

29. M. Mayer, Remarks at the National Seminar on School Security sponsored by the Institute for the Development of Educational Activities, Inc., Belmont House, Maryland, April 30, 1974.

8

Legal and Policy Issues of School Violence

Ivan B. Gluckman

Although school violence has become a growing concern to school administrators, boards, and the public at large in recent years, most legal aspects of the problem have not changed very much. After all, violent acts of any kind are clearly violations of both criminal and civil law as well as of school rules, and carry penalties under each of these parts of our legal system. While murder and rape have occurred on school grounds, the common acts of violence are generally categorized as assault or battery.

Laypeople and, sometimes, even law enforcement personnel often use these two terms interchangeably, but they have somewhat different characteristics. Battery is the actual physical injury of one person by another with an intent to cause harm. Assault requires no physical contact but is, rather, the threat of causing such harm, the placing of a person in fear of physical injury. Thus, to punch a person in the nose is a battery, but even to throw the punch and miss is an assault, and the threat to do so may also be an assault if it is made in a serious manner. All this being said, what are the remedies provided by law for such actions at school?

LEGAL REMEDIES FOR SCHOOL VIOLENCE

Obviously, the intentional physical injury of one person by another is usually a crime and will be prosecuted by law enforcement authorities in all jurisdictions of the United States if the injury resulting is a serious one.[1] In the case of injury of one student by another at the elementary and even secondary school level, however, the perpetrator as well as the victim is usually a minor and can be prosecuted only in a juvenile court. The purpose of juvenile courts is to correct and rehabilitate the young offender and, hopefully, to avoid his or her becoming an adult criminal. For this reason, juveniles committing assault and battery of a less aggravated sort, and who do not have a previous record of such acts, will usually be treated with lenience by juvenile courts, often being placed on supervised probation without any other penalty. In many cases, law enforcement personnel, busy with crimes they consider more serious, will not even seek to press charges against the juvenile offender.

Victims of juvenile assault and battery—at school or otherwise—are not without any remedy, of course. Criminal prosecutions are, after all, acts of the state against citizens who offend public order. They are not intended to directly avail the victim of a harmful act and are, indeed, not under the control of that victim. The person injured by another may pursue a civil remedy, however, generally through a suit for damages. And the same act that may be prosecuted as the crime of assault or battery gives rise to civil suit for torts of the same name. Why, then, do we not hear of such suits against students very often?

The problem here is not one of the legal availability of a remedy, but rather the impracticality of pursuing it. Most minors are what lawyers term "judgment proof"—that is to say without meaningful assets against which a court can levy judgment. While the victim may, therefore, get a civil judgment against a minor who intentionally injures him or her, he or she is unlikely to be able to collect any damages. That being the case, most victims will not want to invest the time, effort, and expense of pursuing this remedy in the first place. What, then, can the student or, for that matter, the teacher, who is attacked by a student do about it?

Physical violence by a student at school will generally be a violation of a school's disciplinary code and subject the offender to school discipline.[2] In most cases, this means suspension from school or, in serious cases involving repeat offenders, even expulsion. The specific punishment depends on state statutes and the provisions of the school code. Hopefully, the student offender—or his or her parents—will regard school disciplinary action as a serious enough penalty to deter further violence by the student and, indeed, even other members of the student body who might otherwise be tempted by violence as a means of resolving their disputes.

Unfortunately, the incidence of student violence has continued to increase. As a result, administrators have sought other remedies that might have greater effect. In some cases where the level of violence has become very high, greater cooperation has been secured from police and juvenile court authorities in removing offenders entirely from the school and the community. In other cases, however, because of disagreement by such authorities as to the seriousness of school problems, or merely because of a lack of appropriate facilities in which to place juvenile offenders, cooperation has not been forthcoming, and the young offender has merely been returned to the school.

Because of the ineffectiveness of criminal, civil, and school disciplinary penalties, some school boards and administrators have sought to find or develop other legal remedies for student violence or other misconduct such as vandalism of school property. One of the remedies tried has been the enactment of parental liability laws that subject the parents of student offenders to financial penalties either in the form of criminal fines or the obligation to pay restitution to injured parties. Most laws of this kind place relatively low limits on the amount of liability to which the parent may be subjected. This is the result of both practical and legal concerns. In many cases, after all, the parent of a violent or otherwise harmful student is "judgment proof," or unable to pay very much by way of compensation to an injured person or school district. At the same time, the parent, particularly of an older juvenile, may reasonably plead that he or she is unable to control the behavior of the child and should, therefore, not be held financially responsible for intentional harm caused by that child. Indeed, it is a longstanding and well-respected principle of Anglo-American law that one person should not be responsible for the intentional harm committed by another.[3]

Partly because of the problems inherent in discouraging violence or even other misconduct by students through criminal and civil legal remedies, and even by school disciplinary actions, and because of the general belief that the best remedy is the prevention of violence before it occurs, most recent attention has been concentrated on just this—prevention. Some of these approaches have raised legal questions too, however, and we turn to these now.

PREVENTION OF SCHOOL VIOLENCE

One of the greatest concerns of school administrators in connection with violence is the presence of weapons and, in particular, firearms in the school. One aspect of this problem, which makes it difficult to control, is the fact that the student who brings a handgun to school is as likely—perhaps even more likely—to be a "good" kid as a "bad" one. These students bring the weapon to school for protection against bigger or older students who abuse them without the use of weapons. The victim then sees the weapon, particularly a handgun, as an "equalizer." Often they have no intention of using it, but in order to have the desired effect, it usually must be loaded and may very well wind up injuring someone—as often the victim who brings it to school or some other innocent student as the bully whom it was intended to deter.

Almost all schools have rules prohibiting the bringing of weapons into the school, and students caught violating such a rule are at risk of serious punishment, including possible expulsion.[4] The problem, of course, is in detecting the presence of the weapon which is usually not carried on the student's person, but is instead kept in a locker or some other hiding place.

To meet this problem, many schools have adopted rules purporting to permit broadscale searches of student lockers, book bags, and, sometimes, even a student's person. Student searches have been given greater support by the courts in recent years, especially since the U.S. Supreme Court sustained such a search by an administrator on the basis of what the court found to be "reasonable suspicion" that a school rule was being broken, rather than the more stringent test of "probable cause" applicable to law enforcement officers.[5] Probable cause means that the officer must obtain a search warrant or meet the specifications of one of the exceptions to that requirement, such as a belief that the suspect is a "fleeing felon" or that the suspected evidence is about to be destroyed.

Even under the more permissive test for constitutional searches, the courts have not been as supportive, for the most part, of mass or random searches as they have been of individual searches. In such situations, even reasonable suspicion of a particular student or students may fail to justify the extensive interference with the rights of a large number of students. Some schools have sought to avoid this problem as it affects student lockers by indicating in their school policies that lockers are regarded as the property of the school rather than the student, and that lockers are consequently subject to search at any time in order to ensure that they are being used only for the intended purpose of storing student books, school supplies, and outdoor garments. Under these circumstances, the argument is made, students can limit the school's intrusion into their privacy by merely not keeping personal or intimate objects in their lockers.[6] Many courts have failed to go along with this theory, however, and have found students, like adult citizens who rent storage lockers, to have a reasonable expectation of privacy in their school lockers regardless of who actually "owns" them.[7]

Even under this approach, however, where the object of a search has been a weapon, and specifically a handgun, recent decisions indicate that the courts will bend over backward to help school officials deal with this problem. In a recent Wisconsin case, for example, in which a Milwaukee high school had been experiencing repeated problems with guns brought into the school and had experienced an incident involving shots fired on school premises following a basketball game and dance at the school, the state court sustained a random search of student lockers aimed at finding and confiscating handguns. Again the court relied heavily on the fact that the school had adopted and promulgated a policy clearly warning students that they should have no expectation of privacy in their lockers and that they were subject to search by school administrators at any time.[8]

Another technique being applied recently by many schools in search of weapons is the use of magnetometers or metal detectors. These instruments, which detect metal by its mass, are generally used for random checks of students entering school for interscholastic athletic contests, or at other times where the risk of weapons being brought in is thought to be high. In some cases, where schools have installed airport-style magnetometer doorways, all students are required to submit to the use of the machines in order to gain entry. Clearly, this procedure is being imposed without any kind of individualized suspicion. To date, however, there have been few legal challenges to the use of these machines. The American Civil Liberties Union did represent a female student in a suit against the Detroit Board of Education back in 1985, and a state court held that the school district's use of permanent metal detectors for random checks for weapons did not meet the then new reasonable suspicion test of *New Jersey v. T.L.O.*[9] Since that time there has only been one reported decision involving a school district's use of magnetometers, and the court not only upheld the school district of the city of New York, but also "applauded" it for using the machines when faced with a documented weapons problem.[10]

The attorney general of California has also produced an advisory opinion indicating that the use of metal detectors in public schools "does not violate the Fourth Amendment or the California state constitution as a *matter of law*, and therefore *may* represent a viable tool for school officials to deter weapons from being brought on school grounds."[11] The attorney general went on to say that he found the use of metal detectors in schools satisfies the standard established by the Supreme Court in *T.L.O.*, and alternatively meets the standard for administrative searches established in cases involving the use of metal detectors in airports and courthouses. Nevertheless, the attorney general set forth some recommended procedures for the use of metal detectors, including (1) a finding of necessity by administrators in specific schools in which they are to be used, and (2) adoption of an administrative plan for the use of the machines that includes, where possible, application to all individuals. If the method used is applied instead on a random basis, there should be assurance that the application is truly random and not based on some criterion that a person might reasonably believe to be discriminatory. Finally, the attorney general recommended adoption of adequate safeguards to minimize the intrusion upon personal privacy, such as advance notice of intent to use the metal detectors, and followup of a positive activation by a permanent "gate" by use of a hand-held wand and the like.

Although there has been no court test of the theory, some observers would argue that the use of magnetometers, in itself, does not even constitute a search in Fourth Amendment terms, but rather should be regarded only as the use of scientific technology to discover whether there is a basis to conduct a search.[12]

One concern administrators have in regard to the conduct of searches of any kind has been the threat of litigation for violation of a student's constitutional rights. From even the very cursory review of some of the cases above, one can see that this threat is not completely unrealistic. School administrators should be equally aware, however, that they can become the targets of litigation in situations in which students are injured by the intentional acts of others. In such situations, what is the administrator's duty to the students?

LIABILITY OF SCHOOLS AND SCHOOL ADMINISTRATORS

One of the most common types of suit brought by students against school districts and their administrators these days alleges violation of constitutional rights as protected by the Civil Rights Act of 1871 (Section 1983 of Title 42 U.S. Code). This act, originally passed by Congress to protect the rights of freed slaves, has been more recently interpreted to protect all citizens against any act by a public agency or its employees that interferes with civil rights protected by the Constitution or by federal laws. The act further provides that such violations are punishable by the award of civil damages, by injunctive order, or by any other remedy within the authority of a federal court.

Predictably, such a broadscale statute has resulted in an enormous growth of civil rights suits brought in federal courts. Public education has not been exempt from it, and in recent years a growing number of student suits has been brought under this statute. But why would injured students seek to bring a federal claim under Section 1983 rather than the usual personal injury suit in a state court, which is usually easier and less expensive? The main reason is that the federal suit permits the plaintiff to recover not only damages, but also all of their attorney fees if they are successful. This is rarely possible in the usual personal injury suit. Another reason for claiming constitutional violations rather than ordinary personal injury is that, in many states, the legislature has provided school districts and their employees with immunity against negligent actions arising out of the performance of their duties. Such immunity cannot be provided by state legislatures against alleged violations of the U.S. Constitution.

The big legal question involved in such suits is: What constitutional right is involved? In cases involving student searches, this is easy: the Fourth Amendment. In student discipline cases involving even short suspensions, the Supreme Court has recognized a right to due process under the Fifth and Fourteenth Amendments. But it is far less clear what constitutional right is involved in incidents where a student is physically injured at school. For the most part, the courts have extended an old doctrine called "substantive due process," loosely based on the due process clause of the Fourteenth Amendment. The problem is that no one can really define "substantive due process" with any specificity. What is clear is that it is not intended to protect against ordinary negligence. Rather, it is meant to be a remedy for governmental conduct that is clearly objectionable.[13]

Most recently, the U.S. Supreme Court has indicated that the concept is to be applied in a limited manner—for example, refusing to find liability by a child welfare agency where one of its employees released a child to a noncustodial parent, even though it had reason to know that the parent had previously beaten the child, and subsequent to the release the parent administered a beating to the child that resulted in his death.[14] While the Court recognized the unfortunate nature of the situation, it indicated that the due process clause is not intended as a guarantee of any particular level of safety and security for citizens, and cannot be extended to impose an affirmative obligation on the state to ensure the protection of individual interests. Only in cases where the Court finds that the state has assumed a special duty to protect citizens will such an obligation be imposed. For the most part, such "special relationships" have only been found to exist where the relationship between the state agency and the state is a custodial one, as in the case of prisoners or mental patients in a state hospital.

In recent years, attorneys have attempted to apply this concept in the public school context by arguing that students are in a relationship with their schools that should be regarded as "special," so as to confer the protection of substantive due process whether or not that relationship is actually custodial. Most of the federal courts that have reviewed the question have refused to find such a special relationship to exist, reasoning that public school students typically live with a parent or guardian to whom they have access each day, and to whom they can complain if they are being victimized by someone at school.[15] Although a few courts have been willing to recognize some sort of relationship as being sufficiently "special" as to confer constitutional protection, this has been limited to incidents in which the individual injuring the student has been a teacher or other employee of the school district, and the conduct involved was either the result of a school district-approved policy, or such misfeasance as to meet the standard of "deliberate indifference."[16] Even then, for some reason, most of the cases in which liability has been attached to the district have involved sexual offenses and not ordinary physical injury.

In any event, no federal court has yet imposed legal liability on a school district on the basis of "substantive due process" in cases in which a student has been injured by either another student or by a third party not employed by the school district. These are, of course, the primary source of injury in incidents of violence at school.

STATUTORY IMPOSITIONS OF HIGHER LEVELS OF RESPONSIBILITY

As indicated previously, even in the absence of immunity statutes, individuals and school districts are not normally held legally responsible for the negligence of other individuals. To succeed in a negligence action, a plaintiff must show that his or her injury was proximately caused by the action or omission of the defendant himself or herself (or itself) that owed some kind of duty to that plaintiff.

In the case of school districts and administrators, the claim has been based on an argument that the district or administrator failed in his or her (or its) duty to supervise or train the employee adequately in order to have prevented the injury. This theory has not usually been successful in cases where the plaintiff has been the victim of intentional harm, because despite any reasonable effort by the district and its employees, it could not have prevented an employee from intentionally harming a student. In only a few cases in which the plaintiff could clearly show that defendants knew or should have known of the dangerous or harmful behavior of the person actually injuring a student have courts been willing to attach liability to the school defendants.

Public concern about the danger presented by school employees who might harm students either by physical assault or sexual molestation has led to a recent spate of state legislation that seeks to codify the terms on which school districts will be liable even for hiring persons who commit such acts. The basis for liability is usually the negligence standard of knowing or failing to find out about an employee's dangerous propensities, and that this negligence was the proximate cause of the injury. The idea is to place a legal duty on the employer to know whether an employee is unfit for a particular job. Such statutes place new and heavy burdens on school districts, some ramifications of which are still unclear.[17] If a person had been convicted of rape, for example, would that preclude his hiring to do maintenance work for a school district? Probably not, as long as it would not be part of his job to interact with students. And how thoroughly is the employer required to check out a job applicant's prior background? Again, this will vary with the specific responsibilities of the position involved.[18]

California went beyond other states by adding an amendment to its constitution that would provide each student with the right to attend a school in a safe and secure environment. In a subsequent effort by plaintiffs to interpret this provision as the imposition of strict liability on school districts for any and all injuries students sustained at school, the Supreme Court of California demurred on the grounds that such a far-reaching change in the law could not be imposed by the courts and would have to await specific statutory enactment by the state legislature. To date, this has not occurred.

CONCLUSION

Without question, the public's growing concern about violence in the schools has, and will continue to have, legal ramifications for school districts and their administrators. But the major focus of efforts to combat school violence is, and should be, on administrative rather than legal approaches to the problem. As in the case of metal detectors and even of drug testing, the courts will lend their support to any reasonable effort made by school administrators to prevent and reduce violence in their buildings, even if it causes minimal interference with student privacy or other constitutionally protected rights.

At the same time, school officials must be aware of the counterbalancing obligations increasingly being placed on them by a frightened public to be responsible for student injury, physical or emotional,[19] especially if the person causing that injury is a school employee. The wise school official will therefore make all reasonable efforts to improve screening, hiring, and supervision of employees, especially those whose duties bring them into contact with students, and to prevent employees with past records of dangerous or harmful conduct from being placed in positions in which such incidents might reoccur.

NOTES

1. There are some exceptions to the general rule that the intentional physical injury of one person by another is a crime, and some exceptions have specific applicability to schools. Corporal punishment, for example, where not prohibited by statute, is a situation in which adults are permitted to strike children. Even in this case, however, the exception is generally proscribed very carefully to allow only certain kinds of physical force to be used and under very specific conditions, all of which fall short of causing any permanent injury to the child. Even the parental right to physically discipline a child has been sharply reduced by statutes and court decisions defining child abuse. A third exception that sometimes applies in the school context is self-defense, which permits even a teacher or other adult to exercise physical force to prevent being injured by a violent person—even if it is a minor student. Here too, however, the law proscribes any amount of force that exceeds that reasonably necessary to defend oneself.

2. One exception to this general rule is the special protection afforded children classified as having disabilities under the Individuals with Disabilities Education Act (IDEA). While the act appears to permit disciplinary action to be taken against such students where the act giving rise to the disciplinary action is unrelated to the child's disability, the U.S. Department of Education has taken a contrary position. In any event, where the disability is

an emotional or a mental one, it is very difficult for school authorities to prove that the disability is unrelated to the conduct being punished; where the student's conduct is related to the disability, disciplinary action is limited to ten days' emergency suspension until the student's placement is reviewed under the process set out in the statute, or unless a court order can be secured.

3. Where one person injures another unintentionally, one person may be held financially liable to the victim under civil law. However, this is usually true only where the negligent party is acting as the agent of another person or entity known as the principal. An individual may also be liable for his or her own failure to provide training or supervision adequate to have prevented the injury from occurring. This doctrine is often applied to educational administrators as well as to parents.

4. The U.S. Congress has recently enacted the Goals 2000 Act which conditions the receipt of educational program funds provided by the act on adoption by the applicant of a school rule requiring expulsion of any student found in possession of a firearm on school property.

5. *New Jersey v. T.L.O.*, 469 U.S. 325 (1985).

6. *Commonwealth v. Carey*, 554 N.E.2d 1199 (Mass. 1990).

7. *In Interest of Dumas*, 515 A.2d 984 (Pa. Super. Ct. 1986).

8. *Isiah B. v. State of Wisconsin*, 500 N.W.2d 637 (Wis. 1993).

9. "Detroit to Use Metal Detectors," *Education Week* (December 11, 1985).

10. *People v. Dukes*, 580 N.Y.S.2d 850 (N.Y. City Crim. Ct. 1992).

11. Synopsis of Attorney General's Opinion Concerning Metal Detectors in Schools, State of California Department of Justice, October 6, 1992.

12. The argument that the use of a machine to aid in investigation of possible violations of law is not a search has been used successfully in other kinds of cases. It is clear, for example, that the use of a flashlight by a police officer to look into an automobile at night is not a search but merely the use of technology to aid a law enforcement officer in deciding whether to conduct a search. This argument has also been used successfully in at least one federal case involving the use of dogs trained to sniff out the presence of drugs. *Doe v. Renfrow*, 479 F. Supp. 1012 (N.D. Ind. 1979), aff'd 631 F.2d 91 (7th Cir. 1980).

13. See *Daniels v. Williams*, 474 U.S. 327 (1986) and *Davidson v. Cannon*, 474 U.S. 336 (1986).

14. *DeShaney v. Winnebago County Department of Social Services*, 489 U.S. 189 (1989).

15. *J. O. v. Alton Community Unit School District 11*, 909 F.2d 267 (7th Cir. 1990); *D. R. v. Middle Bucks Area Vocational School*, 972 F.2d 1364 (3rd Cir. 1992) cert. denied, 113 S. Ct. 1045 (1993).

16. *Stoneking v. Bradford Area School District*, 882 F.2d 720 (3rd Cir. 1989), cert. denied 493 U.S. 1044 (1990); *Doe v. Taylor Ind. School District*, 15 F.3d 443 (5th Cir. 1994) (en banc) vacating 975 F.2d 137 (5th Cir. 1992).

17. Currently, twenty-four states have statutes making negligent hiring a tort for which employers can be held liable in money damages.

18. For a good discussion of this subject and a summary of court decisions, see "The Tort of Negligent Hiring," *School Safety*, National School Safety Center, Westlake Village, Calif. (Spring 1994).

19. Most courts are holding that sexual misconduct by adults with minor students— even though it may occur with student consent, over a long period of time, and without complaint by the student throughout that time—to be incidents of intentional harm by the

perpetrator. Such acts will not, therefore, be coverable by the perpetrator's professional liability insurance, but his or her employer may still be held liable for negligence in placing the perpetrator in the position where the harm could occur.

Part IV

TOWARD A LESS VIOLENT SCHOOL ENVIRONMENT

9

Safe Schools for All

Gwendolyn J. Cooke

When Killers Come to Class; Teen Violence, Wild in the Streets; and *Violence in the Schools: Staying Alive While Learning Reading, Writing and Arithmetic* are titles appearing on the covers of recent editions of *U.S. News and World Report* (December 8, 1993), *Newsweek* (August 2, 1993), and *Crisis* (April/May 1993). Each is testimony to the public's concern about the rising tide of violence among adolescents. Few Americans are without an opinion about the root cause of this unique challenge of the 1990s. Both "the White House [and] the Centers for Disease Control...now regard guns in America as less an issue of individual rights than a matter of national health."[1]

WHAT ARE TEACHERS SAYING?

Since 1984, MetLife has commissioned Lou Harris and Associates each year to ask teachers their opinions on a wide range of issues in order to fill a void by including teachers' voices in the debate on education reform. In 1993 MetLife asked the Harris organization to take a look at violence in American public schools, violence against teachers, and violence against students. Highlights of the survey's findings include:

- Twenty-two percent of students (6.8 million) and 11 percent of teachers (273,000) have been victims of violence in and around schools.

- Boys are twice as likely as girls to have been victims of violence (30 percent versus 16 percent).

- Seventy-four percent of teachers believe students react to violence by watching, not doing anything, or encouraging it. Sixty-three percent of students believe that students react in these ways.

- Twenty-two percent of boys have carried weapons to school, while only 4 percent of girls claim to have done so.

- The major reason students believe weapons are carried is in order to impress friends/to be accepted (66 percent), for self-esteem/to feel important (56 percent), and for self-defense on the way to and from school (49 percent).[2]

THE ROLE OF GOVERNMENT

At the national level, the debate about crime is traditionally a phony one. The positions of conservatives and liberals are predictable. Conservatives demand "get tough" measures such as more prison cells, lengthy mandatory sentences, and the death penalty. Liberals call for prevention through programs that treat poverty, drug addiction, and other social causes of lawlessness. The reality is that most crime, like politics, is local. There are signs that a new and more honest politics of crime is emerging, however.

Democrats are talking more openly about crime and its links to illegitimacy and welfare dependency; in 1994 six Republicans joined Democrats and voted for the crime bill, which banned nineteen types of assault weapons. The crime bill also provides funds for one hundred thousand new police officers on city streets over the next five years. The most dramatic symbol of change was the passage in 1994 of the Brady Bill after a bruising seven-year fight with the National Rifle Association (NRA). The measure established a five-day waiting period on handgun purchases so that buyers can be screened for criminal records or mental instability.

The first issue on many policymakers' agendas for school safety is antigun measures, but none so far have cut the mayhem. Congress passed the Gun-Free School Zones Act in 1990, barring the possession of guns in or near a school. One court has declared it unconstitutional. Separately, eighteen states have enacted laws prohibiting gun possession by juveniles.[3]

Education Secretary Richard Riley has sent Congress two bills that would help educators in their crusade. The Safe Schools Act, which cleared its first congressional hurdle in November 1993, would provide $175 million to school systems trying to beef up security. The second bill would launch long-term funding beginning in 1995. The bills earmark much of their funding for violence prevention curricula and training in peer mediation and conflict resolution. Ten percent of the funding could be used to purchase metal detectors and hire security guards.[4]

Another effort of the Clinton administration is a special task force bringing together some 150 people from five departments—Education, Labor, Justice, Housing and Urban Development (HUD), and Health and Human Services (HHS)—to address violence. The task force has identified five cities that will be allowed to design a master plan to combat violence using federal funding. The task force also has adopted a broad definition of violence that includes domestic, child abuse, street crime, media, and firearms. The belief is that if a frontal attack is leveled on each type of violence, benefits will accrue more quickly and be long-lasting.

The Clinton administration also has adopted the policy of discontinuing the sale of confiscated and governmental weapons to gun dealers. Instead, the guns are to be burned and sold as scrap metal.[5]

The Colorado legislature, meeting in a five-day special session in September 1993, established a *separate* penal system for juvenile weapons offenders and ordered that some juvenile records be made public. Also in 1993 California required that the records of violent students transferring from one school to another under a second-chance program be shared with their new teachers after one such student nearly killed his eighth-grade history teacher.[6]

In 1993 at least eight states had legislation proposed to address citizens' possession of handguns. In Virginia legislators enacted an anti-gunrunning measure that limits handgun purchases to one a month. In Connecticut certain military-style assault weapons were banned. Connecticut also became the fourth state to enact a ban on semiautomatic assault weapons, joining California, New Jersey, and Hawaii. The New York State Assembly approved a bill that would ban assault weapons, although opposition in the state senate severely modified it.

Other states where legislators have taken a stand against the powerful National Rifle Association lobby included New Jersey, Minnesota, Indiana, Missouri, and Texas. Former Texas Governor Ann Richards vetoed NRA-backed legislation that would have allowed people to carry loaded concealed weapons in public.

THE ROLE OF PROFESSIONAL AND COMMUNITY ASSOCIATIONS

Professional associations have taken a strong stand that the causes of violence are multiple and that government, the private sector, and citizens as individuals must act aggressively to curtail it. Similarly, school and community leaders across America are not idly wringing their hands, but are focusing diligently on the violence issue and exploring creative solutions.

In November 1993 the National Association of Children's Hospitals and Related Institutions released a report stating that the average cost of treating a child struck by gunfire was more than $14,000—the approximate cost of a full year at a private college. The association called for funding for education programs to curtail the violence. "We'd rather see that money ($14,434) spent on educating these kids than treating them for gunshot wounds," stated Lawrence A. McAndrews, president of the association.[7] To make a difference, the group is now asking its 132 member hospitals and pediatric units to track firearms injuries and deaths in order to heighten public awareness of the problem.

The American Psychological Association released a report, "Violence and Youth: Psychology's Response," focusing on how violence affects children. The statistics were sobering. Among the "violence toxins" putting children at risk, as noted by the association, were: child abuse, bad parenting, witnessing violence, socioeconomic inequality, racism, substance abuse, and access to guns. The association concluded that "aggression is primarily a learned behavior, and since it is learned, it can be unlearned or conditions can be set up so that is not learned in the first place." The association also proposed five strategies for school districts and state education agencies:

1. Shut down opportunities at school for bullying, fights, and other violence by strengthening students' academic and social skills and teaching conflict resolution.

2. Take a long view of violence prevention, starting with early childhood programs.

3. Ban corporal punishment in school, encourage behavior management, and teach parents alternative discipline methods.

4. Offer after-school programs and recreation at schools with high proportions of students at risk of gang initiation

5. Require all staffers to take violence-reduction training.[8]

In January 1993 the National School Boards Association reported that violence in our nation's schools extends to all communities—urban, suburban, and rural. Based on survey results from some seven hundred districts nationwide, alcohol and drug abuse, easy access to guns, poverty, the breakdown of the family, and the portrayal of violence by the media were cited as major causes of violence.[9] The association considers legislative remedies—at federal and local levels—as essential for adequate attention to the problem.

The Citizens Task Force on TV Violence has recommended a ban on violent network and cable TV shows for sixteen hours a day—from 6:00 A.M. to 10:00 P.M.—in order to protect children. The task force consists of these groups, among others: the National Association of Elementary School Principals (NAESP), National Association of Secondary School Principals (NASSP), American Medical Association, American Academy of Child and Adolescent Psychiatry, American Psychiatric Association, National PTA, National Council of Churches, and Americans for Responsive Television. In November 1993 Attorney General Janet Reno received the task force's recommendations, which follow:

1. Adoption of a tough, voluntary entertainment violence code by the media, public interest groups, and government.

2. An agreement, as part of the code, not to program gratuitous violence, to exercise severe restraints on violence in children's programming, and to ban violence on television from 6:00 A.M. to 10:00 P.M.

3. Development by the FCC of an antiviolence code if the entertainment industry refuses to cooperate.

4. Access to mechanical and electrical devices to allow parents to block violent programming.

5. Viewer warnings to be aired before and during violent programs.

6. Development of a violence rating system.

7. FCC hearings on TV violence.

8. Strengthened FCC support for children's television, in order to provide alternatives to violent shows.

9. Prohibitions on showing violent programs in prisons.

10. A White House summit on the epidemic of violence in America to include a "specific focus on media violence."[10]

In response, representatives from the cable TV industry agreed in principle in January 1994 to develop a voluntary rating system for their programs and to establish an outside monitor for violent content.[11]

The National Crime Prevention Coalition, with some funding from the Justice Department, has joined with the Advertising Council to sponsor a public service campaign against violence. Two thirty-second spots featuring President Clinton and children ran for eight weeks in 1994, one of which ended with the tag line: "We must give our children back their childhoods. Working together, we can."[12]

The NASSP Board of Directors has adopted two position papers addressing violence: "Weapons in Schools" and "Violence in the Media and Entertainment Industry." The board affirms in the papers that students have a right to attend school without fear of weapons, and that it is opposed to violence and insensitive behavior and dialogue in the entertainment industry. NASSP also developed and disseminated a Student/Parent/Principal Contract for Eliminating Weapons from Schools. (The position statements and contract appear in the appendices.)

Citizens in Kansas City, Missouri, have agreed to use their community as the prototype for the "SQUASH IT" initiative—a new campaign to be woven into prime-time entertainment television programming. The message is that it is "cool" to walk away from a confrontation, that differences can be resolved without violence. The Kansas City Chiefs have promised a prominent player to act as spokesman for the "SQUASH IT" campaign, and local television stations and rap stars will participate, as will the *Kansas City Star*. The AMC Theaters chain, based there, has agreed to show a "SQUASH IT" slide in 1,618 theaters across the country. The program is being jointly backed by the local United Way and the Greater Kansas City Community Foundation. It is being funded by a $375,000 grant from the Joyce Foundation of Chicago and $75,000 from the Max Factor Family Foundation of Los Angeles.[13]

"Can you recognize violence?" is the question posed by the Turn Off the Violence Project in Minneapolis, Minnesota. With a grant from the Bureau of Justice Assistance, Office of Justice Programs, and the U.S. Department of Justice, October 14 was declared "Turn Off the Violence Day!" In widely distributed literature, citizens were requested, for just one day and one night, to turn off the violence in all of its ugly forms:

- Physical violence
- Sexual violence
- Verbal violence
- Violence in music
- Family violence
- Gang violence
- Hate crimes
- Playground violence

The project addressed people's concern about censorship as follows:

"Turn Off the Violence" is NOT A CENSORSHIP project. As an organization, we will not compile lists of music, movies, or TV shows we think are violent. Instead, we ask people to make careful, informed, personal choices about entertainment. We encourage people to voice their opinions to media and entertainment producers not only about what they believe is unacceptable, but also about what is good. We believe that if enough people begin expressing their preferences for non-violent media, the market for violent entertainment will shrink and those in the media industry will get the message.

"Turn Off the Violence" is NOT a Cure-All. It's an awareness campaign encouraging public action. Violence in entertainment is one kind of violence we all have the choice to turn off. By educating our young people about how to resolve conflicts without violence we can help provide hope for the future.[14]

THE ROLE OF RELIGIOUS ORGANIZATIONS

On the religious front, umbrella organizations and theological schools are challenging both the conscious and personal and collective behaviors of its members.

In September 1993 the Jewish Theological Seminary of America placed a one-page ad, suitable for framing, in *Newsweek* magazine. Some quotes from the ad are as follows:

Schoolyard murders. Child abuse. Runaways. Children having children. Teenage suicide. If God hears the child in crisis, couldn't we?

The truth is every child's life is shaped not only by its parents but by neighbors, classmates, by the schools, and ultimately by the whole civilization.

And we need to face it: We are guilty, all of us, of neglecting the children.[15]

The National Council of Churches, based in New York with a membership of thirty-two Protestant and Orthodox denominations, met with U.S. Attorney General Reno in December 1993 to discuss violence in the media. In New York, early in December 1993, sixty-five Catholic, Protestant, and Jewish officials met at the capitol in Albany to seek religious responses to violence that they termed "a scandal of monumental proportions."[16] The New York clergy promised to launch a campaign against handguns and semiautomatic weapons, and to work against the death penalty. They also planned to meet with media executives to complain about the violent language, action, plots, and reporting common in movies and TV films, and on news shows. Part of their plan is to encourage boycotts of advertisers.

Similarly, "Stopping the Violence" is the adopted 1994 theme of the Washington-based policy and advocacy group Interfaith Impact for Justice and Peace.

THE ROLE OF PRIVATE CITIZENS

Everyday citizens and businesspersons also have taken individual initiatives to stop the violence. Throughout this country, campaigns to trade in guns for money, tickets, and merchandise are underway. The District of Columbia, New York City, and Baltimore, Maryland have received national attention for their efforts. In 1933, the 34th precinct in New York City, carpet merchant Fernando Mateo bought $100 toy store certificates and offered them in trade for guns. By the end of the year, other business owners had joined the effort, and more than 850 guns had been collected in one New York precinct.[17] "Give Violence the Boot" is the slogan for the gun collection in Washington, D.C. Those who turn in a gun are given a $75 certificate toward the cost of purchasing a pair of Timberland boots, an item popular with young adults.

THE ROLE OF EDUCATORS

Violence has been declared a public health issue. The pressure is on us, as educators, to intervene and make sure our schools are safe and orderly. Indeed, the sixth national education goal outlined by the president and the nation's governors states that: "Every school in America will be free of drugs and violence and will offer a disciplined environment conducive to learning."[18]

This is not an issue of money—we cannot buy new values for our children. We must first model, then teach, and, finally, protect our children so they are not forced to grow up enveloped in the violence created by adult neglect. The front end of prevention is far less than the back end costs of healing. Yet, according to the Center for School Counseling Practitioners, we must acknowledge and question the social myths that perpetuate and reinforce violence if we truly want to make a difference:

Myth 1. *Violence works.* Seeing violence on television, in movies, and at home gives young people the impression that violence is an accepted and effective way to achieve one's goals. This myth may sometimes be reinforced by national militaristic traditions—especially when international conflicts are deemed best handled through violent armed attack that seeks to achieve its goals at the costs of innocent victims.

Myth 2. *Violent acts go unpunished.* Inconsistencies in the juvenile justice system convey the misguided message that young people often get away with violence, because many adults do not find it offensive, do not take it seriously, or cannot control or correct it.

Myth 3. *Relationships are normally sexist and imbalanced.* Exposure to family violence, in which women are generally the victims, reinforces social inequalities and creates the impression that unequal relationships—in which one partner controls and manipulates the other—are the norm.

Myth 4. *Violence relieves stress.* The commonly held notion that violence relieves stress in the short run and is an acceptable way to express tension overlooks the fact that it always has harmful long-term consequences. This myth, like others, works to perpetuate the first myth—that violence works.

Myth 5. *Victims bring trouble on themselves.* This is perhaps the most insidious of myths about violence because it serves to shame the victim into silence and passivity at the same time that it justifies the violent behavior.

Myth 6. *Success is conquest.* Success in our culture is usually predicated on one person's power over another. Although there are ways to reach goals that depend on collaborative effort and sharing rewards, the cooperative process is much less celebrated in our society than the myth of the extraordinary individual who achieves success at the expense of someone else.[19]

The consequences and costs of violence in schools are enormous for students and staff. Confronting these myths annually, in a formalized way, may augment or be integrated into the ten steps recommended by the National School Safety Center for preventing or reducing violence in schools:

Step 1: Create Awareness
—Is there violence in my school? Of what nature is it? Fighting? Bullying? Verbal interchanges between students to students? Students to adults? Adults to students? Parents to staff?

Step 2: Perform an Assessment
—In the past three years, in my school, has a survey been conducted with students, staff, and parents to determine how they perceive the safety of my school?

Step 3: Use a Comprehensive Approach
—Does my school have a comprehensive approach to school violence?
  • Are students and staff involved in discussions on security problems and plans of action?
  • Are the police used as a resource?
  • Are parents and community groups key stakeholders in our antiviolence programs?

Step 4: Encourage Curricular Intervention
      —Is the teaching of positive social skills part of the school's curriculum?

Step 5: Offer Conflict-Resolution Training and Services
      —Are staff trained to defuse violent situations?

Step 6: Harden the Target
      —Is there a plan to control and monitor physical access to my school?
      —Do staff emphasize the importance of self-protection?

Step 7: Establish Disciplinary Standards
      —Are standards of discipline clearly communicated to staff, parents, and students; and enforced fairly and consistently?

Step 8: Address Gang Activity
      —Is there a systematic plan to discourage gang activity?
      —Are parents provided information about signs of gang involvement?
      —Are there alternatives to gangs for students?
      —Do students have caring adults whom they may approach in crisis situations?

Step 9: Prevent Weapon Concealment
      —Do we conduct periodic searches to locate and confiscate weapons and implement other strategies that make it difficult for students to conceal weapons? Are there strict penalties for possession of weapons on school grounds?

Step 10: Institute Alternative Education Programs
      —Do we require students suspended for violent acts or gang activity to attend an alternative educational program that teaches nonviolence outside of the students' usual environment?

Positive answers to these questions can become ten steps for preventing or reducing violence in your school. It is important to remember, however, that our schools are populated by adolescents—adolescents who are entitled to discipline with love and compassionate attention to them as *individuals* who will be dealt with fairly and consistently. Adopted strategies should not become bureaucratic and insensitive because of the public's outcry. As principals try to make schools humane, free of drugs and violence, and conducive to learning, they should reflect on the words of Frederick Douglass:

If there is no struggle, there is no progress. Those who profess to favor freedom, and yet deprecate agitation, are men who want crops without plowing up the ground. They want rain without thunder and lightning. They want the ocean without the awful roar of its many waters. This struggle may be a moral one; or it may be a physical one; or it may be both moral and physical; but it must be a struggle. Power concedes nothing without a demand. It never has and it never will.[20]

CONCLUSION

The list of causes of violence is long, as is the list of remedies/solutions. The responsibility for change rests with every facet of our society. Gun manufacturers, filmmakers, educators, parents, police, health providers, legislators, and the media—none is exempt from the challenge. The totality of our national community must agree to remove guns and lethal weapons from our children's lives, to eradicate violent images in film and video, to educate parents and children in the skills of nonviolence, and to negate the culture of violence that is threatening to overwhelm us.

And it can be done—if the will and commitment to expend the energy to make the sacrifices necessary is present. We know this will not be done without all of us learning to value each human being and understanding that an injury to any member of our community is unacceptable.

NOTES

1. M. Safer, "Arms and the Woman," *60 Minutes* (October 10, 1993).

2. L. Harris and Associates, *Violence in America's Public Schools,* MetLife Survey of the American Teacher, 1993.

3. Center to Prevent Handgun Violence, 1994.

4. C. Gutscher, "Violence in Schools: Death Threat for Reform?," *America's Agenda* (Fall 1993): 10.

5. *60 Minutes* (December 1993).

6. "Colorado's New Gun Law Shows the Way for Others," editorial in *USA Today* (September 16, 1993), 12A.

7. Associated Press, "Cost to Treat a Wounded Child: $14,000," *Washington Post* (November 26, 1993), A15.

8. American Psychological Association Commission on Violence and Youth, "Violence and Youth: Psychology's Response" (Washington, D.C.: American Psychological Association, Public Interest Division, 1993).

9. National School Boards Association, *Violence in Our Schools: How America's School Boards Are Safeguarding Our Children* (Alexandria, Va.: NSBA, 1993).

10. J. Price, "Senator Leads Groups' Cry Against Violence on TV," *Washington Times* (December 16, 1993), A1.

11. "Cable Leaders to Develop Violence Ratings," *Washington Post* (January 11, 1994), B1.

12. "TV, Clinton Team Up Against Violence," *Washington Post* (March 16, 1994), C1.

13. E. Edwards, "Campaign Beats Up on Violence," *Washington Post* (December 8, 1993), C1.

14. National Crime Prevention Council, *Working Together to Stop the Violence* (Washington, D.C.: Presstar, 1994), 13–18.

15. *Newsweek* (September 13, 1993), 55B.

16. Price, "Senator Leads Groups' Cry Against Violence on TV."

17. Edwards, "Campaign Beats Up on Violence."

18. "America 2000, an Overview," a pamphlet put out by America 2000.

19. Center for School Counseling Practitioners, *Coping with Violence in the Schools* (Cambridge, Mass.: Harvard University Graduate School of Education, 1994), 7–8.

20. J.C. Bell, *Famous Black Quotations* (Chicago: SABAYT Publications, 1986), 13.

Appendix A: NATIONAL ASSOCIATION OF SECONDARY SCHOOL PRINCIPALS

STATEMENT OF POSITION

Weapons in Schools

WHEREAS, students have a right to attend school without a fear of weapons' violence to themselves or others;

WHEREAS, safe schools enhance the learning environment, necessary for quality schools, which are essential to a successful democracy;

WHEREAS, the causes for violence are multiple: chronic poverty, the lack of jobs and role models, the disintegration of families, the loss of moral values, and a popular culture that seems to glorify violence at every turn;

WHEREAS, a major 1993 Louis Harris poll about guns among American youth reports that 1 in 25 students have taken a handgun to school in a single month, and 59% know where to get a handgun if they need one;

WHEREAS, violence is exacerbated with the increase of weapons in our schools resulting in some 31 deaths from guns during the 1992–93 school year; be it therefore known that,

The position of the National Association of Secondary School Principals:

- supports passage of the Brady Bill which requires a waiting period and background check before legal purchase of a handgun;
- urges full enforcement of the Gun-Free School Zones Act of 1990;
- calls on Congress to pass the Safe Schools Act of 1993, with an amendment that will ban the purchase of a handgun and semi-automatic guns for any person under the age of 21;
- urged schools to provide staff training for weapons situations arising in school, and to implement student awareness programs which challenge youths' falsely held beliefs that they are invincible;

- challenges schools to implement apprehension, prevention, intervention, and counseling programs to combat possession of weapons and violent acts;

- encourages school-based parent involvement programs to include violence prevention strategies that emphasize the issue of easy access to handguns;

- exhorts school districts to establish violence prevention curriculum, grades K-12, and promote articulation among levels to ensure continuity in policies and practices;

- challenges Schools of Education to add conflict resolution and violence coping skills to their teacher preparation programs.

* Where principals appear in this statement, it refers to assistant principals, vice principals, and deans (where the role is that of administrative support to the principal).

Appendix B: NATIONAL ASSOCIATION OF SECONDARY SCHOOL PRINCIPALS

STATEMENT OF POSITION

Violence in the Media and Entertainment Industry

WHEREAS, in 1979, the National Association of Secondary School Principals urged the broadcasting and motion picture industries to work with educators and parents in moving toward a significant reduction of violent acts in television and film programming;

WHEREAS, the nation is experiencing an unrivaled period of juvenile violent crime perpetrated by youths from all races, social classes, and lifestyles;

WHEREAS, the average American child views 8,000 murders and 100,000 acts of violence on TV before finishing elementary school, and by the age of 18, that same teenager will have witnessed 200,000 acts of violence on TV, including 40,000 murders; and,

WHEREAS, the entertainment industry (movies, records, music videos, radio, and television) plays an important role in fostering anti-social behavior by promoting instant gratification, glorifying casual sex, encouraging the use of profanity, nudity, violence, killing, and racial and sexual stereotyping; be it therefore known that,

The National Association of Secondary School Principals:

- appreciates the efforts of the U.S. Attorney General to focus on the problem of increasing violence in the media;
- stands in opposition to violence and insensitive behavior and dialogue in the entertainment industry;
- commends television broadcasters who have begun self-regulation by labeling each program it deems potentially offensive with the following warning: DUE TO VIOLENT CONTENT, PARENTAL DISCRETION IS ADVISED; and producers of music videos and records who use similar labeling systems;
- encourages parents to responsibly monitor and control the viewing and listening habits of their children with popular media products (records, videos, TV programs, etc.);
- calls upon advertisers to take responsible steps to screen the programs they support on the basis of their violent and profane content;

- supports federal legislation designed to decrease and monitor TV violence including:

    a. H.R. 2888, sponsored by Representative Edwin Markey (MA) and Jack Fields (TX), requiring TVs to be equipped with a V-chip enabling viewers to completely block programs classified as violent by the networks;

    b. S. 942, sponsored by David Durenburger (MN), requiring the Federal Communications Commission (FCC) to develop and codify standards to reduce TV violence; and

- calls upon the Federal Communications Commission to initiate hearings on violence in the media, and to consider as part of those hearings the establishment of guidelines for broadcasters to follow during prime time and children's viewing hours; furthermore, the FCC should use its licensing powers to ensure broadcasters' compliance with guidelines on violence and establish a strict procedure to levy fines against those licensees who fail to comply.

**Appendix C: STUDENT/PARENT/PRINCIPAL CONTRACT
FOR ELIMINATING GUNS AND WEAPONS
FROM SCHOOLS**

Guns and other weapons clearly are a hazard to a safe learning environment and the welfare of human beings. According to the National Center for Health Statistics, every day 14 young people, age 19 and under, are killed as a result of gun use. According to the Metropolitan Life Survey of the American Teacher, 1993: Violence in America's Public Schools, 11% of teachers and 23% of students say they have been victims of violence in or near their schools. While the elimination of guns and weapons from schools is the responsibility of all segments of the school and society, three individuals have especially crucial responsibility: the student, principal, and parent. This contract draws attention to the specific responsibilities of those three individuals.

**WE, THE UNDERSIGNED, AGREE TO THE FOLLOWING
COMMITMENTS:**

STUDENT

- I agree not to bring a gun or any weapon to school or to any school event.

- I will tell my peers to seek adult assistance when conflict situations begin to get out of control.

- I will not carry another person's gun or weapon.

- If I see a gun or other weapon on campus or at a school event, I will alert an adult about its existence.

Student Signature_____

PARENT/GUARDIAN

- I will teach, including by personal example, my teenagers about the dangers and consequences of guns and weapons use, and I will keep any guns and all weapons I own under lock and away from my children.

- I will support the school's policies to eliminate guns and weapons and work with the school in developing programs to prevent violence.

- I will carry out my responsibility to teach my children how to settle arguments without resorting to violence, to encourage him/her to use those ideas when necessary, and to follow school guidelines for reporting guns and weapons they see to an appropriate adult.

Parent Signature_____

PRINCIPAL

- I will ensure that students have an anonymous way to report to an adult any guns or other weapons they see on campus.

- I will promote conflict resolution instruction for all students as part of the curriculum.

- I will communicate the school's policies on guns and weapons to all participants in the school community and focus upon the responsibilities we all have.

- I will use the school's student leadership groups and student meetings to obtain ideas to develop a safe school environment.

- I will report all guns and other weapons violations to law enforcement officials, according to established procedures.

Principal Signature_____

Signed:

Student_____ Date_____

Parent _____ Date_____

Principal _____ Date_____

10

Communities, Schools, and Violence

Deborah Prothrow-Stith and Sher Quaday

Safety is a concern shared by all Americans, regardless of color or income level. Constantly fed a barrage of media stories about increases in the violent crime rate, people are afraid. This fear is based on some frightening statistics. Homicide is the twelfth leading cause of death in America, the second leading cause of death for teenagers and young adults, and the leading cause of death for African-American men and women ages fifteen to thirty-four.[1] More than twenty thousand people die each year from homicide, hundreds of thousands are injured by assault, and millions are fearful of the risks and potential destruction of intentional injury.[2]

The causes of violence are complicated and deeply rooted. The complex interaction between poverty; racism; drugs and alcohol; the loss of jobs and living wages; gangs; unrestricted and overabundant supplies of guns; lack of personal opportunity and responsibility; disinvestment in communities, schools, and after-school activities; family violence; and our national admiration for violence plays a critical role in sustaining our culture of violence. There is no easy answer to this problem. What is needed to begin curbing this epidemic is a commitment from educators, parents, community leaders, politicians, public health professionals, and, of course, children and teenagers.

CHILDREN: WHO IS AT RISK?

Violence in schools is certainly not new; almost every adult remembers the school bully. But today's school violence is increasingly lethal. In a recent nationwide survey, 50 percent of tenth-grade boys claimed they could get a handgun if they wanted one. Firearm homicides have increased 61 percent for fifteen- to nineteen-year-olds in one decade! Twenty years ago students may have engaged in a typical playground brawl and sustained some injuries. Today, it is more likely that those students will carry weapons and that the event will end in homicide.

Adolescent violence, in particular, should be a major concern for all Americans. The decade from 1980 to 1990 saw the juvenile violent crime arrest rate increase by 19 percent for blacks and by 44 percent for whites. The FBI predicts further increases in the crime rate through the next decade. And violent crime is not particular to any one group. The increase in adolescent crime rates in the last several decades cuts across race, class, and lifestyle.[3]

Some children are more at risk for violence than others, however. Factors that increase children's risk include gender (males are at a higher risk), poverty, residence in an urban area, and having witnessed or been the victim of violence during early childhood. In particular, the social condition of poverty is a factor for many adolescent high-risk behaviors.

One child in five lives in poverty; among children under age six, one in four is poor. One-third of these children are black. There are 13.4 million poor American children.[4] Teenagers, in particular, will understand and respond to opportunity. But if there is no hope and opportunity for a better future, adolescents may choose what makes them feel better, what the media portray as glamorous and exciting, and what counteracts the grinding boredom of poverty.

These problems are not unique to the inner city. In all settings—rural, suburban, as well as inner city—children witness or are victims of violence on a regular basis. Communities that seemed insulated from the epidemic of violence are becoming increasingly aware of their vulnerability.

MINORITY YOUTH: AT SPECIAL RISK

Adolescents often experiment with a variety of roles without making a commitment. Some adolescents are given the benefit of what Erik Erikson, author of *Identity, Youth, and Crisis*, calls a social moratorium from responsibility.[5] This moratorium allows adolescents to engage in experimental behavior without compromise of future options. It is debatable as to whether this moratorium occurs at all, yet in the situation of poverty, it surely does not. The poor adolescent struggles with developmental tasks without the protection of a social moratorium.

Minority youth must develop a healthy racial identity in addition to the developmental tasks of adolescence. Contact with racism results in anger that appears to contribute to the overrepresentation of black youth, in particular, for interpersonal violence. According to psychologist Lewis Ramey, these youth feel a "free-floating anger" that is generated not by a specific individual event but by global factors such as racism and limited opportunity.[6] This anger is the excess baggage an individual brings to an encounter which lowers his or her threshold for direct danger and violence. This concept is helpful in that it attempts to account for the environmental and socioeconomic factors behind such violence and does not simply label the individual as deficient; the anger is considered normal and appropriate. Attempts to prevent violence should be designed to achieve a healthier response to anger, to redirect anger and not suggest that we can just eliminate it.

Violence-prevention programs that are developmentally appropriate for adolescents and have a realistic cultural context can be expected to be effective. Such programs use peers in education and counseling and reflect an understanding of the stages of adolescent development. The cultural context must acknowledge the violence, racism, and classism that many adolescents experience.

CHARACTERISTICS OF VIOLENCE

The characteristics of violence may surprise some. If we accept the stereotype of violence often promoted by the media and some politicians, we will conclude that the perpetrators of most violence are strangers or "bad guys." The fact is that in the United States much of the violence occurs in the context of personal relationships. A typical homicide involves two people who know each other, who are under the influence of alcohol, and who get into an argument that escalates with the presence of a gun or knife. Only 15 percent of homicides occur in the course of committing a crime, as compared to the over 50 percent that stem from arguments among acquaintances—family relationships (that is, child abuse, elder abuse, spouse abuse) or among friends (interpersonal peer violence). For the remaining 35 percent, the relationship between victim and perpetrator is unknown.[7]

Again, our media-fed image of perpetrators and victims of violence often promotes the image of black perpetrators preying on white victims. In reality, the victim and perpetrator share many traits. They are likely to be young and of the same race (more than 90 percent of the time).[8] They may be depressed and use alcohol or drugs. And they are likely to have been exposed to violence in the past—especially family violence.[9] The result of this incongruity between public perception and actual characteristics of violence has contributed to our overall failure to design effective solutions to the problem. The traditional political response has focused on resources—police, courts, jails and prisons—that address only part of the problem. Although we ought not to discard punishment and incarceration, effective policy and programs should be implemented to address the circumstances of violence.

APPROACHES TO PREVENTING VIOLENCE

Many law enforcement experts now assert that the traditional criminal justice approaches to violence must be augmented with solutions from other disciplines, including those of public health. These experts acknowledge that social conditions such as family stability, education, and other societal institutions directly affect the behavior of juveniles and the safety of communities.

Our society's current approach lacks a comprehensive, coordinated vision. No single institution or discipline can bring about the changes needed to restore a sense of safety and order to everyday life. Violence demands not only continued attention but also new and creative approaches and partnerships. Crafting these new approaches and forging effective coalitions in each community depends on understanding the problem of violence in America.

The Role of Schools

The school is part of the community and should become part of such a comprehensive, coordinated vision for violence prevention. Schools play an important role in nurturing our children, especially our most vulnerable—those most prone to cause disruption in the classroom or to act out violently. We must ensure that every child is given the opportunity, support, and encouragement to meet with success in a setting where discipline is fair but firm, where teachers are imbued with high expectations for every child, and where parents are drawn into the education orbit so that learning can take place. From such a place we can teach our children the skills needed to prevent violence.

In the school setting, teachers and administrators must be trained for the challenges of providing an adequate multicultural education for all students. The training requires educators to evaluate and improve their own knowledge, competence, and tolerance skills by examining personal attitudes, behavior, and knowledge. To address issues of conflict resolution and mediation, school-based violence-prevention programs must incorporate multicultural values and experiences for students.

The basic charge to schools is to provide all children with an academically sound program in a safe environment for learning. In addition, there is perhaps no better place than schools to house and nurture community coalitions to improve the quality of life of families. A school that is responsive to community needs and respectful of cultural differences provides a natural environment and an existing resource for multidisciplinary programs. It is a place where diverse groups of children, parents, and elders can congregate and promote community interests, a place to gain practice and experience with getting along with diverse groups.

Many schools around the country have employed innovative strategies to help families develop skills and a sense of community. These schools tend to subscribe to the philosophy that successful families (used in the broadest sense) are critical to a community's survival in this time of dwindling social resources. They work to develop community/school partnerships that are dynamic, diverse, and driven by the needs of the families within. They provide parents with an active voice in school policies and planning. They may offer an array of programs including after-school programs for children, adult education courses, family counseling services, recreational programs, or job skills training. They become a vital hub of neighborhood activity.

Schools willing to take on the challenge of education amidst adversity should use existing knowledge of school-based community programs. Administrators must build coalitions to ensure that meaningful, long-term, and multifaceted approaches be implemented to bring about peaceful schools and safe communities.

Education

Education is a vital tool of violence prevention. The child who achieves in school learns skills that can help him or her navigate through dangerous and stressful situations—favoring words over force as a strategy to deal with conflict. Our most vulnerable students, those growing up in poverty, must be given extra attention through tutoring, nurturing, after-school programs, and conflict-resolution programs.

It has been shown that learning cognitive skills helps prevent violence. Children develop cognitive skills while studying English, social studies, math, and science. These skills help them reason their way through stressful and dangerous situations. Those with superior language skills and analytic abilities are less likely to use force to persuade and more likely to use creative and intellectual exercises to imagine and respect different points of view. They are also able to more clearly envision the consequences of certain actions and possess a greater repertoire of alternatives to violent behavior.

Many adults are anxious to blame the child for his or her inability to learn. But most teachers agree that children begin school in first grade excited and hungry to learn. This is as true for minority as for nonminority children, and as true for boys as girls. All children want to learn, feel valued, and succeed in school. But many encounter circumstances that lessen the appetite for learning. Jeff Howard, a Harvard-trained sociologist now with the Efficacy Institute, says that negative expectations and the uneven reinforcement of some students by teachers clearly play a part in destroying the enthusiasm of young blacks for school. He calls these incidents "spirit murder."

School-Based Activities

Schools have been an effective and useful forum for youth health education, particularly for recent prevention campaigns against risky behavior. Schools provide a setting where the targeted age group can be easily reached. Prevention programs such as those dealing with substance abuse, heart disease, and sexually transmitted diseases have been implemented with measurable success. School-based approaches have been employed in the prevention of interpersonal violence with the hope of similar success. These violence-prevention programs can include a number of activities: classroom curricula, teacher training, and peer-led instruction. In addition, coordinated efforts among schools, parents, and community groups can provide a comprehensive program of complementary, reinforcing messages to youths.

Classroom Curricula

Early health education campaigns focused primarily on providing factual information about the negative effects of health risk behaviors, but research found that using scare tactics is generally ineffective in preventing risk behaviors. Based on theories that risk behaviors are socially influenced/learned, health education programs now attempt to change the conditions under which the behaviors are acquired.

Many violence-prevention curricula employ the social skills approach. Multiple influences are thought to contribute to the development of violent behavior.

including neurobiological, cognitive, and social components. Current social influence prevention programs are based on the ideas that (1) aggression is a learned behavior in response to stress and conflict situations; (2) adolescents who lack skills in communication, negotiation, and problem-solving have a limited range of alternatives with which to solve interpersonal problems; and (3) such adolescents have learned that violence is an appropriate way to solve interpersonal problems.

Prevention programs are designed to counteract the development of attitudes, cognitions, and behaviors that lead to violence. These programs train children and adolescents in areas like stress management, problem-solving, communication, and boosting of self-esteem. Noteworthy recent additions to some curricula are programs to curb the use of abusive language and training to respond to verbal abuse. A lot of violent behavior, including homicide, begins with verbal provocation. Eliminating abusive words may eliminate the trigger for aggressive behavior. Through such programs, students also learn words and skills to defuse verbal conflict and avoid volatile situations.

A number of communities are already using conflict-resolution curricula. The results of these programs' short-term reviews are promising. The Education Development Center, Inc., of Newton, Massachusetts compiled a report of twelve case studies describing promising violence-prevention programs across the country. In general, positive effects have been seen (as indicated by preliminary program evaluations) on student knowledge, attitudes, and behavior; teacher attitudes and competence in violence-prevention skills; school climate; school statistics in violence/misbehavior; program implementation; and general response to/support of programs.

Teacher Training

Essential to the success of these school curricula are teacher training programs. The School Health Education Evaluation, a comprehensive assessment of the status of school health education (using twenty states), as well as studies of individual prevention programs (smoking, substance abuse), have found that teacher in-service training is related to more complete health program implementation and, consequently, to more successful program outcome. Because many of the current social skills prevention programs have a nontraditional approach involving demonstration, modeling, and role-playing, teachers accustomed to the traditional lecture and discussion format may need to master new instruction strategies in order to feel comfortable with the innovative programs. Teacher training should include a presentation of the theory underlying the program, a demonstration of the skills to be learned, a chance to practice the new skills being taught, feedback, and coaching.

In addition to learning methods specific to teaching students violence-prevention skills, teacher training programs provide a forum for changing the school atmosphere—teachers get a chance to learn violence-prevention strategies themselves for use in their own classrooms. For example, in Chicago teachers attend fifteen seminars per semester, receiving college credit for their participation. They are taught how to reduce the level of violence in the schools, how to respond to violent situations, and how to teach children alternative ways of behaving. Teachers can thus be taught to effectively mediate the atmosphere of their own classrooms.

In general, teacher training not only provides educators with skills to instruct a new program and to use in their own classroom, but also can increase their enthusiasm for a program and their *self-confidence* to teach a new program.

The Public Health Model

Public health practitioners and school personnel have a longstanding alliance in working to ensure the health of children. Together, they have designed and implemented proactive prevention programs covering vision, hearing, tuberculosis screening, vaccinations, and so forth. In the classroom, health education teaches children about fitness, human reproduction, nutrition, and substance abuse. It is in this setting that public health strategies can be used to educate and ultimately prevent violence both in and out of school.

Some public health and education academics have criticized stand-alone violence-prevention curricula as ineffective. These critics are right. A ten-hour curriculum taught in tenth grade is not enough to provide a measurable change in youth attitudes and behavior. It is, however, a step in the right direction. A violence-prevention curriculum plays a role in the overall school-based approach, but it should not be considered the solution to this complex problem. Ideally, a schoolwide violence-prevention program would include the teaching of social skills, problem-solving, peer-mentoring programs, conflict-resolution programs, afterschool activities, parenting courses, and early intervention programs such as Head Start.

A public health model offers strategies that could complement and strengthen the traditional criminal justice approach. Public health recognizes that violence has become a major contributor to mortality and morbidity. In fact, homicide and intentional injury may represent as much as $60 billion in short- and long-term health care costs and lost productivity of those who are injured or disabled by violence in just one year.[10] These facts alone warrant attention by public health professionals and give society even more reason to be concerned about violence.

Public health has also developed techniques of analysis and prevention that may be useful in our efforts to prevent violence. This analytical approach identifies risk factors that could become the focus of preventive interventions. It touts a record of accomplishment in controlling accidental (unintentional) injuries through both environmental and legal interventions (for example, seat belts and childproof caps on medicines) and behavioral change (for example, educational campaigns to reduce drunk driving). These techniques may be valuable in the analysis and prevention of violence as well. As we learn more about violence and its causes, these techniques seem more plausible.

The public health approach to violence prevention is similar to the methods used to stop people from smoking—by using primary, secondary, and tertiary prevention interventions. Although some programs must be targeted at our most vulnerable children and families, we must also develop and promote primary prevention for those at moderate to low risk in order to keep these children and families from becoming high risk. The following comparison between preventing smoking and preventing violence describes the phases of the public health prevention model:

Primary prevention programs encourage a negative view of smoking to keep people from starting to smoke. Violence-prevention programs promote redefining the "hero" and nonviolent problem-solving. These types of violence-prevention programs may include mass media messages that realistically portray the effects of violence and reinforce the concept that violence is not a smart way to solve problems.

Secondary prevention programs attempt to get people to quit smoking through behavior modification programs or therapy. In violence prevention, secondary prevention methods include counseling or mentoring programs for children at risk of violence—for instance, those who have gotten into fights at school or been suspended from school.

Tertiary prevention programs are the last step for smokers with cancer, offering surgery or chemotherapy as a treatment option. The last step in violence prevention is to offer rehabilitation programs to incarcerated violent offenders.

In violence prevention, as in smoking prevention, early intervention is safer, preferable, and more cost-effective. It is smarter to teach kids not to smoke, or conflict-resolution skills and nonviolent methods of dealing with anger, than to run programs in treatment facilities or perform surgery to remove a lung or a bullet.

THE TIME IS NOW

We have come a long way in the past ten years. Politicians are beginning to listen to the logic of prevention. We now have money for violence prevention in both the new crime and education bills. Existing violence-prevention programs are expanding. New programs are being developed. More and more people and communities are demanding a different response to the violence in our society. New antiviolence television programming, curricula, and other educational tools are being developed.

Joint collaborative programmatic efforts will move this process even further and will help establish concrete working relationships between the disciplines. A concrete example of a collaborative effort could be accomplished in joint community training efforts. Police officers could provide violence safety training to low- to moderate-risk children and adolescents on safety behaviors as part of a violence-prevention curriculum in the schools. Joint federal interagency funding and promotion of interdisciplinary program development will greatly enhance collaboration. Some individuals within each of these professions have recognized the need for a comprehensive agenda and have begun this important dialogue. More individuals need to enter this process, and the institutions that greatly influence the bigger picture and provide the resources for all of our work must create the opportunities for this to happen. There is so much to be gained.

We must allow our current approaches to violence prevention to continue to evolve. We need to nurture the national grassroots violence-prevention movement to change our social norms. With this support, communities can advocate for the necessary resources and legislation to address the excessive violence in our communities, schools, and entertainment. The most sophisticated and well-funded arrest, prosecution, and incarceration strategies will not prevent violence. Prevention requires attending early to those at risk and changing our culture of violence so that we develop better skills for getting along and no longer promote, encourage, and celebrate violence.

We can learn much from the communities, individuals, and programs across the country that have charted new ground in their responses to community violence. These include gun buy-back programs, targeted media messages, citizen watch groups, economic development strategies, and gang and violence prevention programs. Some of these approaches include opening, staffing, and offering positive programming in schools from early morning to late at night; opening schools for community education programs; installing streetlights in targeted neighborhoods; incorporating community policing strategies; and offering job training and violence-prevention skill training to at-risk youth.

We must apply those successful public health strategies and expand those that show promise. Above all we must be creative, flexible, and patient. The unlearning of violence in society will be a long-term effort. It is time to begin.

NOTES

The authors wish to acknowledge the research and editing assistance of Jacqueline T. Kral.

1. Center for Disease Control, "Homicide among Young Black Males—United States, 1978–1987," *Morbidity and Mortality Weekly Report* 39 (1990): 869–73.

2. Federal Bureau of Investigation, *Uniform Crime Report: Crime in the United States* (Washington, D.C.: U.S. Department of Justice, 1981).

3. Federal Bureau of Investigation, *Uniform Crime Report: Crime in the United States* (Washington, D.C.: U.S. Department of Justice, 1992).

4. Children's Defense Fund, *Child Poverty: Comparative Nationwide and State Data from the 1990 and 1980 Censuses* (August 11, 1992).

5. E. Erikson, *Identity, Youth, and Crisis* (New York: W. W. Norton, 1968).

6. N. Akbar, "Homicide among Black Males: Causal Factors," *Public Health Reports* 95, No. 6 (1980): 549.

7. *Uniform Crime Report,* 1992.

8. Akbar, "Homicide among Black Males."

9. D. Prothrow-Stith and M. Weissman, *Deadly Consequences: How Violence is Destroying Our Teenage Population and a Plan to Begin Solving the Problem* (New York: HarperCollins, 1991).

10. D. P. Rice, E. J. Mackenzie et al., *Cost of Injury in the United States: A Report to Congress 1989* (San Francisco: Institute for Health and Aging, University of California and the Injury Prevention Center, Johns Hopkins University, 1989), 37–85.

11

From Fight or Flight to Collaboration: A Framework for Understanding Individual and Institutional Development in the School

Steven Brion-Meisels and Robert L. Selman

In September 1977 twelve students emerged from yellow school buses to begin the year in a classroom at the Manville School in Boston. The eight boys and four girls shared all of the typical developmental interests and needs of early adolescence: hesitantly self-conscious and yet impulsive, mature and yet childlike, insightful and yet oblivious to the world around them, full of ideas, values, and strong feelings about right and wrong. Although they came from different social, economic, and racial backgrounds, they also shared a clinical label: they were acting out and emotionally disturbed." Therefore, they shared a special set of experiences, including a social and school history of rejection. They were and felt disempowered, marginalized, and left to survive through one of two simple strategies: fight or flight. However, as adolescents, they also shared a common desire to become part of a "crowd" and make friendships, to discover and exercise their personal power as young people facing a complex and difficult social world.

One of us (Steven Brion-Meisels) was their new classroom teacher. After the first conflict of the first day of school, he understood that his primary job was to create a learning community where the children's basic academic and social needs could be met in a context that emphasized collaborative transformations: that is, a shared life in which all of us would change—for the better. The other of us (Robert Selman) was director of the Manville School. He brought with him a background as a clinical and developmental psychologist and, more recently, a researcher investigating how children's developing ability to coordinate interpersonal perspectives affected their ideas about such important social issues as friendship, trust, loyalty, and conflict resolution, as well as their behavior.

Both of us shared a belief that the worlds of research and practice, too long held at arm's length, needed to be brought together. During the next seven years, we worked with colleagues, parents, students, graduate assistants, and members of the community to try to help and understand and to integrate practice with research—to inform each with the other.[1]

In doing so, we confronted the need to help not only students but also staff, to move from an impulse toward fight or flight toward an attitude of collaboration. We wrote and implemented curriculum;[2] conducted classroom and schoolwide community meetings; initiated parent support workshops; started an after-school program; led teacher workshops; conducted research and evaluation projects;[3] and struggled with the slow, uneven, and dialectical pace of both individual development and institutional change.

Since 1983 we and our colleagues have worked to extend as well as deepen our work with students, educators, and parents in a broad range of public school and residential settings. We have constructed a developmental model of socialization that we believe is more sensitive to both specific contextual and general sociocultural forces than that of our forebearers. We have tried to apply our model in preventive work with children, adolescents, and school staff in public schools. In these settings, we have used curriculum,[4] discipline strategies,[5] pair counseling,[6] peer mediation,[7] and staff support programs.

We have developed a conceptual vehicle, a part of which we call interpersonal negotiation strategies, in order to help us integrate a social developmental approach in the tradition of Dewey, Piaget, and Kohlberg. The focus of this approach is on the development of individual children, with a political and sociological approach to social institutional change represented by the work of Paulo Freire and Alfred Alschuler.

We have worked with children and adolescents to understand and then support the development of new and more adequate interpersonal negotiation strategies. We have approached this work sensitive to the role of developmental, relational, and contextual factors: how children think and feel about these strategies is related to their interactions with significant others in their social context. In recent years we have used this same framework to understand and improve the institutional strategies used by schools, because we believe that interpersonal and institutional development are deeply linked—both for students and adults in the school community. If either is to be improved, both must be nurtured.

Students (over the course of their social development), teachers, and the schools where they both work can all move from strategies of fight or flight to a collaborative orientation that can truly transform both the individuals and the institution itself. This chapter shares some of what we have learned from the past two decades of work in schools and suggests ways in which practice and theory can inform each other.

Piaget documented the metamorphosis in children's developing ideas and reasoning about areas ranging from mathematical logic to moral reasoning.[8] From Mead[9] and from Dewey,[10] we take the core notion of perspective-coordination; the belief that children actively construct ideas about social relationships through their interactions with peers and adults; and the tenet that understanding the natural course of the development of children's ideas is central in the creation of good schools. Kohlberg[11] and Gilligan[12] provide us with a dialectic by painting contrasting pictures of children's development in moral judgment and action. From

Kohlberg we take the constructivist notion that the development of moral ideas follows a universal sequence; from Gilligan, the contextualist caution that, even if so, we must listen carefully for and give power to the diverse voices that make up the school community. From the work of Paulo Freire,[13] we take the understanding that gender, race, social class, and role all deeply affect how children and adults understand and act in the social world. Our own work has focused first on how the developing ability to coordinate social perspectives affects children's ideas about friendship, trust, and groups,[14] and more recently on how new social perspectives generate new and alternative social strategies.[15] In sum, our pedagogy is designed to help children gain a broader *social perspective* and to use the perspective gained to understand *their own point of view* and to speak more clearly in their own authentic voice.

Although we have followed the Piaget/Kohlberg focus on qualitative and sequential development, our own theoretical orientation tries to bridge, or include, what goes on inside the child's mind with what goes on between the child and others (the relationships and roles in which he or she finds himself or herself, the ways in which he or she and other people treat one another). We are as interested in the diversity of the ways children express their developing social understanding as we are in their structural similarities. First, we are aware that children's ideas about the social world do not develop uniformly across all domains: ideas about conflict or jealousy in a friendship may be more or less developed than ideas about trust or fairness or authority. Second, these new ideas about the social world can be forgotten or unused when a child feels sad or angry, or when the situation is not supportive. Thoughts do not equal behavior; children, like adults, are complex persons and respond in different ways to different contexts and feelings.

Dewey and Kohlberg shared with Freire a conviction that knowledge (and skills) must be used for the common good, and be understood in the context of core social/political questions. Dewey writes that "all the members of a group must have equal opportunity to receive and take from others.... Otherwise, the experiences which educate some into masters, educate others into slaves."[16]

And Freire writes: "Education as an act of knowing confronts us with a number of theoretical–practical, not intellectual questions: What to know? How to know? Why to know? In benefit of what and of whom to know?"[17]

In alignment with the recent work on critical theory and feminist perspectives,[18] and the political perspective articulated by Freire, we ask what *level* of perspective a child uses, *whose* perspective is being considered, and *what value* that perspective taker holds—for the individual and the community. Questions of role, voice, and perspective become increasingly important when we try to apply a developmental lens to the world views of adults. Where one stands depends not only on where one sits, but also on how well one can see.

CHILDREN'S DEVELOPING VIEW OF THE SCHOOL AS A COMMUNITY

The school is a community in constant flux and change. These changes are both interpersonal (for students and staff) and institutional, and each change may create changes in other aspects of the school community. For example, developmental changes in children's social awareness create strategies that are more inclusive and effective in dealing with a broader range of social problems. These changes in turn affect school climate and may influence the way the school as an institution negotiates problems.

Individual faculty members also change their perspectives, and with these changes come changes in the institution itself. Some changes in each faculty member's attitude are developmental with respect to personal and professional growth. New perspectives may or may not lead to strategies that are more inclusive and effective in dealing with longstanding professional problems. For example, a first-year teacher will often be concerned primarily with his or her own performance in an immediate and personal way: Will the students listen to me? Will my lessons work? Will my principal support me? Master teachers often have incorporated these concerns into broader perspectives, and they become concerned about the welfare of colleagues, the climate of their classroom and school, and changes in the system over time.[19]

Together, these changes in individual students and faculty create changes in the school as an institution, because new ideas and new demands come to the fore. *Institutional development* affects the ways in which children and adults relate to each other, and, in turn, the ways in which children's psychological development is fostered or stifled. Although there has been a good deal of research about effective schools and about the institutional climate of schools, we believe that there has been little research or practice that relates the developmental changes of children and adults to the institutional improvement of schools. Kohlberg's later work on the Just Community School,[20] the research and teaching of Fritz Oser in Switzerland,[21] and the little known but crucial projects of Alfred Alschuler and his students[22] are important exceptions to this pattern.

Children's Developing Theories about What Makes a Good School

Many students use words such as the following when they describe what makes a good school: *fair, friendly, safe, people listen to me, people are nice, people help each other, everyone is accepted, people work together, I learn here.* But these words mean different things to children at different ages and in different social contexts and roles within the school.

For preschool children, a good school may be based largely on perceived physical characteristics. A school (or a daycare center) may be good because it has a good slide, or good snacks, or pretty colors, or a good playground, or a nice teacher, or a great rabbit. These views have important personal meanings for the young child. However, because they are largely focused on physical (instead of psychological) qualities of interpersonal relationships, these young children also are limited in their ability to resolve problems. When the teacher tells them to follow the lead child on a walk, chaos may reign without direction, because, as one child notes, rushing to the front of the line, "we all can be the leader." Without adult intervention, serious problems between young children are often solved by fight or flight; lesser issues are often solved when one child is distracted or when the two engage in parallel play.

For a kindergarten child or first-grader, a good school usually centers around one good teacher and one good friend. Relationships are becoming more psychological, but they are still individualized, still taken one person at a time. Fairness issues center around fairness "to me"—or to my "best friend." A fair teacher is one who is "not mean"—especially "to me." This unilateral view of the social world often translates into strategies that are similarly unilateral: fight or flight is replaced by command or obey as the alternatives for resolving conflicts. Whether commands are gentle or harsh, the kindergarten room is filled with the voice of authority: "Everyone follow me," "Let's play follow the leader," "Look at what I brought for show and tell," "I want to jump rope now," "She's being mean; she always wants to go first!"

For a third-grade student, social life is becoming more of a two-way street. A friend is a person one can trust to make an "equal" exchange: of secrets, snacks, goods, time, and interests. Friends take turns; friends protect each other. Fairness is also built on reciprocity and the capacity to take a second-person perspective: I understand what you want, and you understand what I want, so we can get along as long as each of us gets what we want. These social relationships and the strategies they engender focus on *partners* as the foundation for interpersonal relationships.

For a young adolescent, the social world revolves increasingly around the peer group collaboration. Therefore, the school community becomes a series of minicommunities: teams, cliques, lunch table partners, friends and foes, them and us, teachers versus kids. At this age, too, differences related to gender, race, and social class, with their clear connections to questions of power and status, become increasingly potent and visible. For most young adolescents, to be fair and act fairly now means taking into account the good of the group. However, *which* group and *which* role are often important issues as the young adolescent struggles to find and then save a space for himself or herself in the social group. The cumulative effects of parenting and schooling often informally teach different strategies for group survival based on race, gender, and social position.

These ideas and strategies include learning how to take a third-person perspective on the social world, what George Herbert Mead called the perspective of the "generalized other," and how to focus on the group as the key social unit. Moreover, adolescents begin to glean collaboration and transformation as the twin mechanisms for solving problems: "we need to work together so everyone is satisfied," and the best solutions are those that transform our own individual wants and desires into a common view of the situation that caused the problem in the first place. For them, a good teacher works to make the classroom a place "where everyone learns and gets along, and everyone is listened to." A good school addresses meaningful issues of adolescent development: "people know what's going on in our lives, and they want to make things better."

The ideal of collaborative transformation is deeply held by all adolescents, no

168 Toward a Less Violent School Environment

matter how "troubled" or "stable" they are. As is often the case, however, if this ideal is not easily achieved, adolescents act out in ways that use their earlier developed, less effective strategies: fight or flight, command or obey, trade and exchange. At times, situations, feelings, and limited practice skills obstruct the adolescent's ability to carry out his or her goals. At other times, the adolescent's desire to collaborate is obstructed by the institutional patterns of the school. Schools are often built on a one-way approach: one text, one time for class change, one kind of schedule, and one boss (the teacher or principal). A one-way or unilateral institutional pattern does not readily allow for collaboration, let alone reciprocity. It will inevitably create conflict with those adolescents and adults who seek to collaborate as part of their life in the school.

We believe that each of these views of the good school captures a piece of the totality of the complex school community. However, our developmental lens leads us to believe that each new view of what constitutes a "good school" is more inclusive and has more potential productivity than the previous one. In other words, the developmental changes in children's and adolescents' ideas about the school as a community facilitate new ways of negotiating interpersonal problems, as well as new feelings about the social relationships imbedded in the school. These ideas will turn cynical if the institutional perspective on social relationships does not support them.

It is important to remember that children's ideas about the good school are norms and ideals. We do not argue here that children *always* believe in or live according to these norms and ideals. There is anger, fear, unfairness, jealousy, and more in the minds and hearts of children, as well as adults. Like adults, children often lose or forget their best perspective and therefore fall short of their own norms and ideals. We do believe, however, that these developing ideas and norms can be a solid foundation on which to build more successful and supportive school communities.

Relationships Between Children's and Adults' Views of the Good School

Children's ideas about a good school are related *both* to their naturally developing social capacities *and* to the social realities of their lives—including the climate of the school itself. A healthy climate for students also depends on the quality of the climate for staff. Therefore, in helping to create a more supportive and collaborative school community, we need to understand how the adults in the school community understand this same question: What makes a good school?

Conversations with teachers, parents, and administrators inevitably uncover some persistent patterns of response. For them, a good school may be one where:

- "People leave me alone and don't bother me."
- "There are no fights, and kids get along."
- "Students work quietly and respect staff."
- "Teachers get support from the administration."

- "I have a colleague I can count on."
- "I have a good class this year."
- "Parents make sure kids are prepared for school."
- "Kids are learning and succeeding."
- "Everyone is respected and feels safe."
- "People work together to solve problems."
- "We are always asking how to make the school better and
- looking for ways to help each other."
- "People are willing to take risks and make mistakes so
- they can improve the place."
- "Students learn to work together and be independent learners."

We believe that each of these views of the school as a community can be represented by a level of perspective on the totality of the school as a community. We also want to make a developmental claim about these views—one that remains untested and may strike some as presumptuous. This claim is also more sociological than psychological. If development involves the creation of strategies that are increasingly inclusive and effective, but in a way that is not totally age-related and more subject to the variations of school climate, then two implications follow.

First, we believe that faculty perspectives on the good school often develop with professional experience; they move from egocentric and physical concerns (Will I be safe? Will I have enough pencils?) to unilateral views (Will my students listen to me and do what I say? Will I be a good enough teacher?) to reciprocal concerns (Who can I hook up with for support?) to collaborative ideas (How can we engage with each other to make this school better for everyone?). As with the natural development of children's *psychological* understanding, we believe that these adult *sociological* views on institutional life can also be organized structurally as to their inclusiveness and functionally as to their effectiveness.

Second, we suggest that there are parallels between the ontogenesis of individual views of school held by children and the sociogenesis of institutional views of the good school that are created by the beliefs espoused by the adults who work there. In other words, we believe that both children and adults think about the good school in ways that range from fight or flight to collaboration. Together, these ideas help create a language children and adults use when they talk about the climate of their school.

What parallels exist between student and adult ideas about the good school? For some adults, the good school is based only on physical criteria. In this view, the good school is one that is physically safe, surroundings are pleasant, and things work. Other adults take a unilateral view where the good school is a school that is good for *me*: "My class is a good one," or "Students are quiet because I demand respect," or "I get support from my administrator," or "Parents support what the school wants to do."

Sometimes adults talk about the good school as being built on reciprocal relationships, both with students and with colleagues: "I like it here because I have people I can trust and work with," or "My principal listens to me even if he or she disagrees," or "Kids get along with each other and that makes my work easier," or "Students respect me and I respect them."

Less frequently, adults talk about the good school from a third-person and collaborative perspective: "Here everyone helps each other, we all pitch in to work together," or "I feel this school is working well because I see kids and teachers working out problems with each other," or "This school finds ways where everyone is respected and can learn," or "The principal treats us as a team, and we respect him or her for that."

For children and adults, a fight or flight view of school leads to isolation and helplessness; a unilateral view leads to "taking care of myself (only)"; a reciprocal view leads to alliances that, though supportive, cannot support institutional change. Only a collaborative view of the good school allows for the possibility that each and every member of the community can be supported in achieving excellence.

Therefore, the ideas held by children and adults, in interaction with the feelings they have about the school and the roles they play in it, help determine the kinds of strategies they will use in dealing with school-related problems. In other words, we believe that a developmental lens can be used to describe the institutional strategies used in dealing with school conflicts and can in turn help us improve the school for everyone in it. We now take a closer look at the action strategies engendered by these views of the good school.

FROM SCHOOL THOUGHTS TO SCHOOL TRANSFORMATION

In trying to trace the link between thought and action, our work focuses on three distinct but related factors that contribute to the development of negotiation strategies: ideas, relationships, and context. As we have just seen, ideas about how to relate to the social world are rooted in the developing ability to coordinate social perspectives. For us, the developing perspectives used by children and adults when they think about the good school help create strategies for dealing with school-related conflicts.

Interpersonal Negotiation Strategies

Social relationships in the school often are affected by how the individual copes with feelings of helplessness or competence in dealing with other members of the community at each developmental level. We have identified two different orientations to interpersonal relationships. In a *self-transforming orientation*, one seeks to resolve problems by changing one's own behavior: "I'll let you go first all the time, so you won't be mad at me" (unilateral), or "If I have a fight with my friend, it's over if we both apologize, but I'm willing to apologize first" (reciprocal). An *other-transforming orientation* also can operate at each new level of negotiation. However, in this orientation one seeks to solve problems by changing the other person's behavior: "You have to let me go first on the slide or I won't be your friend," or "When my friend and I have a fight, it's only over if he or she apologizes first."

These two orientations become integrated only as a mutual or collaborative approach to negotiations begins to take place: "When we have a fight, we both know that we are still friends and so we just accept our part, apologize, and go on; as long as both of us feel we have moved from our different perspectives to a common understanding, the issue is resolved." As we shall see, these orientations also can be used to characterize institutional negotiation strategies.

Orientation-in-action, more than the developmental structure of the student's (or teacher's) thought, is more often associated with and influenced by the political forces of race, gender, status, power, and oppression—in the school as well as in the larger society. When all other things are equal, in our society girls and women are more likely to use a self-transforming orientation than are boys and men. Power differences in roles as well as individual differences in personality also affect orientation.

The orientation used is often a product of the context in which a negotiation takes place, as well as the history of personal, interpersonal, and institutional relationships that precede it. The first component (ideas) speaks about the inner, psychological part of our model, and the second component (orientation) speaks about the social relationship part of our model. The third component (context) speaks to the external forces (contextual and sociocultural) that act on both the individual and the institution. Negotiations may be greatly affected by the situation in which a child finds himself or herself. Is he or she negotiating a contentious issue with a friend whose feelings he or she understands (ideas) and whom he or she trusts (relationships) away from peers who might goad them to fight (context), or does the negotiation take place with a new teacher who is nervous, in a public place (context)? The strategies and outcomes of each negotiation may be very different.

These three factors—ideas, sociocultural relationships, and context—combine to create a dynamic framework for assessing and explaining any series of interpersonal negotiation strategies that are directly observed. In turn, the framework can be used to improve the quality of the school for both students and adults. Next, we try to show how the three components interact to shape the ways in which students, staff, and the school as an institution deal with the problems of the school day and the long-term challenges of school transformation. We will look at both interpersonal and institutional negotiation strategies.

Levels of interpersonal negotiation, or those used to describe children's and staff's ideas about the school community, are not meant to be restrictive labels: children (and adults) are complex and respond in different ways to complex situations. The levels of negotiation strategies are intended to serve as a guide to thinking about ways to improve school—especially when we focus on strategies and behavior.

Fight or flight characterizes the strategies often used by young children. However, young children occasionally do use unilateral (command or obey) or even reciprocal (persuade or permit) strategies,[23] and older children sometimes revert to fight or flight strategies. In other words, young children sometimes solve problems by giving orders or following them, or even by sharing. Older children sometimes see the world only from their own point of view rather than from that of the group.

The earliest and simplest kinds of strategies (known as fight or flight) are impulsive. They also can be only physicalistic, because the very young child is not yet able to take the psychological perspective of a second person; therefore, only physical solutions are possible. A self-transforming orientation will lead to flight, an other-transforming orientation will lead to a fight strategy, and the choice of strategy may depend at least in part on the perceived power of the other person in the relationship (Is he or she bigger or smaller than me? Is this an adult or a younger peer?).

One-way (unilateral) strategies represent an advance, even though they are still one-way and are also often win/lose. These strategies (known as command or obey) define the problem from only one perspective and focus on resolving the problem in a way that satisfies only one person's needs at a time. Some children are most likely to look for solutions in which their own view can dominate (an other-transforming orientation). Students who use such one-way strategies may often argue or even fight, but they may also respond well to an adult (teacher, principal, parent) who uses a similar strategy because the adult is bigger, has more authority, and uses a strategy that is familiar. Other children may hold a one-way perspective in which they tend to resolve the conflict by automatically giving in or obeying (a self-transforming orientation).

Two-way (reciprocal) strategies represent what we have called trade/exchange, or persuade/permit strategies. In these strategies, the two individuals seek equal gain from the negotiation. In this sense, they seek solutions where each person both gains and loses a bit: "I'll play basketball today if we can play football tomorrow," or "I'll help you with your homework if you'll teach me how to dance like you do." Strategies here involve establishing trust between the two parties: keeping confidence, trading equally, taking turns, and so forth. With adults, children use and respond to strategies that establish various kinds of two-way contracts. They may wheedle, whine, cajole, or seek to make bargains. However, they use these strategies in a framework that recognizes the needs of both the child and adult: "I'll finish my homework tomorrow if you just let me go this once," or "I'll stay after to finish my homework now because I know I promised I'd have it to you today." The two orientations (self- and other-transforming) here begin to come closer together. Our research suggests that by around ages eight to ten, children can move more flexibly and consciously from one orientation to the other and more generally seek solutions that will serve both sets of interests. At this age most children begin to take control of and manage their repertoires.[24]

Collaborative (mutual) strategies require and are built on a third-person perspective of the interpersonal relationship and the negotiation itself. The adolescent can imaginatively step outside of the dyadic conflict and see it as a third person might. From this new perspective, strategies and solutions have to take into account what is fair for an imagined third person in this situation, and what is fair for the group. The negotiation becomes much more complex—one must give to get—but the solutions are more inclusive and stable because they truly seek win/win outcomes. Strategies involve language such as, "It's not fair that you always go first, because everyone wants a turn sometimes," or "You can join our dance group even though we are already full, but you need to promise to not skip out on practices."

We believe that collaborative interpersonal strategies are more inclusive and successful in resolving interpersonal problems: they allow each individual to feel that he or she has gained and given something, and they take into account the broadest set of perspectives. In addition, these strategies are more successful in strengthening the school as a supportive community. However, the creation of a just and supportive school community requires institutional strategies that build collaboration among all parties. If students are the only group required to be collaborative, then collaboration is a mislabeled conformity and not a truly mutual transformation: you (students) must collaborate with us because we (adults) know what you should do.

Institutional Negotiation Strategies

Patterns of institutional negotiation have profound impacts on the ways in which adults and youth work together within the school as a community. Institutional levels of negotiation can exacerbate the isolation, name-calling, and blaming (whether of self or other) that plague some schools; or they can establish a climate within the school that pulls for collaboration among all its members— from the very youngest to the most senior or powerful.

Our analysis of the levels and orientations of institutional negotiation strategies derives from our interpretation of two important educational approaches. The first is Paulo Freire's work in which he analyzes what he calls the "pedagogy of the oppressed" and creates a pedagogy for liberation. The second is the little-known research and intervention project conducted by Alfred Alschuler and his colleagues who worked for years in urban school systems to develop what they called "social literacy"—in our words, the ability to liberate ourselves and others through negotiation strategies that use and nurture collaborative transformations.

For those who may be new to the work of Freire and Alschuler, a brief word about the context of their efforts may be helpful. Freire began his work on literacy in poor urban areas of Brazil in 1959. He discovered that many of his students reflected (in their own value systems and their behavior toward others) the same oppressive structures that were present in the broader society of which they were victims: "some of us are rich, while others are poor; some are powerful while others are weak; that's the way it is and will always be, so I must accept it." Freire also found that those who broke out of their own oppression simply replicated the model and became oppressors themselves: "I am now more powerful, so I will strive to keep that power for myself and use it to have control over others." In our framework, this situation parallels the situation in which an adult uses a self-transforming strategy when dealing with a supervisor ("I'll do what you tell me"), and then turns around to use an other-transforming strategy with children ("And now you'll do what I tell you to do"). Freire believed that both models would only continue the oppressor-oppressed relationships that he saw all around him. He believed, as we do, that the central change required was the shift from oppressive relationships to liberating ones—in our framework, from fight or flight to collaborative transformations.[25]

In the early 1960s, Alfred Alschuler was asked to help out a public school system in Massachusetts where suspension rates had risen dramatically and in which African-American males from low-income families were disproportionately represented. Alschuler had visited a Freire-based school in the mountains of Ecuador and understood intuitively that Freire's work had deep relevance to the lives of urban public school systems. He and his colleagues thus began the Social Literacy Project, in which they worked with public school teachers and students to analyze the social realities of the school (what they called "naming the game") and to develop, with the teachers, collaborative strategies to change the rules and roles that created unhappiness and oppression for all.[26]

Our fight or flight strategy level of psychosocial development parallels what Freire called a *magical conforming* strategy. Here, problems are denied or avoided; difficulties are accepted as fate—a part of existence. The only strategies available are either shutting out others ("I'm not listening to anything you say, it's useless!") or shutting the self in ("I'll just close my classroom door and wait for June."). These strategies exacerbate the isolation felt by teachers, students, and administrators. In our view, they are present when:

- A teacher says, "It's not my problem; all these kids are lazy."
- A student says, "It's not my problem; teachers are always unfair."
- A teacher says, "It's useless; I just give up trying to do anything."
- A principal says, "It's not my problem; it's always like this in public education—families don't support us and neither do our bosses."
- A teacher feels the only way to cope is to shut the door until he or she can ask for a transfer.
- A student finds rage to be the only way to express his or her sense of powerlessness in creating a better role for himself or herself in the school.
- An administrator says, "We'll never raise scores because poor kids (or Hispanic kids or these kids) have no support at home."
- A student, teacher, or administrator drops out of school.

Institutional fight or flight strategies, like interpersonal ones, also come in both self- and other-transforming orientations. Naming this kind of strategy accomplishes several positive steps. First, it helps us understand that everyone feels this way at times and that most institutions function this way at least some of the time. Second, we are reminded that this kind of strategy is a social dead end: it cannot create working relationships. Institutional fight or flight is disempowering to the individuals and to the community; it prevents transformation or development of any kind—for staff as well as for students.

What we have called one-way strategies reflect what Freire and Alschuler speak of as *naive-reforming* approaches. In this approach, problems are seen as the fault of individuals within the system. Therefore, change requires "reforming" the individual-echoing the notions connected to youth "reformatories." We hear one-way (or naive-reforming) strategies when:

- A teacher says, "If only Billy were not in this class."
- A student says, "If only they fired Mr. Bironi."
- A principal says, "If only Mr. Bironi could manage his class."
- Mr. Bironi says, "If only the principal were tougher on these kids."
- A student says, "If only I worked harder. I must be stupid."
- A teacher says, "If only I were a better teacher. I must be doing something wrong."
- A principal says, "Kids just have to learn to be more responsible."
- A parent says, "If only I were a better parent, Billy would pass."

Again, these strategies can be self- or other-transforming: an individual can blame oneself, or he or she can blame all problems on others. As Freire and Alschuler point out, the rules and roles of the situation often determine the orientation of the strategy used by those confronting a problem. As sociologists make clear, the quality and power of the individual's voice is often deeply affected by his or her role and the social rules of the setting. The cold, harsh wind of an oppressive school climate can easily silence the voices of the disempowered—regardless of the maturity of their understanding or the beauty of their song.

One important aspect of a unilateral institutional strategy is that on a surface level it "works." For example, a school can be run along the lines of this kind of strategy and be orderly, quiet, safe, even productive—usually when a strong teacher or principal asserts an other-transforming strategy to keep things, and people, in line. If an institution is in severe distress, this may be the proper initial course of treatment. However, our view is that this kind of institutional negotiation pattern has severe limitations in the long term. With young children, it provides a safe foundation for further growth (remember our view that young children look to a single authority who is fair, "nice," and safe). But the *sole* use of one-way institutional strategies can also create a hostile overdependence to solve all problems, leaving children without the foundation they need to create positive peer relations (our reciprocal strategies) on their own or with help.

Even more problematic is the counterproductive effect of a one-way institutional pattern of negotiation when dealing with adolescents. Students at this point in development are striving to create for themselves a workable model of reciprocity, and to move toward collaboration. Adolescents look to adults as models of collaboration. When, as teachers, we fail to reciprocate (among ourselves or with our students), adolescents become disconnected; their search for power and relationship turns elsewhere. It often turns into rage or withdrawal, or to affiliation with other groups, including gangs. Adolescents may respond to a one-way institutional strategy by staying in line (a self-transforming strategy) or by active resistance; or they may revert back to a fight or flight strategy—with tragic consequences for all.

Both Freire and Alschuler see the next level of institutional negotiation in collaborative terms—what they call *critical transforming,* and what we call mutual and collaborative. From this approach, problems are named as systems problems; individuals are not blamed, though they are still seen as responsible and as the locus for change. Oppression is now understood as a product of societal relationships and roles that are unequal and unjust: rich–poor, powerful–weak, landlord–peasant, and—by extension in too many schools—principal–teacher, teacher–student. The solution to such problems lies in restructuring the social relationships, not simply in changing the individuals. Therefore, problems must be analyzed and approached in a collaborative way:

As an individual, I can not solve this alone. I need to talk with other teachers, students, and administrators. I need the cooperation of others to resolve this pattern of conflict and play a new game in which we all can win.[27]

We also see collaborative strategies as necessary for creating a supportive school community. From our point of view, they best address the developmental needs of adults and youth in schools; and they plant the seeds for future growth for younger students as well. We hear this kind of strategy when:

- A teacher says, "We need to work as a team to deal with our discipline problems; that includes the kids and parents too."
- A student says, "Kids and teachers don't respect each other, so we need to let all of us say how to make it better."
- A principal creates structures where staff, parents, and students can work collaboratively on shared problems and goals.
- A teacher says, "I want him to do the work but he doesn't want to look stupid, so how can we both get what we want?"
- A student says, "I know not all teachers are unfair, so let's try to work together in this class to make it better for all of us."
- A principal works to make sure that the expectations, goals, and rules of the school are clear, fair, and democratic.

The positive potential of school restructuring and school-based management efforts lies in the promise of a more collaborative, democratic approach to negotiation and decisionmaking. In our view, if school-based management simply transfers power from a superintendent to a principal, the one-way model will be maintained—though localized—and the results will be no better than now. If the structures of collaboration are in place without the institutional and personal commitment to democratic transformation, then school reform will be one more lost promise.

We have come to believe that, in schools, the institutional side of our analysis needs one more level—to mirror the interpersonal side. What we might call a *reciprocal* or *partners* strategy seems to us to be the missing transitional step from a one-way (naive-reforming) to a collaborative (critical-transforming) institutional strategy. Just as children moving toward early adolescence initiate their social relationships by seeking and finding a "best friend" (a partner or buddy), school staff often reach out initially to a single colleague for support, ideas, and consolation. The partners strategy has elements of both a one-way and collaborative approach. For example, sometimes the partnerships are made in response to feelings of anger, isolation, and blame: "If the principal (central administration, other teachers) won't work together, at least WE can support each other—for our own sanity!" At other times, the partner strategy is seen as a first step toward more collaborative approaches: let us start small, by teaming, and then build on that. (The same kind of sequence can be seen when teachers start with peer tutoring and move to cooperative learning models.) We hear partner strategies when:

- Two teachers decide to team-teach or share preparations.
- A student and teacher create a tutoring schedule.
- A principal creates a buddy or mentor system for new teachers.
- Two teachers help each other with behavior problems; for example, making a pact that neither will send students to the office, or just talking strategy with each other.
- Two students are given permission to work together on a project.
- Two principals pair their schools for common staff development.

At this level, the self- and other-transforming orientations begin to converge. One teacher may initiate the partnership, but both must be active and reciprocal members for it to work; each must give a little to get a lot more. Where there was once helplessness (fight or flight) or isolation (one-way), there are now connections, alliances, and a new kind of strength.

VIOLENCE PREVENTION IN MIDDLE SCHOOLS

In thinking about the transition from reciprocal (two-way) to collaborative (third-person) strategies, we can bring to bear current school-based practices in areas of violence prevention and peacemaking. The strategy called peer mediation continues to gain popularity across the nation as a way to reduce violence. Although peer mediation has important limitations (for example, when it stands alone, isolated from other strategies, it will not markedly reduce levels of violence), the process itself—and the strategy for teaching adolescents to become peer mediators—has both practical and theoretical promise.

Peer mediation involves two adolescents (usually age ten and up) working as a team, whose task is to help two other students, called parties or disputants (usually the same age or younger), resolve a problem. Peer mediators must stay neutral and avoid making judgments; they must be active listeners, reflecting and reframing the often angry words of the disputants. Although they can follow a basic script for the process, peer mediators must be able to shape and re-create their strategies in ways that respond to the evolving process between the parties. This mediation process has been described in Fisher, Ury, and Patton's pioneering work *Getting to Yes* (1991),[28] and in subsequent papers dealing with cultural, contextual, and developmental aspects of negotiation.[29]

For our purposes, peer mediation helps us understand the complexity of the shift from reciprocal (two-way) to collaborative (third-party) strategies, because peer mediation involves a combination of both levels. The mediators themselves are challenged to act as third parties. They must step back from the dispute to see it from a neutral and encompassing perspective. They must refrain from unilateral strategies ("All you need to do is apologize.") or even reciprocal/self-reflective ones ("I used to feel angry about that stuff myself, and I just tried to get over it: if I can do it, you can!"). Neither of these strategies will help the disputants themselves come to resolution. They may be appropriate strategies for other contexts (counseling a friend with hurt feelings, separating two younger peers in a playground fight), but they do not work for the peer mediation context.

This aspect of peer mediation, in turn, helps us integrate our understanding of developmental and contextual issues. The difficulty most often faced by peer mediation trainers and supervisors in working with young adolescents is in part developmental: third-person, collaborative strategies are the cutting edge for most young adolescents; these tasks stretch the cognitive and social abilities of most peer mediators, and the mediators' frustration often demonstrates this in graphic and moving ways. At the same time, the struggle to implement peer mediation programs is a cultural and contextual challenge. Our culture reinforces win–lose outcomes and most often rewards those who "take care of number one." Schools, and the adults in them, are practiced in unilateral problem-solving: students look to adults for answers (with respect both to tests and to personal problems), and adults feel obligated to give themto take care of the problem before it escalates. Effective peer mediation programs must go beyond both these developmental and cultural/contextual barriers. Breaking new ground is often difficult.

The cultural issues that emerge from observing peer mediation are both exciting and challenging, and they connect this work to other areas in both research and theory. For example, our anecdotal experience suggests that boys more quickly revert to a counseling or teacher mode. They are more quick to say things like "You just need to forget it and go play a different game" than are female mediators. The young female mediators we have worked with, perhaps because they are more comfortable with relational issues, seem to more easily understand the special "third-arty/active listener" role of the peer mediator. Therefore, for example, they are more likely to use open-ended questions: "Is there anything else you might try?" "Have you thought about walking away as another way to deal with this?"

In addition to these gender-based cultural issues, there are ethnic ones as well. For example, Hawaiian approaches to peer mediation make use of the reciprocal/collaborative shift in a somewhat different way, relying more on nested and complex familial and elder relationships as one source of support for the disputants.[30] But, from a developmental perspective, for the disputants in the mediation the goal is neither tradeoffs nor collaboration, but compromise. Here we begin to see a transitional step between our reciprocal and collaborative levels of negotiation strategies. Compromise is more than a simple trade, because it creates a third solution in which both disputants move toward the middle—both give a little to get more.[31] Because it does not involve the transformation of initial objectives on the part of the two parties, we consider it a reciprocal strategy. Yet, because it opens up a third way—the compromise that is neither a win–lose nor a simple trade—it functions as a transition from reciprocal to collaborative strategies.

An example may help. If two fourth-grade students have a dispute about name-calling, the following outcomes might be seen:

- *Fight or flight:* One hits the other; one walks away and feels threatened.
- *Unilateral:* One bosses the other; one gets a teacher to settle the problem.
- *Reciprocal/trade:* Each promises not to name-call "if the other promises too"; each will apologize if the other will first.
- *Reciprocal/compromise:* Both agree that they like to tease each other but that they will stop for a while, and be sure to tell the other if the teasing bothers them.
- *Collaboration:* Both parties understand that name-calling is not a good thing for anyone, so they will look for other ways to deal with their anger when they feel this way.

This brief exploration of the peer mediation practice suggests both research-able and theoretical areas for future work and helps us understand the limits as well as the benefits of this developmental framework. A developmental frame-work helps us to understand the process by which negotiation strategies develop—both over time and even during the mediation process itself. And it helps us under-stand why compromise is both a challenging and powerful strategy for young adoles-cents. Finally, it helps us to understand that the ways in which compromise takes place—and the meaning it has in the lives of children—shifts as children mature. Five-year-olds compromise, just as do adolescents and adults. But for the adoles-cent mediator, compromise is understood in a way that is very different from the way a five-year-old understands it. Five-year-olds can compromise but not clearly articulate the logic that underlies it.[32] The adolescent sees compromise as one step along a relational path—he or she can reflect on the process itself and place it in a broader interpersonal context. But can he or she understand it in a systemic and sociocultural context, as do teachers?

As practical as this theory may be, we see the limitations of the developmen-tal framework. Understanding the transition from trade to compromise to collabo-ration does not answer questions about how to support this process across cultures or contexts. For example, showing up at 6:30 rather than 6:00 for a meeting may seem appropriate to someone from one culture and yet feel disrespectful for some-one from another. Setting the meeting for 6:15 (as a "compromise") does not resolve this kind of problem. Nor does this theory help us very much in under-standing—or dealing with—conflicts that may arise from issues that are very indi-vidual and personal, rather than cultural and contextual. For example, it does not help us to fully understand how a grudge at school between a boy and a slightly older peer may be difficult for that boy to work through because he (unknowingly) associates the event with his feelings about an older brother who is perceived to get all the attention at home. Finally, it should be clear from this developmental analysis of peer mediation that the practice–theory road is a two-way street. In this case, the practice of peer mediation has led us to rethink not only the variations in mediation skills by gender, race, and ethnicity, but also the levels in our developmental theory—even to the point of studying empirically the possibility of revising the notation and number of theoretical levels that have practical value.

NEXT STEPS: FROM ANALYSIS TO IMPLEMENTATION

Although we believe that our analysis of interpersonal negotiation strategies can be used to help us understand institutional strategies, it is important to point out that the social (and political) factors involved in these analyses become more and more complex as the systems become larger. Therefore, our sociological analysis of institutional levels is even more exploratory than our psychological analysis of children's and early adolescents' interpersonal levels, and our suggestions about its potential for social change remain modest because they have been tested only in our own experience.

As we continue to work on ways to help schools transform themselves, using a developmental model, we face a series of difficult questions. Perhaps the most important ones revolve around one central question: How can we respect and accept the ideas and relationships children and adults bring to the school community, while at the same time seeking to transform them into ideas, relationships, and contexts that are truly collaborative? How can we see children and adults as resources (rather than problems) at the same time as we recognize that real collaboration involves deep change in ourselves and each other—change that is often painful, contentious, confrontational, and unpleasant?

One way to put this question into concrete terms is to return to the voices of children and adolescents. Let us walk back through our analysis, returning in the end to the place where we began: the yellow school bus and its children. First, let us revisit the transition from reciprocal to collaborative strategies: from the buddy to the group. This is an extremely difficult transition in the best of contexts because it involves leaving behind a fundamental part of the dominant North American culture: that every interaction is built around the question "What's in this for me?" In reciprocal or buddy relationships, we give in order to get: "I'll take care of you because I want you to take care of me," or "I'll give in a little on my view of classroom management because I want to get something in return from you." Collaboration and transformation are qualitatively different kinds of interactions from these exchanges because they require that each individual redefine his or her needs in a way that both encompasses and is encompassed by the needs of others. Instead of trades, collaboration requires that we transform our own understanding of the situation, and therefore our own behavior as well, so that it can be integrated with the views of the other.

For example, we can listen to this difference in the words of both students and adults. When a teacher and student negotiate about an academic expectation, they are most likely to use a reciprocal strategy: "You can turn this assignment in late if you promise to turn the rest in on time," or "I expect you to stay after school for me today to finish this, and then we will wipe off the late marks on your progress report." Each person gives to get. In a truly collaborative relationship, this same negotiation might take place, but it will take place with a different meaning in a different context. Real collaboration between this student and teacher will require that each *understands* and *values* the perspective, role, needs, and goals of the other. Real collaboration involves the teacher understanding the student's needs and goals; it requires that the teacher use the power of his or her role and relationship to help the student find his or her own strength, rather than simply to enforce a demand. Real collaboration sounds something like this: "I know it can make you angry when an adult enforces this kind of rule, and I understand that in many ways this work seems irrelevant to what you value right now, but at the same time we need to do this together so you can achieve your goals. How can I help you achieve your goals? How can our work together be a way for you to get what you want out of school?" Real collaboration involves the teacher seeing the student (or in other contexts, his or her peers or principal or parent group) as resources from whom he or she as a teacher can continue to learn.

From a student's developing point of view, real collaboration involves the ability to understand that the teacher's enforcement of expectations and limits has less to do with arbitrary power and more with helping him or her (the student) reach goals that he or she has stated as important. It sounds like this: "I know you're trying to get me to finish this work because you believe I need it, but you need to see that I've got a lot on my mind right now and it's hard to concentrate. I will try, but I need you to understand what's happening for me as well. And even when I act angry or stupid to you, I do understand that you're trying to help me."

Real collaboration involves transformation and often painstaking, if not painful, change. Real collaboration is very difficult, even for adults. For most students, including teens, it will be possible only in fits and starts in contexts where they are particularly competent, feel especially safe, and have developed patterns that provide a foundation for collaboration. This is why the behavior of students and teachers across contexts often seems irreconcilable: the teacher who barks at students and then spends the weekend comforting a colleague who has lost a parent; the student who insists on his or her way in class but then can facilitate inclusion of a shy new schoolmate in the recess basketball game. Roles, relationships, and contexts are powerful determinants of how our competence in understanding negotiation strategies is translated into action.

The question we raised to end this chapter involves creating strategies for personal and institutional change. How do we help individuals and institutions who may be struggling to overcome unilateral patterns of negotiation move toward real collaboration and transformation? How do we help the children, fresh off the yellow school buses, for whom life is a series of win–lose (mostly lose) power struggles characterized by unilateral perspectives and outcomes, create a climate and culture where their needs are met not at the expense of others but in collaboration with others? The move from unilateral to reciprocal, the development of friendships and buddy relationships, is the central ingredient here. It is a step that is often neglected in school settings—a mistake that makes the jump from a unilateral to a collaborative institution seem impossible. The neglect of a buddy system leads to one of two unacceptable outcomes: we either maintain a unilateral system (where those in power hold on to it because it doesn't "work" to share it) or we create a system that *looks* collaborative (with councils and committees and community meetings) but where there are really only multiple sets of unilateral negotiations taking place. In the first case we fail because we did not try. In the second case we fail because we are not doing what we say we are doing. Collaboration, like other educational styles, will then be relegated to the junk heap of education reform before it has ever really been tried.[33]

The next steps in our work must therefore include an honest, and perhaps painful, look at the commitment required to move from fight or flight to collaboration. This commitment must realistically understand the interdisciplinary (and interactive) nature of individual development and sociological change. First, we need to understand that development takes time and is often a question of deconstructing before reconstructing. "She's a jerk," when spoken about a peer, parent, or teacher, may be the first way in which a student (or parent or teacher) says, "I don't like what I'm experiencing here; it's not right or fair and I want to try something different." As educators, our task is to listen to this statement both developmentally and sociologically: to hear it and understand it as a step along a path toward collaboration, and to nurture that forward movement.

Second, we need to understand that both psychology and sociology have much to contribute to our understanding and our strategies. We cannot transform institutions without transforming the individuals who make them up. If we change only institutional structures without respecting, listening to, and helping the individuals within them to develop, we will be left with an empty shell—with a collaborative structure that has no collaboration within it. At the same time, individuals will not risk developmental change—or even reconstruct their ideas, relationships, or behaviors—in institutions they see as dangerous, oppressive, or unsupportive.

Too often the language of collaboration is used to mask what may otherwise be a respectable cooperative venture, or less respectably, unilateral autocracy.[34] When a teacher says, "We're all listening now, aren't we?" the "we" refers to the students. When an administrator says to a colleague, "When you talk with parents, you need to give them the *appearance* of collaboration," both the language and the meaning of collaboration are transformed into a unilateral manipulation. When a school or school systems create group goals that reflect only the institutional needs, expectations, perspectives, or culture, the collaboration, and hence the context for development, is absent.

So, in helping individuals move from fight or flight to collaboration, we must create institutions that model that vision even before it is realized. "We" who want to be allies for developmental change (whether we are teachers, administrators, parents, or peer leaders) must take the risk of looking weak or wishy-washy (self-transforming) when we listen to and share power with those who have less power, or who understand power with only a limited perspective. "We" who want to help individuals and institutions develop must think and act carefully about what constitutes the next step forward, both psychologically (individually) and sociologically (institutionally), even if this step seems to us only a "half-step." These questions will continue to provide the framework for our work as we try both to understand how schools can transform themselves, and to help in the process.

NOTES

1. For the past sixteen years, a number of colleagues at the Judge Baker Children's Center, the Harvard Graduate School of Education, and the Cambridge Public Schools have contributed to the discussions leading to this chapter. We appreciate their generous help and their commitment to children—especially the early contributions of Beth Rendeiro, Gwen Lowenheim, and Sarah Freedman—in our struggle to understand.

2. S. Brion-Meisels, G. Lowenheim, and E. Rendeiro, *Adolescent Decisions* (Boston: Judge Baker Children's Center, 1982); S. Brion-Meisels, G. Lowenheim, and E. Rendeiro, "Student Decision-Making: Improving the School Climate for All Students," in *Programming for Adolescents with Behavioral Disorders,* eds. S. Braaton, R. Rutherford, and C. Kardash (Council for Exceptional Children, 1984).

3. R. L. Selman and L. H. Schultz, *Making a Friend in Youth* (Chicago: University of Chicago Press, 1990).

4. S. Brion-Meisels and M. Jacobs, *Yo! Let's Make Some Decisions* (University of Oklahoma, National Resource Center for Youth Services, 1991); S. Adalbjarnardottir, "Promoting Children's Social Growth in the Schools: An Invention Study," *Journal of Applied Developmental Psychology* 14 (1993): 461–84.

5. S. Brion-Meisels, "Reasoning with Troubled Children: Classroom Meetings as a Forum for Social Thought," *Moral Education Forum* (Winter 1979).

6. R. L. Selman, L. H. Schultz, M. Nakkula, D. Barr, C. Watts, and J. B. Richmond, "Friendship and Fighting: A Development Approach to the Study of Risk and Prevention of Violence," *Development and Psychopathology* 4 (1992): 529–58.

7. S. Brion-Meisels, *Peer Mediation Manual*, unpublished manual (Cambridge: Cambridge Public Schools, 1994).

8. J. Piaget, *The Moral Judgment of the Child* (New York: Free Press, 1965).

9. G. H. Mead, *Mind, Self, and Society* (Chicago: University of Chicago Press, 1936).

10. J. Dewey, *Democracy and Education* (New York: Free Press, 1944).

11. L. Kohlberg, "Moral Stages and Moralization: The Cognitive and Developmental Approach," in *Moral Development and Behavior: Theory, Research and Social Issues,* ed. T. Lickona (New York: Holt, Rinehart and Winston, 1976).

12. C. Gilligan, *In a Different Voice* (Cambridge, Mass.: Harvard University Press, 1982).

13. P. Freire, *The Pedagogy of the Oppressed* (New York: Continuum Press, 1970); P. Freire, *Education for a Critical Consciousness* (New York: Continuum Press, 1973); P. Freire and I. Shor, *A Pedagogy for Liberation* (Gamby, Mass.: Bergin and Garvey, 1987).

14. R.L. Selman, *The Growth of Interpersonal Understanding* (New York: Academic Press, 1980).

15. S. Brion-Meisels and R. L. Selman, "Early Adolescent Development of New Interpersonal Strategies: Understanding and Intervention," *School Psychology Review* 13, No. 3 (1984); Selman and Schultz, *Making a Friend in Youth.*

16. Dewey, *Democracy and Education.*

17. Freire, *The Pedagogy of the Oppressed.*

18. A. Rogers, "Voice, Play, and a Practice of Ordinary Courage, Girls' and Womens' Lives," *Harvard Education Review* 63, No. 3 (1993).

19. D. C. Berliner, " The Nature of Expertise in Teaching," in *Effective and Responsible Teaching: The New Synthesis*, eds. F. Oser, A. Dick, and J. Patry (San Francisco: Jossey-Bass, 1992), 227–48; T. Sizer, *Horace's Compromise: The Dilemma of the American High School* (Boston: Houghton Mifflin, 1985).

20. F. C. Power, A. Higgins, and L. Kohlberg, *Lawrence Kohlberg's Approach to Moral Education* (New York: Columbia University Press, 1989).

21. F. Oser, "Morality in Professional Action: A Discourse Approach for Teaching," in *Effective and Responsible Teaching: The New Synthesis*, eds. F. Oser, A. Dick, and J. Patry (San Francisco: Jossey-Bass, 1992), 109–125.

22. A. Alschuler, *School Discipline: A Socially Literate Solution* (New York: McGraw-Hill, 1980); A. Alschuler, "Creating a World Where It Is Easier To Love: Counseling Applications of Paulo Freire's Theory," *Journal of Counseling and Development* 64 (April 1986).

23. G. Spivack and M. Shure, *The Social Adjustment of Young Children* (San Francisco: Jossey-Bass, 1974).

24. The children on the bus to Manville we spoke of earlier were not so fortunate. Even if they had the idea of reciprocity, it was hard for them to implement it. Even if they saw the other side (self- and other-transforming), it was hard for them to break the old habit of rigidly externalizing or internalizing a situation.

25. Freire, *The Pedagogy of the Oppressed;* Freire, *A Pedagogy for Liberation.*

26. Alschuler, *School Discipline*; Alschuler, "Creating a World Where It Is Easier to Love."

27. Alschuler, *School Discipline.*

28. R. Fisher, W. Ury, and B. Patton, *Getting to Yes: Negotiating Agreement Without Giving In* (New York: Penguin Books USA, 1991).

29. T. Kovac-Cerovic and S. Brion-Meisels, Conflict Resolution and Negotiation in the Cultural-Historical Framework, unpublished manuscript (Cambridge, Mass.: Harvard Graduate School of Education, 1994).

30. M. Meyer, Ho'oponopono—To Set Right: A Hawaiian Peacemaking Process, unpublished manuscript (Cambridge, Mass.: Harvard Graduate School of Education, 1994).

31. P. Walker, personal communication, October 3, 1994.

32. S. Kane, "Shared Meaning on Young Children's Peer Relationship: The Development of Practical Social-Cognitive Know-How," a paper presented to the Twenty-Fourth Annual Symposium of the Jean Piaget Society, Chicago, 1994.

33. R. Barth, *Improving Schools from Within* (San Francisco: Jossey-Bass, 1991).

34. J. Kozol, *Savage Inequalities: Children in America's Schools* (New York: Crown Publishers, 1991).

12

Learning to Care and to Be Cared For

Nel Noddings

Learning to care and to be cared for is a major developmental task. There have always been people—some of them highly successful in other ways—who have never learned to care for human beings. For example, the great philosopher Ludwig Wittgenstein said of himself that he needed love but was unable to give it. However, he did care deeply about human suffering. Today many young people not only fail to develop the capacity to care, but also seem not to know what it means to be cared for. Some confuse coercion with care, some deceive themselves that they are cared for in highly exploitative situations, and some have simply given up hope that anyone will care. James Comer has described the feelings expressed by inner-city high school students toward their teachers: "They don't care!"[1]

It seems obvious that, for most people, being cared for themselves is a prerequisite to caring for others. There are exceptions—some neglected children draw on a heroic inner capacity for care that allows them to care for others despite their own deprivation. Other children who have been well cared for nevertheless fail to develop the ability to care. But it is clear that our society might greatly reduce the widespread violence and alienation so characteristic of life in the United States by caring more effectively for its children. This chapter explores ways in which schools should be involved in helping children learn how to care and be cared for.

A CLIMATE OF VIOLENCE

Many publications today present horrifying statistics on violence in the United States. A recent *Carnegie Quarterly* report states that "nearly one million adolescents between the ages of twelve and nineteen are victims of violent crimes each year."[2] Marion Wright Edelman tells us that an American child is killed every two hours by guns, and thirty more are injured each day.[3] The figures vary some from report to report, but they are never less than appalling.

Sociologists, educators, and others who study the phenomenon of violence blame it variously on poverty, doing poorly in school, lack of social skills, hopelessness with respect to getting a job, the influence of television and movies, and a general failure of morals in society at large. School programs aimed at reducing delinquency sometimes target one of these presumed causes—for example, doing poorly in school—and try to prevent violence by removing the cause. More often, schools provide protection by installing metal detectors, hiring guards, and locking doors and fences. It is estimated that the cost of such protection runs to $300,000 per year per school in New York City.[4]

It is not at all clear that violence prevention programs are working. The Carnegie report suggests that some are, but a recent *Harvard Education Letter* article raises serious doubts about all such special programs.[5] The best course of action seems to be to transform the whole school climate. In a caring climate, in a "full-service school," violence prevention programs may add the skills and knowledge needed to resist particular forms of violence. Basically, however, students must believe that the adults in their schools and communities care about them, that their well-being and growth matter. Kids seem able to survive material poverty, and many can ignore much of the violence in the media—or, at least, keep its effects to a minimum—if they have continuing relationships with adults who obviously care about them.

LEARNING TO BE CARED FOR

One of the essential elements in learning to be cared for is continuity. All children need the security of knowing that particular adults will be a positive presence in their lives over time. They need people who recognize their vulnerability, adults capable of what Sara Ruddick calls "holding": "To hold means to minimize risk and reconcile differences rather than to sharply accentuate them. Holding is a way of seeing with an eye toward maintaining the minimal harmony, material resources, and skills necessary for sustaining a child in safety."[6]

Today, when so many children lack continuity in their family lives and when conditions in the larger society exacerbate the need for continuity, schools must give greater attention to this requirement. Teachers, like good parents, must engage in holding. There is no good reason why teachers and students should not stay together (by mutual consent) for several years rather than for the one year typical of U.S. schools. Elementary schools in much of Europe have operated this way for years. The hard work of getting to know twenty-five or thirty children has little payoff in one short year, but over several years a relationship of trust can be established, and teachers can talk to students in ways that would seem intrusive in shorter periods of time.

Continuity is important not only in the elementary school grades but also at the middle and high school levels. Here students see their teachers only briefly, and teachers often deal with more than 150 students each day. If math teachers, English teachers, and other subject matter specialists could stay with the same groups of students throughout their high school years, caring relationships would have a chance to develop. Many of the teachers whose students report them as "not caring" really do care, but the structure of schooling makes it impossible for the caring to be completed.

If we think seriously about the need of children and youth for care and continuity, we will begin to assess all of our educational policies in its light. Should we bus students in order to achieve the laudable goal of racial integration? Perhaps not. If our efforts are likely to destroy the sense of community and make it virtually impossible for students and teachers to form relationships of care and trust, we must reject busing. However, there may be ways to constitute racially diverse groups that will, by general consent, remain together in a given building even though some of the students must be bused for years, and there may be ways of compensating students and parents who are willing to accept this hardship. The important point here is not the particular solution but the commitment to find methods that will not jeopardize the heart of the educational enterprise—the relationship between teachers and students.

Now, of course, a plan to keep teachers and students together for several years will not help those students who are constantly moved from place to place by their families or social agencies. But the *need* for continuity remains. Under such circumstances, the school has to intensify its efforts to care. It has to work with social agencies to care for the families, and it has to welcome impoverished and often lonely parents (usually mothers) into its community life. (For a powerful description of what can be done when schools, religious communities, and social agencies work together, see Sharon Quint, *Schooling Homeless Children.*[7])

The discussion so far implies a point that is often implicitly (or even explicitly) rejected by many policymakers and educational theorists: schools must be thought of and restructured as multipurpose institutions. They cannot exist merely to provide academic resources. Many policymakers blame the academic failure of today's schools on the fact that schools must "do everything" in this troubled society and, therefore, cannot perform the task for which they were constituted—namely, academic instruction. I think this assessment is dead wrong. Indeed, evidence suggests that schools that accept full-service, family-like obligations also do better academically.[8] If we want children to learn how to be cared for, so that eventually they will have the capacity to care for others, we must make it a primary goal of schools to care for them.

Continuity by itself cannot guarantee caring. By insisting that students and teachers stay together by mutual consent, we reduce the likelihood that continuity will be accompanied by cruelty or neglect. However, a school dedicated to caring for its children must encourage continual discussion of what it means to care. Teachers must have time to talk with one another about the problems they encounter, and students must learn how to detect and appreciate caring.

In a phenomenological analysis of caring, it becomes clear that the consciousness of "carers," in moments of care, is characterized by two features. First, there is a special form of attentiveness that I have called *engrossment*; this form of attention is acutely receptive and is directed at the "cared-for."[9] Second, there is a motivational shift; the motive energy of the carer begins to flow toward the needs of the cared-for. Children who are genuinely cared for learn early to detect these signs in adults around them.

For a relationship—even a very brief encounter—to be caring, the caring must be received. The consciousness of being cared for shows up somehow in the recipient of care—in overt recognition, an attitude of response, increased activity in the direction of an endorsed project, or just a general glow of well-being. This response then becomes part of what the carer receives in new moments of attention.

If this analysis is correct, it is easy to understand why so many students complain that their teachers "don't care." The structure of schooling, especially at the secondary level, makes it impossible for teachers to give individual students the attention caring requires. Furthermore, in attempts to overcome their perceived academic failure, schools have become more and more coercive with respect to what is studied, where, and when. We have already discussed the need for continuity. Because continuity by itself is insufficient to guarantee caring, we must also consider how coercion affects attempts to care.

As teachers and students study the nature of caring and the variety of its manifestations, both may begin to question the degree of coercion in today's schools. Should all students be forced to take certain subjects? Can coercion be a sign of caring? Many teachers insist that the coercion they exercise in assigning and evaluating work is indeed a manifestation of caring. It is "for their own good." Correspondingly, many students assess teachers' caring in a similar way: teachers who care will insist that their students do the work. However, we must press the analysis further.

Alice Miller has written powerfully on the damage that can be done by what she calls "poisonous pedagogy."[10] Such pedagogy is rigid and coercive; it seeks to substitute the will of the teacher for that of the student. Throughout the process of "educating," teachers guilty of poisonous pedagogy take a highly moralistic tone, insisting that what they are demanding is right and that coercion and cruelty, if they are used, are necessary "for the child's own good." Most of us have heard from some teacher or adult, "Some day you'll thank me for this." In all too many cases, we accept this pronouncement (or reject it) without analysis or criticism, and then, as adults, employ the same line of justification in our own relations with the young.

With careful analysis, we can sort out the worst forms of coercion from more innocent ones. Where a task is clearly connected to a purpose espoused by the student, coercion is usually unnecessary. For example, students who move from standard academic classrooms to vocational classes of their own choice often show an amazing increase in motivation. Their teachers do not have to coerce and threaten them. But sometimes, even in their chosen fields, students will resist certain tasks as too boring, tedious, difficult, or apparently peripheral. Then teachers may have to say, "Look, if you want to become a carpenter (mathematician, dental assistant, English major, or whatever), you have to be able to do this." Many times, as a high school mathematics teacher, I had to say to otherwise energetic and highly motivated students, "I know this stuff is tedious, but learning it will make the next material exciting and much easier to tackle." In such situations, we apply a reasonable type of coercion. We say, "You have to *if...*" That "if" is all important. It calls on students to recognize and reassess their own goals. It reminds them that they have come to us with purposes in mind and that they have entrusted us to help them fulfill those purposes.

Notice, again, how important care and trust are in the situations just described. Because we care, we detect the reluctance of our students to engage in the given activity; we allow them to express their reluctance. But we teachers know (or *should* know) that the prescribed task is really important to the goals sought, and so we insist on its completion. If students trust us, they will usually accept such coercion in good spirit.

Not all forms of coercion in school are so innocent. In the form just described, students are allowed to express their feelings, and teachers take those feelings into account as they offer justification for their coercion. Teachers attend to both students' feelings and objective needs. Simone Weil said that the form of attention required by caring or love is very rare:

The love of our neighbor in all its fullness simply means being able to say to him, "What are you going through?" It is a recognition that the sufferer exists, not only as a unit in a collection...but as a man, exactly like us.... This way of looking is first of all attentive. The soul empties itself of all its own contents in order to receive into itself the being it is looking at, just as he is, in all his truth.[11]

A question we must put to ourselves as educators is whether this form of attention must be so rare. Why do we so often fail to develop it and substitute instead an almost self-righteous belief in our own authority and the goodness of our coercive methods? Open discussion and analysis of caring might yield an answer to this question and lead to the abandonment of unhealthy forms of coercion.

What are these forms of coercion that I have labeled not so innocent? Anytime we force children to do something that is not connected to their own purposes, the coercion is at least questionable. Sometimes it is easy to connect our coercion to a child's best interest, despite his or her lack of purpose or understanding. We forcibly keep young children out of the street, for example, and we force them to undergo inoculations and trips to the dentist. Even in these obviously necessary instances, caring adults allow children to express their reluctance and pain, and we sympathize as we coerce. As we force children to go to school, the coercion becomes more questionable, and when we force adolescents to take particular subjects in school, the coercion should definitely be challenged.

Let us consider an example. Authorities in New York City schools recently decided that all students must take algebra and geometry. The New York schools are not alone in this decision; districts all over the country have made similar decisions. In the name of equality, in trying to care equally for all its children, a district decides that all students—regardless of interest, purpose, or capacity—

will take the course of study intended originally for those planning to attend college. The decision is meant "for their own good," but it suggests strongly that their own interests, purposes, and talents are not highly valued—that to be valued themselves, children must conform to a particular model of success. This kind of coercion is at least questionable, and it is the sort that should be the focus of lively discussion among both teachers and students.

Clearly, I am not arguing against all forms of academic requirements. If students have made a well-informed choice to pursue a particular career or goal, it is reasonable to require that they meet the standards of their chosen enterprise. But a requirement that assumes a particular goal without the consent of students verges on poisonous pedagogy. Without listening to what students are going through, what they really want to know, we treat them as units in a collection and force them into a mold they resist.

Many good-willed educators argue that adolescents of high school age are too young to make decisions about their careers paths. "Suppose they change their minds?" is the question repeatedly asked. The well-intentioned implication is that if a student prepares for a trade, he or she may some day regret that he or she did not prepare for college, and so, in just the way we yank a toddler off a busy street, we assign adolescents to algebra and geometry—for their own good. What we overlook in exercising this coercion is that students following their own purposes learn a good deal not only about the subject studied but also about learning itself, and they may also learn something about themselves as learners. If they change their minds (as many people do), they will know better how to pursue their new goals, and they may well have greater confidence in doing so as a result of prior experience. Students forced to take algebra and geometry may or may not "be prepared" for college study. Many will fail (the rate in New York City even before the universal requirement was about 50 percent), some will finish with a credential of sorts but little knowledge, and some will actually be inspired and adopt the goals suggested by their teachers. This last effect could probably be achieved, however, without coercion. In an atmosphere of care and trust, students likely to manifest special academic interests can be informed, enticed, and encouraged.

Care, I would argue, requires attention to individuals, and individuals have different needs and interests. John Dewey argued the case this way:

The general aim translates into the aim of regard for individual differences among children. Nobody can take the principle of consideration of native powers into account without being struck by the fact that these powers differ in different individuals. The difference applies not merely to their intensity, but even more to their quality and arrangement. As Rousseau said, "Each individual is born with a *distinctive* temperament.... We indiscriminately employ children of different bents on the same exercises; their education destroys the special bent and leaves a dull uniformity. Therefore after we have wasted our efforts in stunting the true gifts of nature we see the short-lived and illusory brilliance we have substituted die away, while the natural abilities we have crushed do not revive."[12]

The result of academic coercion, even the best-intentioned coercion, is often frustration and a pervasive feeling of "being dumb."[13] These feelings play a role in triggering violence. If a youth's own legitimate interests and talents are not admired and encouraged, he or she may never really learn what it means to be cared for. All care then seems to be contingent and associated with psychological or physical coercion. Young men try to coerce sex from young women by saying, "If you really cared about me..."; women remain in abusive situations because they feel it is their duty to care, or because they have no sense of what it means to care for themselves; evangelical advocates of religion try to force others to accept their beliefs in the name of caring for their souls. Readers can probably offer many more examples. Certainly, these aberrations of care are not entirely caused by the school's coercive curriculum, but that coercion plays a part in the misunderstandings that arise, and it leads also to a waste of real talent and energy.

Teachers and students must be given time to discuss these matters. Whether they agree with my analysis of care and coercion is not so important as their addressing the issues and reflecting on them. Indeed, from the perspective taken here, teachers and students who know what it means to be cared for will resist coercive instruction or care as well as other topics, but they may respond enthusiastically to an invitation to join in the discussion.

LEARNING TO CARE

When we look at the world as it is today, we might well wonder why learning to care is not at the heart of the school curriculum. Humankind has not yet learned how to avoid war, nor even to resist the most familiar forms of psychological manipulation that help make war possible. Perhaps worse, we have not learned to give and receive the joy and emotional support that should be part of family life. Of course, these forms of learning—all forms of learning to care—are difficult. May Sarton has the narrator of one of her novels say: "Family life! The United Nations is child's play compared to the tugs and splits and need to understand and forgive in any family. That's the truth, I am sure, but, like every hard truth, we all try to pretend it isn't true."[14]

Perhaps in keeping with this need to pretend, despite the fact that such a great proportion of today's violence takes place in families, schools virtually ignore family life and learning to care for intimate others. When schools do offer courses on the subject, the courses are considered frills, nonacademic additions to the curriculum. Completing such courses counts nothing toward college entrance.

Learning to care is not a sequential process like, say, learning mathematics. (For that matter, although schools organize the mathematics curriculum sequentially, learning math may not be a sequential process either.) It is probably true that one must learn how to be cared for and to care for oneself before learning to care for others, but the process is not linear. As we begin to care for others, we learn more about what it means to be cared for. As we learn how to care for ourselves, we become more discerning in assessing the efforts of others to care. Sarton describes an elderly woman, Jane, who has learned in old age to accept care gracefully. Her narrator says:

I have learned so much from Jane over the years, and the last thing is this seraphic way she has of accepting dependence—it can't have been easy for a woman of her spirit. How does she do it? She floats—why do I say that? I mean she lets herself be carried by Hannah, yet never becomes a baby, the baby Hannah wants her to be. It takes wisdom to be able to do that with grace.[15]

Children today need desperately to know how to care for themselves and for intimate others. I think it would be hard to exaggerate the mistakes schools are making in this domain. Instead of helping students to identify and develop their own talents, schools try, quixotically, to prepare everyone for college. Instead of tackling the subject of human life and love holistically, schools respond to various crises with drug education, sex education, and violence prevention courses. Religious and existential questions are rarely discussed, and English teachers debate whether literature should be taught for itself (complete with analysis), for its contribution to competence in reading and writing, or for its great existential messages. Some actively resist the last. Even philosophy teachers often insist that they do not intend to produce better people by teaching ethics. "I'm not a moral educator," says the philosopher, "I teach philosophy." But cannot one teach philosophy or literature with the clear understanding that one's aim is to help students search for wisdom and for better moral selves? And cannot this be done without imposing a particular view of morality on one's students?

It is not reasonable to suppose that the school curriculum will be entirely reorganized around themes of care in the near future. But such themes can be introduced into traditional classes with salutary effects. The subject itself may become of interest to a greater number of students, connections can be made with other subjects, and students will feel encouraged to explore the eternal questions.

The question "Who am I?" must be encouraged, and as students explore their own interests and capacities they should be advised and supported. It is not enough to take a few aptitude tests (which are then ignored by the school placement process), browse through computerized descriptions of occupations, and have an annual talk with a career counselor—although some unlucky students do not get even this much help.[16] Someone has to care about the individual kid who is asking the question; someone has to be proud of the answer that is emerging.

But, in addition to the personal connection, self-knowledge can be encouraged in academic classrooms. For example, religious and existential questions can be discussed in mathematics and science classes. Through biographical and historical accounts, students can learn how great mathematicians approached such questions. Mathematics students can be asked to analyze Descartes's proof of the existence of God. If the proof fails, does this mean that God does not exist? They should hear about Pascal's alternative approach, too. Pascal, one of the founders of probability and gaming theory, said that we should wager on God's existence: If we bet that God exists and live our lives accordingly, and God does exist, what do we stand to gain? If God does not exist, what have we lost? Stories of this kind can enrich ordinary math classes and help students feel less alone in their existential struggles.[17] The great mathematicians become more human as we hear them explore questions about God's existence, the problem of evil,[18] the Bible's status as historical record,[19] and the nature of the infinite.[20]

Teachers at a given grade level can work together to plan units of study that are intellectually rich, interdisciplinary, and full of potential for personal meaning. For example, while a math teacher shares Leibniz's study of God and evil, an English teacher might read parts of the Book of Job with the students. A social studies teacher might help students explore historical views of evil and how people in various times understood and tried to cope with it. A science teacher might discuss ways in which Social Darwinism replaced earlier views of evil while retaining the basic idea that the poor somehow deserved their poverty. Together, the team of teachers might guide students through such works as Harold Kushner's *When Bad Things Happen to Good People*[21] and Elie Wiesel's *Night*.[22]

For students immersed in a violent society, the search for meaning is especially important. Just to engage in such a search is a sign of caring for one's self. Teachers who are familiar with the music and films that young people patronize can relate that material to the academically acceptable topics I have suggested. At present, however, we do not use even the academic material that is available. How many students ever discuss existential questions in mathematics or science classes?

In learning to care for oneself, self-image and self-esteem are, of course, important. Current educational emphasis on self-esteem has become the object of both caricature (in *Doonesbury*, for example) and serious criticism. Critics are right to question some of the strategies educators use to raise self-esteem, but they are wrong to ridicule its importance. Again, educators have too often gone at problems of self-esteem directly, much as they have approached problems of drugs, alcohol, sex, and violence. A wiser approach recognizes that a measure of self-knowledge is necessary for self-esteem and that there are features to deplore as well as to admire in most selves.

Adolescents need to understand how they seek self-esteem. Why do so many young men act tough? Why do so many young women permit themselves to be abused? Serious study of gender differences in self-image, and how these differences are exaggerated and used by the media, should be part of the secondary curriculum. For example, students might profitably discuss the four basic rules of American manhood as described by Michael Kimmel (attributed by Kimmel to Robert Brannon):

(1) No Sissy Stuff: Men never do anything that even remotely suggests femininity. Manhood is a relentless repudiation and devaluation of the feminine. (2) Be a Big Wheel: Manhood is measured by power, wealth, and success. Whoever has the most toys when he dies, wins. (3) Be a Sturdy Oak: Manhood depends on emotional reserve. Dependability in a crisis requires that men not reveal their feelings. (4) Give 'em Hell: Exude an aura of manly daring and aggression. Go for it. Take risks.[23]

A unit of study that begins with this paragraph might be followed by books, films, and personal accounts that describe very different pictures of manhood—some that illustrate the rules Kimmel criticizes and still others that simplify a modification of the rules.

Both girls and boys need to understand the social construction of femininity, too. Several of the female writers in the volume containing Kimmel's chapter emphasize the need for women to develop a vocabulary of resistance. Louise Erdrich puts the point this way:

To hold the *no* in my mouth like a gold coin, something valued, something possible. To teach the *no* to our own daughters. To value their *no* more than their compliant yes. To celebrate *no*. To hold the word *no* in your fist and refuse to give it up. To support the boy who says *no* to violence, the girl who will not be violated, the woman who says *no, no, no. I will not*.[24]

bell hooks and Ntozake Shange express the point in ways particularly powerful for black youth. hooks refers to "the dick thing"—the idea celebrated in parts of black culture that to prove his manhood a man has "to rape and assault black women and brag about it."[25] She reminds black women that they play a role in maintaining this attitude when they favor brothers who fit the image. Shange tells a wonderful story in which "mandy" teaches "ezra" a thing or two about resistance and the language of consent. Fighting ezra off both physically and verbally, resisting her own contradictory physical desire, mandy sets her house in order. At the end of the story, "there are no more assumptions in the house."[26]

The pursuit of self-knowledge—knowledge of the self as an individual, as a male or female, as a member of a race and community, as part of a particular age group—blends easily into a study of relations with others. Part of learning to care for one's self is a concomitant learning to care for others.

Schools can encourage this learning by providing a climate of care and trust as described earlier. Within that climate, teachers can use pedagogical strategies such as cooperative learning, noncompetitive grading, and service learning. But, again, the strategies by themselves will not accomplish the learning we seek. The strategies have to be part of a dedicated drive to produce caring, competent, loving, and lovable people.

This dedicated drive should guide everything we do in schools. As we have seen, it should influence the structure of schooling by maintaining continuity of people and place; it should suggest an emphasis on teacher–student relationships; it should affect how parents and other community members are received in classrooms; and it should transform the curriculum.

How might the curriculum be transformed? We have already considered topics that might be introduced to aid students in their search for self–knowledge. As we assist them in learning to care for others, further topics may be studied. I will briefly consider three such topics here.

Consider *love*. Here is a topic that fascinates most teenagers, and teachers could construct wonderful interdisciplinary units on it. For those who worry about intellectual rigor, it may be important to include the poetry of the Brownings, *Romeo and Juliet, The Scarlet Letter, Wuthering Heights*, the stories of John and Abigail

Adams and Marie and Pierre Curie, and perhaps even *The Mill on the Floss*. Students could also see great films and listen to Berlioz's *Romeo and Juliet*, Wagner's *Tristan and Isolde,* Bernstein's *West Side Story*, and Gershwin's *Porgy and Bess*. Students could also study patterns of love and marriage in different times and places. The topic can be as intellectually rich as we care to make it, but the important point from the perspective of our dedicated purpose is that it is existentially rich. It connects to our lived experience and not just our conceptual experience.

A valuable exercise for teachers planning such a unit is to create a network of ideas and resources connecting the present topic, love, with another, say, violence, since that is our interest here. How are love and violence connected in *Romeo and Juliet*? Concepts that might emerge include hatred, feuds, honor, despair, suicide, and regret, and each of these concepts can be filled out with further reading and study. How are "feuds" and "honor" connected to violence? If the school in which the teachers work has gangs, a new unit may emerge rapidly. Similarly, if there have been suicides or attempted suicides, planning may turn in that direction. *The Scarlet Letter* might suggest adultery, compassion (and lack of it), fidelity, and community prejudice. *Wuthering Heights* might produce ambition, jealousy, passion, gratitude, loneliness, and mental health. As teachers discuss the possibilities, they may be amazed at what can be contributed by math and science teachers who are usually left out of such units.

Friendship is another topic that might be used to build an interdisciplinary unit. What does it mean to be a friend? How is friendship connected to violence? What do we owe our friends? This unit might begin with a newspaper story—one in which some act of violence was committed in the name of friendship, or in which an act of violence was covered up to protect a friend. In addition to the moral dilemmas inherent in such stories, students might want to discuss friendships involving people of different races, ages, and sexes.

Again, the unit can be academically, as well as practically, rich. It can include a study of Aristotle's analysis of friendship. Especially important in that analysis is Aristotle's claim that friends help one another to be better people. What might that mean for a boy who thinks he must cover up a friend's criminal activity? What might it mean for a girl who tolerates the abusive behavior of her boyfriend?

Literature can, once again, make a great contribution. Friends are usually drawn from a group like oneself, but occasionally incongruous friendships are formed. Consider Huckleberry Finn and the slave, Jim; Miss Celie and Shug in Alice Walker's *The Color Purple*; Lenny and George in Steinbeck's *Of Mice and Men*; Jane and Maudie in Lessing's *The Diaries of Jane Somers*. What characterizes each of these friendships? Can friendship be part of a personal quest for fulfillment? When might personal interest destroy a friendship?

A book like John Knowles' *A Separate Peace* can help students understand the forms of violence associated with friendship. Envy and misunderstanding lead the unhappy protagonist, Gene, to suppose that his friend, Finny, has the same competitive attitude that he has. In reality, Finny is innocent of such longings. What Gene learns from the tragic events that follow is that human misunderstanding contributes to violence at every level of human activity. Even war between nations can be traced to misunderstanding, to the narrow drawing of lines between people who perceive one another as reprehensibly different, to the mistaken notion that oneself and one's friends must be protected from these others. As an adult looking back on the events of his school years, Gene realizes that his schoolmates saw enemies and rivals everywhere:

All of them, all except Phineas [Finny], constructed at infinite cost to themselves these Maginot Lines against this enemy they thought they saw across the frontier, this enemy who never attacked that way—if he ever attacked at all; if he was indeed the enemy.[27]

Finally, in transforming the curriculum toward one that will reduce violence and support a climate of trust and care, much more attention should be given to *women's traditions*. Teachers can draw effectively on women's traditions of care without claiming that women are inherently more caring than men or that all women are, by nature, inclined to care. Not all women have participated in the care tradition—any more than all men have participated in the military tradition. But there is such a tradition, and many beautiful examples can be drawn from it.

The tradition is illustrated in the character of Mrs. Shelby in Harriet Beecher Stowe's *Uncle Tom's Cabin*. Mrs. Shelby argues against her slaveholder husband that Uncle Tom and little Harry should not be sold. But she does not plead on the basis of an abstract argument in favor of abolition (which her husband is prepared to counter with a logical argument *against* abolition). Rather, she argues on the grounds of love and compassion. A tradition of care and compassion forbids an act that will separate mother and child, father and family. The tradition is illustrated not only in Stowe's characters, but also in her own life and in the work of her sister, Catherine Beecher.

The tradition we are talking about here has not been laid out comprehensively as an argument, and there is some question whether it should be. However, it is vividly revealed in the life of Jane Addams; in the novels of Virginia Woolf, Mary Gordon, Doris Lessing, Alice Walker, and Toni Morrison; and in biographical accounts such as Anne Morrow Lindbergh's *Gift from the Sea*. Pearl Buck's biography of her mother (*The Exile*) illustrates it again and again; in it we see an articulated Christian tradition and an unarticulated women's tradition sometimes working together in charity, sometimes in great conflict where the first insists on adherence to rules of law and the second insists on responding more directly to human need. The second steadfastly opposes violence of all kinds, although its proponents occasionally fail—as all people do—to sustain their commitment. If we are serious in our own commitment to reduce violence and to help students learn how to care and be cared for, women's traditions of care must receive a prominent place in the school curriculum).[28]

CONCLUSION

Violence has many roots, but it seems obvious that people who feel cared for and who have learned to care for others will be less likely to engage in violent acts. I have argued here that the first obligation of schools is to make care manifest in their structure, relationships, and curriculum. I have also argued that an emphasis on producing caring, competent, loving, and lovable people need not reduce the intellectual dimension of the curriculum. On the contrary, such emphasis should enrich the lives of both students and teachers intellectually, morally, and spiritually. As we approach the twenty-first century, we must make human relations the first priority of our intellectual and moral efforts. Schools can contribute by helping students learn how to care and be cared for.

NOTES

1. J. P. Comer, "Is 'Parenting' Essential to Good Teaching?," *NEA Today* 6 (1988): 34–40.

2. F. Hechinger, "Saving Youth from Violence," *Carnegie Quarterly,* 39, No. 1 (1994): 2–15.

3. M. Wright Edelman, "Cease Fire! Stopping the Gun War Against Children in the United States," *Religious Education* (1994).

4. Hechinger, "Saving Youth from Violence."

5. M. Posner, "Research Raises Troubling Questions about Violence Prevention Programs," *Harvard Education Letter* 10, No. 3 (1994): 1–4.

6. S. Ruddick, *Maternal Thinking: Towards a Politics of Peace* (Boston: Beacon Press, 1989), 78–79.

7. S. Quint, *Schooling Homeless Children* (New York: Teachers College Press, 1994).

8. Posner, "Research Raises Troubling Questions"; Quint, *Schooling Homeless Children.*

9. N. Noddings, *Caring: A Feminine Approach to Ethics and Moral Education* (Berkeley: University of California Press, 1984).

10. A. Miller, *For Your Own Good,* translated by Hildegarde and Hunter Hannun (New York: Farrar, Straus, and Giroux, 1983).

11. S. Weil, "Reflections on the Right Use of School Studies with a View to the Love of God," in *Simone Weil Reader,* ed. George A. Panichas (Mt. Kisco, N.Y.: Moyer Bell Ltd., 1977), 44–52.

12. J. Dewey, *Democracy and Education* (New York: Macmillan, 1916), 116.

13. Posner, "Research Raises Troubling Questions."

14. M. Sarton, *Kinds of Love* (New York: W. W. Norton, 1970), 49.

15. Ibid., 50.

16. J. Kozol, *Savage Inequalities: Children in America's Schools* (New York: Crown, 1991).

17. N. Noddings, *The Challenge to Care in Schools* (New York: Teachers College Press, 1992).

18. Leibniz, "Theodicy," in *The Whys of a Philosophical Scrivener,* ed. Martin Gardner (New York: Quill, 1983).

19. See Newton in *Men of Mathematics,* ed. E. T. Bell (New York: Simon and Schuster, 1965/1937).

20. R. Rucker, *Infinity and the Mind* (New York: Boston: Birkhauser, 1982).

21. H. Kushner, *When Bad Things Happen to Good People* (New York: Schocken Books, 1981).

22. E. Wiesel, *Night*, translated by Stella Rodway (New York: Hill and Wang, 1960).

23. M. Kimmel, "Clarence, William, Iron Mike, Tailhook, Senator Packwood, Spur Posse, Magic... and Us," in *Transforming a Rape Culture,* eds. E. Buchwald, P. R. Fletcher, and M. Roth (Minneapolis, Minn.: Milkweed Editions, 1993), 123.

24. L. Erdrich, "The Veils," in *Transforming a Rape Culture,* eds. E. Buchwald, P. R. Fletcher, and M. Roth (Minneapolis, Minn.: Milkweed Editions, 1993), 338.

25. b. hooks, "Seduced by Violence No More," in *Transforming a Rape Culture,* eds. E. Buchwald, P. R. Fletcher, and M. Roth (Minneapolis, Minn.: Milkweed Editions, 1993), 353.

26. N. Shange, "Comin' to Terms," in *Transforming a Rape Culture,* eds. E. Buchwald, P. R. Fletcher, and M. Roth (Minneapolis, Minn.: Milkweed Editions, 1993), 373.

27 J. Knowles, *A Separate Peace* (New York: Boston Books, 1975), 196.

28. J. R. Martin, *The Schoolhome: Rethinking Schools for Changing Families* (Cambridge, Mass.: Harvard University Press, 1992).

13

Victims of Violence: Helping Kids Cope

Melba F. Coleman

One November morning at a large elementary school in the Los Angeles Unified School District (enrollment 1,100–plus), children kept coming into the office and reporting that they had seen a dead body on the way to school. As this story kept surfacing, the principal decided that she had better investigate the situation. As it turned out, the story was indeed true, and the principal's actions led to a whole chain of events that eventually led to the creation of a grief and loss counseling program entitled *Children Grieve, Too.* This program is described later in this chapter.

This scenario opens up a whole range of questions that relate to violence and raises the possibility of an array of solutions for schools to help children, the innocent victims of violence, cope. This chapter addresses the following questions:

- How bad is the problem of violence as it relates to children?
- What kinds of violence do children encounter?
- How are children affected by violence?
- What factors affect children's response to violence?
- What can schools do to help children cope?

THE SCOPE OF THE PROBLEM

Violence is a pervasive force in American society; it appears to be an integral part of its fabric. We glorify the "Lone Ranger" character, the "make my day" mentality, and the vigilante attitude. Institutions that were once considered safe havens have become battlegrounds where violence flourishes: hospitals, churches, and, yes, schools. No segment of our population suffers more from this culture of violence than our children and youth.

Violence is an equal opportunity tragedy. It cuts across socioeconomic and ethnic lines; it affects men, women, and children of all religions and races. It is not limited to the poor inner-city neighborhoods, but invades suburban as well as rural

America. Children all over this country are suffering from the pain and trauma of unresolved grief. The National Childhood Grief Institute reports these facts:

> Ninety percent of children in chemical dependency programs have lost a parent by death or divorce.
> One-half million children in the United States lose one or both parents by death before the age of fifteen.
> Over thirty thousand children per year lose a sibling through death.
> More than 916,000 children are being raised by widowed parents.[1]

Further evidence of the perils facing America's children comes from the Children's Defense Fund. It reports that every day in America:

- 13 children die from guns.
- 2,868 babies are born into poverty.
- 101 babies die before their first birthday.
- 7,945 children are reported abused or neglected.
- 3 children die from abuse.
- 2,768 teens become pregnant.
- 2,255 students drop out of school.
- 100,000 children are homeless.[2]

Despite the staggering statistics, most of these children are left to navigate the stages of grief on their own. Because death, grief, and loss are dealt with very poorly by most adults in Western cultures, not much is done to help children get over their sense of grief and loss. Therefore, there is no opportunity for them to get on with their lives in a "normal" fashion. In many cases, children are being victimized again and again by the lingering effects of tragic events that were never dealt with. Subsequent events can cause them to relive the original incident. For example, children in housing projects like the one described by Alex Kotlowitz in his book *There Are No Children Here* (1991) live with the ever-present sounds of gunfire, police sirens, helicopters, and other sounds of urban violence on a daily basis.[3] Garbarino states that in Chicago "the rate of 'serious assault' increased 400 percent from 1974 to 1991. Most of this violence takes place in poor, inner-city neighborhoods and public housing projects."[4]

THE FACES OF VIOLENCE

Violence has many faces; it is multifaceted and complex. It is a societal, community-based, and school-based problem as well as a personal and interpersonal concern.

Societal Violence

Daniel Patrick Moynihan suggested in an *American Educator* article that society must have a certain number of deviants; however, when the "amount of deviant behavior in American society has increased beyond the levels the community can 'afford to recognize'...we raise the 'normal' level in categories where behavior is now abnormal by any earlier standard." He goes on to say that, "as a society, we have become accustomed to alarming levels of crime and destructive behavior," and that we have "redefined" deviancy so as to "exempt much conduct previously stigmatized, and also quietly raising the 'normal' level in categories where behavior is now abnormal by an earlier standard."[5] Society, therefore, "normalizes" increasingly higher levels of violence so that our collective psyche becomes desensitized. Murder and mayhem that previously would have shocked and dismayed us is shrugged off, especially if it does not touch our lives.

Community-Based Violence

Toby offers one explanation for community violence. He posits that the "circumstances of life...the lack of jobs that pay a living wage, the stigma of race, the fallout from rampant drug use and drug trafficking, and the resulting alienation and lack of hope for the future" breed violence in many communities. He goes on to describe the conditions under which aggressive behavior is born, nurtured, and thrives, especially where children and youth are concerned. He offers a notion of the "code of the street," in which youth, especially males, engage in whatever activity is necessary in order to gain and keep "respect." The so-called street people define respect in this context as being "treated right" and with appropriate deference. Respect is gained by fighting back, solving interpersonal problems by hitting, taking valued property from others, and prevailing over peers by force and intimidation.

By contrast, Toby describes the "decent" people in these communities as those who:

tend to accept mainstream values more fully and attempt to instill them in their children. Whether married couples with children or single-parent (usually female) households, they are generally "working poor" and tend to be better off financially than their street-oriented neighbors. They value hard work and self-reliance and are willing to sacrifice for their children. Because they have a certain amount of faith in mainstream society, they harbor hopes for a better future for their children, if not for themselves.

Toby would argue that the degree to which a youngster internalizes and lives by either the "code of the street" or the "code of the decent people" determines the degree to which violence will be used as a problem-solving strategy.[6]

Garbarino describes community violence as it relates to children as follows:

[Y]oung children are enmeshed in this problem of community violence in many ways. They are witnesses to it: by age five, most children have had first-hand encounters with shootings. By adolescence, most have witnessed stabbings and shootings, and one-third have witnessed a homicide. Many of these children are also witnesses to or victims of domestic violence: rates of child abuse are substantially higher in these poor, inner-city communities than in other areas. And most of these children know, and in many cases depend upon, the perpetrators of community violence: gang members are also their brothers, their cousins and uncles, their fathers, or their mothers' boyfriends. "Them" is "us" for many inner-city children. These youngsters are in and of the community; the "problem" of community violence is the fabric of their lives. Victimization and loss are rampant. Homicide is the leading cause of death for young males in these communities.[7]

School-Based Violence

While riding in my car one afternoon, the bumper sticker on a truck in front of me caught my attention. It read, *"MY KID CAN BEAT UP YOUR HONOR STUDENT."* This sickening statement and the attitude behind it is all too indicative of the environment in which many children find themselves in today's schools. School crime statistics reported by the California Department of Education from July 1, 1987 through June 30, 1988 show the following:

- There were 4.4 million students in California public schools.
- The dollar loss to school districts as a result of a variety of property crimes was reported to be $24,471,680. (Nearly one-half of this dollar loss was the result of arson.)
- A total of 162,061 school crimes were reported. This figure most likely underrepresents the actual number of school crimes.
- Reported incidents of vandalism totaled 41,331.
- Incidents of assault, attack, or menace totaled 59,973.
- There were 789 reported incidences of handgun possession.
- (This figure represents a 28 percent increase from the previous year.)
- There were seven reported homicides involving student victims that occurred on public school campuses or on the route between home and school.[8]

Since these figures were compiled, the level of violence in schools has increased dramatically. For example, 13 percent of the students who responded to the 1993 Metropolitan Life Survey regarding Violence in America's Public Schools indicated that they have carried a weapon to school:

Twenty-two percent of boys and young men, compared to 4% of girls and young women, claim to have carried a weapon to school at some time. Nearly one-fourth (23%) of America's public school students say they have been the victim of an act of violence in or around school. Boys and young men are twice as likely (30%) as girls and young women (16%) to have been victims of violent acts that occurred in or around school.[9]

The causes of school violence are varied. Toby identifies "disorder" as a cause of everyday school violence:

What school disorder means in concrete terms is that one or both of two departures from normality exists: A significant proportion of students do not seem to recognize the legitimacy of the rules governing the school's operation and therefore violate them frequently; and/or a significant proportion of students defy the authority of teachers and other staff members charged with enforcing the rules.[10]

According to the Metropolitan Life Survey, the following factors contribute to violence in schools:

* Lack of parental supervision at home.
* Lack of family involvement with the school.
* Exposure to violence in the mass media.
* Boredom or lack of motivation to learn.
* Gang or group membership, or peer group pressure.
* Poverty.
* The sudent's achievement level.
* The student's racial or ethnic background.
* Involvement with drugs or alcohol.
* Overcrowding or lack of supervision in school.[11]

Personal and Interpersonal Violence

Given the level of violence in society, the community, and schools, it is inevitable that the amount and kinds of interpersonal violence would increase. Some examples of interpersonal violence in schools are verbal insults; threats to students; threats to teachers; pushing, shoving, grabbing, or slapping; kicking, biting, or hitting someone with a fist; threatening someone with a knife or gun; using knives or firing guns; and stealing.[12]

THE EFFECTS OF VIOLENCE ON CHILDREN

The groups that are suffering the most from the rampant violence in our society are children and youth. The physical, psychological, and emotional damage that they endure contributes to the repetition of the cycle of violence. Garbarino observes that children's feelings about community violence are complex.[13] These feelings range from fear and terror to admiration and excitement. Not only do these youngsters suffer from the effects of violence in the short run, but also they and society suffer the long-term effects in terms of the cycle of antisocial and deviant behavior in which these youngsters may engage. The cycle of violence is perpetuated by children who were once victims of violence. These are the students who are disruptive and aggressive, and who fight, destroy property, and intimidate other students in the schools. Maintaining discipline and order is a major problem in schools where societal, community, school, or interpersonal violence is prevalent.

Another serious residual effect of violence is unrelieved grief in children. According to Kubler-Ross, the "normal" stages of grieving are denial, anger, bargaining, depression, acceptance, and hope.[14] Crenshaw identifies seven tasks of mourning:

Task 1:   Acknowledge the Reality of the Loss
Task 2:   Identify and Express the Emotions of Grief

Task 3:   Commemorate the Loss
Task 4:   Acknowledge Ambivalence
Task 5:   Resolve the Ambivalence
Task 6:   Let Go
Task 7:   Move On[15]

Grief may manifest itself in physical, social, and emotional responses. Unresolved grief may have the effect of prolonging these patterns of behavior.[16] Physiological responses may include frequent uncontrollable crying; sleep disturbances, insomnia, nightmares, fear of sleeping alone; bedwetting and other bowel and bladder problems; increased heart rate; thumbsucking; breathing problems, shortness of breath, rapid breathing; increase in colds, ear infections, allergic reactions; impaired concentration and hearing; increased adrenaline flow; high blood pressure; deep and frequent sighing; gastrointestinal upset; feelings of exhaustion; restlessness; general illness, aches, and pains; and headaches.

Social responses that may occur include withdrawal from "normal activities"; mechanical, numb, "flat" responses; staring into space; radical change in interpersonal relationships; concern for other victims and their families; desire for revenge; clinging to parents; decrease in talking; change in school achievement, over- or underachievement.

Emotional reactions may include general feeling of fear and anxiety; extreme emotional reactions such as anger, depression, sadness, guilt, shame, detachment; helplessness and passivity; unprovoked violence and overactivity; compulsive, ritualistic, robotlike behavior; antisocial behavior; drug and alcohol abuse; temper tantrums; adultlike behavior; reckless, risk-taking behavior; retelling and replaying of the traumatic event; feeling disturbed, confused, and frightened by the grief responses; and fear of ghosts.

In addition to these responses, researchers have recently uncovered evidence that children who live with ongoing community violence may also suffer from post-traumatic stress disorder (PTSD).[17] Children who live in violent communities are particularly at risk of developing PTSD. The American Psychiatric Association defines PTSD symptoms as follows:

1. The person has experienced an event that is outside the range of usual human experience and that would be markedly distressing to almost anyone.
2. The traumatic event is persistently reexperienced in dreams, flashbacks, intrusive memories, or distress when confronted with reminders of the event.
3. The person becomes "desensitized" by avoiding thoughts or feelings associated with the trauma, activities or situations that arouse recollections of the trauma, or inability to accurately remember aspects of the trauma. The person may also experience loss of interest in daily activities, feelings of detachment from others, and a sense of a foreshortened future.
4. Persistent symptoms of increased arousal (not present before the trauma), as indicated by at least two of the following:
      a. difficulty falling or staying asleep

b. irritability or outbursts of anger
c. difficulty concentrating
d. hypervigilance
e. exaggerated startle response
f. physiologic reactivity upon exposure to events that resemble
   an aspect of the traumatic event
5.   Duration of the disturbance (symptoms 2–4) of at least one month.[18]

Many of our students who live in urban areas suffer from PTSD simply by virtue of where they live. This fact alone is indicative of the magnitude of the problem, because the largest percentage of America's students are enrolled in urban schools.

In addition, a large percentage of these students live in poverty and have limited access to mental health services. Therefore, the burden of helping these children to heal falls on the classroom teacher.

FACTORS THAT AFFECT CHILDREN'S RESPONSE TO VIOLENCE

In spite of what many adults think, *children do grieve*. The manner in which they grieve, however, is different from the way in which adults grieve. The grief and recovery process is profoundly affected by a child's age and developmental level, gender, poverty, and cultural factors such as family, community, and social context.

Age and Developmental Level

The way in which children react to grief, loss, and separation is determined largely by their age and developmental level. Many researchers start with age two and describe children's reactions to grief in terms of Piaget's stages of cognitive development.[19] In the book *Children Grieve, Too*, the effects of age and developmental levels on the grief response are described as follows:[20]

Ages Two to Five. Children at this age grieve intermittently. They may grieve for a while, play "normally," and then return to grieving. Observers of their behavior may assume, therefore, that they are not grieving or that they have "gotten over" the tragedy.

Because children at this age level may not fully understand the permanence of death, they may ask inappropriate questions or accept the news of death in a matter-of-fact manner. They may ask repeatedly where the deceased has gone and even when they will return.

Anger and sadness are frequent emotions experienced by youngsters in this age group. Their world has suddenly become insecure and unpredictable, and they do not fully understand why. It is important, therefore, to explain death in concrete terms to these children, taking care to avoid euphemisms such as "She has gone to sleep." It is also critical that children's play be used as a way of expressing their feelings.

Ages Five to Eight. To children in this age group, death is more understandable. They know that death is final and irreversible. They may also feel guilty that they could not do anything to stop the death. These children may attempt to hide their feelings in order not to be labeled "babyish." Expressions of grief may be done in private rather than in public. As a result, adults may think the child is unaffected by the death.

Because these children may not have opportunities to express their feelings, it is important to let them know that it is O.K. to have these feelings, and to provide them with safe, supportive environments in which to express these feelings. Art work is one of the ways in which children may express what they cannot say.

Ages Eight to Twelve. Independence and coping may be part of a facade adopted by children in this age group to convince observers that they can handle the tragedy in an adultlike manner. However, they may feel helpless and exhibit evidence of longing and yearning. Although they know that death is permanent and irreversible, they may try to hold on to a relationship with the deceased through fantasy. As a result of unresolved grief, these children may become quiet and withdrawn, perhaps deferring their grief and mourning for a time when they feel it is appropriate to mourn.

These children need ample opportunities to express their feelings. They need to feel secure enough to talk about what they are feeling and to share their feelings of yearning, longing, and "survivor guilt." "Active listening" is an extremely important technique for helping these children to heal. In addition, these children should be allowed to participate in mourning rituals and to create memorials for the deceased.

Adolescence. Adolescence is often a time of tremendous physical, emotional, and psychological upheavals. This stage of development is often characterized by "highs" and "lows." Peer pressure and the need to fit in play a significant role in how the adolescent behaves. Adolescents also deal with such weighty matters as relationships with parents, sexuality, and substance abuse. How they handle these issues often determines how they will handle grief and recovery.

Another startling phenomenon is the incident of adolescent suicide. According to Gollnick and Chinn, the rate of suicide among young males in the United States is the highest in the world.[21] The ratio of male suicide to female suicide is five to one. White males between the ages of fifteen and nineteen have a suicide rate that is over twice the rate of suicide for African-American males in the same age group.

These factors have a profound effect on how the adolescent responds to grief and loss. At a time when the young person is struggling to develop independence and adultlike behavior, tragedy may cause him or her to retreat into childlike, helpless behavior that may result in expressions of extreme anger and other heightened emotional responses. Rando indicates that the bereaved adolescent may be expected to comfort others, thereby causing his or her own grief and recovery process to be repressed.[22]

Culture

Cultural norms dictate to a large degree how people think, feel, and behave. Culture encompasses an individual's socioeconomic status, level of education, and income. Other factors influenced by culture may include religious beliefs, ethnic identification, power, and social standing.

The way in which children work through their grief may often be affected by their cultural identification. For example, Gibbs found that African-American youth exhibit a "cultural paranoia" because of their marginal status in society. She indicates that they often are "[f]earful and suspicious of the clinical staff, withhold pertinent information, engage in verbally abusive and threatening behavior, and refuse medication or treatment." She goes on to observe that these youth are often victims of multiple risk factors that are "psychosocial" more than "psychological" in nature.[23]

Some minority groups exhibit an antipathy toward counseling and mental health services and agencies. They express suspicion about letting others into "their business." Also prevalent in some of these groups is the idea that talking about death is taboo. Religious beliefs also play an important role in how some cultural groups treat the subject of death and dying.

Given these cultural underpinnings, the school is often the one institution of socialization that provides a common experience for children and youth. The school may be the only place that has the potential for reaching hard-to-serve populations. The teacher needs to recognize that culture exerts a strong pull on the grieving and recovery process.

Poverty and Urban Communities

According to U.S. Census Bureau data for 1990, one in four children in the United States lives in poverty. The significance of this statistic is that poverty often dictates living conditions that include low-income neighborhoods characterized by consistent violence. These communities are like "war zones" where children live in constant danger and fear. Garbarino quotes Bell as follows:

For inner-city children, the risks of living in the midst of violence are compounded by the risks of living in poverty—risks that include malnutrition, unsuitable housing, inferior medical care, inadequate schools, family disruption, family violence, and maladaptive child-rearing patterns. Because many of the developmental consequences endemic to inner cities—for instance, poor school achievement, aggression, and self-destructive behaviors—occur almost routinely, the contribution of community violence to developmental harm is often overlooked.[24]

Children who live in poor communities may be exposed to multiple risk factors such as low birthweight, unmarried mothers, teenage mothers, low-energy physical and psychological child-rearing practices, increased child abuse, family violence, and the effects of chronic and pervasive poverty.[25] Such exposure has a major impact on how these children respond to chronic violence.

Teachers need to recognize the special problems of children who live in poverty. They need to be aware of the conditions in which the children live that may cause them to respond differently to grief and loss. Constant exposure to violence and death creates different emotions than occasional or no such exposure.

Gender

Gender identification affects the way children and youth grieve and recover. In addition to the fact that young adolescent males commit suicide at a rate five times greater than young adolescent females, other factors have an impact on the grieving process that males undergo as opposed to females.

Gender identity is learned through the process of socialization. The thoughts, feelings and actions of males and females are learned responses to the expectations of society, family, friends, and even schools. Males and females in this society are socialized differently from birth. "Masculinity" and "femininity" are clearly defined. Gender expectations are transmitted to the young and reinforced through a system of rewards and punishment, approval and disapproval. Boys are taught to be aggressive, self-reliant, independent, and emotionally stable. They are also trained for leadership roles. On the other hand, females are taught to be nurturing, responsible, dependent, emotionally vulnerable, and followers.

Based on these factors, it naturally follows that the manner in which males and females move through the grieving/recovery process would be different. Males are supposed to remain tight-lipped, dry-eyed, and in control at all times. Even very young boys are urged to "take it like a man." They are often expected to be the "man of the house" if the father is lost through death or divorce. It is not socially acceptable to exhibit signs of grief; this is not "masculine." The fact that boys and young men are more frequent perpetrators as well as victims of violence is cause for increased attention to their responses.

Females, on the other hand, may be allowed to show signs of grief. It is socially acceptable for them to cry, talk about the loss, and exhibit their feelings (to a certain extent). However, even females may be expected to keep the demonstration of feelings to a minimum, which is conveyed by words such as "Don't cry," "Be a big girl." They, too, may be expected to fulfill the role of the departed.

The bottom line for teachers when helping children and youth work through the grief and recovery process is to be aware of gender differences. They can reassure these students that it is all right to have certain emotions and that it is acceptable to express the feelings generated by those emotions.

SCHOOL-BASED SOLUTIONS: VIOLENCE PREVENTION, INTERVENTION, MANAGEMENT, AND POSTVENTION

In days gone by, schools were considered one of the safe havens in society. Parents sent their children off to school secure in the belief that they would be safe. They fully expected the school staff to take care of their children while in their keeping. After all, teachers and administrators served *in loco parentis* (in the place of parents).

Increasingly, schools have become less and less the bastions of safety that parents and the community have come to rely upon. The school environment has changed markedly from the days when the six hours children spent at school were unmarked by social upheavals and community problems. As Doll observes, "Schools are continually affected by forces and influences from American society and the culture at large."[26] These forces and influences affect the school environment, curriculum, students, and staff.

Violence, natural disasters, trauma, and grief have been frequent visitors to school campuses. Administrators are often called upon to handle these crises with as much proficiency and authority as they handle the educational programs of their schools. Indeed, students, staff, and the community at large expect the school administrator to take charge, take care of everyone, and make sure that things "get back to normal" as soon as possible. Teachers interact with students on a daily basis and are, therefore, the ones who must detect the emotional problems and provide the solutions, while still teaching the subject matter for which both they and the students are held accountable.

According to Garbarino et al., the task is further "complicated by the fact that inner-city teachers and child-care professionals often have feelings and ideas about community violence that overlap with the children's. They themselves are often victims of violence, or at least they confront the threat every day. They too must live with the power of the gangs and the limits of the police to protect them."[27]

It is increasingly clear that school personnel can play an important role in violence prevention, intervention, and postvention. Breaking the cycle of violence is impossible without breaking the patterns of aggressive, antisocial, and inappropriate behavior that result from children acting out their feelings in negative ways. These responses must be replaced with strategies that promote positive expression of feelings.

The overarching goals of violence prevention, intervention, management, and postvention programs are: (1) to break the cycle of violence and (2) to transform children and youth from *victims* into *victors*. Although some may argue that the schools' mission is educating children, not solving society's problems, many educators are optimistic that schools can and should make a difference in helping kids cope with social ills, including the effects of violence.

Some of the solutions that are currently being tried include metal detectors, surveillance systems, and other security and control devices. It is my belief that *mental* detectors instead of *metal* detectors are the prevention strategies that children and young people need to break the cycle of violence. Mental detectors can be described as those strategies that tap into the feelings that children have about themselves and the events that happen to them. Feelings dictate attitude, behaviors, and actions. It is important, therefore, to detect negative feelings and provide a variety of opportunities for dealing positively with these feelings. It is not the anger that causes the problem, but rather the expression of that anger.

What Can School Faculty and Staff Do to Help Children Cope?

Historically, society has expected schools to be responsive to social problems. Curriculum and instruction have been adapted to address all kinds of social ills—from nuclear education to AIDS education. Once again schools are being called upon to address yet another critical social problem: dealing with stress, grief, and trauma in children and youth. The optimum solution is to provide counseling and psychological support to these students. Unfortunately, the problems are too numerous and counselors and school psychologists too few to take care of all the young people who need help. Therefore, it is incumbent upon school personnel to identify effective programs and strategies and to train teachers and other school staff members in implementing these techniques.

Administrators (Principals, Assistant Principals, Deans). As managers and leaders of people, school administrators are expected to handle every situation at their site, whether planned or unplanned. Grief, loss, and trauma are no exception to this rule. While most school districts have established policies and procedures for handling natural disasters and other emergencies, few districts have clear guidelines for administrators in what to do when grief strikes the campus.

Policies and procedures governing the management of grief and trauma at school should include the following:

- Formulate a crisis management team.
- Develop a well-defined communication plan.
- Involve all mental health personnel and agencies.
- Provide support plans for students and staff that include prevention, intervention, and postvention.
- Identify and use appropriate external agencies.
- Develop a well-publicized parent-outreach program.
- Identify resources for ongoing assistance.
- Identify and use support systems for yourself and the other administrators on your staff.
- Develop a plan for interacting with the media.

Mental Heath Professionals (Counselors, Psychologists, Psychiatric Social Workers, Social Workers, Probation Officers). Grief and loss issues are mental health concerns and, therefore, fall under the domain of mental health professionals. The problem in most schools is that either there are no mental health professionals on staff, only part-time mental health professionals, or full-time mental health professionals with extremely high caseloads. For example, the ratio of counselors to students in secondary schools can range anywhere from 1:100 to 1:500. Many elementary schools do not have counselors at all.

In many schools, the job of the psychologist is to test students for special programs. In addition the school psychologist may be assigned on only a part-time basis. With regard to psychiatric social workers, social workers, probation officers, and other mental health professionals, very few schools employ these workers.

If the school is fortunate enough to have the services of a mental health professional, the following services should be included for grieving children and staff:

- Serve as a key resource on the crisis management team.
- Develop a counseling/support plan for students and staff.
- Provide support to the administrator related to prevention, intervention, and postvention activities.
- Serve as a liaison to parents.
- Refer students, staff, and parents to appropriate outside agencies.

Teachers. Teachers are the first line of contact for students. They are often the first to know when something is wrong. When students are suffering from pain due to a loss, their behavior and achievement may change in the classroom. When teachers do not know what to do to help grieving students, they feel frustrated. They realize that, unless the healing process takes place, academic achievement may plunge.

Although teachers' time, energy, and efforts are severely overtaxed, many teachers have expressed a desire to learn strategies to help their students deal with problems related to grief, loss, and trauma. This chapter provides ideas for teachers that can be integrated into existing curricula. For example, thematic units can easily be modified to include activities that focus on feelings associated with grief and loss.

Support Staff (Secretaries, Education Aides, Teacher Assistants, Nurses, School Police, Itinerant Teachers). Everyone employed by a school can help students cope with grief, loss, and trauma. While it should always be remembered that support personnel are *not mental health professionals,* they, too, can play an important role in the healing process. The following guidelines are recommended for school support personnel:

- Serve on the school crisis management team.
- Be knowledgeable about school policies and procedures for handling grief and loss situations.
- Learn how to be "active" listeners.
- Refer grieving students, staff, and parents to the appropriate school personnel.

What Types of School-Based Solutions Are Recommended

School-based solutions can be classified as either *environmental* or *program.* Environmental solutions focus on school climate and physical characteristics. Among the most important environmental concerns are safety, sense of community, order, and well-being. Program solutions focus on methodologies and strategies that provide positive responses to negative occurrences.

Environmental Solutions. Increasing attention is being paid to the issue of school *safety.* Indeed, student achievement is directly correlated to student safety. Students who are fearful of physical attacks in and around school cannot perform at their optimal levels. School safety, therefore, has become a local, state, and federal priority.

One safe school model developed by the California State Department of Education and the California Office of the Attorney General listed the following components of a school environment:

- Personal characteristics of students and staff
- The school's physical environment
- The school's social environment
- The school's cultural environment.[28]

The model then describes the planning steps, school strategies and actions, worksheets, safety code references, and questionnaires for each component.

Safe schools also have in place crisis management plans.[29] Such plans may include establishment of a crisis management team; description of the role and responsibilities of the principal, counselor, and teachers in managing crises; and specific activities and resources for resolving the crisis. The *School Safety Check Book* published by the National School Safety Center recommends the following safety plan components:

- School climate and discipline
- School attendance
- Personal safety
- School security.

Each component is discussed in terms of the issues; problem assessment; prevention strategies; prevention response strategies; and sample programs. The publication also offers a variety of surveys and policies that should be helpful to school safety planners.[30]

The old African proverb "It takes a whole village to raise a child" strikes at the heart of what *a sense of community* is about. Community is also called "school culture" and "school climate." One of the most urgent needs of human beings is the need to belong. Children must feel that school offers them a chance to be valued, nurtured, and supported. Numerous opportunities must be made for students to have a "safety net" that is there for them whether or not they are doing what they are supposed to do, or whether they need the guidance to do the right thing. School ought to be a place where children and youth can find many positive groups in which to enroll.

Successful strategies for building community in schools are abundant. The short list that follows describes just a few of the techniques I found effective in schools where I was the principal:

Establish daily routines such as lining up in predetermined locations.

Create rituals, school songs, school colors, spirit days for wearing school sweats and t–shirts, school songs.

Develop and publish school goals.

Divide school into teams or houses for instruction; create small groups out of large ones.

Create curricular and extracurricular clubs, programs, and activities.

Create special celebrations such as Wonderful Wednesdays, Fabulous Fridays.

Create school campaigns where all students work toward a short-term, rewardable goal.

Observe established traditions (those that still work well), but do not be afraid to establish new traditions.

One of the tenets of an "effective" school is an *orderly environment*. Toby says that a disorderly school, such as one "in which students wander the halls during times when they are supposed to be in class, where candy wrappers and empty soft-drink cans have been discarded in the corridors, and where graffiti can be seen on most walls" breeds everyday school violence. In such a school:

One connection between the inability of school authorities to maintain order and an increasing rate of violence is that—for students who have little faith in the usefulness of the education they are supposed to be getting—challenging rules is part of the fun. When they succeed in littering or in writing on walls, they feel encouraged to challenge other, more sacred, rules like the prohibition against assaulting fellow students. If the process goes far enough, students come to think they can do *anything*. The school has become a jungle.[31]

By contrast, an orderly school is one in which the rules are known and accepted by students, staff, and parents. The rules cover not only student conduct and behavior, but also the cleanliness of the school. When every stakeholder has a role in developing rules of conduct and disciplinary standards, school becomes an orderly, inviting place to be. Orderly schools promote a sense of well-being among students and staff members.

Program Solutions. Among the most promising violence prevention programs and practices are peer counseling; conflict resolution and mediation; gang reduction; and grief, loss, and support programs. This section describes an effective counseling program and offers suggestions to teachers for developing a curricular-based support approach.[32]

Children Grieve, Too was initiated in 1987 as an intervention response—*a counseling approach*—to the problem of unresolved grief due to losses suffered by the students. Approximately 10 percent of the 1,100 students enrolled in a large inner-city elementary school in Los Angeles were exhibiting behavior that was classified as "high-risk." All of the students enrolled were considered "at-risk" because they were minorities; lived in a high-crime, gang-infested neighborhood; and were, mostly, poor. The high-risk children, however, were those who were further affected by the conditions in which they lived. The behaviors they exhibited included unprovoked tantrums, sleeping difficulty, mood swings, withdrawals, and other antisocial—even pathological—behaviors.

Quite by accident, we discovered one of the root causes of this high-risk behavior. The event that uncovered this was the shooting of a young man across the street from the school one night in November 1987. Because the coroner would not come into this neighborhood after dark, the body of this young man laid out uncovered until after 8:00 A.M. the following morning. Hundreds of children saw the body on their way to school. A team of school psychologists was immediately called in to administer psychological "first aid." As the team went from room to room, they kept hearing from the children that many of them had relatives and friends who had died—many by violent means.

As a result of this discovery, the elementary school counselor, school psychologist, and psychiatric social worker made a concerted effort to develop an intervention program to address this need. They were already conducting counseling sessions dealing with social skills and self-esteem. Their program, entitled Showing Caring About Myself and Others (SCAMO), gave students a safe place to share their problems and work through their grief.

It was determined that a school-based mental health program was crucial to the healing and recovery of these children. Program goals and procedures were established for this intervention:

- Provide a needed service to children who have experienced the death of a significant other.
- Provide a vehicle to help children cope with the effects of death.
- Provide a supportive environment for children to grow and develop a positive, healthy attitude about themselves and school.
- Serve as facilitators/consultants in implementing a grief and loss program in the school setting.

Teachers need to be prepared to deal with single-incident occurrences using a *crisis approach*. When a loss occurs to a student or within a school, strategies need to be implemented that will help the victims to heal. Such activities may be conducted on an individual basis, or with small groups or the entire class.

Often a single child in the classroom is affected by a single incident involving a personal loss. Teachers have expressed their sense of frustration at wanting to help the grieving child, but not knowing what to do. They do not want to make the situation worse for the child, yet, on the other hand, they want to do something that will ease the child's pain.

Techniques and strategies will depend on the child's age, gender, type of loss (that is, a sibling, parent, or other), recentness of the loss, and so on. The following list offers a starting point for the teacher who wants to do something for the child in mourning:

- Listen, Listen, Listen. Let the child talk.
- Give the child "permission" to grieve, feel sad, mourn.

- Allow the child to express his or her feelings in a variety of ways.
- Be available for the child when he or she needs you. Show support, caring, and concern.
- Talk to the child privately from time to time.
- Answer the child's questions truthfully. Forget euphemisms.
- Attend the funeral services.
- Reach out to the family—write or call them.
- Allow the other students to do something for the bereaved child and/or family.
- Encourage the child to keep a journal.
- Allow the child to create commemoration rituals.
- Give yourself, the teacher, permission to grieve.
- Be alert to changes in the child's physical, emotional, social, and academic performance.
- Refer the child to the school mental health professionals or nurse.

Many children suffer from chronic grief and pain. They may not exhibit any of the symptoms described previously, or their symptoms may have gone unnoticed. It may not be appropriate, therefore, to single them out individually to focus on their situation. They can be helped, however, through participation in regular curriculum that is adapted to include some of the themes related to loss. *An integrated, thematic approach* is recommended for teaching about social issues and current problems.[33] Language arts and the social sciences lend themselves quite nicely to the thematic approach. Language arts are especially important in helping children to express their feelings; reading, writing, speaking, and listening can be used as tools for helping children to heal.

Thematic units can be developed or adapted to include a variety of activities. It is important to set the tone for group participation; establish group goals; and provide a relaxed, safe environment for participants. In a thematic approach, students are provided many concrete methods for self-expression designed to help them to build effective coping skills.

Whole-class activities are often used to address an urgent, immediate need of students. This strategy can also be used to introduce new concepts, reinforce, and extend concepts. In addition, whole-class activities can be used to access prior knowledge of the group and to introduce and demonstrate small-group activities. Whole-class activities include:

- Language arts (reading, discussing, listening/viewing tapes and videos, writing).
- Art (drawing/painting; modeling with clay, etc.; building/constructing).
- Music (listening, dance/movement).
- Drama (role-playing and presenting plays).

Small-group activities provide a different dynamic, allowing students the freedom to express emotions and feelings in a more intimate setting—one that is less likely to invite ridicule or humiliation. Activities performed in small groups seem more personalized. Also, all children are allowed to participate in a more in-depth manner. Suggested procedures for a two-day, small-group cycle are as follows:

1. Introduce all activities to the whole class first.
2. Divide the class into four heterogeneous groups.
3. Decide on the amount of time that will be spent on activities in a given day. (Each group will rotate to two activities per day.)
4. Establish rotation and stop procedures.
5. Establish traffic patterns.
6. Select and train group leaders.
7. Establish evaluation procedures for independent group work.

The thematic units presented in Appendix A provide selected activities that demonstrate how the language arts and visual/performing arts can be used to incorporate themes related to the grief and recovery process into existing curriculum. (Appendix B provides a list of selected support groups, organizations, and agencies for grieving children and their families.)

CONCLUSION

Violence in and around schools is a growing problem. Children are fearful for their safety. Teachers and administrators are increasingly embracing the notion that they can and should help children develop coping skills for dealing with the pain and anguish of violent environments. While there have been no studies directly linking school violence with lower student achievement, the connection is obvious. When students and school staff are preoccupied with issues of personal safety, it is reasonable to assume that less time and energy is spent on academic concerns. Also, when people are in a state of constant anxiety, their mental state precludes optimum academic performance. The indirect results of violence, therefore, can lower student achievement and teacher effectiveness. It is therefore imperative that school personnel learn strategies for helping kids cope.

Appendix A: THEMATIC

Theme: Loss
Subjects: Language Arts, Visual/Performing Arts
Resources: *Everett Anderson's Goodbye*, by Lucille Clifton (New York: Holt
and Co., 1983).

Concepts/Generalizations
1. Many people suffer losses.
2. Losses are painful.
3. Grief results from loss.
4. Grief generates many different feelings.
5. Expressing feelings is O.K.

Skills/Processes
- Accessing prior knowledge
- Writing
- Reading
- Analyzing
- Responding

Language Arts Activities
- Listening—Children listen to the story *Everett Anderson's Goodbye*.
- Writing—Children write a letter to Dad from Everett, from mother to Everett, from Dad to Everett regarding Dad's death.
- Speaking—Each character sits on a chair ("hot seat") and answers questions about his feelings related to the loss of Dad.
- Children then brainstorm how people feel when someone dies.
- Discussion—In a discussion circle, children are asked to tell about a time when they lost something. They then tell how they felt.
- Reading—Children read letters from a writing assignment, re-read the story selecting the passages that describe Everett's feelings, and write about and read their own stories about a loss that they suffered and how they felt.

Visual Arts Activities
- Drawing/Painting—Children fold a piece of paper into five sections and then draw a picture in each section that shows how Everett feels during each stage of grief. Children paint using colors that reflect feelings Everett had throughout the story. This activity may also be combined with music activity.

- Music—Select and play music that depicts each stage of the grief process. Children then demonstrate how each musical selection makes them feel.
- Drama—Children role play or use puppets to express the different feelings in the story.

**Appendix B: SUPPORT GROUPS, ORGANIZATIONS AND
AGENCIES**

American Association of Suicidology
2459 South Ash
Denver, Colo. 80222
(303) 692-0985

Bereavement Magazine: A Magazine for Hope and Healing
Bereavement Publishing
350 Gradle Drive
Carmel, Ind. 46032

Camp Amanda (grieving children)
4217 University Avenue
Des Moines, Iowa 50311
(515) 279-5444

Caring About Children (teacher training)
6709 La Tijera Boulevard, Suite 437
Los Angeles, Calif. 90045
(213) 882-1257

The Compassionate Friends (bereaved parents)
P.O. Box 3696
Oak Brook, Ill. 60522
(312) 990-0010

The Dougy Center (grief recovery for children ages 2 to 17)
3903 S.E. 52nd Avenue
Portland, Oregon
(503) 775-LOVE

Fernside (grieving children ages 3 to 17)
P.O. Box 8944
Cincinnati, Ohio 45208
(513) 321-0282

The Good Grief Program
Judge Baker Children's Center
295 Longwood Avenue
Boston, Mass. 02115
(617) 232-8390

Mothers Against Drunk Driving (MADD)
(magazine and materials for grieving children and adults)
669 Airport Freeway, Suite 310
Hurst, Tex., 76053
(817) 268-6233

The National Childhood Grief Institute
(grieving children—death and divorce)
6200 Colonial Way
Minneapolis, Minn. 55436
(619) 920-0737

National SIDS Foundation
8240 Professional Place
Landover, Md. 20785

Psychological Trauma Center, Cedars–Sinai Medical Center
(mental health consultations—schools, families, and individuals)
8730 Alden Drive, Room C–106A
Los Angeles, Calif. 90048
(310) 855-3506

Rainbows (grieving children—death and divorce)
Marilyn Scott, Certified Director
8309 Bevan Street
San Gabriel, Calif. 91775
(818) 287-9282

Rothman–Cole Center for Sibling Loss, The Southern School
(Individual, Group and Family Counseling)
1456 West Montrose
Chicago, Ill. 60613
(312) 769-0185

The Warm Place (grieving children ages 2 to 18)
1510 Cooper
Fort Worth, Tex. 76102
(817) 870-2272

NOTES

1. National Childhood Grief Institute Fact Sheet.

2. "We Are Making a Difference in Children's Lives," Children's Defense Fund Fact Sheet.

3. A. Kotlowitz, *There Are No Children Here* (New York: Doubleday, 1991).

4. J. Garbarino et al., *Children in Danger, Coping with the Consequences of Community Violence* (San Francisco: Jossey-Bass, 1992).

5. D. P. Moynihan, "Defining Deviancy Down. How We've Become Accustomed to Alarming Levels of Crime and Destructive Behavior," *American Educator*, American Federation of Teachers (Winter 1993/94): 10–18.

6. J. Toby, "Everyday School Violence: How Disorder Fuels It,"*American Educator*, American Federation of Teachers (Winter 1993/94: 4–9, 44–48.

7. Garbarino et al., *Children in Danger*.

8. School Climate and Student Support Services Unit and Crime Prevention Unit, California State Department of Education, *Safe Schools: A Planning Guide for Action* (Sacramento: California Department of Education and the Office of the Attorney General, 1989).

9. L. Harris and Associates, *Violence in America's Public Schools* (New York: Metropolitan Life Insurance Co., 1993).

10. Toby, "Everyday School Violence."

11. Harris and Associates, *Violence in America's Public Schools.*

12. Ibid.

13. Garbarino et al., *Children in Danger.*

14. E. Kubler-Ross, *On Death and Dying* (New York: Macmillan, 1969).

15. D. Crenshaw, *Bereavement, Counseling the Grieving Throughout the Life Cycle* (New York: Continuum Publishing Co., 1990).

16. M. Coleman, J. Freeman, and L. Duncan, *Children Grieve, Too* (Los Angeles, Calif.: Caring About Children, 1994).

17. R. Pynoos and K. Nader, "Psychological First Aid and Treatment Approach to Children Exposed to Community Violence: Research Implications," *Journal of Traumatic Stress* 4 (1988): 445–73; Garbarino et al., *Children in Danger.*

18. American Psychiatric Association, *Diagnostic and Statistical Manual of Mental Disorders*, 3rd ed.-revised (Washington, D.C.: APA, 1987).

19. E. B. Kelly, *Dealing with Death: A Strategy for Tragedy* (Bloomington: Ind.: Phi Delta Kappa Educational Foundation, 1990); T. A. Rando, *Grief, Dying and Death* (Champaign, Ill.: Research Press Co., 1984).

20. Coleman, Freeman, and Duncan, *Children Grieve, Too.* (This excerpt is reprinted by permission of the publisher.)

21. D. Gollnick and P. Chinn, *Multicultural Education in a Pluralistic Society* 3rd. ed. (New York: Macmillan, 1990).

22. Rando, *Grief, Dying and Death.*

23. J. T. Gibbs et al., *Children of Color, Psychological Interventions with Minority Youth* (San Francisco: Jossey-Bass, 1989).

24. C. Bell, "Traumatic Stress and Children in Danger, " *Journal of Health Care for the Poor and Underserved* 2, Vol. 1 (September 1991),175–88, in Garbarino et al., *Children in Danger.*

25. Garbarino et al., *Children in Danger.*

26. R. C. Doll, *Curriculum Development* (Boston: Allyn and Bacon, 1989).

27. Garbarino et al., *Children in Danger.*

28. California Department of Education, Office of the Attorney General, *Safe Schools.*

29. S. Peterson and R. L Straub, *School Crisis Survival Guide, Management Techniques and Materials for Counselors and Administrators* (New York: Center for Applied Research in Education, 1992).

30. National School Safety Center, *School Safety Check Book* (Malibu, Calif.: Pepperdine University Press, 1990).

31. Toby, "Everyday School Violence."

32. This section is excerpted from Coleman, Freeman, and Duncan, *Children Grieve, Too*, with the permission of the publisher.

33. S. M. Drake, *Planning Integrated Curriculum: The Call to Adventure* (Alexandria, Va.: Association for Supervision and Curriculum Development, 1993).

Part V

SOME SPECIFIC APPROACHES

14

NEA's Perspective and Policies on Violence in Schools

Keith Geiger

The statistics on violence in America are sobering. The homicide death rate increased from 8.3 per 100,000 persons in 1970 to 9.2 in 1989, the last year for which data are available. Perhaps the most striking fact about these trends is the homicide rate for black men. The homicide death rate for black men in 1970 accounted for an astounding 67.6 percent of all homicide deaths, its highest in the years covered; it declined to about 61 percent in 1989. Moreover, although the homicide death rates are considerably lower for women than for men, they are highest for black women.

Another way to examine increasing crime in the United States is by victimization rates per one thousand population of persons twelve years of age or older. Data show that males are about one and one-half times more likely than females to be victims of violent crime.

There are several important demographic differences in victimization: younger people are more likely than older people to be victims; blacks are more likely than whites and other races; Hispanics more likely than non-Hispanics; the poor more likely than the more affluent; and residents of central cities more likely than residents of suburbs and nonmetropolitan areas.

What about violence in schools? It appears that schools are increasingly becoming places where students act out violent behaviors. In a national survey of teachers, the U.S. Department of Education notes that about 28 percent of teachers responding indicated that physical conflict among students was a serious-to-moderate problem.[1] The percentage increased to 32 percent in elementary schools and to 44 percent in city schools.[2]

Interestingly enough, a vast majority of teachers feel safe in their schools. For example, 88 percent of teachers feel safe in the school building during school hours. The percentage drops to 68 percent *after* school hours, however.[3]

Nevertheless, it is actual violence and the potential for violence that concern the NEA and that drive NEA policy and position on the topic. This chapter describes what the NEA had been doing to address violence in schools. As such, this chapter has two objectives: (1) to describe NEA's overall framework and (2) to present a very general description of NEA policies and programs.

NEA POSITION ON VIOLENCE IN SCHOOLS

When Lee Brown, the current U.S. drug czar, was chief of police in Houston, Texas he sought to reduce violence in that beleaguered city by initiating a new program: "neighborhood-oriented policing." Brown felt that the function of police was not simply to react to crimes in the community, but to behave proactively by helping communities solve the problems that have led to violence. The NEA's approach is in the same spirit: not to react solely to crime in the schools, but to address the families and communities where crime originates.

The statistics on crime clearly point out that schools are not violent environments; indeed, schools are environments for teaching and learning. Instead, the data point out that certain community and family factors increase the probability of violence and that students bring these problems with them to schools. Based on these facts, the NEA's position can be captured in the following equation:

$$\text{Safe Neighborhoods} + \text{Safe Homes} = \text{Safe Schools}$$

In other words, safe schools are a function of those institutions from which students originate: their homes and communities. It is in those environments, not schools, that students learn the attitudes and behaviors that increase the likelihood of violent behavior. This is not to say that the NEA does not acknowledge the existence of violence in schools, but it does say that violence does not *originate* in schools.

COMMUNITY PROBLEMS

Five factors account for a large amount of the crime and violence in communities: gangs, drugs, the culture that has developed around the community, the media, social factors such as racial or religious intolerance, and poverty. This section summarizes what the NEA considers the most crucial elements contributing to violence.

Gangs

Four characteristics of gangs form the basis for adequately dealing with the gang violence that infiltrates schools. First, gangs tend to form in communities whose members are not fully integrated, economically or socially, into the American mainstream.[4] Second, although it appears that violence is not a major function of gangs, members of gangs are more likely than nongang members to participate in acts of crime and violence.[5]

Third, gangs tend to operate as important socializing agents in their communities. They tend to recruit from among young members of the community. Gang members also act as role models. Indeed, many gang rituals stress certain kinds of behaviors and attitudes that emphasize aggressive behavior when confronted with interpersonal problems.[6]

Fourth, the characteristics of gang behavior and attitudes are also formed by the culture within the community.[7] Interestingly, not all gangs function for the same reasons. Some function as quasi-families for their members, others have economic motives (usually involving illegal activity), and still others operate for social reasons.[8]

Drugs

Drugs are a problem in many communities, being the cause of much crime and violence. What is generally known about drugs and their relationship to crime and violence may be summarized in the following four points:

1. Users of drugs are more likely than nonusers to commit violent crime such as robberies and assaults.[9]
2. There is a correlation between drug use and homicide, but it varies from place to place, depending on predisposing and situational factors.[10]
3. There is a relationship between the economics of drugs and crime/violence. Drug users commit crimes to obtain drugs or money for their purchase or use.[11]
4. Drugs and violence are related to other kinds of illegal markets characterized by crime and violence: prostitution and loan sharking, for example.[12]

Cultures

Culture is a group characteristic that defines and filters world views and the group's place in it. The world view is defined by group norms, values, mores, myths, and folkways. It is expressed in a variety of ways, including language, art, social behavior, and social organization.[13]

Communities develop their own unique cultures, with some of them coinciding nicely with mainstream American culture, whereas others are oppositional. In communities characterized by family disorganization, high population turnover, high levels of unemployment, and other kinds of social dysfunction, cultures emerge that impede its inhabitants from developing the social skills they need to enter the mainstream culture.[14]

Three major traits of oppositional cultures make it difficult for their members to enter the mainstream culture:

1. *Language and social behavior.* Coarse, rough language that was acceptable in some old manufacturing industries as a sign of being tough or manly is virtually unacceptable in today's service and professional occupations.

2. *Illegal markets and gang membership.* Significant proportions of young people in oppositional cultures are involved in illegal markets and gangs. Both activities also have their own languages, which serve two functions: (1) they identify an individual as a member of a group or some underground activity, and (2) they serve as a means of communication accessible only to members.[15]

3.   *Alienation*. Members of oppositional cultures feel alienated from the larger mainstream culture. They sometimes believe that there is a conspiracy to reduce their numbers, evidenced by police brutality, AIDS, high unemployment, and drugs.[16] The feeling that the wider society does not respect members of their community or that the lives of members of their community are viewed as cheap by the wider society contributes to this sense of alienation.

Urban social scientist Elijah Anderson summarizes these oppositional cultures eloquently as follows:

Of all the problems besetting the poor inner-city black community, none is more pressing than that of interpersonal violence and aggression. It wreaks havoc daily with the lives of community residents and increasingly spills over into downtown and residential middle-class areas.... The inclination to violence springs from the circumstances of life among the ghetto poor—the lack of jobs that pay a living wage, the stigma of race, the fallout from rampant drug use and drug trafficking, and the resulting alienation and lack of hope for the future.[17]

The Media

Mounting evidence shows that violent or aggressive behavior is related to several kinds of media outlets: television, movies, and video games. The heroes or villains from such media outlets become role models for children and, in some cases, for adults. Viewers may begin to mimic behavior they see onscreen. For example, some recent summaries suggest a link between television viewing and aggressive or violent behavior among children.[18]

Social Factors

Aside from the factors proposed and discussed thus far, other social factors—such as racial or religious intolerance—motivate crime and violence in our society. These result in what I would call hate crimes, or crimes based on issues of race and ethnicity, sexual orientation, religion, or gender.

Defining hate crime is complex because certain kinds of hate-motivated behavior, such as racial slurs, are not illegal. Nevertheless, Bodinger-deUriarte offers the following definition:

A hate crime is any act, or attempted act, to cause physical injury, emotional suffering, or property damage through intimidation, harassment, racial/ethnic slurs and bigoted epithets, vandalism, force, or the threat of force, motivated all or in part by hostility to the victim's real or perceived race, ethnicity, religion, or sexual orientation.[19]

Hate crime and violence differ from other kinds of crime and violence in seven important ways: First, victims of hate crime rarely know the assailants.[20] Second, hate crime seems to involve two or more perpetrators.[21] In fact, Pierce indicates that there are, on average, four assailants to one victim in hate-motivated crime.[22]

Third, assailants tend to attack people who are somewhat helpless—that is, those either much younger or otherwise unable to defend themselves.[23] Fourth, hate-motivated crimes are exceedingly violent.[24] Fifth, whereas in property crimes something of value is taken, in hate-motivated crime property is damaged or destroyed.[25] Sixth, hate-motivated crime and violence are characterized by a "no gain" trait: there is no profit or gain. Instead, hate-motivated crime is symbolic in nature. Finally, hate-motivated crime is more likely to occur where victims congregate: churches, schools, mosques, synagogues, and so forth. These seven traits indicate that hate-motivated crime is largely violent, symbolic behavior against groups of people who are considered "different."

Though data are rare, many organizations believe that hate-motivated crime is on the rise. Indeed, Pasternak states:

Wherever such statistics are kept, across the United States, bigotry cases have become more commonplace. . . . The incidents have ranged from anonymous spray-painting of slurs to cross burnings to murder. What they have in common is their motivation: fury directed at those that are different because of their race, their religion, or their sexual orientation.[26]

In formulating policy against hate-motivated crime, we need to know its causes. In general, it may be said that hate-motivated crime is rooted in psychology that depersonalizes victims and uses them as scapegoats for existing social, economic, and political instability. The changing demographics in cities, states, and neighborhoods creates social unease. Rather than leading to greater understanding, these changes often lead individuals to resort to stereotypes when negotiating with others of different religious, ethnic, or racial backgrounds.[27]

Economic instability is also a factor in hate-motivated crime, for social unease occurs when various groups—ethnic or racial groups, for example—vie over scarce and desired resources such as jobs and education. At least two important traits of economic instability predict hate crime. First, there is the sense that social programs aimed at assisting minorities are unfair. This leads to resentment and, at times, to hate-motivated violence or crime. Second, immigrants often are seen as "stealing" jobs from nonimmigrants and placing a heavy burden on an economy already bursting at the seams.

Finally, political instability can lead to hate-motivated crime and violence. The foreign policy of the United States in the Middle East has resulted in a number of hate-motivated crimes and violent acts against Middle Easterners in this country. For example, in Los Angeles, students of Middle Eastern background were the objects of much name-calling and intimidation following the Persian Gulf War.[28]

Poverty

Finally, poverty or socioeconomic factors are important contributors to the crime and violence in America that spills off into our schools. Why is poverty implicated? To begin with, statistics indicate that the overriding common denominator among those committing crime and violence is individuals from lower socioeconomic groups. Individuals from such communities are not in the mainstream of economic or social life in America and tend to be extremely alienated from the American mainstream.

Shaw and McKay found that three structural factors were related to crime and delinquency, mainly because these factors disrupted community organization and cohesion: low economic status, ethnic heterogeneity, and residential mobility.[29] Subsequent studies have, indeed, found high associations between violent crime and poverty.[30] But these studies, though important contributions, beg the most interesting and important question: How is poverty related to violent crime?[31]

Despite some of the methodological problems in attempting to examine the influence of poverty on violent crime, research finds several community traits associated with violent crime in poverty areas. These include:

- The high density of multihousing, high residential mobility, and the prevalence of disrupted family structures.[32]
- Almost any kind of change that disrupts community organization.[33]
- Poverty and its correlates in the inner city.[34]

FAMILY DYSFUNCTION

Being raised in an environment of violence and abuse (emotional, sexual, and physical) has at least two consequences for school violence: (1) it can perpetuate a "cycle of violence," and (2) it can lead to social psychological problems that can be linked to aggressive, antisocial, or violent behavior.

The "Cycle of Violence"

A major research hypothesis surrounding family violence is the "cycle of violence," which states, simply, that children raised in violent/abusive families become violent/abusive adults themselves, with a plethora of personal and social problems. For example, there is an increased risk of suicide[35] and mental illness[36] in such adults.

It is, however, the perpetuation of violence that is of greatest concern. Straus et al., in a study of adults who were abused as children, found that about 20 percent abused their own children.[37] Using a longitudinal design, Widom found that abused or neglected children had greater probabilities of being arrested for violent offenses.[38] In a later policy piece, Widom also found that the type of maltreatment a child received was related to the type of criminal activity he or she became involved in. Thus, for example, 16 percent of physically abused children were later arrested for a violent offense; 13 percent of those who were neglected were later arrested for a violent offense, as were 6 percent of those who were sexually abused as children.[39] There is ample evidence to corroborate both the cycle of violence hypothesis and the correlation between type of maltreatment and the probability of committing certain criminal acts.

Mental Illness

Although there is a link between family violence and mental illness, there are at least two nagging issues that have not, as yet, been resolved. First, it is difficult to determine the extent of the connection, for certain biological factors are also related to mental illness. Second, there is a genetic link to mental illness; certain types of mental illness often characterize families—depression, for example.

With these confounding issues aside, it appears that certain kinds of mental illnesses—such as depression—are related to violent behavior.[40] It is, therefore, not too much to assume that for some children mental illness may result from being raised in a violent family, which may in turn trigger violent behavior in school.

Regardless of the origin, causes, or other antecedents to family violence, the consequences are the same for many children: they are raised in a violent environment where they learn certain norms, values, roles, and ways of handling problems. They interpret these as the normal way to resolve problems and issues, and they conduct themselves accordingly outside of the family. Unfortunately for students and educators, such behavior often gets exercised at school.

NEA'S POLICIES AND PROGRAMS FOR DEALING WITH VIOLENCE IN THE SCHOOLS

The mission of the NEA is given in the following statement:

To fulfill the promise of a democratic society, the National Education Association shall promote the cause of quality public education and advance the profession of education; expand the rights and further the interests of educational employees; and advocate human, civil, and economic rights for all.[41]

The NEA's concern with violence in schools touches on each concept embedded in its mission statement. Violence in schools detracts from the development of a quality public education; it places educational employees at risk of injury or fatality; and it violates the human, civil, and potential economic rights of educational employees, victims, and perpetrators of crime and violence.

The NEA provides a variety of services to meet the needs of its constituency. These include advocacy, in the form of legislative lobbying and funding; technical assistance, in the form of information and research; and training. The following sections briefly describe the work of two NEA work groups and present a general, overall scheme as to how NEA policies, practices, and positions have been marshalled to handle violence in schools.

NEA Work Groups

In the past few years some of the NEA membership has felt a greater urgency regarding safety on school grounds. Consequently, the NEA has formulated a strategy to address both the immediate, short-term needs of a small proportion of our members and some long-term policy recommendations for the remainder. The

NEA leadership addressed both areas by forming two NEA work groups: the cross-unit work team, which was composed of NEA staff from various divisions; and the NEA Special Committee on Discipline, Order, and Safety, which was composed of NEA members with the assistance of NEA staff.

Both groups worked closely with one another, but each had its own objectives. The cross-unit work team focused on developing short-term solutions and providing assistance and information to NEA's membership. The committee, on the other hand, spent nearly a year developing long-term recommendations for NEA to pursue.

The NEA Cross-Unit Work Team. The NEA's cross-unit work team was organized to handle the immediate needs regarding violence in schools. At its first meeting, the work team put together a list of eleven activities it would undertake:

1. Conduct an assessment of affiliates to find out what their antiviolence activities are and what they are doing that works. HCR (Human and Civil Rights) and Research would collaborate to condense the information, ready it for review by the work team, and use it with activities planned by the work team. The NEA would establish or use the ongoing clearinghouse apparatus in HCR to serve as an information source for NEA affiliates. The assessment would be initiated in late November, with information available before the holiday break.
2. Create a subgroup to develop a "how-to" booklet identifying solutions that work, appropriate evaluation and documentation, experts and organizations in the field, and instructions on using the information. CRUE (Center for the Revitalization of Urban Education), HCR, the Center for Teaching and Learning, and PSP (Professional Standards and Practice) are likely resources. Units would merge funds for distribution of the information kit to states and the three hundred largest locals immediately. If funds are not available, they would have to be appropriated.
3. Endorse the "standards for children's programming" guidelines on TV violence established by DIC
4. Publish a lead story on antiviolence in *NEA Today*.
5. Incorporate in NEA training, UniServ, and governance curriculum the how-to concept of combatting violence. Provide workshops with UniServ in January, March, and April of 1994.
6. Develop and implement a National Conference on Antiviolence in Schools.
7. Incorporate antiviolence and how-to activities in the national conference coordinated by the Center for the Revitalization of Urban Education, the conference coordinated by the Center for the Preservation of Public Education, the Joint Conference on the Concerns of Minorities and Women coordinated by Human and Civil Rights, NEA national conferences, and the Regional Minority Leadership Training Seminars.
8. Make training programs on teaching tolerance available to affiliates.
9. Begin implementing a two-pronged telephone survey of members and administrators on the status of programs on antiviolence in schools.
10. Form coalitions with national groups such as the Council on Urban City Schools, the National School Boards Association, and the American Federation of Teachers in order to share resources and collaborate on other activities.
11. Work with Teacher TV in creating a program on antiviolence in schools.

In subsequent meetings, it became evident that long-term planning and policy would have to be addressed, and the work team began that process. Of special importance was the need for models and solutions to actual and potential violence in schools in order to protect both educational employees and students. Several long-term products were deemed crucial: a how-to manual on what teachers could do to reduce the probability of violence (the manual would include a video); a resource guide; and training sessions on the topic. These products are being developed.

In the midst of its work on violence in schools, the cross-unit work team was asked to work closely with the Center for the Preservation of Public Education (CPPE). Staff on the work team were asked to make available three products for NEA state leaders at a conference being coordinated by CPPE: (1) a how-to manual and accompanying video on school violence (to provide educational employees with plans, solutions, and models for making their schools safe); (2) a briefing package that could be used by local, state, and national NEA leaders in addressing violence in schools (and containing a sample of talking points, an editorial, some background information, and answers to the most frequently asked questions about violence in schools); and (3) an organizing manual (to be used at the building level as a tool for organizing education employees about violence in schools). With the exception of the how-to manual, all products are to be available in late summer 1995.

A second issue emerged that also involved the extensive participation of NEA staff. NEA joined forces with other education and advocacy organizations in planning the television documentary "Kids Killing Kids." The CBS and Fox television networks spearheaded this effort.

The NEA Special Committee on Discipline, Order, and Safety. The Special Committee on Discipline, Order, and Safety was convened as a result of a motion by a teacher member at the NEA's nine-thousand-member annual Representative Assembly. The committee was established on September 1, 1993 and given the following charge: "This committee was authorized by the 1993 Representative Assembly to study discipline and safety issues in the public schools, colleges, and universities. The committee will report to the 1994 Representative Assembly."[42]

After about a year of work in which members read and evaluated numerous reports and studies, listened to the presentations of experts in selected fields, and evaluated videos on crime and violence, the committee began the process of making recommendations in the areas with which it was charged: discipline, order, and safety. The committee's general recommendations are as follows:

1. Extend the life of the Special Committee on Discipline, Order, and Safety.
2. Form an Institute on Discipline, Order, and Safety.
3. Hold a national conference on discipline, order, and safety.
4. Schedule in all NEA conferences at least one session on discipline, order, and safety. Work with the Institute on Discipline, Order, and Safety.
5. Support the cross-unit work team's efforts to publish its three manuals: How to

Deal with Violence in Schools; Organizing and Training Manual on Violence; and Briefing Manual on Violence.

6. Begin a national media campaign that focuses on awareness of violence in schools.
7. Survey all members (pre-K to 12) on the effectiveness of teacher education programs and pre-service and in-service training.
8. Establish a national clearinghouse with at least one full-time employee in the Institute on Discipline, Order, and Safety. Assign staff to read, file, prepare, and distribute materials and data on discipline, order, and safety, and school environments. File and distribute materials.
9. Network with other agencies (on schools, home, discipline, order, and safety issues).
10. Develop joint legislation with network agencies on discipline, order, and safety.
11. Develop curriculum on discipline, order, and safety (to include pre-K, higher education, and adult education).
12. Develop model plans for discipline, order, and safety that include due process for students and staff.
13. Work with the U.S. Department of Education and other federal agencies to develop criteria for designing and constructing school buildings that promote discipline, order, and safety.
14. Develop prototype language for state and local affiliates for use in securing local and state legislation that promotes discipline, order, and safety in school environments.
15. Support NEA's resolutions and amendments on discipline, order, and safety, including C-17, C-18, B-47, and B-48.
16. Form a coalition including the Special Committee on Discipline, Order, and Safety; the cross-unit work team; and other staff/member groups.

In addition to these general recommendations, the committee made several policy and action recommendations. The main difference between the work of the committee and the cross-unit work team is that the committee focused on broad, long-term NEA policy. Although not all of its recommendations will be accepted, some will be acted on and will form the basis for future work by NEA staff.

Other Activities

In addition to the work of the cross-unit work team and the committee, the NEA has been working closely with government and private nonprofit organizations that are concerned with violence not only in schools, but also in society. For example, NEA staff have been working closely with the National Institutes of Justice, the Center for the Prevention of Handgun Violence, the American Bar Association, and the American Medical Association. The NEA also has been instrumental in lobbying for and writing such legislation as the Safe Schools Act, the Brady Bill, and legislation guiding the content of television and video games.

The NEA has been concerned with issues of safety in school for some time. As a result, it has formulated a number of policies, activities, and positions on violence and related topics.

Communities. The NEA has taken positions on all six community issues related to crime and violence in schools: gangs, drugs, culture, media, social factors (hate crime), and poverty. As we have pointed out in previous sections, each of these areas contributes significantly to crime and violence in our society. Unfortunately, the behaviors and attitudes that young people learn and acquire through these sources move onto school premises and increase the likelihood of violent and aggressive behavior.

Although the NEA has taken positions on each of these areas, through resolutions, legislative programs, and new business items, there is much we can still do. Indeed, at our annual Representative Assembly, many new activities on violence in school were passed and were implemented in fiscal year 1994–1995.

In the meantime, we have taken the initiative to strengthen and broaden our relationships with other advocacy organizations. Clearly, the NEA cannot and should not address community issues alone. Consequently, we have been attempting to form policy relationships with a variety of outside organizations, such as the American Medical Association, the American Bar Association, the National Council of La Raza, Aspira, and the NAACP. In addition, as violence in our society becomes an even more important issue, we shall make our concerns known to President Clinton.

Families/Homes. Our concern with family issues centers on the impact that growing up in a violent or abusive environment has on the attitudes, behaviors, and safety of children. Children being raised in violent and abusive families may come to believe such behavior is normal and thus deal with social relation problems in a violent or aggressive manner.

The NEA has thus taken a number of positions on family violence, spousal assault, and child abuse. Our positions in these areas are not merely ideological, but have included providing information to our members and leaders (and other policy and advocacy organizations) on such issues as child abuse and teenage suicide.

Schools. Even though schools are not inherently violent places, they can benefit from a number of policies and activities designed to alleviate persistent violence or the potential for violence. The NEA has not only taken positions in favor of such programs as peer mediation and conflict resolution, but its cross-unit work team is currently analyzing these programs in order to offer recommendations to members and leaders who are attempting to create safe school environments.

If I were to suggest the two most important strategies, they would be, first, that schools and school districts develop an overall plan. The plan must be extremely detailed so that mistakes and errors are avoided in emergency situations. For example, it is important to identify who is to handle the media in the event of a crisis; where the media are to congregate; and who is to inform the district, parents, students, and other staff. These are tough issues, and ones that we as educators attempt to avoid. But as violence in schools becomes a problem, potentially or actually, they are nonetheless issues that we must address.

The second important strategy is to increase the outreach activities of schools. Such outreach would be extended not only to parents, but also to protective, religious, business, welfare, and other agencies that have a stake in the community and the violence that has caused—or will arise and cause—much social disorganization. To reduce violence significantly, community issues must be addressed, since such issues as drugs, poverty, and social alienation appear to be major causes of violence—whether in communities or in schools.

CONCLUSION

Crime and violence in America have been increasing in recent years. These trends also appear to characterize schools. In the past several years, we have read about countless crimes and violent acts on school grounds. These crimes place our children and educational employees at risk of injury or fatality and detract from the ultimate aim of our educational system: to train and educate our youth.

The NEA has marshalled its resources in addressing crime and violence in schools. However, rather than viewing schools as inherently violent places, the NEA believes, and has provided considerable evidence in corroboration, that crime and violence in schools are the result of community and family problems. Only by addressing such problems can we begin to stem the tide of crime and violence in schools. The problem, ultimately, is a societal one, and we all share in some of the responsibility. As Caesar said to Brutus in Shakespeare's play, "The fault, dear Brutus, is not in our stars, but within ourselves."

NOTES

1. W. Mansfield, D. Alexander, and E. Farris, *Teacher Survey on Safe, Disciplined, and Drug-Free Schools* (Washington, D.C.: U.S. Department of Education, 1991), 3.

2. Ibid., 4.

3. Ibid., 15.

4. F. M. Thrasher, *The Gang: A Study of 1,313 Gangs in Chicago,* abridged ed. (Chicago: University of Chicago Press, 1927); G. Schwartz, *Beyond Conformity or Rebellion: Youth and Authority in America (Chicago:* Chicago University Press, 1987); M. Sullivan, *Getting Paid: Youth and Crime and Work in the Inner City* (Ithaca, N.Y.: Cornell University Press, 1989); A. J. Reiss, Jr., and M. Tonry, *Communities and Crime (* Chicago: University of Chicago Press, 1986).

5. M. Klein and C. Maxson, "Street Gang Violence," in *Violent Crime, Violent Criminals,* eds. N. A. Weiner and M. E. Wolfgang (Newbury Park, Calif.: Sage Publications, 1989), 198–234; Schwartz, *Beyond Conformity or Rebellion;* M. S. Jankowski, *Island in the Street: Gangs and American Urban Society* (Berkeley: University of California Press, 1991); J. Fagan, "The Social Organization of Drug Use and Drug Dealing Among Urban Gangs," *Criminology* 27, No. 4 (1989): 633–69.

6. J. Hagedorn, *People and Folks: Gangs, Crime, and the Underclass in a Rustbelt City* (Chicago: Lakeview Press, 1988); Jankowski, *Island in the Street;* J. W. Moore, "Variations in Violence among Hispanic Gangs," in *Research Conference on Violence and Homicide in Hispanic Communities,* eds. J. F. Kraus et al. (Los Angeles: University of California, 1987); J. D. Vigil, "Street Socialization, Locura Behavior, and Violence among Chicano Gang Members," in *Research Conference on Violence and Homicide in Hispanic Communities,* eds. J. F. Kraus et al. (Los Angeles: University of California, 1987): 231–41; F. Padilla, "Going to Work: The Entrepreneurial Side of the Gang," unpublished manuscript,

1990; J. MacLeod, *Ain't No Makin' It: Leveled Aspirations in a Low-Income Neighborhood* (Boulder, Colo.: Westview Press, 1987); R. Horowitz, *Honor and the American Dream* (New Brunswick, N.J.: Rutgers University Press, 1983); J. F. Short and F. L. Strodbeck, *Group Process and Gang Delinquency* (Chicago: University of Chicago Press, 1965).

7. Ibid.

8. Hagedorn, *People and Folks*; Jankowski, *Island in the Street*; Moore, "Variations in Violence"; Vigil, "Street Socialization"; Padilla, "Going to Work"; MacLeod, *Ain't No Makin' It;* Horowitz, *Honor and the American Dream*; Short and Strodbeck, *Group Process and Gang Delinquency*; J.W. Moore et al., *Homeboys: Gangs, Drugs, and Prisons in the Barrios of Los Angeles* (Philadelphia: Temple University Press, 1978); K. Chin, *Chinese Subculture and Criminality: Non-Traditional Crime Groups in America* (Westport, Conn.: Greenwood Press, 1990).

9. A. Blumstein et al., *Criminal Careers and "Career Criminals"* (Washington, D.C.: National Academy Press, 1986); D. S. Elliot and D. Huizinga, "The Relationship Between Delinquent Behavior and ADM Problems," *National Youth Survey Report* No. 26 (Boulder, Colo.: Behavioral Research Institute, 1984).

10. H. Harwood et al., "Economic Costs to Society of Alcohol and Drug Abuse and Mental Illness," *Final Report*; Alcohol, Drug Abuse, and Mental Health Administration, unpublished manuscript, 1984; P. J. Goldstein and D. Hunt, *The Impact of Drugs on the Health of the Nation: Final Report* (Atlanta, Ga.: Emory University, 1984); P. J. Goldstein, "Drugs and Violent Crime," in *Pathways to Criminal Violence*, eds. N. A. Weiner and M. E. Wolfgang (Newbury Park, Calif.: Sage Publications, 1989): 16–48; J. A. Inciardi, "The Crack/Violence Connection Within a Population of Hard-Core Adolescent Offenders," a paper presented at the National Institute on Drug Abuse Technical Review on Drugs and Violence, Rockville, Maryland, September 25–26, 1989.

11. P. J. Goldstein et al., "Crack and Homicide in New York City, 1988: A Conceptually Based Event Analysis," *Contemporary Drug Problems* 16 (1989): 651–87; Blumstein et al., *Criminal Careers*; D. Chaiken and M. Chaiken, "Drugs and Predatory Crime," in *Drugs and Crime, Crime and Justice: A Review of the Literature*, Vol. 13, eds. M. Tonry and J. Q. Wilson (Chicago: University of Chicago, 1990), 203–39.

12. B. Johnson et al., *Taking Care of Business: The Economics of Crime by Heroin Users* (Lexington, Mass.: Lexington Books, 1985); Fagan, "The Social Organization of Drug Use"; Chin, *Chinese Subculture and Criminality*.

13. This definition can be compared with two formal definitions. First, there is the definition provided by Kroeber and Kluckhon in their massive analysis of culture (A. L. Kroeber and C. Kluckhon, *Culture: A Critical Review of Concepts and Definitions* [New York: Vintage Books, 1963], 357). Summarizing a multitude of research on the topic, the authors offer the following definition:

Culture consists of patterns, explicit and implicit, of and for behaviors acquired and transmitted by symbols, constituting the distinctive achievement of human groups, including their embodiments in artifacts; the essential core of culture consists of traditional (i.e., historically derived and selected) ideas and especially their attached values; culture systems may, on the other hand, be considered as products of action, on the other as conditioning elements of further action.

Another, shorter definition is provided by T. Shibutani and K. M. Kwan in *Ethnic Stratification: A Comparative Approach* (New York: Macmillan, 1965), 58:"Culture consists of the assumptions with which people in a particular group approach their world, assumptions that are learned by each new generation while participating in organized transactions."

14. W. G. Skogen, *Disorder and Decline: Crime and the Spiral of Decay in American Neighborhoods* (New York: Free Press, 1990); E. Anderson, *A Place on the Corner* (Chicago: University of Chicago Press, 1978); E. Anderson, *Streetwise: Race, Class, and Change in an Urban Community* (Chicago: University of Chicago Press, 1990); E. Anderson, *Alienation and Crime among the Ghetto Poor*, unpublished report prepared for the Panel on the Understanding and Control of Violence, 1991; W. J. Wilson, *The Truly Disadvantaged: The Inner City, the Underclass, and Public Policy* (Chicago: University of Chicago Press, 1987).

15. Anderson, *A Place on the Corner*; Anderson, *Streetwise*; Anderson, *Alienation and Crime*; Sullivan, *Getting Paid*; Wilson, *The Truly Disadvantaged*.

16. Anderson, *Streetwise*.

17. E. Anderson, "The Code of the Streets," *Atlantic Monthly* 273 (1994): 81–94.

18. L. Heath et al., "Effects of Media Violence on Children," *Archives of General Psychiatry* 46 (1989): 376–79; G. Comstock and H. Paik, *The Effects of Television Violence on Aggressive Behavior: A Meta-Analysis*, unpublished report to the National Academy of Sciences Panel on the Understanding and Control of Violent Behavior, Washington, D.C., 1990.

19. C. Bodinger-deUriarte, *Hate Crime: Sourcebook for Schools* (Los Alamitos, Calif.: Southwest Regional Laboratory, 1991), 10.

20. R. Berk, "Thinking about Hate-Motivated Crimes," *Journal of Interpersonal Violence* 5 (1990): 334–49; J. Mann, "The Statistic No One Can Bear to Believe," *The Washington Post*, December 1990, D3; O. Clayton and V. Webb, "A Longitudinal Look at Homicides in a Midwestern City: Has It Changed?" *Sociological Practice Review* 2 (1991): 40.

21. Berk, "Thinking about Hate-Motivated Crimes"; N. R. Pierce, "Recurring Nightmare of Hate Crimes," *National Journal* 3045 (December 15, 1990); H. Daughty, "Who Really Killed Yusef Hawkins?," *New York Times* (August 29, 1989): A19.

22. Pierce, "Recurring Nightmare."

23. Bodinger–deUriarte, *Hate Crime*, 11.

24. Pierce, "Recurring Nightmare."

25. Berk, "Thinking about Hate-Motivated Crimes."

26. J. Pasternak, "How Hate Comes to Full Boil," *Los Angeles Times* (December 9, 1990): A1, A42–43.

27. Berk, "Thinking about Hate-Motivated Crimes."

28. Los Angeles County Office of Education, Attendance and Pupil Services, and the Los Angeles County Commission on Human Relations, *Intergroup Conflict in Los Angeles County Schools*, 1990.

29. C. R. Shaw and H. D. McKay, *Juvenile Delinquency and Urban Areas* (Chicago: University of Chicago Press, 1942).

30. R. A. Gordon, "Issues in the Ecological Study of Delinquency," *American Sociological Review* 32, No. 6 (1967): 927–44; H. S. Bullock, "Urban Homicide in Theory and Fact," *Journal of Criminal Law, Criminology, and Police Science* 45 (1955): 565–75; R. W. Beasley and G. Antunes, "The Etiology of Urban Crime: An Ecological Analysis," *Criminology* 11 (1974): 439–61; K. Mladenka and K. Hill, "A Reexamination of the Etiology of Urban Crime," *Criminology* 13 (1976): 491–506.

31. There have been at least two methodological problems in linking poverty to violent crime. First, there is the problem of separating ethnic/racial status from community influences. Blacks and Hispanics, for example, tend to live in high poverty areas to a greater extent than do whites. For example, Reiss and Roth (A. J. Reiss and J. A. Roth,

eds., *Understanding and Preventing Violence* [Washington, D.C.: National Academy Press, 1993], 132) note: "In 1980...in the five largest U.S. cities, 85 percent of poor blacks lived in poverty areas, compared with only 30 percent of poor whites; nearly 40 percent of poor blacks lived in areas characterized by extreme poverty, compared with 7 percent of poor whites."

Second, the communities in which various ethnic and racial groups reside are vastly different culturally and structurally. These differences are extremely difficult, if not impossible, to measure, and include differences in job quality, access to information about jobs, and access to high-paying jobs (see Wilson, *The Truly Disadvantaged*).

32. R. J. Sampson, "Structural Density and Criminal Victimization," *Criminology* 21 (1983): 276–93; Sampson, "Neighborhood and Crime: The Structural Determinants of Personal Victimization," *Journal of Research in Crime and Delinquency* 22, No. 1 (1985): 7–40; Sampson, "Personal Violence by Strangers: An Extension and Test of the Opportunity Model of Predatory Victimization," *Journal of Criminal Law and Criminology* 78 (1987): 327–56; D. R. Smith and G. R. Jarjoura, "Social Structure and Criminal Victimization," *Journal of Research in Crime and Delinquency* 25 (1988): 27–52.

33. R. B. Taylor and J. Covington, "Neighborhood Changes in Ecology and Violence," *Criminology* 26, No. 4 (1988): 553–89; K. Land et al., "Structural Co-Variates of Homicide Rates: Are There Any Invariances Across Time and Space?," *American Journal of Sociology* 95 (1990): 922–63.

34. L. E. Lynn, Jr., and M. G. H. McGeary, *Inner-City Poverty in the United States* (Washington, D.C.: National Academy Press, 1990); M. G. H. McGeary and L. E. Lynn, Jr., *Urban Change and Poverty* (Washington, D.C.: National Academy Press, 1988).

35. E. Stark and A. Flitcraft, "Medical Therapy as Repression: The Case of the Battered Woman," *Health and Medicine* 1 (1982): 29–32.

36. E. Stark, "The Battering Syndrome: Social Knowledge, Social Therapy, and the Abuse of Women," Ph.D. diss. (Binghamton, N.Y.: State University of New York, Binghamton, 1984); I. H. Frieze and A. Browne, "Violence in Marriage," in *Family Violence*, eds. L. Ohlin and M. Tonry (Chicago: University of Chicago Press, 1989), 163–218.

37. M. A. Straus et al., *Behind Closed Doors: Violence in the American Family* (Garden City, N.J.: Doubleday, 1980), 11.

38. C. P. Widom "The Cycle of Violence," *Science* 244 (1989): 160–66.

39. C. P. Widom, *The Cycle of Violence*, a research in-brief (Washington, D.C.: National Institute of Justice, 1992).

40. Stark, "The Battering Syndrome."

41. National Education Association, *Handbook 1993–1994* (Washington, D.C.: NEA, 1993).

42. Ibid., 30.

15

Waging Peace in Our Schools: The Resolving Conflict Creatively Program

Linda Lantieri, William DeJong, and Janet Dutrey

THE ANGEL OF REDHOOK

It was the morning of December 17, 1992. I was returning the last of several telephone calls at my office before I hurried out to Long Island to be with my Dad, who had been taken to the hospital once again because of heart trouble. As I thought of my Dad and my need to be by his side, little did I know what the morning would actually bring: a friend's violent death, followed by profound feelings of hopelessness and doubt about the value of my life's work.

Shortly after 11:00 A.M., at an elementary school in Redhook, Brooklyn, a third-grade boy erupted in anger, ran out of his class, and left the school building. His principal, Patrick Daly, got word of what happened and quickly went to find the boy. Within minutes, as Pat walked through the housing project that surrounds the school, he was caught in the crossfire of a drug deal gone sour and killed almost instantly. I rushed to P.S. 15 as soon as I heard the news.

Ironically, P.S. 15 was one of three schools that had worked with me and Tom Roderick, Executive Director of Educators for Social Responsibility Metro, to pilot the Resolving Conflict Creatively Program (RCCP) in 1985. Tom and I knew Pat Daly to be a man of courage who took Goethe at his word: "Whatever you can do or dream you can do, begin it. Boldness has magic, power and genius in it. Begin it now." As I walked through the doors of Pat's school, a place that had become an oasis of peace for kids and families in the neighborhood, I was hit by the bitter realization that I would never see the "Angel of Redhook" walking those hallways again.

The next several weeks are a blur to many of us who knew and loved Pat. Those weeks after his death hit me in the part of my being where all my feelings of self-doubt and helplessness live. I wondered, How can RCCP's message of non-violence, empowerment, and hope ever match the grinding and relentless violence that has become such a pervasive force in our lives? But giving in to despair has never been my style. I also remember these words by Goethe: "Of freedom and of life one is only deserving, who every day must conquer them anew."

Almost two years after Pat's death, under the strong and committed leadership of principal Mary Manti, Pat's legacy lives on at P.S. 15, now called the Patrick Daly School. Although Pat's death was a heartrending reminder of how far our work must still go to change the climate of violence that surrounds us, I am also aware of how far we have come in just one decade. I will always remain grateful for Pat Daly's example, his courage and inspiration. I still hold the vision that one day we will all live in communities where we will always be able to walk safely.

—Linda Lantieri
Co-founder and National Director,
The Resolving Conflict Creatively Program

Violent crime is commonplace in the United States, a public health problem of true epidemic proportions. It is street crime that often haunts us, making us fearful and undermining our sense of community, but we should be equally concerned about the violence that occurs among people who know and often love one another. More than 60 percent of the homicides in this country are committed among people who know each other.[1]

What especially alarms Americans is that this epidemic of violence now touches our children so deeply. Homicide has become the third leading cause of death for children five to fourteen years old, and the leading cause of death for young African-American men. Counting suicides, a gun takes the life of an American child every two hours, so that our children are fifteen times more likely to be killed by gunfire than children growing up in Northern Ireland.[2]

A number of factors contribute to this problem. Among the most important is the value our society places on violent solutions to conflict. By example (and sometimes through explicit instruction) we teach our children several deadly lessons:

- Conflict produces a winner and a loser.
- Using physical force to get what you want is legitimate.
- Force must be met by even stronger counterforce.
- Avoiding violence is a sign of weakness.

Reinforcing these lessons, television and movies—a dominant influence in the lives of most young people—provide graphic images of countless ways to hurt, maim, and kill, often in the name of heroism, manliness, and righteousness. Studies of television violence have found that, on average, 5.3 violent scenes are shown on prime-time network television every hour. Fifty-two percent of the characters in dramatic programs engage in violence. Children's Saturday morning programming averages twenty-three violent scenes per hour, with 83 percent of the characters engaging in violence.[3]

Unfortunately, our schools are no longer a safe haven from violence. The U.S. Department of Justice estimates that each day one hundred thousand children carry guns to school. In a nationwide survey of students ages twelve to nineteen, researchers found that 9 percent of the students became crime victims in or around their school over a six-month period. Fifteen percent of the students said their school had gangs, and 16 percent claimed that a student had attacked or threatened a teacher at their school.[4]

No school seems immune. A 1993 Harris poll of students in grades 6 through 12 found a widespread fear of violence at school, even in suburban and rural areas.[5] This fear is not unreasonable. More than four hundred thousand violent crimes are reported in and around our nation's schools each year, with still far more crimes going unreported.[6]

The toll this violence takes on our children's psyche is clear. More than one-third of the students in the Harris poll said they believe their lives will be cut short by violence. Miguel Sánchez, a student from New York City, described his fear during the 1993 National Hearings on Violence and the Child in Washington, D.C.: "When I wake up in the morning, I ask myself, am I going to survive this day? So every day I try to make it seem as if it is my last day on this earth. So far I've been lucky. I don't know when my luck is going to run out."

THE SEARCH FOR SOLUTIONS

As our nation approaches the year 2000, our children face an ever increasing likelihood of involvement in violence, both as victims and as perpetrators. Working to reduce this problem must be at the top of our nation's educational agenda. In a recent visit to RCCP, Deputy Secretary of Education Madeline Kunin explained that the school reform movement could not move forward without paying attention to the social problems that affect our children and their ability to learn. Chief among these problems, she said, is the threat of violence.

Although the problems facing our children are complicated, immense, and horrifying, we do know a great deal about what causes violence, and this knowledge can help direct our search for solutions. First, we need to teach our children ethical and moral values that emphasize respect and concern for others, principles that are universally acknowledged as the basis for any just society. Second, children need to learn the emotional and social skills that will help them gain understanding and control over their potentially disruptive emotions, and help them manage the conflict they will continue to face in their lives. In short, we must teach our children ethical and emotional literacy.

The Resolving Conflict Creatively Program (RCCP) has proven its effectiveness in accomplishing these goals, and is now regarded as one of the most promising school violence prevention programs in operation.[7] In this chapter we describe RCCP's educational approach to prepare young people with the knowledge, understanding, beliefs, and skills they need to be "citizens of peace" in the twenty-first century.

Those interested in replicating RCCP's approach should keep two points in mind. First, RCCP and other violence-prevention programs cannot be "parachuted" into a school. Building an effective program takes time. Although teacher training, staff development, and other resources provided by outside agencies are necessary, the process of developing an effective program must ultimately be driven by leadership from within. Only the school's principal, teachers, students, and parents can create a sustainable program that will have a strong impact on the learning environment.

Second, while RCCP has demonstrated that principals, teachers, and students can work together to create "peaceable schools," this work must eventually be carried outside the schools to create "peaceable neighborhoods." An African proverb teaches us that "it takes a whole village to raise a child." Similarly, we are convinced that it will take the "whole village" working together to rescue our children from the epidemic of violence.

RCCP: THE PEACEABLE SCHOOL

RCCP began in 1985 as a collaboration of the New York City Public Schools and Educators for Social Responsibility's New York City Chapter (ESR Metro). Now in its tenth year, RCCP teaches lessons in creative conflict resolution and intergroup understanding to students, teachers, school administrators, and parents in five school systems: the New York City Public Schools, the Anchorage School District, Alaska; the New Orleans Public Schools, Louisiana; the Vista Unified School District in Southern California; and the South Orange-Maplewood School District in New Jersey.

Participating in RCCP during the 1993–1994 school year were 120,000 young people in over three hundred schools, making RCCP the largest school-based program of its kind in the country. ESR National established the RCCP National Center in September 1993 to support national replication efforts already begun, and to provide technical assistance to additional school systems as they develop and implement conflict-resolution programs.

RCCP is based on a relatively simple idea, but one that is often hard to carry out: people should listen to one another when there is a problem and work toward a peaceable solution. By encouraging open discussion in a supportive atmosphere, RCCP helps students, teachers, school administrators, and parents better understand conflict and its roots. Most important, RCCP teaches practical skills that can facilitate the discovery of creative solutions to conflicts. In short, RCCP helps people realize that they have many choices other than passivity or aggression for dealing with conflict, and gives them the skills they need to make those choices in their own lives.

From the beginning, the RCCP curriculum has focused as much on issues of diversity as it has on conflict resolution. One of the most pressing problems in schools and among youth in general involves issues of cultural and racial bias. RCCP has found that conflict-resolution skills are extremely useful in enabling students of different races and cultures to work through their disputes. RCCP is unique in covering both arenas.

What is also different about RCCP is its focus on changing the total school environment to create a community that lives by a credo of nonviolence. Unlike most school-based programs, RCCP is institutionalized within the school, and its nonviolence message is seen as part of the school's central mission. RCCP's hope is that the lessons of peace and intercultural understanding will eventually become a basic part of every school's curriculum, with as much emphasis devoted to teaching negotiation and other conflict-resolution skills as is given to other academic subjects.

By creating a "peaceable school," a safe environment where students are encouraged to experiment with peaceful ways of resolving conflict, RCCP teachers strive to give their students a new image of what their world can be. For this to happen, however, the teachers themselves must change. They must learn, and then apply, a new set of skills for heading off and resolving conflict. Even more difficult, they must adopt a new style of classroom management, one that fundamentally involves a sharing of power with students so that they can learn how to deal with their own disputes.

To this end, RCCP's comprehensive approach includes the following components: (1) a K-12 classroom curriculum; (2) a student-led mediation program; (3) professional training and ongoing technical assistance and support for teachers; (4) parents' training; and (5) administrators' training.

RCCP costs annually just over $33 per student. To educators accustomed to buying packaged curricula that sell for a few hundred dollars, this might seem expensive. It should be remembered, however, that RCCP is much more than a curriculum. Rather, it is an intensive effort at school reform, with a strong emphasis on teacher training and professional development.

Regular Classroom Instruction Using a K-12 Curriculum

RCCP's K-12 curriculum stresses the modeling of nonviolent alternatives for dealing with conflict, teaching negotiation and other conflict-resolution skills, and demonstrating to students that they can play a powerful role in creating a more peaceful world.

Accordingly, RCCP concentrates on teaching several key component skills: active listening, assertiveness (as opposed to aggressiveness or passivity), expressing feelings in appropriate ways, perspective-taking, cooperation, negotiation, and countering bias. Because learning these skills requires weekly practice, teachers are encouraged to do at least one "peace lesson" a week, to use "teachable moments" that arise because of what is happening in the classroom or the world at large, and to "infuse" conflict-resolution lessons into the regular academic program.

RCCP lessons involve role-playing, interviewing, group dialogue, brainstorming, and other experiential learning strategies, all of which require a high degree of student participation and interaction. Since the elementary and secondary curricula require good verbal skills, several adjustments are necessary to accommodate the variety of cognitive and communications abilities of special needs students. With that in mind, the RCCP curriculum for special needs students breaks the lessons into smaller steps and makes greater use of visual and kinesthetic learning modalities (that is, art, mime, and nonverbal communication). In 1993 RCCP in New York embarked on an exciting pilot of its work in the bicultural and bilingual domain as well.

RCCP seeks to address racism and other root causes of violence through lessons on "multicultural appreciation" and "bias awareness." Teachers help their students become aware of their prejudices and to see that stereotypes are based on inaccurate or incomplete information. Differences among people are acknowledged, but RCCP urges that they be seen as a cause for celebration and respect rather than as an excuse for prejudice and discrimination.

Most important, RCCP seeks to foster a classroom climate in which students are affirmed and respected for who they are. RCCP staff works with teachers to create a "multicultural classroom," where teachers make a special point of identifying and celebrating the diversity of their students. In such a classroom, expressions of racial, ethnic, or gender bias are not tolerated. Teachers stay vigilant to spontaneous comments or actions that seem motivated by bias, and use these opportunities to teach about prejudice and discrimination.

Peer Mediation

A key component of RCCP's plan for school change, the student mediation program provides a strong peer model for nonviolent conflict resolution and reinforces students' emerging skills in working out their own problems. Ultimately, by reducing the number of fights between students, the mediation component can contribute to a more peaceful school climate. It is important to note that student mediation is not a substitute for an effective school discipline policy, for if strictly enforced sanctions against fighting are not in place, students are unlikely to turn to the mediators for help.

RCCP embraces the concept of "principled negotiation" outlined by Fisher and Ury in their best-seller, *Getting to Yes*.[8] With this approach, mediation is not a contest of wills to see whose position will prevail, but an opportunity for mutual problem-solving. The ultimate goal of mediation is not to force one of the parties to give up something or to find a way of "splitting the difference," but to forge a "win–win" solution that meets the underlying interests and needs of both parties.

RCCP initiates the mediation component only in schools that have been participating in RCCP for at least a year and have a group of teachers who regularly use the curriculum. As explained by ESR's philosophy, "School mediation programs are best implemented as part of a larger effort to train staff and students in conflict resolution." This is a significant strength over mediation-only approaches used elsewhere in the country.

Although the mediation component is an important part of RCCP's approach, funding limitations have prevented its widespread implementation. An elementary school mediation program costs an average of $10,000 per year to run, which covers training of faculty coordinators; staff time for supervision and support; ongoing consultation by RCCP staff; and various supplies, including tee-shirts and manuals. Mediation programs are in operation in about one-third of RCCP schools nationwide.

Professional Development for Teachers

RCCP uses both formal training sessions and one-on-one consultation to teach regular classroom teachers how to present the curriculum. Equally important, the teachers are led to reexamine how they handle conflict in their own lives, particularly in their relationships with students. With a strong commitment from the principal to make the school violence-free, and with changes in the teachers' style of classroom management, students are provided a supportive environment for working on their emerging conflict-resolution skills.

RCCP first provides twenty-four hours of introductory training in a series of after-school or full-day sessions. The training introduces the RCCP philosophy and the curriculum; teaches communication, conflict resolution, and intergroup relations skills; and demonstrates "infusion" strategies for integrating these concepts and skills into social studies, language arts, and other academic subjects.

Training also covers effective teaching techniques—in particular, role-playing, interviewing, group dialogue, brainstorming, and other experiential approaches. Teachers are encouraged to use cooperative learning groups, assigning teams of students to study, work on projects, and learn together. Such teams provide diverse groups of students with a common purpose, which can lead to new friendships and a reduction of prejudice.

A key to RCCP's success is the follow-up support that teachers receive. Use of the curriculum requires teachers to relinquish some control over what happens in their classroom. Because many teachers are uncomfortable with this, at least at first, RCCP provides continuing consultation and support during the school year. Each new teacher is assigned to an RCCP staff developer who visits between six and ten times a year, giving demonstration lessons, helping the teacher prepare, observing classes, giving feedback, and sustaining the teacher's motivation. In addition, the staff developer convenes bimonthly follow-up meetings after school so that teachers can receive additional training, share their experiences, discuss concerns, and plan schoolwide events. During a teacher's second year, the staff developer visits only two or three times. The 1990 evaluation of RCCP in New York City by Metis Associates, Inc. found that the support of staff developers was regarded by teachers as the single most important aspect of the program.

Parents' Training

No one would disagree that parents and teachers should work together to teach children how to resolve conflict nonviolently. The reason is clear: If students are to use their emerging conflict resolution and intergroup relations skills outside of school, they must have family support. The problem in bringing parents into the process is equally clear. It is not that parents actively resist a message of nonviolence, though some might do so. Rather, it is that parents who are busy making a living and raising a family have difficulty finding the time to be involved.

In the last five years, parent education has become a top priority for RCCP. Staff recently launched a Parent Involvement Program that was piloted in New York City and is being disseminated to other RCCP sites nationwide. A team of two or three parents per school is trained for sixty hours to lead four two-and-one-half-hour workshops for other parents on intergroup relations, family communication, and conflict resolution. Through this "training-of-trainers" program, nearly two thousand parents nationwide have received training to date.

Administrators' Training

This component of RCCP introduces school administrators to the concepts and skills of conflict resolution and bias awareness and shows them how they can achieve effective implementation of the program. RCCP's primary aim is to encourage administrators to embrace and model the humane and creative approaches to dealing with conflict and bias that students are learning through the classroom curriculum. RCCP has also learned that the more principals understand and "buy into" the program, the more willing they are to provide the flexibility and administrative support needed to make RCCP work at the school level.

Evaluation

Since the movement to introduce this work in violence prevention into schools is relatively young, hard evidence on the effectiveness of school-based programs is scant. Quality research in the fields of conflict resolution and emotional literacy need to be supported and encouraged. There is a great need for comprehensive studies to provide an in-depth picture of the impact this work is having on the lives of young people. It is equally important to investigate critically what is working and what is not.

In 1992 the Centers for Disease Control (CDC) identified ten promising programs to evaluate in the next three years in the field of violence prevention, allocating close to $2.5 million. RCCP in New York City was one of the grant recipients chosen from among more than four hundred applicants.

Prior to the CDC grant, Metis Associates, Inc. conducted two independent evaluations of New York City's RCCP in 1988 and 1990. Uniformly, these evaluations showed high enthusiasm among RCCP teachers who reported decreases in name-calling and physical violence among their students. In 1990, for example, about 71 percent of the teachers surveyed said RCCP led to less physical violence in the classroom. Furthermore, over 98 percent of the teachers agreed that mediation had given children who were trained as mediators an important tool for dealing with the everyday conflicts that surface among students.

Student achievement tests have confirmed the teachers' view, showing that most RCCP students learn the key concepts of conflict resolution and are able to apply them in responding to hypothetical conflicts. In addition, the RCCP students themselves have reported having fewer fights and engaging less frequently in name-calling, as compared to a matched control group.

Teachers report that they have changed, too. In the Metis evaluation, roughly nine out of ten teachers said they had an improved understanding of children's needs and were now more willing to let students take responsibility for solving their own conflicts. Many also said that they had applied their increased knowledge of conflict-resolution techniques in their personal lives.

THE PEACEABLE NEIGHBORHOOD

Can students use these conflict-resolution lessons in the outside world, where the ethic of the streets supports the rightness of power over "win–win" solutions to conflict? Truthfully, some students, owing to the circumstances in which they live, will find it impossible to apply what they have learned. But many others will be emboldened to try, and that is an important first step. In fact, when they do try, many students are surprised by the success they have.

In the end, however, young people will consistently apply these lessons in their everyday lives only when they become convinced that nonviolence can work. To convince them, we must create not only "peaceable schools," but also "peaceable neighborhoods." To achieve that, we must try to change the climate of violence that drives antisocial behavior. More than that, we must also address the social and economic conditions that feed that climate.[9]

School administrators and teachers have a critical role to play in making this happen. First, they can reach out to the leaders of community-based youth programs to instruct them in violence prevention and mediation strategies. One of the keys to effective prevention is for young people to hear a consistent message of nonviolence from multiple sources.[10]

Second, more educators must get involved with parents, police, religious leaders, and neighborhood coalitions to create after-school and weekend programs that focus both on violence reduction and more broadly on problems such as low academic achievement and poor self-esteem.[11] Ultimately, these programs—athletic leagues, tutoring, mentoring, and so forth—will help restore and sustain community life.[12]

Third, working in conjunction with local leadership, more school administrators and teachers must become advocates for bringing new resources to the neighborhoods they serve. Creating a "peaceable neighborhood" requires that residents of all neighborhoods have access to preventive health care, readily available treatment for alcoholism and drug addiction, better housing, and greater economic opportunity.[13] This is a politically charged perspective, but one that, ultimately, seems unavoidable. Educators should not (and cannot) carry this burden alone, but they must lend their voice to the cause.

A teacher in an RCCP high school in the South Bronx was recently conducting a "go-around" in which she asked the students to share one goal they each had for the future. One young man, Eugene, said, "My goal is to be alive at 21." He was then eighteen years old. As educators and concerned citizens, we have to help turn this tide of violence around enough so that young people like Eugene can have a vision of their future that goes beyond their very survival. Working to create safer schools and neighborhoods through violence prevention can help make that happen.

CAUSING CHANGE

Marian Wright Edelman, founder of the Children's Defense Fund, tells the story of meeting a seventy-five-year-old man who was waiting outside in the rain to pay his last respects to Thurgood Marshall, the first black Supreme Court justice, who died in 1993. "He didn't just witness change," the man said of Marshall, "he caused change." That is what we also hope to do as the RCCP National Center continues to provide desperately needed leadership for school systems across the country. We expect to cause quite a bit of change.

For additional information, please contact: The Resolving Conflict Creatively Program, 163 Third Avenue #103, New York, New York 10003. Phone: (212) 387-0225; Fax: (212) 387-0510.

NOTES

This chapter was adapted from *Peacing Our Schools*, Janet Dutrey and Linda Lantieri (Boston: Beacon Press, forthcoming February 1996).

1. D. Prothrow-Stith and M. Weissman, *Deadly Consequences: How Violence Is Destroying Our Teenage Population and a Plan to Begin Solving the Problem* (New York: HarperCollins, 1991).

2. Children's Defense Fund, *Cease Fire in the War Against Children*, a brochure published by the Children's Defense Fund, 1994.

3. University of Pennsylvania, Annenberg School for Communication, *Television Violence Profile* No. 16 (January 1994).

4. L. D. Bastian and B. M. Taylor, *School Crime: A National Crime Victimization Survey Report* (Washington, D.C.: U.S. Department of Justice, 1991).

5. L. Harris, *A Study of Experiences, Perceptions and Apprehensions about Guns among Young People in America,* a study prepared for the Harvard School of Public Health (New York: L. H. Research, 1993).

6. New York City Board of Education, Chancellor's Working Group on School-Based Violence Prevention, *Draft Report* (New York: New York City Board of Education, 1994).

7. W. DeJong, *Preventing Interpersonal Violence among Youth: An Introduction to School, Community, and Mass Media Strategies* (Washington, D.C.: U.S. Department of Justice, 1994); Prothrow-Stith and Weissman, *Deadly Consequences*; R. Wilson-Brewer et al., *Violence Prevention for Early Teens: The State of the Art and Guidelines for Future Program Evaluation* (Newton, Mass.: Education Development Center, 1990).

8. R. Fisher and W. Ury, *Getting to Yes: Negotiating Agreement Without Giving In* (Boston: Houghton Mifflin, 1981).

9. M. A. Bailin, "Attributes of Successful Programs for Adolescents: What Works," *Bulletin of the New York Academy of Medicine* 67 (1991): 583–94; R. J. Haggerty, "Health Policy Initiatives in Adolescence," *Bulletin of the New York Academy of Medicine* 67 (1991): 514–26.

10. Prothrow-Stith and Weissman, *Deadly Consequences*.

11. Haggerty, "Health Policy Initiatives in Adolescence"; R. Wilson-Brewer and B. Jacklin, *Violence Prevention Strategies Targeted at the General Population of Minority Youth* (Newton, Mass.: Education Development Center, 1990).

12. B. Webster and E. F. Connors, *Research in Brief: The Police, Drugs, and Public Housing* (Washington, D.C.: U.S. Department of Justice, 1992).

13. L. A. Curtis, "Neighborhood, Family, and Employment: Toward a New Public Policy Against Violence," in *American Violence and Public Policy: An Update of the National Commission on the Causes and Prevention of Violence*, ed. L. A. Curtis (New Haven, Conn.: Yale University Press, 1985).

16

Strategies to Reduce School Violence: The New Mexico Center for Dispute Resolution

Melinda Smith

The proliferation of mediation and conflict programs for children and families throughout the United States over the past decade is an indication of their potential to address the crisis of youth violence in our society. It is estimated that over five thousand schools throughout the country are now implementing some form of conflict-resolution or peer mediation program.[1] The agencies that have been instrumental in this growth are community mediation centers in cities throughout the United States, which have grown from a handful in the mid-1970s to an estimated five hundred programs today.[2]

Community mediation programs train local volunteers to mediate interpersonal and neighborhood disputes referred from the community and the courts. In the mediation process, a neutral third party intervenes in a dispute with the consent of the parties to assist them in reaching a mutually satisfactory agreement. Mediators help the parties vent feelings, express their points of view, clarify needs, and resolve their conflicts. The community mediation field has adapted this process for use with children in schools and in other settings.

THE NEW MEXICO CENTER FOR DISPUTE RESOLUTION

The experience of the New Mexico Center for Dispute Resolution (NMCDR), a community mediation agency that specializes in programs for children and families, is illustrative of the growth of youth mediation programs. In 1984 two elementary schools in New Mexico began piloting peer mediation programs; ten years later, nearly 250 elementary and secondary schools throughout the state had initiated programs with assistance from NMCDR.

New Mexico is among the most violent areas in the country for teens. The state ranks the worst, except for the District of Columbia, in the violent death rate for children between fifteen and nineteen: there were 121 deaths per one hundred thousand youths in 1990. New Mexico ranks forty-ninth in the country in percentage of students graduating from high school.[3] Truancy, family dysfunction, and teen pregnancy and poverty all contribute to this statistic.

NMCDR is attempting to create opportunities for young people to learn and practice conflict-resolution skills in a range of environments. It has developed a continuum of prevention and intervention programs that introduce conflict-resolution processes into the lives of children and families in the home, the community, and the juvenile justice system. These programs include:

— The Parent/Child Mediation Program, which helps families negotiate concrete agreements of daily living and prevent runaway, truant, and incorrigible behavior.

— The Victim/Juvenile Offender Mediation Program, which brings together offenders and their victims to negotiate restitution agreements with the help of trained volunteer mediators.

— The Violence Intervention Program, which teaches conflict-resolution skills to violent juvenile offenders and their parents while the offenders are on intensive probation.

— Mediation in Juvenile Corrections Settings, which trains staff and residents of corrections and detention facilities to mediate youth conflict at the facility.

There is a growing consensus in the field that for youth mediation and conflict-resolution programs to have an impact in reducing violence, practitioners must design approaches that are consistent with the following principles:

• School-based conflict-resolution programs must change the culture of the schools, not just the students. School staff must be committed to model and reinforce the skills for students and create a school community that adheres to the positive expression and resolution of conflict.

• Violence-prevention programs must be reframed as positive youth development programs that involve young people in the design, decisionmaking, and implementation.

• There is a need for interdisciplinary, broad-based, and community-driven responses to violence. Collaborative efforts among schools, community agencies, policymakers, and other stakeholders must be initiated. We must go beyond the classroom if we are going to make an impact in reducing violence.[4]

In its programs and approaches, NMCDR is attempting to adhere to these principles. This chapter focuses on NMCDR's experience in several areas in which it has developed school-based models or approaches, including:

• School peer mediation and conflict-resolution programs
• Mediation of gang disputes
• School-based parent/child mediation
• Suspension mediation
• School/neighborhood mediation

Each of these program approaches and their relationship to violence prevention is described, program evaluation results are presented, and implementation issues are discussed.

SCHOOL MEDIATION

NMCDR operates one of the largest and oldest school mediation programs in the country. This program has been cast alternately as a delinquency prevention, child abuse prevention, and violence prevention program by the state agencies and other sources that have funded it. As a prevention program, its purpose is to create a school environment committed to the value of positive expression and management of conflict, and to impart essential communication and problem-solving skills to students and staff.

The New Mexico model combines classroom conflict-resolution curricula with a mediation component. At the elementary level, selected students are trained in a simple mediation process and take turns patrolling the playground to offer their conflict-resolution services to their peers who are having fights. At the secondary level, student mediators meet with disputants in a supervised but private setting, such as a counselor's office, to help fellow students resolve differences. At both the elementary and secondary levels, a conflict-resolution curriculum can also be integrated into the ongoing classroom curriculum so that all students have an opportunity to increase their communication and problem-solving skills. Teachers are provided with sets of curriculum materials that teach a range of skills, including listening and communication skills, understanding feelings, problem-solving, anger management, and understanding others' points of view.

From the beginning, the strategy in New Mexico was to maximize the program's potential impact in communities by developing a statewide program. Currently, thirty-nine communities in the state have implemented school mediation programs. Significant funding has been obtained during the past several years from the New Mexico Department of Children, Youth, and Families to expand the program to many more districts and schools. The program has been established not just as a school program, but as an important prevention model in the spectrum of programs in the social service and juvenile justice systems. The New Mexico program has reached diverse communities in the state: multicultural urban settings, the rural Navajo reservation, ranching communities, small Hispanic towns in northern New Mexico, and Indian pueblos.

Another important strategy has been to encourage and assist school districts in implementing the program at all levels of instruction in order to reinforce conflict-resolution skills through the entire educational experience. Furthermore, when NMCDR staff work with schools, there is a school-level requirement that 80 percent of the staff vote to implement the program in order to maximize commitment to long-term implementation. School staff must be willing to use and model the conflict-resolution processes they expect the students to use.

In order to institutionalize programs so that they are integrated into the daily life of the school on a long-term basis, NMCDR works at the school-district level to develop long-range implementation plans. District teams are formed to do planning and to identify district trainers who are responsible for training teachers and students to expand the program to new schools. The results of this approach have been mixed. Some districts have accomplished districtwide implementation and operate with little outside assistance from NMCDR, while other districts lack the leadership and commitment to fully implement the program. Ultimately, statewide mandates may be the only way to fully institutionalize these programs. Illinois, for example, has recently mandated violence-prevention and conflict-resolution instruction in grades 4 through 12 in all public schools.

What is the impact of these programs on school violence and fighting? Practitioners and researchers throughout the country agree on the need for long-term research to answer this question. In New Mexico, as well as in other states where school mediation programs are implemented, there is plenty of anecdotal evidence to suggest that such programs are having a positive impact on school climate as well as on individual students who participate. One Albuquerque elementary school principal commented: "We were having 100 to 150 fights every month on the playground before we started the program. By the end of the year, we were having maybe 10."[5] Observations like this are common. In fact, some programs at the elementary level reduce playground fighting to such an extent that mediators find themselves out of a job.

Other positive reports come from parents of mediators. A mediation program at an Albuquerque high school with a large "at-risk" population did a survey of parents of mediators to see if there had been any impact on the students' behavior at home. The mother of one mediator reported:

My daughter behaves better than before. She is no longer involved in problems... she no longer spends times with her negative friends. She tries to help people like her friends, her nieces and nephews, and her family. She has become a role model in our family. I would recommend the mediation program in order to have a better community and school.[6]

Principals of schools implementing mediation indicate that the biggest program impact is in increased self-confidence and problem-solving abilities among students. These results were found in a 1991 survey conducted by the New Mexico Department of Education. Sixty-six principals rated the effectiveness of the program in a range of categories listed in the accompanying table:

Criteria	Percentage of Effective or Highly Effective Responses
Increased self-confidence	93
Increased problem-solving skills	90
Improved self-esteem	88
Developed leadership skills	87
Improved communication skills	86

Provided alternative to student violence	82
Resolved school-based disputes	81
Promoted active listening	81
Changed attitude toward conflict	79
Helped students deal with peer pressure	66

Several studies of the New Mexico program have been conducted by independent evaluators to assess the program's impact. The first study, conducted in 1987, compared elementary (N=331) and middle school (N=53) students participating in the program as mediators with a control group of elementary (N=193) and middle school (N=181) students at nonparticipating schools. Students completed questionnaires both before and after mediation training and program implementation, responding to questions grouped into four broad areas: (1) students' attitudes and approaches to conflict and problem-solving; (2) students' self-concept and peer relationships; (3) students' attachment to school; and (4) students' perceptions of their social skills. Results showed that at the middle school level there were statistically significant differences between the pre- and post-test gains of the two groups in the first three areas. There were similar differences between the elementary school program and control groups, but the only significant difference at the elementary level was in students' attitudes and approaches to conflict and problem-solving.[7]

A second study, based on interviews with school personnel and students participating in the program, was conducted in 1990. It showed reductions in school conflict and violence, and it reduced reliance on administrators to handle conflict. The study also examined the impact of the program on participating special education students and found that their serving as mediators helped them integrate with regular education students and increased their self-esteem.[8]

One of the questions that has been raised in the field is the comparative difference between teaching young people to be mediators and teaching conflict-resolution curriculum in the classroom. While NMCDR's evaluations of its school mediation programs have not addressed this question, research of NMCDR's Youth Corrections Mediation Program does. NMCDR assisted several juvenile corrections facilities in the state to implement mediation programs, which also included a conflict-resolution curricular component. The preliminary research found that youth who were trained as mediators and were taught conflict-resolution curriculum had fewer disciplinary referrals than youth who had been taught just conflict-resolution curriculum. In turn, the group that had received curriculum instruction had fewer disciplinary referrals than a control group of nonparticipating youth. Similar results were obtained when examining the recidivism rates of the three groups six months after release from the facilities. Thirty-five percent of the control group was rearrested for criminal offenses or technical violations, as compared with 33 percent of the conflict-resolution group and 28 percent of the mediation group.[9]

These results suggest what we know from experience—that if young people have an opportunity to practice skills by becoming mediators, they will probably internalize conflict-resolution skills better than students who only receive classroom instruction in conflict resolution. The implications are that as many students as possible should be trained as mediators and be given an opportunity to serve. Logistically, this might be difficult, particularly at secondary levels. Some elementary schools have implemented models in which entire classes are trained as mediators and serve on rotations within classrooms as well as on the playground.

Another implementation issue relates to youth involvement in mediation program management. In keeping with the principle that young people need to be involved in the design and decisionmaking of programs that affect them, the experience of NMCDR suggests that some of the most successful school-based mediation programs involve students directly in program management.

In 1992 student mediators assumed most of the management duties of a peer mediation program at a high school in Albuquerque that had a history of rampant truancy and gang and intergroup conflict. Students receive credit for serving as mediators each semester, and in addition to mediating cases they manage all of the scheduling, followup, and recordkeeping duties. Students selected as mediators represent a cross-section of the student body, and a number of youth who participate as disputants eventually become mediators. The program mediates 150 to 200 cases per year, many of which could have resulted in serious violent fights, according to one of the adult supervisors. So much trust has been developed in the program that some students who are suspended for fighting request mediation before they return to school. The level of student involvement in this program seems to have made a difference in its success.

GANG MEDIATION IN SCHOOL SETTINGS

Gang conflict and violence are of concern to a growing number of schools in New Mexico, as well as throughout the country. A range of strategies are routinely tried by administrators to decrease gang rivalry and violence, including suspension and expulsion, metal detectors, banning colors, and restricting the assembly of more than four or five students at a time. While these methods have been implemented with varying degrees of success, some of the underlying issues of intergang rivalry—the need for safety and protection, the need for respect and identity among gang-involved youth—do not go away.

The use of mediation to manage multiparty, intergang disputes in both school and community settings is in its early stages of development. An intergang dispute is defined as a conflict involving two or more gangs. While mediation has been used in schools throughout the country to resolve interpersonal disputes between gang-involved youth, little has been reported or documented on multiparty, intergang mediation.

NMCDR has designed a number of interventions in multiparty gang disputes during the past six years. In the first such intervention, the staff at an Albuquerque middle school asked NMCDR to mediate an ongoing conflict with three rival gangs that involved turf issues and complaints against the school administration. Conflict among the gangs had escalated to the point that the student body and staff feared for their safety. Guns and knives were confiscated daily, and older gang members from the neighborhood gathered near the school threatening students as they left school. Students were afraid to be alone in restrooms and hallways, and parents were requesting transfers for their children because of gang harassment.

The middle school had an ongoing peer mediation program which encouraged the staff to seek mediation for the more serious intergang conflict. In addition to calling upon NMCDR mediators, the school asked gang intervention specialists from a youth development agency in Albuquerque to serve as translators for students not fluent in English and to provide support and encouragement to the participating gang members. The process was initiated through separate meetings with each gang to identify key concerns and persuade the gangs to participate. Each gang selected a team of three representatives and three alternates to participate at the mediation table. The school was also asked to select a team of three staff members to be present.

A series of meetings took place over a four-week period during the school day. The mediators set up the proceedings to create a dignified and serious venue for dispute resolution—tables in a circle, name tags, pitchers of water, notepads, butcher paper—in short, all the trappings of any large, multiparty mediation. The process established common concerns of all the gangs, including fear of weapons and concern for the safety of families and homes, anger at being intimidated and put down by rival gang members, and concern about perceived unfair treatment by the administration.

The mediation resulted in two major agreements. The first was a "no first strike" agreement in which gang members pledged not to provoke fights. They agreed not to start rumors, use name-calling, make threats, deface gang graffiti, call in outsiders, or "mad-dog" (provocational looks or stares). The second agreement dealt with the administration's dress code. If no gang-related fights were reported in a two-week period, gang members would be permitted to wear their gang attire on Fridays.

The result of the mediation was immediate. There was a marked reduction in fighting and violence. Some of the gang members were subsequently trained as mediators for the peer mediation program. The school counseling staff has continued to offer mediation for gang-related conflict, and the school has become a neutral zone for gang members. A subsequent intergang mediation was held three years later to avert potential violence. In addition, a gang leadership council was created at the school which has met bimonthly to provide a forum for discussion of differences and to manage conflict through communication. The mediation process has helped this middle school become a safer educational environment.

Those who support zero-tolerance approaches to gangs will no doubt be skeptical of this approach, because acknowledging gangs through mediation will give the appearance of condoning their existence and activities. However, there are numerous benefits to using mediation to respond to school-based gang conflict. The mediation process creates a learning experience for youth in constructive and nonviolent methods of resolving conflict. Many of these young people have never experienced alternatives to violence for gang-related problems. The mediation process teaches by modeling and brings together all of the parties who have a stake in the problem. It allows for open dialogue of all of the issues, and it permits underlying issues to be fully discussed. Finally, it can bring together school and community groups such as community mediation centers and youth agencies to share their collective resources and expertise in the improvement of conditions that affect young people's lives.

From the experience of NMCDR, mediation can reduce gang violence among middle school age students in the school environment. The commitment to an ongoing peer mediation program, the presence of trained staff who can monitor and handle intergang conflict as it arises, and collaboration with community agencies are critical to the long-term success of such interventions. Whether it can be effective for older youth and in community settings is a question that challenges schools, community mediation agencies, and youth workers.

SCHOOL-BASED PARENT/CHILD MEDIATION

Students bring not only gang conflict to school, but also the effects of family conflict. Unresolved family conflict and family dysfunction in general are leading causes of school behavior problems. Moreover, students who act aggressively in a conflict at school most likely learned this behavior at home from example or even exhortation. Parents who have not learned anger management skills are likely to act with physical or verbal aggression toward family members and to model these behaviors for their children. In addition, many parents encourage their children to fight in response to aggressive acts by other children.[10]

Parent/child mediation has proven to be a highly effective process, not only for helping families resolve the conflicts of everyday living in constructive ways, but also for teaching parents and children to learn new ways of handling the strong emotions that surround most family conflicts. In the parent/child mediation process, families work with trained volunteer mediators to discuss issues such as school attendance and performance, curfew violations, social life, household chores, privacy, sexual activity, and family interaction patterns. Family members work toward a concrete agreement that each family member feels is fair and realistic. The process is based on the premise that compliance with agreements of daily living increases trust between parents and children and facilitates negotiation on larger issues in the future.

Follow-up studies of parent/child mediation programs have shown that there is a high rate of adherence to mediated agreements and improved family functioning. In a research study of the very first parent/child mediation program developed in Massachusetts, over half of the families studied said they had changed the way they handled conflict. Seventy percent of the family members said that there was less arguing and fighting after the mediation.[11] In an evaluation of a similar program in Washington D.C., 62 percent of the parents and 68 percent of the adolescents felt that the problem had been solved through mediation. Over 75 percent of the families believed that mediation had made a difference in how family members were getting along.[12]

In an effort to create a program model that provides school-based access to these services and that includes school personnel and community members in the delivery system, NMCDR is piloting a school-based parent/child mediation at a middle school in Albuquerque. This pilot was initiated as part of a collaborative effort created by the Albuquerque public schools and public and community-based social service providers. Called the Human Services Collaborative, it was designed to bring a range of services to families in a targeted neighborhood in Albuquerque.

The following case study illustrates one family's involvement in the process and how NMCDR, the school, and the community interact to provide parent/child mediation services:

> Carlos, a twelve-year-old attending middle school, was referred to the parent/child mediation by one of his teachers because of his dropping grades and his aggressive behavior. The teacher sensed that the boy was having family problems and told the school counselor who had been assigned the job of scheduling intake interviews for families referred to the program. An NMCDR case manager was contacted about the referral and went to the school to meet with the mother and son. The father refused to participate. After an hour of explaining the mediation process and assessing the family's needs, the case manager determined that mediation was appropriate and scheduled a mediation. He identified two mediators from the neighborhood who had been recruited and trained by NMCDR for the program. The mediation took place at the school in the late afternoon, after the mother got off work.
>
> Some of the issues that were uncovered in the mediation involved Carlos's father and his treatment of his family. The father, an unemployed Vietnam veteran and an alcoholic, had been emotionally abusive to Carlos and his mother. Carlos's mother, who worked full time, was considering divorce because of the deteriorating relationship. She complained of lack of support in raising Carlos and motivating him to succeed in school. Carlos complained that his father's behavior made it difficult to concentrate in school. The mediators were able to identify two issues that could be made concrete and could result in agreements: Carlos's need for school motivation and the family's need for emotional support. After two sessions, Carlos and his mother reached an agreement on the following points:
>
> 1. Carlos would prepare weekly progress reports in his classes that would be signed by his teachers.
> 2. Mom would reward Carlos weekly if he remembered to present her with the progress reports.
> 3. Mom would monitor Carlos's homework regularly and provide assistance if needed.
> 4. Carlos would get TV privileges if his progress reports from school showed that he was completing his work and performing satisfactorily.

5. Carlos and his mother agreed to attend separate support groups for families of alcoholics.

The case manager also referred Carlos and his mother to the appropriate support groups. Six-week and six-month follow-up phone reports indicate that they are keeping the agreement and attending the support groups. In addition, Carlos's grades have improved, and he and his mother are reporting improvement in their communication skills and relationship.[13]

Without the collaborative program, the family might not have been referred to mediation, or even if they had, they might not have participated if it was not held at the school. One of the benefits of this model is that by recruiting parents and local residents to serve as volunteer mediators in the program, mediation services are delivered by members of the community and the mediation skills are spread throughout the community. There is reduced reliance on "professionals," and the service provision is cost-effective. This is an example of how the school, a community agency, and community volunteers can work together to assist families whose problems were likely to increase. While mediation is not a panacea for all the family's problems (indeed, the father did not even participate), it can strengthen and support those family members who choose to participate and lead them to other services that might provide them with additional assistance.

OTHER PILOT PROGRAMS

One of the criticisms of school-based conflict-resolution programs is that they are not combined with complementary efforts to address other areas of young people's lives that foster violence, such as home, community, and peer relationships.[14] NMCDR has initiated several pilot youth mediation programs in an attempt to involve parents and community members in violence-prevention activities and to develop program models that bring schools and communities into greater contact.

In Santa Fe, New Mexico, NMCDR is bringing volunteer mediators into the junior high schools to mediate conflicts between students who have been given automatic three-day suspensions for serious fights. These schools have ongoing peer mediation programs, but the conflicts are beyond the scope of what the mediation programs can handle.

In many cases, the fights are conflicts that are carried to the school environment from the community. In order to return to school after suspension due to violence, students and their parents must participate in the mediation process. These are often multiparty mediations with several sets of students and parents. Parents typically defend their child's actions and are sometimes hostile toward their child's adversaries as well as toward the school administration. The mediation process allows both the parents and the children to experience constructive problem-solving. The participants listen to each others' points of view and create agreements aimed at ending the hostilities. The parent involvement is crucial because they can take the skills home with them and practice and reinforce them with their children.

Furthermore, as in other types of mediation, it allows all parties to share in the responsibility for the conflict and the solution. According to the principal at one of the participating schools, the program has improved the subsequent behavior of suspended students and has reduced overall fighting substantially.[15]

Another pilot effort, initiated in a neighborhood of Albuquerque, is a collaborative effort among the local high school, the neighborhood association, the city-run neighborhood community center, the police department, and NMCDR. Ten students from the high school were trained (and received course credit) along with adult mentors from the neighborhood to serve as mediators for school or community conflicts. The community center has served as the site for the mediations, and its staff provides the case management. Program staff from the community center take case referrals and manage the day-to-day program operations. The program will mediate disputes involving juveniles in the school and community setting, as well as common neighborhood disputes such as barking dogs, trespassing, and noise problems. In addition, the police are playing an important role in the program by referring parties to mediation. Two officers who work the neighborhood beat were trained with the mediators to enable them to fully understand the process and refer appropriate cases to mediation. This program is still in its early stages of development, but it serves as an example of a broad-based community effort that involves youth in its development and implementation.

CONCLUSION

Mediation program models for children and families build on young people's strengths and focus on skills development rather than deficits. Current trends in youth policy stress the need to view youth as resources rather than as problems that need to be remediated. Youth are not only "at risk," but also "at strength."[16] Mediation programs are consistent with this thinking in that they can engage young people's energies and skills and enable them to increase their responsibility and social functioning.

A caution for practitioners of youth mediation programs is that we must know more about the impact of our programs in order to "sell" them as violence prevention programs. Most practitioners, as well as academics, agree that research and development funds must be appropriated to assess the long-term impact of mediation programs on children, families, schools, and communities.

While many mediation programs and approaches have proven effective, they must not be offered as a panacea. There is general consensus that while mediation and conflict-resolution programs have gained in popularity because of the rise in youth violence and the imperative to reduce it, these programs alone will not reverse the violence in our society. The underlying causes must be addressed and responded to through broad-based community efforts and new social and economic agendas.

NOTES

1. M. Pont, "The Origins and Growth of School-Based Conflict Resolution Programs," unpublished thesis, Stanford University, American Studies Department, 1994.

2. M. Smith, ed., *Youth Mediation Resource Guide* (Tulsa, Okla.: National Resource Center for Youth Services, 1994).

3. Center for the Study of Social Policy, *Kids Count Data Book* (Washington, D.C.: Center for the Study of Social Policy, 1993).

4. R. Sherman, "Dispute Resolution: Providing for Positive Youth Development and the Prevention of Violence," *Forum*, No. 35 (Spring 1994).

5. M. Smith, "Mediation and the Juvenile Offender," *Update on Law-Related Education*, American Bar Association (Spring/Summer 1991).

6. Survey (1993) conducted by T. Elizalde, former mediation counselor at Highland High School, Albuquerque, New Mexico.

7. J. Jenkins and M. Smith, *Mediation in the Schools Program Evaluation Report 1986–87*, New Mexico Center for Dispute Resolution, 1987.

8. S. Carter, "Evaluation Report on New Mexico Mediation in the Schools Program," unpublished report, 1990.

9. P. D. Steele, *Youth Corrections Mediation Program, Final Report of Evaluation Activities*, New Mexico Center for Dispute Resolution, 1991.

10. D. Prothrow-Stith and M. Weissman, *Deadly Consequences: How Violence Is Destroying Our Teenage Population and a Plan to Begin Solving the Problem* (New York: HarperCollins, 1991), 23.

11. S. Merry, *The Children's Hearings Project Research Findings* (Cambridge, Mass.: The Children's Hearings Project, 1985).

12. G. J. Stahler, J. P. DuCette, and E. Povich, "Using Mediation to Prevent Child Maltreatment: An Exploratory Study," *Family Relations* (July 1990).

13. Case file from NMCDR parent/child mediation program.

14. D. Webster, "The Unconvincing Case for School-Based Conflict Resolution Programs for Adolescents," *Health Affairs* (Winter 1993).

15. E. Martinez, Principal, Alameda Junior High School, Santa Fe, New Mexico, phone conversation, August 9, 1994.

16. M. Sherraden, *Community-Based Youth Services in International Perspective* (Washington, D.C.: Carnegie Council on Adolescent Development and W. T. Grant Foundation Commission on Work, Family and Citizenship, 1992).

17

The New York City Board of Education and Violence Prevention

Ramon C. Cortines

The first priority of the Board of Education of the City of New York is to improve teaching and learning. But students cannot learn if they are frightened for their safety—just as they cannot learn if they are hungry or ill. We must therefore ensure that every student in every school feels safe, secure, and ready to learn.

New York City's public school system, the largest in the nation, has an enrollment of approximately 1,035,000—representing an annual increase of ten thousand to twenty thousand students for each of the past several years. Enrollment increases are primarily due to the city's rising immigration rates. With a budget of over $8 billion, a staff of over 120,000, and nearly 1,100 schools, ours is a huge and complex system.

The Board of Education employs over three thousand School Safety Officers, a force equivalent in size to the ninth largest police force in the country. School Safety Officers are certified as peace officers and are trained in strategies of peace-keeping in schools. There were 17,046 school safety incidents reported for the 1993–1994 school year, or an average of approximately fifteen such incidents per school. The incidents reported range in severity from simple misconduct to felony-level offenses. There were no school homicides during the 1993–1994 school year, the first time since the 1990–1991 school year.

The problems of crime and disorder plaguing neighborhoods continue to affect the schools profoundly. We at the Board of Education of the City of New York believe that a comprehensive approach to violence prevention—including instilling values and a sense of responsibility, teaching skills for nonviolent conflict resolution, and providing measures to enhance students' safety and security—is necessary to effectively reduce the number of violent acts young people commit and to which they are exposed. Ambitious programs to increase the safety and security of students and staff are already in place at the Board of Education, but much more needs to be done.

Our school staff is largely unsung for their efforts, day in and day out, in providing children with as supportive a learning experience as possible. Teachers, guidance counselors, deans, and school safety officers all come into regular, close contact with students. We have them to thank for a system that is, after all, considering its vast size and the extraordinarily challenging social conditions that many of its students face, largely an orderly one.

But our staff alone cannot stave off the school problems caused by society's disorder. We need help from the state and city governments in fostering interagency and community cooperation to respond to the violence that is encroaching on our schools. Appropriate services to students, promoting their safety and security, must be increased. Funds must also be provided for expansion of program models that work.

STUDENT RIGHTS, RESPONSIBILITIES, AND DISCIPLINE

Values and a sense of responsibility are critical to a safe, violence-free environment. An important component of safety in our schools is awareness on the part of students and their parents that certain types of behavior are expected of members of a school community, and that other types of behavior are unacceptable. Furthermore, it is crucial that we make children aware that their actions have consequences.

It is also critical that we give our students due process and that we make all experiences learning experiences, including those in which we teach students to not commit violent acts. Our Code of Student Discipline, which provides comprehensive guidelines for determining unacceptable behaviors and appropriate disciplinary measures, also describes the due processes to which students are entitled— including hearings, appeals, and so forth.

All schools are expected to incorporate information about the Code of Student Discipline into their curriculum, as well as to address issues related to our Student Bill of Rights and Responsibilities. Students' responsibilities include:

- Regular, punctual, well-prepared attendance.
- Participation in and the promotion of a cooperative school community.
- Adherence to school rules and guidelines for appropriate conduct.

Students' rights include:

- The right to a free public school education.
- The right to freedom of expression and person.
- The right to due process.

Punishments, when they are meted out, must be fair and consistent, and must encourage, not discourage, appropriate behavior in the future. Later in this chapter we will describe some of the ways in which our system helps students who are not succeeding—by providing counseling, alternative educational sites, and so forth, in addition to suspensions from school. When students have committed acts so serious that they enter the criminal justice system, then the city, the state, and the Board of Education must work together to ensure that each offender is given the best chance possible to turn away from crime and begin a life as a productive member of society.

CONFLICT-RESOLUTION/VIOLENCE-PREVENTION PROGRAMS

Giving students skills for nonviolent conflict resolution is the most critical component of any effort to reduce violent behavior in the long term. We have instituted programs for nonviolent conflict resolution throughout the system, but these will not be sufficient until every student develops skills in resolving conflicts without violence. Conflict-resolution programs are a long-term solution, not a quick fix. Experts indicate that several years of commitment are required before we can expect these programs to yield significant systemwide counteraction of the violent behavior students see all around them in society.

At the elementary and middle school levels, preventing the development of violent reactions is crucial. About 20 percent of New York City high school students believe that carrying a weapon is an effective way to avoid a physical fight, according to a 1992 Centers for Disease Control report, and only about 55 percent believe that avoiding or walking away from someone who wants to fight is an effective way of avoiding such a fight. The way to prevent the development of such attitudes is to teach children, beginning when they are very young, that the violence and hate that may pervade their environments can be dealt with in peaceful and constructive ways.

The New York City school board has had conflict-resolution programs aimed at these issues in place for several years, and we have expanded them significantly over the last two years. Our two main programs, Schools Teaching Options for Peace and the Resolving Conflict Creatively Program, are operating in twenty-eight of our thirty-two community school districts, but they currently reach fewer than forty thousand elementary and middle school students—only about 5 percent of the total. We still have a long way to go before everyone who needs these programs has access to them.

The Resolving Conflict Creatively Program, which operates in about 150 elementary and middle schools, works collaboratively with students, parents, and school staff to incorporate the knowledge, attitudes, and skills of conflict resolution into a school's culture. Its core components are:

- Classroom instruction aimed at increasing caring and cooperative behavior, using peaceful conflict-resolution techniques, intergroup understanding, and appreciation of differences.
- Peer mediation programs (in which "playground mediators" are created).
- Training of parents.
- Staff development.

Plans for expansion include piloting a bilingual conflict-resolution program. In a 1990 outside evaluation, 84 percent of the mediators surveyed said they had learned skills they could use their whole life; 83 percent said that being mediators had helped them to understand people with different views.

Schools Teaching Options for Peace, which operates in approximately fifty middle schools, draws together the best components of three of the city's top programs in conflict resolution and peer mediation, emphasizing:

- Improved communication and understanding among diverse groups of students, their teachers, and their parents.
- Training for teachers to impart conflict-resolution skills to their students.
- Training for school personnel, students, and parents in mediating disputes.

The benefit of parental participation in conflict-resolution programs is stressed by educators at all levels, but it is particularly important for parents of young children. Children model behavior they learn in the home, and the more parents are able to resolve conflicts without a physical fight, the more children will develop the same abilities. Parents who have participated in Schools Teaching Options for Peace report improvements in their ability to talk to their children. Students report that through the program they learn to listen, keep eye contact during conversations, and maintain self-control. We are beginning a longitudinal study of youngsters who participated in Schools Teaching Options for Peace to determine the extent to which violent behavior is reduced in the long term.

Inappropriate behavior, however, continues to be a significant problem, and increased expansion of violence-prevention programs will be necessary to counteract the trend. The rate of suspensions at the elementary and middle level has increased: 3 percent of elementary and middle school students were suspended in the 1992–1993 school year, as opposed to 2.5 percent of students the year before. Some 10 percent of these suspensions were for serious infractions such as possessing weapons, inflicting a serious injury, or selling or distributing controlled substances.

Consistent with the view that interventions should be repatriative, not simply punitive, we have called for the development of "alternative to suspension" programs in each district for middle school students on extended suspensions (more than five days). Rather than allow students to fall farther and farther behind in school, these programs provide instruction in core subjects, guidance services, and violence-prevention components—sometimes within the student's existing school building. Children must realize that negative actions have negative consequences, but giving them punishments without helping them develop the skills to cope and succeed only starts them on a pattern of repeated failure. However, some students who, even at the middle school level, have committed very violent acts might not be appropriate candidates for remaining in their existing school setting. Alternative programs for middle school students, similar to the alternative high school programs discussed later in this chapter, should be explored.

THE SPECIAL SITUATION OF HIGH SCHOOLS

At the high school level, a broader series of educational strategies is required to reduce and counteract unacceptable student behavior.

Smaller Schools

We must continue to increase the extent to which youngsters come into contact with caring adults, a goal that is often more easily achieved in a small school setting. The New York City school board provides a variety of such programs, with a variety of educational goals. In 1993, in collaboration with local districts and community-based organizations, we began thirty new, small, theme-oriented high schools, for all children—there is no particular emphasis on those who misbehave. We have, for many years, run a broad range of alternative high schools, which comprise smaller programs for a range of at-risk students. Finally, our borough academies provide a case-management approach for chronically misbehaving students, coordinating deans, guidance counselors, academic advisers, and security staff to improve these students' ability to succeed. The trend of creating smaller, more personalized school settings must increase. As children have fewer and fewer caring adults providing them with strong role models at home, schools must do their part to provide these experiences, to impart values whose absence contributes to increased violence.

Conflict Resolution

Most high schools now offer programs designed to prevent violence, but these programs are able to reach only a fraction of our students. The New York City school board is proud of the quality of the programs it runs, but we need to go much farther: every student must receive training in strategies for nonviolent conflict resolution.

The conflict-resolution programs of the City of New York school system have two major elements: (1) infusion of violence-prevention concepts and strategies in the curriculum and (2) peer mediation. Schools provide classroom lessons related to nonviolence, but these reach varying numbers of students. (For example, in some schools, it may be done in health, social studies, or English classes; in others, it might be in ninth-grade seminar classes.) High schools also designate a mediation center, which allows disputes to be addressed nonviolently before they erupt into major conflicts. Starting in 1995, students who were peer mediators at the middle school level will be identified as they move into high school. They will be able to participate immediately in their new school's peer mediation program.

Universal conflict-resolution programs will not be easy to implement. In 1993 the New York City board trained about three hundred professional staff members—two per high school—for a week each in negotiation and peer mediation skills. In addition, each high school principal received three full days of training in conflict-resolution techniques, and about seven hundred students received peer mediation training. The board plans to expand to a full day of training for a parent representative for each high school.

Evaluations for existing programs are very positive—participants report the development of valuable mediation and negotiation skills, many citing positive changes in their ability to interact with others—but again indicate the need for more training, time, and resources, including, perhaps, more involvement of parents.

Providing Continuity for Students Who Have Been Removed from School

A critical issue regarding educating juvenile offenders is the fact that they are pulled out of school at random times and then put back in at random times. This lack of continuity significantly reduces their ability ever to succeed in school, which in turn makes it much more likely that they will be repeat offenders.

Youth who commit crimes are under the custody of non-Board of Education agencies for periods of one night to three years. There is too little coordination at the city or state level between outside agencies and the Board of Education. Schools are not notified when the student is withdrawn, and, although all students who return from institutional settings—including incarceration, drug facilities, and New York State Division for Youth sites—should be referred to us for readmission, we often receive no prior notice of return. Finally, the seriousness of offenses committed indicates that some truly dangerous youth are returned to the schools with little preparation, few transition services, and little supervision after release. These issues should be addressed in several ways:

Students have the greatest chance for success in school when they enter at the start of the school term, or, if this is not possible, if they are enrolled in a program specifically designed to accommodate open-ended admissions and self-paced instruction, followed by routine, timely transition into high school. Although the board operates some programs of this nature, there are not enough.

The New York State Division for Youth, the Department of Juvenile Justice, and the Department of Probation release students to the schools virtually every day of the year. Although the board operates a number of small education programs with each agency, there is no comprehensive plan to serve the needs of youth, and the agencies do not coordinate with one another, even when they are dealing with the same youngsters or youngsters with similar educational needs. The state, together with the New York State Division for Youth, should help facilitate a planning program for receiving, preparing, and articulating students to schools, together with the New York State Division for Youth. A similar effort should take place in New York City, creating a network of school sites to which youngsters returned to school by the agencies can be referred and transitioned to regular school, creating strategies planned for success.

A broad outreach program should be initiated for judges and courts dealing with school age youth, informing them about the realities of schooling and about decisions within their control that might enhance the schooling of offenders.

Many students, while in custody, have become homeless. At present, there is not a single "halfway house" or residential/transitional facility for youth in New York City, which means that adolescents as young as sixteen are left to fend for themselves. Many of these youngsters subsequently become a fiscal responsibility through application to the Human Resources Administration, foster care, or recidivism to the penal system. An interagency, integrated design should be developed to ensure stable, decent aftercare for adolescents returned to the community after incarceration.

General education and special education students are subject to different discipline codes, based on New York State law and commissioner's regulations. Even when a formal hearing process might determine that a given special education student presents a clear and present danger to the safety of the school and students, the student cannot be transferred to another site. We must work with the commissioner of the state education department to modify current regulations; to propose a legislative remedy for the inability to transfer special education students when they exhibit violent, dangerous, or severely disruptive behavior; and to create appropriate alternatives for these students.

PROVIDING ACTIVITIES AFTER SCHOOL HOURS

Students who are productively occupied after school hours are much less likely to become involved in inappropriate activities. By engaging in a positive outlet for their energies, they learn self-reliance and self-esteem, and many extracurricular activities afford the opportunity to learn discipline, leadership, and teamwork skills. Involvement in extracurricular activities also increases the possibility that students will form a meaningful relationship with an adult role model, which is particularly important to children who may not have strong role models at home. Finally, after-school activities such as working on a school newspaper, visiting the library, or making use of the computer room—can add to the knowledge that students gain in the classroom.

Increased after-hours programming opportunities for students could greatly improve their chances of doing well in school and staying out of trouble. Some examples are:

- Expansion of the junior varsity program at the middle school level.
- Expansion of the city's Beacon program, which allows school buildings to remain open and offer a variety of services to the community.
- Allowing students access to libraries and computer rooms after school hours.

Although many school staff members—coaches, newspaper advisers, and so forth—donate time well beyond that for which they are compensated, volunteers cannot sustain a broad extracurricular program. And keeping schools open is a significant expense. Additional funding would be required to make school buildings available after school hours.

ENHANCING SAFETY AND SECURITY

Hand-held weapons detectors are currently in place in sixty-one New York City high schools and middle schools, and we are experimenting with walk-through detectors, which allow more students to be scanned. (Since the current method of wand scanning is very time-consuming, we scan a random sample of incoming students; otherwise, it would never be possible to start classes.) A 1992 study by the Centers for Disease Control shows that metal detectors reduce students' carrying of weapons by about one-half. During the 1993–1994 school year, about 17 percent of the guns confiscated were taken from students at schools that had weapons detection programs, though these comprised 34 percent of high schools—adding further evidence that scanning acts as an effective deterrent.

The New York City board plans to do more to professionalize its three thousand School Safety Officers through improved training, even more stringent hiring practices, and creation of a career track to retain the best officers. But these officers must also be deployed in such a way that they can do the most possible to reduce violent incidents in our school communities.

We are beginning a broad, ambitious series of initiatives to curb violence, combining the concepts of school-based management and community policing. The tenets of community policing—becoming familiar with patterns of crime and places and situations that create the opportunity for crimes to be committed, knowing the ins and outs of a neighborhood, forging partnerships between enforcement services and clients—are being combined with locally appropriate solutions. For example, we have begun creating—in cooperation with the New York City Police Department—School Safety Zones in neighborhoods, which result in increased safety coverage of school entrances in the morning and at dismissal times; of major corridors to the schools; and of train stations and bus stops.

Neighborhood schools usually share common pressures and problems of crime and disorder, but they often do not take joint action to deal with them. High schools and nearby elementary and middle schools, for example, typically share problems but not solutions. The Board of Education will form neighborhood clusters of elementary, middle, and high schools that share common problems. The School Safety Officers and school staff in each cluster will work together to coordinate safety planning, operations, training, investigations, and allocation of resources among schools in the group. Restructuring our safety operations into Safe School Groups will be the conerstone of our effort to decentralize the school safety management, and to develop responsive, creative solutions to problems of crime and disorder.

We are initiating a number of other activities designed to involve the community in the prevention of crime around schools, such as instituting boroughwide advisory councils, including parent councils, to address these issues; establishing a twenty-four-hour hotline for students to report information about crimes; and cosponsoring an after-school athletic league, with School Safety Officers participating as coaches and referees. These are just a few of the initiatives being implemented.

CONCLUSION

Schools mirror the violence that is occurring in society; and so a whole-society approach must be taken to reduce the violence. Collaboration is necessary between the Board of Education, city and state agencies, community-based organizations, the business community, and all other stakeholders in ensuring that our children receive the education to which they are entitled.

18

The Virginia Model: School to Community Intervention Techniques to Prevent Violence

Yvonne V. Thayer

> Most social problems stem in some way from inequalities, which can
> be solved by sharing.
> —James Moffet[1]

Virginia is not unlike other states. We have intercity schools, bedroom-community schools, rural schools, and small town schools. We have magnet schools for the arts; governor's schools for math, science, and technology; vocational-technical schools; and alternative schools. Our students complete high school and choose Ivy League institutions, community colleges, and state universities for higher education. Our students also choose to fish the Chesapeake Bay, work in coal mines, farm, or engage in high-tech industries. Virginia's students speak the dialects of the mountains and flatlands, the drawl of Richmond, and the languages of a hundred cultures. It is a diverse state, Virginia, cloaked in lifestyles from west to east that reflect Appalachian simplicity to Washingtonian complexity. Yet common threads have always tied Virginia's education efforts into a tapestry that reflected expectations for an educational system that was comparable to any in the nation.

While Virginia reflects much of the diversity of the nation, it also reflects the country's problems. Public schools receive children who are forced to deal on a daily basis with emerging lifestyles that tolerate weapons, drugs, and dysfunctional behavior. These children are now bringing the artifacts of the culture and the accompanying behaviors into the schools; and teachers, administrators and parents are faced with a problem they previously did not have.

The evolution of society is a given, but the stages of the evolutionary process have previously been accommodated by the schools. In the past two decades, as drugs became more accessible to students, their use—though unacceptable and alarming to educators—did not threaten the general safety of the school and the school staff. In addition, as the behavior of students became more provocative and less controllable than in the 1950s and 1960s, discipline in the schools still was maintained at a level of control that did not threaten the safety of anyone. With the emergence of weapons in schools, however, all this has changed. Now the safety of students and sometimes teachers is a paramount concern of school boards and central office leadership, as discipline referrals resound with profane language and personal threats.

The dilemma facing communities is the collective impact of the forces of a changing society: changing values, changing norms, unchallenged behaviors, and unforgiving institutions. Several problems can be teased out of this dilemma regarding the negative impact on the schools. The question can be raised as to how we, educators and community members, react to the appearance of weapons in schools. In addition, the question of what is appropriate discipline for weapons offenders can be discussed. Certainly, the problem of preparing and training staff for emergencies involving violence is worth pursuing. The aggregated result of drugs, dysfunctional families, and weapons has suggested new discussions among school administrators and communities about the security of buildings, the safety of students and teachers, and definitions of who should be allowed to attend public schools.

Any one of these issues, however, no matter how important and timely, still presumes a reactionary stance by school staffs. Should we not be considering the key causes of the problems that created the dilemma; that is, determining measures that could possibly change the course of events, rather than merely reacting appropriately to them?

This chapter explores some of the approaches being taken by public schools to address violence issues. Using Virginia as a case study, the chapter describes specific actions taken to further empower local school leaders to address inappropriate behaviors in the schools. In addition, it reflects the education process that is occurring in Virginia, as school personnel learn about violence and consider what they can do to intervene on behalf of youth. The actions suggested—having stricter rules and regulations, developing alternative schools, safeguarding security in the buildings, and educating teachers and the public—all speak to strengthening the structure of existing schools. These measures are designed to create an infrastructure that reacts properly to the inappropriate behaviors of a few young people while protecting the education of the majority of youth.

But what of the efforts to prevent violent behavior from initially occurring? This chapter briefly assesses information that is available to help design prevention activities or programs. A quick look at the possible root causes of the violence issue will suggest additional research and critical information needed for program design. Looking again to Virginia for one successful model, a systems approach to problem-solving and solution-finding is discussed as a workable process. Community involvement is proposed as a key to long-term solutions. The reader will be left with the question of whether schools can facilitate prevention initiatives, or whether intervention activities represent the extent to which schools should act.

ASSUMPTIONS AND BIASES

Several assumptions and biases direct this work. First, my background is in public education, both at the local and state levels. The limitations of my view are enlarged by my commitment to community involvement in schools. My view of community involvement exceeds participation on advisory councils; I believe that communities have a responsibility to learn about the forces driving change in education and that they should respond only after being educated about the challenges administrators face daily.

Second, while I acknowledge the evolution of societies, I believe that communities create their futures either by abstaining from a role in community development, thereby leaving it to others to direct, or by actively participating in the design of their future. Social action can be defined to match the situation.

Third, I believe that proactive postures solve problems in shorter time periods and, thereby, consume fewer resources in the community. Since problems should be solved rather than ignored (burying one's head only facilitates additional problems), problem-solving is an economical course of action. Problem-solving, though reactive since it is driven by situational data, can lead a group into other proactive, future-setting activities. After all, we must solve the problems in the existing system before we can substantially improve how the system functions. The skills learned in problem-solving and the learning achieved through the process of reflection empower the group to think futuristically.

Fourth, my experience leads me to state that no one really wants to own the problem of violence in society and, consequently, violence in schools. We maintain reactionary positions because it is safer. We can show that we are doing something—taking some course of action—but we do not have to address the key causes that lead to the problems. We can avoid the messiness of problem-solving that challenges assumptions, beliefs, and behaviors. We can avoid the accountability that results from the responsibility of solving problems as long as someone else (or no one) is looking at the real, underlying issues. As school leaders, it is easier to put guards in the high school hallways than to talk about the reasons a sixteen-year-old needs a gun.

Last, social action is not a bad concept. While many of us tend to think of riots and marches as the only courses of social action Americans take, social action is not limited to mass activities. Recognizing the need to change and accepting responsibility that leads to any action can be social action. The presenting problems associated with school violence and violence in society call for social action, which may be defined early on as meetings in communities or discussion groups in schools. The key to gaining interest in the school violence issue is action of some sort, and that action does not have to be highly politically charged.

WHAT SCHOOL LEADERS SAY ABOUT VIOLENCE

The *Executive Educator* conducted a poll of 1,216 school administrators from across the country and reported the results in February 1993. The survey indicated that violence increased in U.S. public schools over the five-year period, 1988–

1993. When asked how school leaders were dealing with the problems of violence, guns, drug- and alcohol-related incidents, "mouthing off," and fighting, the *Executive Educator* reported as follows:

You prefer to stick with tried-and-true approaches. Many school executives (48 percent) are enforcing school disciplinary codes strictly rather than electing extreme methods such as metal detectors or video surveillance equipment.... But nearly one in five respondents has banned gang clothing and insignia—and the same number have closed campuses in response to violence.

In addition, many of you report you prefer to use in-school suspensions... rather than out-of-school suspensions or expulsions.

...But judging by the growth of in-school suspensions and the constancy or decline in out-of-school suspensions or expulsions, you doubt problems can be solved by excluding students from school. Instead, you're attempting to deal with problems internally, with 64 percent of you saying your school districts have counseling programs for students who have committed violent acts.

The majority (58 percent) of administrators say their districts are not training teachers in how to deal with violent student behavior. . . .

...Because schools, as part of society, reflect society's ills as well as its strengths, they cannot be expected to solve the problem of increased school violence alone. Schools must initiate more dialogue among all school, parent, and community groups and must seek a greater degree of parent involvement.[2]

Not having asked Virginia's superintendents the questions that were posed on the *Executive Educator*'s poll, it is not possible to project how close their responses would have been to those reported here. In Virginia, there is a dialogue about metal detectors, security officers, and other precautionary measures that may reflect a need to "police" the schools. In addition, there is great interest in in-school suspension and alternative education, and opinions are mixed about whether it is better to keep disruptive kids in school or move them to a different setting for continued education. Probably all Virginia educators would agree that the problems in the schools are not theirs alone to solve and that parents and community members must help, but few people are stepping forward with a plan for identifying the key causes of the problems and finding workable solutions. Those who have been active in generating discussion within the education community and advocating action through legislation include superintendents' groups in Virginia.

VIRGINIA'S EDUCATION SUMMIT

In May 1992 Virginia's superintendents issued an invitation to several educational associations to join together for an open discussion of concerns related to increased acts of violence and other disruptive behavior in the schools. What resulted was a forum for discussion that led to a collection of recommendations published in October of that year. The process of joining to discuss critical issues was unusual, but these organizations found that they could discuss school violence and agree on courses of action they believed to be important.

The collection of participants was known as the Education Summit, and they represented the following organizations and offices in Virginia: the Association of School Superintendents, the Association of Secondary School Principals, the Middle School Association, the Association of Elementary School Principals, the School Boards Association, the Congress of Parents and Teachers, and the Virginia Education Association (of the National Education Association). The meetings were also attended by representatives from a local school board, the office of the Superintendent of Public Instruction for Commonwealth of Virginia, the office of the Secretary of Education for Commonwealth of Virginia, the House of Delegates of the General Assembly, and a law firm that specializes in education cases. After initial meetings, the organizations chose a committee of working members who forged a plan of action published as *Violence in Schools.*

There were three major purposes of the forum and the subsequent publication: strong disciplinary response, building and managing a safe educational environment, and developing long-term educational and family violence prevention programs. The recommendations published were in response to these purposes and represented a consensus of the participating members. In fact, the document reflected the belief of the participants that the consensus-building and collaboration used by the summit "reflects a path similar to that which each of our communities must travel to achieve the commonly held goal of safe schools."[3] The summit recognized the tendency to blame others for the problems and issues being discussed and the unwillingness felt by some toward shared responsibility for solutions to problems.

The summit's forty-one recommendations were grouped into a number of broad categories that are discussed here under four headings: protection of schools, information for parents, student services, and community involvement. Rather than examining all of the recommendations, a sampling is presented.

The first category, *protection of schools*, includes those items that facilitate information flowing among school divisions[4] in Virginia, recommendations related to local policy, weapons, and building safety. They recommend, for example, that:

- Each school administration and school board take strong and consistent disciplinary action in all weapon, alcohol and other drugs and assault violations by students and that school authorities refer to law enforcement for investigation, automatically and without exception, any student behavior that, if proven, would constitute a criminal act in the Commonwealth.

- The parent/guardian of students enrolling from outside the Commonwealth be required to indicate on local school registration forms if the enrolling student has been expelled or is currently subject to such proceeding for a behavior involvingweapons, alcohol and other drugs, or an assault.

- The General Assembly of Virginia pass legislation that would result in reexamined and strengthened penalties included in the *Code of Virginia* for illegal use of handguns in general and specific strengthening of penalties for the following: 18.2-308.1 Possession of dangerous weapon on school property, property open to public for school activities, or school bus.

- Each school board in Virginia conducts a review of its policies/regulations governing:

  — the conduct and management of members of the public who come onto school property during the school day and for after-school activities.
  — expectations or requirements for adult accompaniment and supervision of young children attending public events on school property in the evening hours.

- School divisions planning for new construction and major renovation include appropriate telecommunication systems.

The broad category of *information for parents* included recommendations such as:

- Every school in the Commonwealth, working cooperatively with parents and other public agencies, develop additional initiatives to provide parental support and outreach services that strengthen meaningful involvement in a constructive home–school partnership.

- Every school in the Commonwealth request the parent/guardian of any child who has been disciplined for a weapon-related offense, alcohol or other drug violation, or an assault, to participate in an appropriate parenting support, counseling, or educational session aimed at rehabilitating these specific student behaviors.

In the category of *student services,* recommendations deal with alternative education programs and support for students identified as "at risk." The report also supports early childhood programs and prevention initiatives in the K-12 curricula. It was recognized that school staff need support in implementing the changes recommended to enhance school safety. For example, it was recommended that:

- The State Board of Education, working cooperatively with local school divisions, the legislature, and the juvenile court system, appoint a task force to develop a specific statewide plan to provide local and regional alternative education programs for severely disruptive and violent youth.

- The Governor of the Commonwealth of Virginia and members of the Virginia General Assembly urge the Virginia congressional delegation to support expanded access for eligible "at-risk" children to programs such as Head Start, Chapter I, or other early intervention efforts known to be successful in increasing school success and subsequently reducing juvenile crime.

- The prevention of violence be an integral part of the K-12 curricula for local school divisions; that this approach be infused across the curriculum; and that students become engaged in cooperative learning strategies related to peer mediation, conflict resolution, citizenship, problem-solving, decisionmaking, and strategies to provide children opportunities for the development and exercise of personal responsibility.

The report from the summit supports *community involvement* and clearly states that "unless individual communities decide to organize and mobilize local resources to change community expectations and youth behaviors, it is likely that schools, working alone, will fail."[5] For example, it was recommended that:

- Each school division analyze and use data being developed by the Department of Education with community teams to identify the type and extent of violent student behavior and related issues as a basis for planning local prevention and intervention efforts targeted specifically to the problems of the individual school community.

The work of the summit was distributed throughout Virginia during 1992–1993, with presentations made to local and regional groups by Dr. William C. Bosher, Jr., the summit chairman and then president of the Virginia Association of School Superintendents. Dr. Bosher, who became Virginia Superintendent of Public Instruction in 1994, states that there were two major outcomes of the summit report, the first being *meaningful collaboration*: "The seven organizations that had come together made a commitment to continue to work together. So often, professionally, we concentrate on our differences rather than concentrating on the issues that we share."

While the first outcome related to process, the second was related to the content of the report, its substance. Dr. Bosher believes that the second major outcome of the summit was the *legislation* to support the summit's work, and the General Assembly of Virginia followed through immediately. *Violence in Schools* concluded with a recommendation that a comprehensive safe school legislative program be developed, based on the findings of the report. By the conclusion of the 1993 session of the general assembly, thirteen pieces of legislation had been passed related to school violence issues.[6] Since funding for programs is always of concern, one can inquire as to what issues require money to forward the recommendations. Dr. Bosher responded that "the two issues that required the greatest funding were alternative education programs and funding for professional development" in order to expand the state's commitment to additional alternative education programs throughout the state, and to initiate and continue training programs for teachers in such things as conflict resolution.[7]

In the state superintendent's mind, one of the most meaningful pieces of legislation passed provides school systems with information regarding expulsion cases. This act establishes communication between schools so that students transferring to a new school have their previous school record follow them. "Before the legislation, a young person could be expelled from the school system, walk across the street, go to another school system, and the receiving school system would have no idea that the young person had brought a gun [to school], or had sexually assaulted somebody, or is a heavy drug distributor," Bosher explains. Throughout the Commonwealth, superintendents have been very supportive of this particular piece of legislation.

With the work of the summit complete and legislation now being implemented, what has been the major impact of *Violence in Schools*? Bosher cites several effects: (1) better communication among schools and stronger expectations for behavior; (2) more pointed penalties for possession of guns in school as well as for adults who enable young people to have guns; (3) intervention efforts for youth, including alternative programs and counseling; and (4) raised consciousness on the part of legislators and other publics about the issues of school violence.

A REGIONAL CALL TO ACTION

The work of the summit called attention to a real problem in Virginia schools and motivated the legislature to begin taking action. Local superintendents joined in the effort to forward legislation that would support school safety. One effort worth highlighting is representative of how Virginia's superintendents can come together to address important issues.

In the fall of 1993, the fatal knifing of a Hampton Roads high school student during the school day on school property brought attention to the problem of violence in schools and renewed the focus of ten local superintendents in proposing remedies to the violence and crime confronting their communities. Hampton Roads is in the Tidewater area of Virginia, recognizable as historic Williamsburg and Yorktown, running through the shipyards of Newport News, to the military bases of Norfolk and Portsmouth. Violence in Hampton Roads schools and communities— primarily urban/suburban communities—has grown over the last few years, and school officials have been concerned about the impact on the public schools, both the perception of safe schools and the reality of changing student behaviors.

In September 1993, in response to the growing concern of citizens regarding incidents of violence in the schools and community, the ten superintendents issued *Ending Violence in Our Schools: A Call to Action* to focus attention on and propose suggested remedies to problems confronting schools. The superintendents attempted to engage all segments—police, courts, parents, schools, churches, and legislators—in the fight to stem the flow of violence. Building on the *Violence in Schools* report, a key component of *A Call to Action* was a pledge to work for legislative solutions to the problems confronting school leaders.

In the original *A Call to Action*, the superintendents called on the citizenry to join the schools in taking responsibility and acting to make schools and communities safer. Four actions were proposed. First, the superintendents said that making safety a priority was a necessary step not only to ensure safe schools, but also to create safe homes and neighborhoods where children could learn to deal with conflict without using weapons. Second, *A Call to Action* stated that citizens, including parents, must be good role models for children, teaching the value of life and the danger of carrying weapons. The third proposal confirmed a strong support of legislative action that would reduce crime and increase safety. Finally, the superintendents urged the media to help promote a positive image of youth, giving greater prominence to the positive accomplishments of youth.

A few weeks after *A Call to Action* was published, the superintendents of Hampton Roads published an addendum that outlined their action plan and established the Safe Schools Regional Task Force. The task force was used to vigorously pursue avenues collaboratively that would lead to reduced violence and crime.

The major portion of the addendum addressed the legislature. Four areas of concern were identified, and legislative action was proposed that provided schools with tools for more aggressively responding to the violence issues. The following summary provides the thrust of the legislative action requested:

> *Gun and Other Weapon Control.* Eliminating student access to guns and other weapons is essential for safe schools to become a reality. The superintendents have called for legislation that would increase penalties for selling guns to minors and tighten access to weapons.
>
> *Increased Parental Responsibility.* Legislation that holds parents more accountable for their children's actions must be pursued. Parental involvement may be the greatest deterrent to crime and violence among our youth. Recognizing that fact, school divisions have the responsibility to keep parents informed of school regulations and discipline guidelines. Conversely, all parents must accept responsibility for providing their children with the necessary attention and guidance.
>
> *Geater Coordination Between Police and Courts and the Schools.* To ensure a safe environment for our students, it is necessary to identify youth who have been charged with serious crimes or violent acts. Legislation must be passed that would provide school divisions with police reports for youth charged with serious crimes. This sharing of youth arrest information would enable schools to take appropriate safety precautions and provide for effective school interventions.
>
> *Alternative Education Programs.* Legislation is needed that would facilitate and speed the admission of students into alternative education programs. Such programs that offer alternative education settings for youth who have committed serious crimes or violent acts have proven beneficial to those youth, to other students, and to the community at large.[8]

The legislative agenda of these ten superintendents supported the summit's report. Their proposals were shared with the general assembly, and, in the sixty days that followed, the legislature acted on bills that gave superintendents across Virginia "the teeth" they perceived were needed to act prudently with violence offenders.

One interesting change that has occurred because of the superintendents' actions has been the elimination of the Category I and II distinction of students' scholastic records. In Virginia, schools historically maintained two sets of files on each student. Category I contained significant factual information pertinent to student development and in some cases was the only information forwarded when a student transferred to a new school. Category II files contained sensitive information such as those reports written by internal and external professionals, court records, and special education information. The elimination of Category II helped ensure that all educationally relevant information would follow a child transferring from one school division to another, including that information on violent or inappropriate school behavior.

STRENGTHENING THE STRUCTURE

The net result of the work of the superintendents throughout the state and those of the Hampton Roads region has been a strengthening of the structure that governs the schools. Better defined rules and regulations, greater access to information, and better coordination among officials and agencies that work with youth all contribute to the structure in which our students must matriculate successfully. While school officials via the legislature and their school boards are able to define the parameters within which the schools will operate to minimize inappropriate behavior, little is being done to involve parents positively in resolving the conditions that lead to violence or other inappropriate behavior. Both reports discussed previously speak of parental involvement in schools and maintain a firm stance about parental responsibility in these matters, but they fall short of endorsing a model for either educating the community or partnering with them. *Violence in Schools* suggests that community coalitions working on substance abuse have the potential for an effective community action model. Later in this chapter, we will look at one such model for its adaptability to this context.

Alternative Education Designed by the Community

A major component of the superintendents' reports, alternative education has become a topic of discussion throughout the state. Although some educators support alternative programs for those students who have developed inappropriate behaviors and cannot be returned to a regular education environment, other educators are asking for programs for students characterized as "at risk," not only at the high school level, but also at the middle school and sometimes even elementary levels. While alternative education programs, including some with separate facilities, have existed in some Virginia localities for many years, there are few programs with a long, successful history that can be viewed as models for other school systems. The violence issue and the deteriorating home situations of many students demand a program that is designed for the student of the 1990s, and good models are difficult to locate. Some educators and parents want to see more "boot camps," such as the program in Hampton Roads that serves a very limited number of students and carries very strict requirements, including uniform dress. Others are interested in school-to-work transition programs for nonviolent students. The focus of some programs, especially at the grades prior to high school, is on prevention of those problems that may lead to either violent behavior or dropping out of school.

One unique approach to alternative education is being planned now in Gloucester County Schools, a rural school division in the Hampton Roads area. Gloucester, with a school population of 6,500, is looking at two approaches to alternative education. The administration of the school division is leading a consortium of adjacent rural divisions in the study and design of a regional alternative school for those students who have committed violent acts and cannot return to regular public schools. However, it is the unique second alternative program that holds the greatest promise. This program is designed to serve secondary students who have not demonstrated acts of violence, but who are habitual discipline offenders and are unsuccessful in the classroom. The intent of the program is to identify those students who are truly at risk of becoming violent offenders and leaving school, and to intervene early enough to provide an alternative program that (1) provides basic skills instruction, (2) is flexible in its structure, and (3) provides school-to-work transition with the development of life skills, the work ethic, and trade-related skills.

The initiators of this project (not yet formally named, but called the Academy for the purpose of this discussion) represent a broad-based community group. They include school administration and teaching staff; guidance and counseling staff; school board, social services, and juvenile court representatives; community leaders; local businesspeople; university and community college representatives; and a member of the legislature (who is also an alternative education teacher). Members of the Academy's steering committee have taken a three-pronged approach to designing an alternative program. First, they are looking at the research on alternative education and matching that which is appropriate to the characteristics and development of their learners in Gloucester. Second, they are mobilizing the community around a site for the program. The proposed site—the former home of a well-known African-American attorney who himself educated young people who were experiencing difficulty—was willed to a local university that is interested in a good use for the property. Those in the community who are particularly interested in honoring the memory of this local leader are energized by the possibility of establishing a model program of such importance at this site.

The Academy's steering committee is incorporating a third element into this project that makes the program unique. The committee has studied a national model that can involve the community in this school on a long-term basis. This program, called Cities in Schools (or Communities in Schools in some states), is the nation's largest nonprofit dropout prevention program.[9] CIS repositions community service providers to work as a personalized team serving alongside teachers to help students who are confronting many problems. Local CIS programs are independently incorporated community public/private partnership organizations led by their own boards of directors. These programs can be alternative education sites where students are enrolled throughout the day.

The Gloucester planning team has visited a CIS program in Chesterfield County, Virginia, whose corporate sponsor is Burger King Corporation. Other large companies sponsor CIS in various locations. The Commonwealth's Department of Education provided planning money to Gloucester County Schools during the 1994–

1995 school year to study the Academy's potential to help prevent inappropriate behaviors and school failure. If the local school board adopts the program and provides the necessary funding, the Academy should begin operating during the 1995–1996 school year.

What makes this alternative education program different? It is driven by community interest in a highly unique way. Often we speak about having a vision for some project or new undertaking, but the Academy is the product of a guidance counselor's vision that was not put to paper at some weekend retreat or written for a grant proposal. The counselor, having worked for years with students who needed this service, was able to generate interest among her colleagues and especially the community for this project. The vision was real and was shared quickly, so that the Academy became a community project and not one solely of the schools. This ownership has sustained the members of the planning team through months of meetings. The leadership for this project belongs to the community, not the public schools.

Regional Education Sessions

The task of educating the community falls on the formal education establishment. Schools must take a leadership role in helping members of the community as well as their own staff learn about school violence. Immediately following the Hampton Roads superintendents' issuance of A Call to Action, a regional seminar was held for educators, school board members, and members of the community. This meeting focused on various community perspectives on school violence and what could be done to address violence in the school and community. Those addressing the conference included the publisher of a local newspaper, the Commonwealth's attorney, a television news director, a community college provost, the chief judge of the juvenile and domestic relations district court, the chief of police, a local minister, an administrator for the community services board, and the state superintendent of public instruction. Comments from these individuals ranged from a concern about the "total lack of discipline" in the home to the need for more programs for at-risk children (that is, Chapter 1, Head Start, alternative education, and peer mediation). The Commonwealth's attorney pointed out that violence is a community problem when he posed the question: What is going on in the community that children feel the need for guns and weapons in order to be safe? The police chief suggested that students should be viewed as a resource in identifying problems and choosing solutions to these problems.

The notion of formal problem-solving and planning was broached by only one speaker, the administrator from the community services board. She suggested that we now have a fragmented system of service delivery for children at risk and that the programs in the different agencies, while good, are often competing for the same program participants and the same money. She cited as an example the programs that seek to promote positive role models to children. Although these many programs have good purposes, the programs may not be what the people in the community want.

Rather than imposing predesigned programs on the community, this administrator proposed that a planning process be implemented that included community members—one that could truly empower the community to solve its problems. She described a process she had used in a community setting. In a one-day meeting of two hundred residents in one neighborhood, the group was able to identify safety as the key concern of the neighborhood and a number of problems related to the safety issue. The group then spent a year analyzing the problems, receiving leadership training, and developing and implementing plans for the neighborhood.

This speaker was singular in presenting a proactive, participatory, collaborative model for community involvement in the identification and solution of violence problems. Most speakers at the seminar discussed the concerns voiced daily in the media, presented another snapshot of what is going on in their communities, and called for agencies and groups to work together. But this one individual suggested a process that could be used, based on previous successes.

As a follow-up to this seminar, the Hampton Roads group sponsored the Regional Safe School Conference in the summer of 1994 for seven hundred educators. Workshop presentations were made by school staff who were involved in initiatives to stem violence and disciplinary problems. Some of the workshop topics were:

> Ways to Manage Disruptive Students
> Peer Mediation Programs
> Sexual Harassment
> Issues of Confidentiality
> Understanding Multicultural Behavior
> Identification of Gang Behavior

An important component of helping adults learn is giving them an opportunity to engage in dialogue. During this conference, "job-alike" sessions were held so that participants could talk with people from other school divisions who held the same job and perhaps had a different (or similar) experience. This was helpful, as security officers, principals, central office personnel, and teachers could share their problems and successes.

Analysis of Safety and Security at the Building Level

The legislation forwarded in Virginia and the open discussion of violence issues have increased the level of awareness throughout the state. As school principals and superintendents in Virginia become more aware of safety issues in their schools, some are choosing to conduct school security studies using the expertise of private consultants. They are seeking to determine the vulnerability of their schools and to minimize opportunities for violent acts to occur based on the facility and staff behaviors. Assessments are conducted by teams of consultants who visit the schools, talk with personnel, gather and analyze data, and make recommendations for improving the security of the building based on both data and perceptions. An example of one organization that conducts these studies is the Center for Safe Schools, Virginia Crime Prevention Association, in Richmond.

One such study was conducted in the spring of 1994 in a Virginia high school of about 1,800 students. The administration of the school chose to conduct the study because the school is growing, and the administration was concerned about the potential for future problems in a large high school setting. Ninety-one recommendations intended to reduce the opportunity for crime, drugs, violence, and disorder within the school were presented to the administration. These recommendations fell into nine categories:

> Data Collection and Analysis (that is, disciplinary referrals)
> Managing Safety and Security
> Law Enforcement Services
> Scurity Related Policies and Procedures
> Entrances to School Property
> Parking Lots and Driveways
> Open Spaces
> Access Control into the School
> Interior Control

The following are some of the recommendations for improvement presented in the report of the visiting team:

- The computerized disciplinary file system should be on a network so that the principal and assistant principals have immediate access to the data.
- Trees at the entrance of the student parking lot should be removed to provide clear visibility.
- All adults within the school should constantly check exterior doors to make sure they are locked.
- Administrators, faculty, staff, and students should be issued picture identification cards at the beginning of the school year.

A review of the ninety-one recommendations points to two important conclusions. First, school safety is everyone's responsibility in the school. Teachers and staff will have to assume a greater role than in the past in order to help the administration provide a building that is secure and that reflects attention to detail and order. Second, implementing safety recommendations is costly to the system. This report recommended rekeying all exterior doors, placing signs throughout the plant, designing new lighting for parking areas, paving parking lots, landscaping, and placing an alarm system in the library, among other actions that require money for manpower and materials.

VIRGINIA'S EFFORTS: WHAT'S MISSING?

Virginia deserves credit for bringing the school violence issue to the attention of their community leaders and insisting on legislation to support their efforts at the local level. The "system" is now working: school administrators can access vital information and act swiftly to deal with violence/drug offenders. The structure is much stronger, with definite guidelines for actions; it is hoped that this strength will send a message to students before they act.

While the school leaders in Virginia want parents to assume more responsibility for their children's behaviors, and many recognize that assistance with parenting is necessary, school leaders have not forwarded a plan or a process for helping communities address the issues that are causing conflicts at school. Perhaps it is not the role of school leaders to do so. After all, schools are but one of the institutions involved in the problem of violence and the task of educating young people. But we must acknowledge that there is a missing component in the efforts to create safe schools. An effort must be made to bring the community together to understand the problems facing teens, the changes in society, and the behaviors being played out in our streets and our classrooms.

Where can we find assistance in developing such a process? Does the literature on school violence address prevention efforts that involve the community? If we find a model for community involvement that helps us know how to begin, is there information in the literature that guides our first steps? If we are going to assume a more proactive position regarding the problems preceding violent actions, do we know why youngsters choose gangs, guns, and violence?

Literature Review

A review of recent articles that address violence in schools reveals several broad categories of information that can be helpful to administrators. Some articles recount specific court cases and legal opinions,[10] and others give detailed descriptions of the dangers for teachers and students on school campuses,[11] suggesting that schools are the staging grounds for hate crimes that can be prevented.[12] Some writers focus on advice for school administrators, suggesting appropriate behaviors when tragedy strikes or proposing appropriate levels of force in confrontations,[13] as well as specifying actions that should be taken after the crisis is over.[14] School security emerges as another important topic.[15]

These topics, though valuable in dealing with the day-to-day circumstances faced by school administrators and teachers, are not very helpful in identifying the issues and solving the problems associated with school violence. Of greater interest are the intervention and prevention strategies available to school leaders. One collection of articles on victimization and bullying offers suggestions for intervention.[16] Smith reports a program that trains students in grades 3 through 6 about bullying and sets up a "student watch" program through which students are taught peer negotiation skills for conflict situations. Floyd proposes, among other activities, a system of incentives called group contingency reinforcement that rewards students as teams rather than as individuals for cooperation and teaming efforts. Greenbaum, who reports on the prevalence of bullying, concludes that "[t]eaching children such skills as conflict resolution, negotiation, legal rights and responsibilities, and simple courtesy can go a long way toward reversing the tragic consequences of the bully victim problem."[17] Prophet recounts efforts in Portland, Oregon to contain gang activity with a broad-based approach that includes students, school staff, parents, and community. Also covered are fourteen youth-related programs coordinated by public and private sector leaders.[18]

An examination of these stories about violence and intervention suggests first, that intervention comes about after the fact, after some act has occurred that reflects inappropriate behavior. While intervention is desirable, it is reactionary, for it occurs early in a developing process that, unarrested, might lead to violence. There will always be a need for intervention such as crisis management and conflict resolution, but intervention cannot be the sole solution to the problems surrounding violence in schools. These problems must be solved as the seeds of violence occur. Second, violence apparently is rooted in power and security. Security, a basic human need,[19] is defined through the family, and in today's world, the gang or other affiliated group serves as a surrogate family for many youth.[20] Thus further study must be conducted on the need for affiliation in youth to determine the relationship, if any, between the dysfunctional family (or families with discernible characteristics) and youth interest in joining a gang:

Gangs are a surrogate family; they give youngsters identity and status they haven't achieved at school; youngsters feel they need the protection of a gang...; youngsters see no employment or recreation alternatives to gangs; and finally, gang membership means money....[21]

Security is a feeling that should begin at home; it begins with children knowing their parent or parents are watching out for them. If they feel no security from home, they will seek it elsewhere.[22]

A return to the literature on school violence begs the question: If intervention strategies suggest that the need for power and security are related to violent behaviors, do the accounts of prevention strategies address the issues of power and security, family and control? In fact, the literature only hints at these issues. Burke, a high school teacher, calls for a curriculum that "incorporates the school into the community and gets the community into the schools," but he does not provide any specifics about what this curriculum would be, other than an attempt to involve the family and improve the home.[23] Hayes describes an Indianapolis program, Security Dads, which was created to offer mentors for students with no male role models in their lives, but Hayes does not go beyond simply reporting its positive impact.[24] Harvard University child psychiatrist Robert Coles, who conducted a survey of five thousand children in 1989, concluded that schools and other social institutions need to address moral education in a generation that is "ethically adrift."[25] His call was issued, however, without elaborating on what should be done. The issues of power and security, family, and control are only beginning to emerge in the discussions of school violence, and apparently few educators have begun thinking seriously about student empowerment and control as it relates to a safe school.

Power and the need for control seem to be related to the carrying of a weapon.[26] Weapons not only convey power, something the powerless want, but also demand respect, something the powerless need. Violence in schools hinges on the issues surrounding personal power and sense of control. In Craig's article on children living with violence, she discusses cognitive and social dysfunction.[27] Craig suggests that youth feel powerless and that they have no sense of control owing to abuse and violence at home, homelessness and poverty, and no feeling of significance and competency. These deficiencies create a sense of "no control" in the individual that may lead to violent behavior. Living with violence creates a lack of self-awareness that leads to a sense of powerlessness, and weapons can provide the personal power the youngster needs. For the youth that feels both the lack of control and the powerlessness, the weapon and the violent behavior can be very empowering.

This discussion of possible root causes of violent behavior in youth is incomplete and is presented only to call attention to the complexity of the violence issue. While the literature reviewed does not propose models for community involvement to identify and solve problems, the literature does suggest that those interested in preventing violent acts—rather than merely responding to them—should engage in a discussion of the cognitive and social needs of children. The nature of such a discussion demands a facilitator who can guide group learning. This effort becomes an educational activity for the community group and probably is necessary as the group examines the assumptions they hold about youth, parents, home, and community. The learning that occurs within the community group undergirds the problem-solving strategies they forward and promote.

The Future by Design

The literature on school violence is emerging, and this review did not find models for organizing groups to problem-solve or methods of community organization as part of the existing school violence literature. The writings on prevention programs are sketchy at best; complete descriptions of good programs should be disseminated. The literature does suggest that issues of affiliation, security, and power in youth are the seeds of youth violence and should be addressed. These are important issues for schools to consider as they debate how students are viewed, treated, and included in the learning process. Moreover, since the issues of power and security have roots in the home and community, these can best, and should first, be addressed by the community as it attempts to solve the root problems causing dangerous and inappropriate behavior in its young.

Let us return to Virginia to find a model for working with communities. When a program administrator for the Portsmouth Community Services Board spoke at the first Hampton Roads conference on violence in schools in February 1994, she quickly outlined a model for engaging the community in a year-long problem-solving process. She spoke with great conviction about the value of having the community identify and solve its own problems. Later, she recommended a model published by the U.S. Department of Health and Human Services called *The Future by Design*. This document presents a community framework for preventing alcohol and other drug problems through a systems approach.[28] Three major themes are included in the framework:

Community empowerment, "doing with" and not "doing for," shifting responsibility for planning and decisionmaking from agencies and professionals to the community.

Inclusion of all community groups, both formal and informal, in all prevention efforts.

Cultural competency, the lifelong process of incorporating, valuing, and celebrating the ethnic and cultural diversity of the community.

This guide presents lessons from successful (and unsuccessful) prevention programs. The framework details initiating a prevention effort, leadership, activities, resources, partnerships, and assessment. The model proposes a management process that includes the continuous cycle of planning, implementation, evaluation, and decisionmaking. Moreover, there is no reason to doubt the model's transferability to community problems other than substance abuse. The essence of the model is not in the topic to be addressed but the process to facilitate the group decisionmaking.

Close to one-half of the school divisions in Virginia already have the tools needed to begin the community problem-solving activity. These school systems have made a commitment to some form of Total Quality Management (TQM) and have either the philosophy in place or the training in process that provides them with the skills needed to facilitate group decisionmaking. Using the TQM process as well as the organizational structure of strategic planning, a school leader can bring together the community to identify key issues.

Although there is probably no one magic way to bring communities together, there are proven strategies for working together that can be helpful. Two key roles must be identified to make this process operable. First, someone must have the belief that a group can come together and solutions will be found. This is the visionary leader, perhaps someone with high visibility or someone who is highly respected, but it must be a person who can get people's attention and articulate a goal. Second, a person with strong interpersonal and group-processing skills should serve as facilitator of meetings. Whether following *The Future by Design*, some other organization's design, or a plan of their own, the group must adhere to a process that lets everyone be heard, considers all the information available, and makes decisions by consensus.

The tools taught in TQM training can assist a facilitator in the problem-solving process. One of the most important steps in problem-solving that is often ignored or passed over quickly is that of analyzing the key causes of the problem. Some of the literature on school violence suggests that the key causes of youth violence revolve around issues of power, security, control, and family, but other causes can surface during a thorough analysis of the data available. Research can provide a facilitator with data to initiate discussions that move beyond the normal rhetoric about violence and young people. It is critical for the group leader to guide the group in a direction that challenges participants' beliefs and assumptions. Using data can aid in this process. A thorough analysis of the problem helps the group better define the problem as well as identify the key causes to be addressed in the solution chosen.

Working with groups of adults requires skill. Adult education literature can provide assistance to those planning decisionmaking activities.[29] Educators and others who support this kind of community effort must be prepared for nonconventional answers to problems and solutions that suggest social action. The problems teased out of the school violence dilemma are complex. Those who respond to the challenge of school violence problems will be asked to look at the situation differently, perhaps creatively, and certainly collaboratively, in order to find meaningful solutions that address the complexity of social change.

PREVENTION OR INTERVENTION?

Teachers and administrators are currently not prepared to address school violence issues. Training in conflict resolution is helpful, but relying on traditional disciplinary procedures may not be adequate. Further research is needed to understand the key causes of youth violence. After those causes are articulated, educators must find help in designing solutions to the problem of school violence that respond to the key causes.

Virginia's efforts to proactively face school violence can be categorized as intervention. Legislation, policies, security measures, teacher training, and community awareness sessions tend to focus on intervention procedures that protect innocent students and provide strong disciplinary measures for offenders. Many educators would say that the recent action taken by legislators and school officials to address violence in schools represents an attempt to stem the growing violence. Prevention may take many forms, but none as serious or as permanent as a community's recognition that the problems of violence belong to the community, and the solutions reside in the heads and hearts, dreams, and expectations of the members of the community. Sometimes it takes a crisis to awaken communities to reality and create a readiness for action. For each community, the threat to its present and its future will be defined differently, perhaps with the assistance of school leaders who are not afraid to talk about the reality of the student's world.

As this chapter was being readied for publication, the Hampton Roads community felt the pain of an innocent five-year-old child, who, while riding his bike one summer afternoon in his grandmother's neighborhood, was caught in the crossfire of a gun battle. The child lies paralyzed, not knowing whether he will ever ride his bike again. There is no intervention strategy to save this child from the effects of violence. He will serve as a symbol for violence in our communities, and perhaps his image will inspire the community action needed to truly prevent further violence by and on our children.

NOTES

1. J. Moffet, *The Universal Schoolhouse: Spiritual Awaking Through Education* (San Francisco: Jossey-Bass, 1994), 26.

2. J. W. Boothe et al., "The Violator at Your Door," *Executive Educator* 15 (January 1993): 20–22.

3. *Violence in Schools* (Charlottesville, Va., 1992).

4. School districts in Virginia are called *divisions*, and are contiguous with city, county, and town governments. There is great diversity in size of divisions and numbers of students served. Each division has its own superintendent and school board. There are 135 divisions in the state.

5. *Violence in Schools*, 23.

6. An excellent summary of the changes in Virginia school law relative to the *Violence in Schools* recommendations was written by T. Page Johnson for the Virginia Association of Secondary School Principals (Richmond, Va., August 1993).

7. Dr. W. C. Bosher, Jr., interview, June 20, 1994.

8. *Ending Violence in Our Schools: A Call to Action* (Newport News, Va., 1994).

9. Cities in Schools, Inc. has been in operation since 1977. For additional information, contact: CIS, 1199 North Fairfax Street, Suite 300, Alexandria, Va. 22314-1436, (703)519-8999. Training is offered at the CIS Training Institute, located at Lehigh University's National Center for Partnership Development in Bethlehem, Pa.

10. D. H. Henderson et al., "The Use of Force by Public School Teachers as a Defense," *West Education Law Report* 54 (March 1989): 773–83; P. A. Zirkel and I. B. Gluckman, "A Legal Brief: Assaults on School Personnel," *NASSP Bulletin* 75 (1991): 101–106.

11. D. Foley, "Danger: School Zone," *Teacher Magazine* (1990): 57–59, 62–63.

12. C. Bodinger-deUriarte, "Hate Crime: The Rise of Hate Crime on School Campuses," *Research Bulletin of Phi Delta Kappa* (October 1994): 1–6.

13. D. Frisby and J. Beckham, "Dealing with Violence and Threats of Violence in the School," *NASSP Bulletin* 77, No. 552 (1993): 10–15; D. Smith, "The Cleveland Elementary School Shooting," *Thrust* 18 (July 1989): 8–11.

14. C. Burns, "What to Do When the Crisis Is Over," *American School Board Journal* 177 (March 1990): 31–32; B. B. Collison et al., "After the Shooting Stops," *Journal of Counseling and Development* 65 (1987): 389–90.

15. K. Bushweller, "Guards with Guns," *American School Board Journal* 180, No. 1 (1993): 31–32; G. J. Gerl, "Thwarting Intruder Violence in Our Schools," *NASSP Bulletin* 75, No. 534 (1991): 75–79; S. R. Sabo, "Security by Design," *American School Board Journal* 180, No. 1 (1993): 37–39.

16. N. M. Floyd, "'Pick on Somebody Your Own Size!': Controlling Victimization," *The Pointer* 29, No. 2 (1985): 9–17; S. Greenbaum, "What Can We Do about Schoolyard Bullying?," *Principal* (1987): 21–24; M. Prophet, "Safe Schools in Portland," *American School Board Journal* 10, No. 10 (1990): 28–30; S. J. Smith, "How to Decrease Bullying in Our Schools," *Principal* 72, No. 1 (1992): 31–32.

17. Greenbaum, "What Can We Do."

18. M. Prophet, "Safe Schools in Portland," *American School Board Journal* 10, No. 10 (1990).

19. A. Maslow, *Motivation and Personality* (New York: Harper and Row, 1954).

20. J. Burke, "Teenagers, Clothes, and Gang Violence," *Educational Leadership* 49, No. 1 (1991): 11–13; P. Ordovensky, "Facing Up to Violence," *Executive Educator* 15, No. 1 (1993): 22–24.

21. V. Robinson, "Violence in Schools: What's the Problem, and Is There a Solution?," *Partners in Education* (February 1994): 4.

22. Burke, "Teenagers, Clothes, and Gang Violence," 12.

23. Ibid., 13.

24. D. W. Hayes, "Reading, Writing, and Arithmetic—An Education in Violence," *Crisis* 100, No. 4 (1993): 8–10.

25. D. Harrington-Lueker, "A Fifth-Grader Is Accused of Trying to Poison Her Teacher," *Executive Educator* 13 (1991): 25–26.

26. Hayes, "Reading, Writing, and Arithmetic."

27. S. E. Craig, "The Educational Needs of Children Living with Violence," *Phi Delta Kappan* 74, No. 1 (1992): 67–71.

28. This publication was prepared by the Division of Community Prevention and Training, Office of Substance Abuse Prevention (OASP) and is in the public domain. It was printed in 1991—DHHS Publication No. (ADM) 91-1760—and is for sale by the Superintendent of Documents, U.S. Government Printing Office, Washington, D.C. 20402, and distributed by the National Clearinghouse for Alcohol and Drug Information, P.O. Box 2345, Rockville, Md. 20852, (800) 729-6686.

29. For additional information on working effectively with adults as they examine their assumptions, see S. D. Brookfield, *Developing Critical Thinkers* (San Francisco: Jossey-Bass, 1989) or S. D. Brookfield, *The Skillful Teacher* (San Francisco: Jossey-Bass, 1989).

19

Violence in Schools: The Texas Initiative

Christie Bourgeois with an introduction by former Texas Governor Ann W. Richards

INTRODUCTION

> What you see depends on where you stand—and what you hear depends on who you listen to.[1]

One of the best things about being governor is meeting with the children who come to the capitol. It made my day to walk out of my office and find a class of first-graders, all wide-eyed and awed and impressed to meet a governor—someone almost as important as their teacher. Those kids are so great that you hope they never lose that first-grade sense of wonder and happiness—that undiluted delight in everything new and challenging.

But you and I know that we live in a world that can be terribly hard on kids. We hear daily stories of tragic crimes: teens assaulting their teachers, drive-by shootings committed by youngsters barely old enough to drive, and young people burglarizing houses during the day—when they should be in school.

When I was growing up, our parents gave us limits. They told us what the rules were. My parents always told me, "There's nothing going on after midnight that you need to be concerned about." That is why I support curfews. Parents have told me that curfews help reinforce their authority. Teenagers have told me that sometimes curfews make it easier for them to get out of difficult situations and into the safety of their homes.

We all know that kids will be kids, but the stories and statistics tell us that the violence done to and by our young people has far outpaced normal youthful antics. The sad fact is that the number of kids committed to the Texas Youth Commission for violent offenses has increased 191 percent since 1988.

With that in mind, I went to those closest to the situation— the kids—and asked, "How can we adults make your lives safer?" On December 7, 1993, at the

Samual Grand Recreation Center in Dallas, I kicked off a series of youth summits in Texas. I invited junior and senior high school students and their parents to meet with police officers and police chiefs, teachers and principals, and criminal justice and education leaders. Over one thousand students and adults worked together throughout 1994 in three regional summits and a statewide youth summit to discover why schools today are often unsafe places to be, and how government might help make them safer.

The youth summit participants proposed realistic and specific solutions to some of the toughest problems facing our state. They told us that we should make punishment meaningful and seek harsher penalties for kids who commit serious crimes. Too many young people believe that being expelled is a permit to skip school legally—that they can commit any crime and get away with it—that punishment is rare, and that when it occurs it is no big deal. Far too often a child with a problem gets our attention— and the use of our services—only after he or she has given up on school or committed a crime. The challenge for government leaders is to find ways to help kids stay on the right track and give them what they need to do the right thing.

We have a system of public education that has remained fundamentally unchanged for forty years. And yet our schools have been asked to absorb wave after wave of social change. Families have changed, kids have changed, work has changed.

We are not living in a "Leave it to Beaver" world where mom waits at home in high heels and pearls with cookies and milk. The only thing holding the middle class together is the two-paycheck family. In our youngest families—families in which most school age children live—real income has fallen in the last decade. Mom and Dad are both working—or if it is just Mom supporting the family, she is certainly at work or trying to find a job.

No matter how good our intentions, life is different for our kids. My daddy was a pharmaceutical salesman, and I can remember him taking me out with him to the drugstores. He said he was showing me off, but, whatever his purpose, I got to see the larger world of work. I saw how people earned a living and what the possibilities were.

Too many city kids walk by tall buildings downtown and have no idea what goes on inside. We think their world is expanded by television—but what career possibilities do they see? Star point guard in the NBA? Impossibly affluent doctor with incredibly attractive lawyer-wife? Renegade homicide detective? Where do these kids see themselves in the picture? Where is the hard-working teacher, the nurse practitioner, the technician, the bookkeeper, the manager, the business man and woman?

Where do these kids go to expand their horizons? And if their horizons do not expand—if they settle for the allure of easy money by dropping out of school to sell drugs, or if they end up in a dead-end job—where does that leave the rest of us?

It leaves us with the frightening image of a Third World American society where the "haves" build walls to keep out the "have not's"—and it leaves us with a workforce that mirrors our worst fears of second-rate economic status. Serious thinkers made this connection even before the statisticians proved it to us.

To understand what we need to do, we do not have to reinvent the wheel. It does not take a rocket scientist to figure out what children want and need. Just ask them. Children need a caring, responsible adult they can depend on. They need someone who will set limits, give them guidance, and listen to them. They need to be fed and clothed and tended when they are sick. All of this sounds suspiciously like a parent. And, indeed, the people who make a difference in children's lives are parents, grandparents, neighbors, and the communities in which our children live. We know that when a parent is positively involved in a child's life and school, the odds turn in favor of that child immediately.

But we have to accept the fact that some parents cannot or will not be involved. And when they are not, we have to do our best to find surrogates or mentors or counselors, or ministers or doctors or teachers, or whatever you want to call someone who is there for a child.

We have a lot of government programs spending a lot of money trying to accomplish that goal. And there are other things that national and state governments can do well. The federal crime bill passed in the summer of 1994 had prevention programs as well as programs to get tough on criminals. In Texas we created a state initiative—the first of its kind nationwide—to ensure that every child in the state can be immunized against childhood diseases, regardless of their family's ability to pay. Texas also passed legislation that will make health insurance affordable for small businesses and their employees—and we hope this will make health care available to more of our children. These are the kinds of actions we can take at the state level that work everywhere.

But too often programs come down as pronouncements from bureaucrats in Washington or state capitals who have little knowledge or regard for what a community needs, or what will work in a certain location. There are circumstances when it simply is better for the higher levels of government to get out of the way and let the people closest to the situation get the job done.

In Texas we have recognized that about our public schools—and we are doing our damnedest to break up the education bureaucracy in Austin and turn the decisionmaking process over to the local schools, where they know what works for their students. To smooth our path, we can take advantage of the incredible variety of successful programs already in place in Texas, as well as in other states. I can cite several examples and still not really touch the surface.

Communities in Schools is a tremendously successful public–private partnership. At an annual cost of about $515 per student—the money comes from both local business contributions and state government—CIS provides help to any child or family that needs it. Whether it is tutoring, counseling, or helping a parent find a job, CIS workers and volunteers are there in twenty-three Texas cities. CIS is growing because it works: 94 percent of kids in CIS stay in school.

At Wheatley High School in Houston, staff from the Texas Department of Human Services work on-site at the school campus coordinating a project to help low-income families and keep kids in schools. The program works because state and local agencies have coordinated their efforts. Since the Wheatley project started, 107 of the students who participated have graduated and only six dropped out. Sixty-four have gotten jobs, thirty-seven have gotten off of welfare, and the number of teenage pregnancies and teenage parents has been reduced by more than 20 percent.

I am proud of the interagency cooperation going on in Dallas in a program called Safe House. The Texas Commission on Alcohol and Drug Abuse, the Texas Youth Commission, and the Texas Juvenile Probation Commission are working with the community to set up houses that will feel and look like a home, not an institution. They are located near neighborhoods with crime and abuse problems, so kids can drop in and encounter responsible adults who will offer them life-skills development training, help with education, recreation, counseling, and many other services. The best thing is that these houses are developed, run, and staffed by the community rather than government.

I am especially proud of a project we helped launch in the Third Ward of Houston. The Casey Foundation has awarded Texas one of only two grants given nationally for the development of a comprehensive, community-driven program for children of an inner-city neighborhood. My staff and representatives from state and city agencies and Houston schools worked with people from the community to get this grant, which will provide $4 million to help the people of the Third Ward address their problems in a way that makes sense for them. We have every hope that the Casey project will develop into a model that will inspire communities across Texas and the nation.

All of these projects have the virtue of bringing the community together and helping kids. The truth is there are a lot of things we can do to change kids' lives, change communities, and—in the long run—change all of our lives.

Churches have always played a vital role in every community. From talking to clergy around the state, I know many Texas churches have undertaken excellent initiatives to benefit children and families. I have asked these leaders to go into partnership with government and make a real commitment to the state's children. Church and community leaders who know their needs best should provide the organization and hands-on care; state and local governments should bring what resources they can to help implement the programs the community says it needs.

Participants in the youth summits held across the state during 1994 recommended many programs to reduce violence in schools; punish young people who commit crimes; and improve education, health care, and social services. But I am convinced that government programs alone cannot solve the problem. I have every faith that the religious and community leaders across the state of Texas will continue to work with local, state, and federal government to save the children and, thereby, save us all.

— Ann W. Richards

Texas Governor Ann W. Richards held a press conference on August 9, 1994 to release a report called, "Safeguarding the Future: A Call to Action." The scene was the Metropolitan Center, an alternative school in Dallas. Everyone who entered the building walked through a metal detector located just inside the doorway. Motivational signs lined the walls, but also signs of warning: "When you have sex with someone, you have sex with their partner, and their partner's partner, and their partner's partner's partner,…"

A bipartisan group of uniformed police officers, sheriffs, state senators and representatives, the mayor, the president of the Greater Dallas Crime Commission, and many other dignitaries were present. Also present was a group of sixty students ranging from elementary age kids to high school seniors. Some of the students came from the Gainesville Texas Youth Commission (TYC) facility; they had been sent there for committing serious crimes. Others were from poor neighborhoods, yet many of those were on a good track nonetheless; for example, Kevin Arrista, a recent high school graduate who presented the report to the governor, was headed to Dartmouth on a scholarship. Others were from middle-class neighborhoods.

The governor released her report in Dallas, because it was where her youth summits had begun back in December 1993. Governor Richards, like everyone else, was distressed by the meteoric rise of juvenile crime in the last few years and tales of young people afraid to go to school, afraid that they might become victims of violence. The first of a series of regional youth summits was launched in Dallas; others were held in El Paso and San Antonio. In May 1994 she called for a statewide youth summit that convened in Austin, the capital of Texas. At each summit, the governor invited experts from the fields of criminal justice and education, not to tell her what to do, but to listen to those who were most affected by the violence: the kids. At the first summit, she gave the group their charge:

We have called this meeting, because we want to hear the truth. And we want to hear the truth as these kids know it. Not like the media reports it. Or like the bureaucracy studies it. But the truth like it is; the truth that students live every day. Because that is the only way we can find out what is wrong and what we can do together to fix it.[2]

THE PROBLEM OF JUVENILE VIOLENCE

We have all heard the grisly statistics. Nationally, between 1983 and 1992, arrests of youth below age eighteen for violent crimes increased by 57 percent; arrests for murder and manslaughter during the same period increased a remarkable 128 percent.[3] And the statistics for Texas are no better. During that same period, arrests of juveniles for violent crimes and arrests of juveniles for murder and manslaughter both increased by 95 percent. Since 1973 the changes are almost unbelievable. That year the predominant offenses for which youngsters were committed to TYC were theft (48.7 percent) and disobedience (27.2 percent). Only 4.9 percent were committed for violent offenses. In 1993, 34 percent of the commitments were for violent offenses, and 31 percent of those admitted had five or more felony arrests prior to commitment. In 1973 only 8.9 percent of youths were committed for alcohol or drug violations; in 1993, 80 percent had used alcohol or drugs and 49 percent were chemically dependent.[4]

These statistics are alarming to students as well as adults. With the explosion in juvenile crime, however, it is often forgotten that the vast majority of young people go through adolescence without once getting into trouble. And that has not changed much over the years. It is not that we have more bad kids today; rather, it is that those kids who are committing crimes are committing more crimes, and more violent crimes. Only 2 to 15 percent of young males commit between 50 to 75 percent of all violent crimes.[5] That is exactly what the kids told us in the youth summits. They said that only about 5 percent of the kids are ruining the schools for the other 95 percent. And they told us that adults should "make punishment meaningful" for the kids who seriously disrupt the schools. As it stands, many kids like to be expelled, and some who go to alternative schools think it is a status symbol, not a punishment.

To "make punishment meaningful," Governor Richards believes that we must expand the Texas Youth Commission (TYC) facilities. TYC deals with the most violent juveniles in Texas, and the governor recommends that the next legislature appropriate $150 million for the next biennium to expand TYC facilities. She also recognizes the need to preserve TYC bed space for the most dangerous offenders. Therefore, she recommends a progressive system of punishment.

One of the more interesting progressive models for dealing with juvenile offenders was developed jointly by TYC and the Texas Juvenile Probation Commission (TJPC). This program ensures that each time a youngster commits a criminal act, there is a consequence. The model is structured to balance public protection, rehabilitation, and offender accountability and consists of six sanction levels, each increasingly more serious than the one before. The six levels allow juveniles to move both up and down the tiers as dictated by their behavior and rehabilitation. Far too often youngsters must commit six or seven offenses before they meet a consequence. With the progressive sanctions model, there will be some consequence each time. For instance, juveniles picked up by the police for status offenses such as truancy will be counseled and released to their parents. A violent felony will land a youngster in a TYC secure facility, a Level 6 sanction. Once a youngster has reached that level, he or she can work down the other side of the ladder, and ultimately to release.[6]

To make communities safer, Governor Richards believes we need to improve access to juvenile records. As it stands in Texas, juvenile records, photographs, and fingerprints are often unavailable to different law enforcement agencies, even within the same county—and these records are never accessible across county lines. Therefore, if a young man commits aggravated sexual assault in Dallas, neither the police nor the district attorney would know that he had committed the same crime in Houston. The governor recommends that the legislature create a statewide juvenile data base so that police officers, district attorneys, and judges in one county will know about the criminal records of young perpetrators in other counties.[7]

Finally, to protect society from the really dangerous kids, Governor Richards wants to expand the determinate sentencing statute to cover all violent crimes. The determinate sentencing statute in Texas currently allows a prosecuting attorney to refer a petition to the grand jury if a child is charged with murder; capital murder; aggravated kidnapping; aggravated sexual assault; deadly assault on a law enforcement officer, corrections officer, or court participant; or attempted capital murder. If found to have committed one of those offenses, the youth may receive a sentence of up to forty years.[8] A youth receiving a determinate sentence is placed under the control of TYC and kept with youth of a similar age until a transfer hearing is held by the juvenile court when the youth is approximately seventeen-and-a-half years old.

The State Bar of Texas Juvenile Justice committee agrees with Governor Richards that if the determinate sentencing statute were amended to include all aggravated offenses, the distasteful alternative of certifying fourteen-year-old kids as adults and sending them into the adult prison system would be unnecessary. Statistics also show that the adult criminal justice system is more lenient on juveniles than the juvenile system.[9]

PREVENTING JUVENILE VIOLENCE

But the real question is, how can we stop violent behavior by young people before they end up in a TYC facility? More than three out of every four schools nationwide—urban, suburban, and rural—reported student-on-student violence during the 1992–1993 school year.[10] The most serious violent acts committed by and against young people involve guns. In fact, 83 percent of murdered fifteen-to-nineteen-year-olds in 1993 were killed with guns.[11] Some children carry guns to school as an aggressive act; sadly, many kids carry guns to school in a misguided effort to protect themselves against aggressors. When you combine impulsive adolescents with the presence of guns, tragedy is often the result.

Youngsters at the youth summits told us that metal detectors in schools made them feel safer and made them feel that adults care about what happens to them. But we have had enough experience with guns in schools to know that metal detectors alone will not keep schools gun-free. One strategy that has proven far more successful is student reporting. If kids who are afraid of aggressive students trust a teacher or administrator to protect them, they will report it if they know that a particular child has a gun at school. Gene Haynes, a school administrator from Omaha, Nebraska, has said that "students are the best kept secret" in keeping guns off campus.[12]

Government Programs

There are certain things that federal, state, and local governments can do to help. For instance, the Federal Crime Bill of 1994 contains not only get-tough-on-crime measures, but also good prevention programs. The Ounce of Prevention program will give grants to cities, counties, school boards, universities, or private nonprofit entities to create or supplement crime prevention programs. There are $380 million available for local crime prevention block grants. Local governments can use this money for myriad programs, from education, training, and research to midnight sports league programs. Some grant funds go directly to eligible communities to provide extracurricular and academic programs, workforce preparation, and other initiatives.[13]

Another good effort on the part of the federal government is the Safe Schools Act of 1993. School districts facing high rates of crime and violence can compete for U.S. Department of Education grants and can receive up to $3 million a year for up to two years to develop a school safety plan for combating and preventing violence. The plan authorizes $75 million in its first year and $100 million in the second year. The grant can be used for a variety of violence-prevention and school safety initiatives, but no more than one-third of each grant can be spent on metal detectors or the hiring of security guards. Governor Richards has urged school districts in Texas to compete for those grants.[14]

Texas Legislation/Initiatives

After the 1993 Texas legislative session, Governor Richards signed legislation that allows for the exchange of information between law enforcement agencies and schools regarding certain criminal activity by students; the law is meant to curtail gang activity. She also signed legislation that enhances penalties for an offender who has drugs or weapons near a school, playground, youth center, swimming pool, or video arcade.[15] The governor recommends that the legislature pass the Texas Federation of Teachers' Zero Tolerance initiative. This legislation would require that a student who, on campus, assaults a teacher or other school employee or commits criminal assault on a fellow student be removed from that school permanently and placed in an alternative learning setting. A student who brings a gun or an illegal drug to school will be permanently removed from that campus and placed in an alternative learning setting apart from the school where the incident occurred. Students could earn the right to reenter regular classes, but they would not be allowed to return to the campus where they committed the original offense.[16]

Key to making the Zero Tolerance proposal work is making sure there are appropriate alternative settings for these children. In "Safeguarding the Future," Governor Richards recommended that these alternative schools not only be strict environments, but also places where kids can learn their way out of trouble. Students there should be responsible for their own learning, and instruction should be self-paced, so that they can either catch up with other youth their age or go beyond their age group if they can. And the teacher should not be the "sage on the stage" who lectures to students sitting in rows of chairs, but should facilitate the students' learning. Counseling should be provided to help these troubled kids face their problems and deal with them in constructive ways.[17]

The Zero Tolerance policy has an excellent change of being enacted into law. At this writing, ninety-two of the one hundred-fifty House members and twenty members of the thirty-one-member Senate support the passage of such a law during the 1995 legislative session. More than 90 percent of Texans, in every area of the state, believe that physically violent and disruptive students should be removed from the regular classroom and placed in an alternative setting. Support for the policy is strong among all ethnic groups: 93.7 percent of whites, 88.4 percent of African-Americans, and 87.4 percent of Hispanics said they would support it.[18] There is evidence that this policy will indeed make schools safer. The Corpus Christi Independent School District implemented the policy and provided an alternative school with two hundred slots for students removed from regular classrooms. One semester after Corpus Christi implemented Zero Tolerance, the incidences of weapons brought on campus in the district fell to two from ten.[19]

Other recommendations in "Safeguarding the Future" include putting peace officers in schools. Young people at the youth summits said they feel safer in school when there are peace officers and metal detectors. The report also recommends that local school districts and juvenile probation officials work together to develop programs that place probation officers on school campuses to monitor troubled youth daily. The report recommended that the State Bar of Texas and law firms work with local school districts to offer pro bono training of students and educators to set up teen courts within schools. Teen courts—operated by students and assisted by lawyers, law students, and law professors—mete out consequences for breaking rules and disrupting schools. The most common recommendation by far coming from students at the youth summits was more counseling for kids. The students wanted the bad kids out of their schools, but they also told the governor that some kids misbehave because they have problems, and that if these kids had a responsible adult to talk to about their problems it might prevent future misbehavior and get them on the right track.

Another recommendation was to extend peer counseling and peer mediation programs which work well and of which there are excellent examples across the state. No one grows too old to remember what an enormous influence our peers had on us when we were growing up, especially during adolescence. If we can turn that influence in a positive direction, we have a powerful tool to reduce violence in our schools. The Peer Assistance Network of Texas (PAN-Texas) is a statewide project launched in 1987 to promote and support quality peer assistance programs. This state-supported project has been successful in helping hundreds of Texas school districts implement programs.[20]

No matter how many programs, police officers, or metal detectors we put in schools, and no matter how tough we get on the kids, we will not succeed in creating the kinds of schools we want until we deal with the problems that many youngsters are bringing to school. So many urban areas are simply unfit environments in which to raise kids. Until we find a way to ensure that our children are nurtured and secure in their own homes and communities, we will not succeed in eliminating violence from our schools and making them places where creativity and learning thrive. Violence in neighborhoods will eventually find its way to school, no matter what precautions we take. A child who sees violence is far more likely to do violence. And a child who is afraid to walk to school for fear she will be a victim of violence has little chance to succeed academically. Charles Sorrentino, policy adviser for the U.S. Department of the Treasury, has compared the borders of the school campus to the borders of our country. We have tried to keep drugs out of our country through interdiction, but interdiction alone has not worked. If we try to make schools safe through metal detectors and violence-prevention strategies in schools alone, we will fail.[21]

During the 1993 legislative session, the state of Texas decided to go beyond passing piecemeal legislation regarding children and violence and take a long look at why there is so much youth violence and what we can do about it. Senate Bill 155 created the Texas Commission on Children and Youth, and the legislation charged the commission with developing a comprehensive proposal to improve and coordinate public programs for children and youth and to achieve specific goals in the areas of education, health care, juvenile justice, and family services. Governor Richards designated Senator Jim Turner from Crocket, Texas to chair the commission, whose members include three senators, three representatives, and eleven public members ranging from a district attorney to city council members, children's advocates, and the retired CEO of Tenneco. Also serving on the commission are eighteen ex officio members from various state agencies.

Between January and June 1994, the commission held a series of public hearings around the state in order to receive comments and suggestions from citizens and experts. Their final report was released in November 1994. Wrestling with the same difficult problems of juvenile crime and lost children that challenge state governments all across the country today, the commission asked many of the same questions that led Governor Richards to call for the youth summits. The commission plans to make recommendations to change the juvenile justice code to reflect the seriousness of the offenses young people are committing, but it is also focusing on how to prevent children from reaching the criminal justice system to begin with. One recommendation is that communities create local children and youth commissions that focus on preventing child abuse and teenage pregnancies and help solve problems for children living in poverty. State funds will be used as seed money to help raise local dollars from the private sector. Senator Turner believes that we must begin to focus significant resources on the prevention side if we are going to make a difference in the crime problem: "I really think that people are waking up to the fact that simply building more prisons is not going to solve our crime problem."[22]

T-CAP

We have an excellent example in Texas of local government helping kids and helping to reduce youth violence. The mayors of eight Texas cities have come together to form Mayors United on Safety, Crime, and Law Enforcement (MUSCLE).[23] This anticrime coalition representing a wide spectrum of political philosophy came together because the mayors realized that their cities faced similar problems with crime, particularly juvenile crime, and that if they worked together they could find some solutions. The MUSCLE cities contain 35 percent of the state's population and almost 60 percent of its violent crime.[24]

In early 1991 senior staff at the National Crime Prevention Council (NCPC) presented a challenge to the MUSCLE mayors: with the help of NCPC, undertake an eighteen-month commitment to develop extensive and detailed crime prevention plans. The initiative is called the Texas City Action Plan to Prevent Crime (T-CAP). During T-CAP planning in the seven cities that participated, representatives from the municipal government sat down with local leaders, private entities, and citizens and came up with recommendations to prevent crime ranging from street lighting and home security surveys to social intervention initiatives such as job training, mandated parenting education, youth recreation, and conflict resolution.[25]

Mayor Richard Greene of Arlington appointed a coalition—the Violent Crimes Task Force—that represented neighborhood associations, the League of United Latin American Citizens, the Asian community, the African-American community, social service providers, the business community, and law enforcement. Polls show that people are most afraid of random violent crime committed by strangers, but the Arlington coalition found that in their community 96 percent of all crime is property crime and that domestic violence accounts for more than half of the violent remainder. Therefore, the task force concentrated not on more jails, tougher laws, and stricter penalties, but on domestic violence prevention. The task force concluded that the domestic violence problem goes far beyond the immediate threat to women and children, because children who see or experience violence in their own homes are much more likely to become violent perpetrators themselves. The task force recommended long-term prevention strategies such as parenting classes, intervention programs, and stronger domestic violence legislation. It also found that youth with nowhere to go and nothing to do spells trouble. In response, the task force recommended crime prevention curricula in schools, after-school programs, business creating jobs for youth, and programs that strengthen connections with parents.[26]

During the youth summits, Governor Richards discovered the influence of domestic violence in perpetuating a cycle of violence that manifests itself in schools and society. Children who grow up in violent homes are more likely to commit violent crimes, use alcohol and drugs, and become perpetrators of child abuse and family violence as adults. Reports of family violence and assault of children, including sexual assault, are increasing in Texas, but protective and counseling services for children and women remain limited, and punishment and counseling for abusers are inadequate. Seventy percent of men who batter their wives also batter their children; being abused or neglected as a child increases the likelihood of arrest as a juvenile by 53 percent. Parenting programs should teach parents to deal with children in a nonabusive manner. Counselors and others who work with kids must be trained to respond effectively when children report abuse or are suspected of being abused.

Law enforcement must take an active role in investigating and reporting child abuse and family violence. Penalties for repeated assaults by family members must be increased. There must be safe places where children and their abused parents or siblings can go while perpetrators of family violence participate in counseling and learn nonviolent ways of interacting with family members.

The Corpus Christi Mayor's Coalition on Crime Prevention included social service providers; a juvenile probation officer; an administrator in the largest school district; an official in the refining industry; and members of neighborhood associations, the United Way, the YMCA, the Housing Authority, and the Boys & Girls Club of Corpus Christi. Mayor Mary Rhodes was heavily involved throughout the T-CAP planning process, traveling with the neighborhood task force to assess conditions in troubled neighborhoods herself:

Friday night at 10:00 p.m., Whataburgers in hand, they had set out to tour the highest crime areas of the city. The members were stunned as they saw drug deal after drug deal occur, then watched young men come up to the bus waving huge wads of cash, despite the presence of a video camera and a uniformed officer. "Why are there no lights here?" members of the task force asked. "Somebody should do something about this," all agreed.[27]

Having local government come down from its ivory tower to really see what is going on in blighted areas of the city is a good idea. Because of that experience, Corpus Christi's coalition focused on what needed to be done at the neighborhood level and allowed those who lived in the neighborhoods to communicate their needs to city hall. A mayor's commission on neighborhoods created a guide to building and running effective Neighborhood Watch associations, a number of which were created to increase the flow of information from city hall and the police department out to the neighborhoods. Many of the specific recommendations centered around initiatives to make neighborhoods and public places safer.[28]

Youth summit participants were also concerned with safe neighborhood issues. One of the youth summit recommendations to keep neighborhoods safe that Governor Richards supports wholeheartedly is curfews. Youth curfews serve two purposes: they cut crime against kids and they cut crime by kids. Even though nighttime curfews are relatively new to most cities, those in place have reduced the number of juvenile perpetrators and juveniles who become victims of crime. Austin, Corpus Christi, Dallas, El Paso, Lubbock, Paris, San Antonio, Seguin, Texarkana, Tyler, and Wichita Falls all enforce nighttime curfews. In San Antonio the number of juveniles who were victims of crime between midnight and 6:00 A.M. dropped by 77 percent in three years owing to the enforcement of a nighttime curfew. After mandating a nighttime curfew, Austin saw juvenile arrests drop 50 percent during curfew hours. Local communities can also adopt daytime curfews to reduce truancy and property crimes. A daytime curfew in Austin reduced juvenile arrests by 25 percent. Police Chief Ben Click in Dallas tells us that the benefits of curfews go beyond just making streets safer in the short term. "I think one other benefit is that the curfew is a way to identify some kids that may need

longer-term attention. The kids who are out at 2 or 3 A.M., you can almost conclude that there is some kind of family issue there, because why are they out so
late? For those kids, I think the curfew is a real warning that if we don't intervene,
we could see them getting into more serious trouble."[29]

Fort Worth decided to focus its T-CAP on targeted high-risk areas and to integrate it with crime prevention initiatives already in place, such as community policing and CODE:BLUE, a program emphasizing police partnerships with other
service sectors. Working groups of residents were then organized in the targeted
areas: Butler Housing Community, Ripley Arnold Housing Community, and the
Near Northside Neighborhood. Many of the neighborhood suggestions were sur-
prising: a store within walking distance; an elementary school to which their children could ride their bikes; an ordinance to ban pint-size liquor bottles and forty-
ounce beer bottles, because at night drunks would litter the children's playgrounds
with the broken glass; a stop sign at the entrance of the project; police foot patrols
so police get to know the residents and their children; a Laundromat; and landscaping. If government had tried to identify the needs of those neighborhoods
without asking those who live there, a very different list would most likely have
resulted.[30]

Community-Based Programs

From these examples, it is apparent that federal, state, and local governments
all have a role to play in fighting violence in schools and communities. But no
matter how many top-down government programs we concoct, no matter how
much money we put into those programs, such actions alone will never solve the
problem. We should have learned that lesson from the 1960s. On January 8, 1964,
in his first State of the Union address to Congress, President Lyndon Johnson
declared an "unconditional war on poverty in America."[31] In March he told Congress that poverty was "a domestic enemy which threatens the strength of our
nation and the welfare of our people." The War on Poverty would be one that
would strike, he said, "at the causes and not just the consequences of poverty, one
which would treat not just poor individuals but poor communities as well."[32]

A cornucopia of federal dollars began flowing from Washington to communities across the nation. Manpower training programs focused on preparing the un-
skilled for jobs. Aid to schools was meant to keep poverty from shackling young
minds. For the first time, many poor people began receiving medical care through
Medicaid. The elderly poor received increased social security payments. Housing
programs provided public housing for poor people. Legal Aid programs provided
much-needed support for the poor, and civil rights lawyers hoped to better the
conditions of life for all black Americans.

It was a generous and well-meaning effort. So what went wrong? Why, in the
1990s, is poverty still "a domestic enemy which threatens the strength of our nation and the welfare of our people"? Perhaps the most important reason is that the
War on Poverty came from the top and left out of the decisionmaking process the
most important constituency: the people it was designed to help. The money

flowed through a new layer of bureaucrats who were more concerned with their own jobs than they were with the poor they were supposed to lift out of poverty. In Texas, we have an excellent example of a group of people who have turned the War on Poverty model on its head.

The Industrial Areas Foundation

The Industrial Areas Foundation (IAF) in Texas was first organized in San Antonio in 1974, and the driving force behind the movement was Ernesto Cortes. Cortes had begun his career as an activist with the United Farm Workers in the early 1960s. Throughout that decade, he angrily watched the Anglo Good Government League (GGL) run city hall with an iron fist, keeping anyone not of their class out of local government. That meant that the mostly Hispanic West Side was generally ignored when it came to city dollars. The mostly Anglo North Side received the money and services, while the West Side could not get even simple improvements such as having their streets paved and repaired, drainage systems, public libraries, or new developments.[33]

Cortes had an idea. He wanted to do something for the West Side neighborhoods, but he did not believe any of the traditional ways would work. He wanted an organization that would be self-perpetuating, not one that would coalesce around one issue, and then, when it won that battle, disappear. He understood that such an organization must be neighborhood-based and would require that the people in those neighborhoods do much of the organizing themselves around issues and values about which they cared deeply. He began to talk with pastors of the West Side Catholic parishes and began to learn the names of their key lay leaders. He wanted leaders in the parish who had much invested in their community. He was looking for the types of leaders who organized church fairs and picnics, were Boy Scout troop leaders, organized their PTAs, and put together baseball tournaments. He envisioned an organization of these parishes that would be self-supporting and not beholden to any politician.

He found the leaders, and they began to research and learn how decisions were made in San Antonio. They perused city hall reports, government documents, and minutes of public meetings. The most pressing problem, they believed, was drainage. Many times after heavy rains, someone on the West Side died in the flood waters that overflowed the inadequate storm drains. Then they learned an astounding fact: the city of San Antonio had approved bonds for West Side drainage improvements way back in 1945. Yet not a cent of that money had ever been spent on the West Side.

One day in 1974 delegates from twenty-seven churches met to give themselves a name and to talk about drainage. They were having trouble coming up with an appropriate name, when someone jokingly said, "Let's call us the COPS. You know, they're the robbers and we're the cops." Someone else suggested a name to fit the acronym: Communities Organized for Public Service. On August 13, 1974, one hundred COPS members challenged city manager Sam Granata, showing him their research findings and asking him why the West Side had been ignored for so long. After he ran out of excuses, he told the protesters that he would put them on the agenda for the next city council meeting. The result was $46 million in new bonds that the electorate approved that fall. Since then, COPS has been one of the most successful community organizations in the country. And even after Ernie Cortes left San Antonio in 1976 to organize in East Los Angeles, COPS did not miss a beat. Cortes did not lead the group; he taught the members how to be leaders themselves.[34]

Today, the Industrial Areas Foundation network of church-based organizations represents over four hundred thousand people in Texas. These people have done marvelous things for their communities. People on the West Side of San Antonio no longer drown during heavy rains, because COPS convinced the city to spend more than $500 million in the area for improvements, including storm sewer systems. One of the IAF organizations in El Paso convinced the city to connect 20,000 people to water and sewer hookups; now children in those areas do not have to drink or bathe in contaminated water. In Houston there are more neighborhood patrols and less flooding in some predominantly black neighborhoods. Fort Worth has more programs to train parents to be involved in their children's schools. The local IAF groups joined together to convince legislators to approve an indigent health care bill that affected two hundred thousand people; now pregnant women who are poor can receive prenatal care. When Ross Perot was leading education reform in Texas in 1984, the IAF convinced him to insist that the legislature appropriate $800 million for poor school districts to try to equalize funding for schools.[35]

Valley Interfaith, the IAF organization in the Rio Grande Valley, has taken on one of the most difficult political tasks imaginable. The four counties of the Rio Grande Valley contain the poorest people in the United States, the lowest per capita income, and the highest unemployment. The poorest of the poorest are one hundred thousand people who live in the Valley *colonias*, the more than four hundred unincorporated rural communities created by developers out to make a fast buck. These developers bought land, divided it up into tracts, and sold it to extremely low-income people on a contract-for-deed basis. In other words, if a buyer misses a payment, the developer can reclaim the land and sell it again. The developers promised that utilities and water would be delivered to the areas soon, but they never came. The *colonias* are outside the extraterritorial jurisdiction of cities and they are unincorporated, so neither cities nor counties provide utilities, water, or sewage.

Valley Interfaith decided to get the attention of state government. The organization invited Governor Richards, then state treasurer, to tour La Meza *colonia* on February 1, 1988. She saw that La Meza's people, mostly migrant farm workers, had no water, no sewers, no paved streets. Sunset Drive-In Grocery sold water from an outdoor spigot for twenty-five cents a jug, but those who could not afford the tap water filled their jugs from irrigation drainage ditches that held water full of pesticides. Overflowing septic tanks fed into shallow water wells, and in times of heavy rains, the water that the people of La Meza *colonia* were drinking contained their own sewage. Incidences of parasitic intestinal diseases are higher in the valley than anywhere else outside of the Third World. Children suffer chronic rashes, lice, and hepatitis. When Governor Richards arrived in La Meza, she saw a woman holding a two-year-old girl on whose left eye was a black tumor the size of a golf ball. A six-year-old boy held a hand-painted sign: "Help us Ann Richards. We need water to drink."[36]

When an IAF organization invites a politician to tour a site like this, it expects actions, not just words. Mary Beth Rogers writes about the IAF in Texas in her book, *Cold Anger*:

The real significance of the IAF's accomplishments is that the political dialogue is shifting in Texas. The questions are no longer whether to help the *colonias*, but *how to do it*; not whether to provide health care to poor women and children, but *how to do it*. And Cortes and the IAF organizations which are training a new group of political leaders...make it possible for these public discussions to be taken seriously.[37]

The IAF is successful because the group always follows their "Iron Rule: Never do for people what they can do for themselves." Critical of government programs that foster dependency while ignoring the abilities of people to act in their own interest, the IAF's mission is empowerment. Cortes likes to say:

Power is such a good thing, everyone should have some.... [O]rganizing is a fancy word for relationship building. No organizer ever organizes a community. What an organizer does is identify, test out, and develop leadership. And the leadership builds the relationships and the networks, and following that, does the organizing.

If I want to organize you, I don't sell you an idea. What I do, if I'm smart, is try to find out what's your interest. What are your dreams? I try to kindle your imagination, stir the possibilities, and then propose some ways in which you can act on those dreams and act on those values and act on your own visions. You've got to be the owner. Otherwise, it's my cause, my organization. You've got nothing![38]

"A Commitment to Texas Children" Initiative

Former Governor Richards knows that the success of the IAF in Texas is due to its being a true grassroots organization, and she clearly understands that people at the neighborhood level are the only ones who can do the real work involved in saving their communities and schools from youth violence. They are the experts; they know what they need. Government can only provide support and resources. Governor Richards, on releasing her youth summit report in Dallas, explained that every one of us must take a hand in solving the problem of youth violence:

We can pass all the bills in the world, we could put a social worker and police officer on every other block, and it would not be sufficient to stop the problems without the support of the whole community. We have to listen to our kids, and convince them that we care about what happens to them. So, we are providing a framework that will help Texas communities make a new commitment to their kids. And we are calling it "A Commitment to Texas Children."

All of us have to take responsibility for their future. The community makes a commitment; the counties, the state make a commitment to incarcerate the worst offenders. Schools make a commitment to remove troublemakers from the classroom and place them in alternative settings. Truancy laws must be enforced. Counties make a commitment to get tougher with juvenile probation. Cities make a commitment to enforce juvenile curfews. Business leaders make a commitment to help our young people find jobs and religious leaders make a commitment to help us design alternative activities to the streets. It is going to take a commitment from all of us.[39]

Governor Richards began her "A Commitment to Texas Children" initiative by calling on ministers across the state to redouble their efforts in working with the families in their congregations and their communities. In a September 1994 letter she told the ministers, "Churches have always played a vital role in every community. From talking to clergy around the state, I know many Texas churches have undertaken excellent initiatives to benefit children and families."[40]

Indeed, churches and synagogues across Texas have been doing wonderful things in their communities. They have paired single pregnant women and single mothers with women in their churches who have agreed to help with prenatal care, parenting classes, and to stay with the young mother during labor and delivery. They have opened their doors to allow their space to be used for clinics for children and families who live in poverty. And most important, they have motivated the families in their congregations to act as mentors to less fortunate families. These mentors can help students with their school work, help troubled kids find ways to solve their problems, take care of the kids for a while when a single parent feels overwhelmed. Male mentors can help adolescent males understand the importance and responsibility of fatherhood. There are so many ways a church congregation can help, but what is most important is that the mentor form a personal bond with those in need; if the relationship becomes too clinical or professional, it will be far less effective.

Governor Richards knows how important religious leaders are in reaching out to their communities. Nationwide, 40 percent of families attend a place of worship each week; over the course of a month this figure rises to 70 percent. There are some 335,000 congregations that reach every county and urban neighborhood in the country.[41] In Texas, Catholic and Baptist churches alone reach 50 percent of the population. In her letter to Texas ministers, Governor Richards identified projects that churches have successfully implemented and projects she hopes other churches will adopt:

— *Teach Nonviolent Ways to Solve Problems.* Within your own congregations and throughout your neighborhood, speak out against violence in the home and in the community. Teach both adults and children the importance of expressing themselves and settling differences without violence.

— Set Up After-School Programs for Children. Within your own churches or in community facilities, invite congregation members to provide snacks, homework assistance, recreation, and adult supervision and guidance for children.

—   Participate in Adult and Peer Mentoring Programs. Ask adults and older youth to become a special friend to a child. Child care workers, teachers, law enforcement officials, and others who work with children can connect you with those who need your special attention.
—   *Set Up Family-Sponsorship Programs.* Ask stable families in your congregations to become sponsors for troubled families, providing someone who will listen and give guidance in dealing with day-to-day problems.
—   *Create Safe Havens for Children.* Open churches and identify homes throughout the community where children can go for protection, or seek help if they feel threatened.
—   *Work with Programs Serving Children.* Ask members of your congregations to volunteer at schools, child care facilities, or youth centers. Learn about public and private programs so you can guide people to sources of the services they need.
—   *Build Church-to-Church Partnerships.* Wealthier churches can be partners to churches with limited resources. Through volunteers and financial or other material contributions, churches with greater resources can support the work of other congregations.[42]

The Casey Foundation

Governor Richards stands ready to help ministers and their communities in any way she can. One initiative that she is particularly proud of is the Casey Foundation grant. Governors' offices around the country were invited to apply for a one-year, $150,000 planning grant and then a $3 million implementation grant. Texas is one of only two states to be awarded the four-year grant. The Casey Foundation had intended to award five grants, but felt that only two state/local groups showed the planning and commitment necessary to make their projects succeed.

The Third Ward of Houston, Texas, has long defined the image that comes to mind when someone says, "blighted urban neighborhood." Children in the Third Ward live every day with drugs, violence, and death. Today, residents of the Third Ward are determined to take back their neighborhoods, and with the help of the Casey Foundation grant they have a very good chance of doing so. This project is different from most such initiatives in two important respects: (1) through the Third Ward Governing Board, the community determines for itself what services are most needed and wanted; and (2) every level of government—city, county, school district, and state—has committed to working together and with the Third Ward neighborhoods to make the project a success. What we are talking about is tailoring existing services, providing them in a way that works, not for the bureaucracy, but for families in need. So far, the Third Ward project has:

•   Established a local governance structure that is a partnership among state and local government interagency groups and a twenty-nine-member neighborhood governing board composed of Third Ward residents and service providers.
•   Established the Family Advocacy Network, composed of a core group of ap-

proximately thirty Third Ward parents, to ensure the inclusion of family members and service users in the project planning and implementation process.

- Designed "Touch Every Home Campaign" block walks to inform residents and promote participation in the project.
- Established an informal system of problem-solving called the In-House Family Assistance programs. Community residents from the Family Advocacy Network identify families that need aid and help them find solutions to their problems using Casey project resources.
- Provided intensive, school-based mental health services for fifteen children in Third Ward schools for six- to eight-week intervals during the 1993–1994 school year. A therapist and child psychiatrist, funded through the Children's Mental Health Plan and the Harris County Mental Health, Mental Retardation Authority provided the services.
- Established the Kick Drugs Out of Third Ward substance abuse prevention program, which works in conjunction with the Houston Independent School District in six Third Ward schools to offer karate and support groups during regular school hours.
- Established the Expressive Arts Series, funded by the Texas Juvenile Justice Commission, which offers mental health and substance abuse prevention services and artistic instruction from members of the Third Ward art community for 125 children at four Third Ward community-based organizations and a church.
- Opened the first Third Ward Family Resource Center at Douglass Elementary School on October 14, 1994. Additional sites were scheduled to open in schools and community-based organizations during 1995.

Plans for the second year of the grant include the Douglass Safe Haven program, a federally funded partnership among the Houston Independent School District, the City of Houston Parks and Recreation Department, and Houston Community College that will provide school-based recreational, academic, and health education as well as conflict-resolution and mediation service. In addition, two Texas Employment Commission staffers will be placed at a Family Resource Center to offer job readiness workshops and one-on-one counseling and coaching; two Ameri-Corp workers will develop a parent education component; and VISTA volunteers will be recruited from the Third Ward to develop a "family cluster" network of support groups for Third Ward families who share common issues and concerns.

CONCLUSION

Nearly everyone understands that if America is to continue to prosper, it *must* have an educated workforce. Gone are the days when an eighth-grade education and a strong back would provide a man the means to support his family working on an oil rig. If we are to have an educated workforce, first we must have schools that are safe havens. No matter what curriculum or teaching methods we employ, if children are afraid to be in school, they will not learn what they must learn to be successful in today's world. And if we are going to have safe schools, we must have safe communities and neighborhoods. We must all make a commitment to keep our children out of harm's way, even when the violence is going on inside the child's home.

The good news from Texas is that we are on the right track. Texans are still concerned about crime and want to see violent criminals locked up for a long time, but many are beginning to realize that building jails alone will not solve our crime problem. It is so much cheaper to save a child than to lock up a juvenile or an adult. So we must begin to invest more of our resources in children. It is the best investment we can possibly make.

NOTES

1. "Safeguarding the Future: A Call to Action," The Governor's Statewide Youth Summit Report, August 9, 1994, 1.

2. Remarks of Governor Ann Richards at the Dallas Youth Summit, December 7, 1993.

3. Federal Bureau of Investigation, *Crime in the United States—1992, Uniform Crime Reports,* 1993.

4. Texas Department of Public Safety, Crime Records Division, *Crime in Texas: Uniform Crime Reporting,* 1983.

5. National Governors' Association, "Kids and Violence," 1994.

6. Texas Youth Commission and the Texas Juvenile Probation Commission, "Progressive Juvenile Justice Sanctions Model":

      Sanction Level 1: Counsel and Release
      Sanction Level 2: Informal Adjustment
      Sanction Level 3: Court Probation
      Sanction Level 4: Intensive Probation
      Sanction Level 5: Community Residential Placement
      Sanction Level 6: TYC Secure Institutions
      Sanction Level 5a: Community Residential Placement
      Sanction Level 4a: Enhanced Parole
      Sanction Level 3a: Parole
      Sanction Level 2a: Support Services
      Sanction Level 1a: Discharge

7. "Safeguarding the Future: A Call to Action," 2.

8. Texas Family Code, Sections 51.09(b)(1)(F) and 53.045.

9. J. Phillips, "Juvenile Justice: Getting Tough on Young Offenders; Tightening Legal Options," *Austin American-Statesman* (October 6, 1994), A1.

10. 1994 National School Boards Association Survey.

11. "Kids and Violence," 19.

12. National School Safety Center News Service, "School Safety Update" (November 1993).

13. Violent Crime Control and Law Enforcement Act of 1994, 103rd Congress, 2nd Session.

14. "School Safety Update."

15. Texas House Bill 23, 73rd Legislature, Regular Session, 1993; Texas Senate Bill 16, 73rd Legislature, Regular Session, 1993.

16. Texas Federation of Teachers Press Conference, August 16, 1994.

17. "Safeguarding the Future," 5.

18. Texas Federation of Teachers Press Release, September 16, 1994.

19. Texas Federation of Teachers Press Conference, August 16, 1994.

20. "Safeguarding the Future," 5–6, 33.

21. "School Safety Update," 1.

22. S. Gamboa, "Turner, Thornton Face Off for Senate: Candidates Differ in Approach to Juvenile Crime," *Austin American-Statesman* (October 4, 1994), B1.

23. The MUSCLE mayors are Richards Greene, Arlington; Bruce Todd, Austin; Mary Rhodes, Corpus Christi; Steve Bartlett, Dallas; Bill Tilney, El Paso; Kay Granger, Fort Worth; Bob Lanier, Houston; and Nelson Wolff, San Antonio.

24. Seven MUSCLE mayors participated; El Paso opted not to participate in T-CAP.

25. The National Crime Prevention Council, "Taking the Offensive to Prevent Crime: How Seven Cities Did It" (November 1993).

26. Ibid., 16–17.

27. Ibid., 5–6.

28. Ibid., 29.

29. "Safeguarding the Future," 17; M. M. Salinas, "Youth Crime Down Since Curfew Started: Night Time Arrests Drop by 50 Percent; Critics Say Numbers May Be Misleading," *Austin American-Statesman* (October 7, 1994); N. Lopez, "Curfew Gives Police Leverage with Youths: Arrests, Offenses Against Teenagers Decline," *Dallas Morning News* (September 25, 1994), 35A.

30. "Taking the Offensive to Prevent Crime," 42; "T-CAP Recap: An Update of the T-CAP Initiative Network, staffed by the National Crime Prevention Council," Summer 1994.

31. L. B. Johnson, *The Vantage Point: Perspectives of the Presidency, 1963–1969* (New York: Holt, Rinehart and Winston, 1971), 75.

32. Ibid., 77.

33. M. B. Rogers, *Cold Anger: A Story of Faith and Power Politics* (Denton: University of North Texas Press, 1990), 76.

34. Ibid., 107–21.

35. Ibid., 26.

36. Ibid., 19–21.

37. Ibid., 26.

38. Ibid., 17.

39. Remarks of Governor Ann W. Richards, Press Conference, Dallas, Texas, August 9, 1994.

40. Letter from Governor Ann W. Richards to ministers, September 1994.

41. National Crime Prevention Council, "Mission Possible: Churches Supporting Fragile Families," August 1993, 4.

42. Letter from Governor Ann Richards to ministers, September 1994.

Part VI

A COMMUNITY-BASED APPROACH

20

Community Safety Zones: A Plan to Curb Urban Violence

William Glasser

If you know anyone who is carrying a gun, selling or using drugs, stealing or joyriding in cars, there is nothing you can do to help that person. Our criminal justice system makes no provision for prevention—only arrest, possible imprisonment, or forced treatment. It does not matter if you are rich or poor; you are helpless to do anything more than report your concern to the police, knowing that you may be doing more harm than good and risking losing the love of those you care about. Until law-abiding citizens can substantially increase their legal options, we will do little or nothing to reduce crime and violence in our society. Community safety zones are a start in that direction.

No one would dispute that what we as a society are doing to deal with violent crime—which is endemic to large areas of our central cities and much of it involving gang activity and disputes over drugs—is not working. We are increasing our prison population while the violence continues to rise. Besides the incalculable cost in human misery, this failure costs huge sums of money that could be better used in places like our schools. At present, the violence is spreading to suburban and rural areas so that no place in our country is free both from it and/or the fear of it. There is no doubt that this unchecked violence is ruining the quality of all our lives.

This chapter discusses a plan—community safety zones—to address urban violence. Because this violence is so visible and dramatic, it infects the media and, in doing so, it spreads the fear of violence everywhere. Reducing it substantially in the inner cities will have a positive effect on all violence, and may lead to the development of similar plans for suburban and rural areas.

People who live in the crime and violence areas of our cities are afraid almost all the time. People who do *not* live in these areas are afraid much of the time and are very afraid if they have to go in or near the areas of violence. Nothing functions normally in these areas; as fear takes over, it becomes a cancer spreading outward from the heart of most of our large cities. In areas like southwest Los Angeles, there is no economic life, schools hardly function, and it is hard to find a person who has any hope that things will ever get better.

We must face the fact that there are no new ideas aimed at solving this problem. All we have is what we have always had: police backed up by an "arrest, try and punish" criminal justice system that no longer works. If there is to be a solution, we need new ideas. All we do now is based on an old psychology (stimulus-response) that depends on fear of punishment and that no longer works at all. The solution I offer is based on a new psychology (control theory) that does not depend on either fear or punishment, but on giving parents, relatives, and friends of the problem people new options as well as eliminating the sources of the violence. If it works, it will make any designated area or zone of any city a safe place to live, work, and attend school.

To begin, we must accept as an axiom that, to solve any human problem, the people who are most affected by it must be totally involved in its solution. Any solution imposed from the outside will not work. What we on the outside can do is give the affected people some new information that makes enough sense to them that they will try to use it to solve their own problem. They must be in charge of implementing any solution. We can and must give them help, but if they are not willing to try to take charge of their own destiny, no solution is possible.

The first thing we have to do is to face the obvious: our criminal justice system does a totally inadequate job of protecting anyone from street violence. Over and over, the offenders are caught and imprisoned for their crimes, but numerous others are not deterred. The thrill of having a weapon and being willing, if not eager, to use it for protection, revenge, or "fun" as well as to safeguard the huge profits from the sale of drugs far outweighs the protection or deterrence of our criminal justice system. Unless we can both disarm the weapons carriers, whatever their motivation, and eliminate the drug traffic in areas where these crimes are common, nothing will change.

We also fail to pass realistic gun control laws because the power associated with owning a gun is so much a part of so many voters' lives that politicians are unwilling to risk their wrath. The more fear pervades the whole society, the less willing gun owners are to consider any alternative to total access to weapons whose sole purpose is to kill people. While gun control might reduce violence among family and friends—bad as it is, this violence does not cause much fear among potential criminals—it would not deter criminals who would still arm themselves illegally and who would not be deterred by the possibility of arrest and imprisonment. When a criminal buys a gun, there is often no background check and usually only a five-day waiting period.

What we refuse to face is that the ancient system of law enforcement based on punishment does not work for people who do not fear arrest, who are willing to take a chance because they believe they will not be caught, or whose lives are so bleak that they pay no attention to the threat of punishment. What is needed, and what I offer, is a totally new system that does not depend on arrest and punishment.

The law enforcement system does not even work for those who are normally thought of as law-abiding; many of them will take a chance if the likelihood of getting caught is slim. For example, many people do not pay all the federal income tax they should because, for small transgressions, they have no fear of being caught. These same people, however, never cheat on their property or sales taxes. *This is not because they are more honest where these taxes are concerned; it is because they have no opportunity to cheat.* What is needed to reduce the violence that plagues the centers of our large cities (and plenty of small cities as well) is not to try to increase either fear or respect for the law, but to reduce or even eliminate the opportunity to break it.

To do this, however, would require a willingness on the part of the residents of those areas—the vast majority of whom are not violent and fear the violence more than anyone else—to get involved in the process of protecting themselves and their loved ones. Currently, they feel powerless to do this. They realize that what they are living in and through is beyond the power of the police and prisons to control, yet no one has offered them any alternative to this failed system. Besides, for many reasons, they tend not to trust the police; a substantial minority see them more as oppressors than as protectors of their safety. Only if we can give these people a chance to get involved in protecting themselves by supporting a new way to reduce the opportunity for violent crime may there be a chance to solve this problem.

BACKGROUND AND GOALS OF THE
COMMUNITY SAFETY ZONE PLAN

More and more, we are seeing people of all political persuasions support the use of our armed forces to police troublespots overseas. Many of these places (like Bosnia, Somalia, and Haiti) are very dangerous, and few of these places have even a vestige of the law-abiding citizens who make up a large majority in even our most crime-ridden neighborhoods. We may not succeed in policing the world, but we could succeed in our own cities if we were willing to try a new approach based upon reducing the opportunity for violence to exist.

In the community safety zone plan, small, specially trained units of a neighborhood protection force (NPF) would patrol the neighborhoods that voted for their services. They would report only to the elected neighborhood safety board that hired them, and they would serve only as long as the people in the neighborhood voted to keep the plan in effect.

While their duty would be dangerous, it would not be nearly as dangerous as what police face now in the same neighborhoods, and there would be no trouble recruiting them. In what will be called voluntary community safety zones (from now on referred to simply as zones), the NPF would do the three things that are absolutely necessary if we are to reduce the opportunity for crime and violence in these zones. They would:

1.   Disarm the community by removing all illegal firearms, long-bladed knives, and other dangerous weapons from the hands of people who walk or drive the streets of each zone.
2.   Confiscate all illegal drugs from the people who walk or drive the streets of the zone.
3.   Remove all illegal vehicles and illegal drivers from the zone streets.

The NPF would not be allowed to search for and confiscate any property other than weapons or drugs. The NPF would be allowed to stop cars and to impound and return to its legal owner any stolen or illegally driven car that was found. Anyone driving a car illegally would be removed from the car and sent on his or her way on foot, or given bus fare to get home. If, in the process of accomplishing this, the NPF discovered individuals in the possession of what appeared to be other illegal property, that property would be impounded, not confiscated, as will be explained in detail later.

With almost all illegal weapons, drugs, and cars and drivers removed from a zone, the chances of anyone seriously hurting anyone else outside of his or her home in that zone would be reduced to the point where few residents would worry about personal safety. When this occurred, the change in the community would be dramatic. Businesses would be able to function, and safe recreation would again be possible. Real estate prices would rise and insurance rates would fall. With less fear, integration of the races would be more likely, and more people would choose to live and work where they wanted to and not be concerned about whom they were living or working near. The stereotype that this group or that group is dangerous would also drastically diminish.

INTRODUCTION OF THE PLAN

All the leading citizens (for example, elected officials, ministers, and school administrators) who live or work in the large areas of the community where most people believe crime is out of control and the fear of personal harm is excessive— such as the southwestern section of Los Angeles—would be informed of the plan through the newspapers, television, and signs posted throughout parts of the city where crime and violence are endemic. The signs would say that a neighborhood safety plan will be offered to any neighborhood that wants it. All residents of the posted areas would be urged to come to one or more of a series of meetings that would be held in a neighborhood school, community center, or church.

An effort would be made to have the information presented in these meetings also reported in the newspapers and, perhaps, shown on local television. If, after hearing the plan and having a chance to ask questions, a substantial group of citizens from a neighborhood within the larger community were interested, that area would be designated as a community safety zone.

It might be suggested at the meeting that the first zones be the areas that feed a large high school, for it is envisioned that students, especially high school students, should be invited to help get the process started. I suggest that we start with young people because their support would be vital to the success of the plan. I strongly believe that the majority of high school students do not like the present crime and violence any more than anyone else and would welcome the chance to be involved in making their neighborhood safer. This plan would also be attractive to them because it is so different from the present law enforcement approach, which few of them trust.

Once such a zone was designated, the students could begin by using their social studies and/or health courses to discuss and critique the plan. This should take a few weeks. If a majority of the students, in a secret ballot, voted both to endorse the plan and to volunteer to explain it to everyone in the community, then students, assisted by their teachers, trained in the details of the plan would lead public meetings in all the schools of that zone to explain the plan to interested members of the community. This would also address the complaint of many students that what they do in school has nothing to do with their lives.

Student involvement would go a long way toward convincing a skeptical community of the credibility of the plan. Since personal safety is on the minds of almost all the residents of a zone like this, these meetings would most likely be well-attended. Questions would be encouraged and the community would be told over and over that unless there were overwhelming support for the plan, it would not be implemented.

These meetings would go on for about a month. At the end of each meeting, an informal secret ballot would be taken to see how many of the attendees would be interested in pursuing the plan in their zone. If at least 25 percent of the registered voters in the designated safety zone attended at least one meeting during the information month and a majority of these people voted for the plan in a secret ballot at the end of each meeting, the plan would be endorsed enough to move to the next stage. The fact that this happened would be publicized in the newspapers and on television, and the residents of the zone would then be given a chance to take a legal vote on the plan. At these information meetings, unregistered voters would be given the chance to register.

A community voting week for all interested zones would then be announced and be widely publicized in the newspapers, on television, and on signs posted all over each designated zone. The citizens would have all week to vote at the high school, but there would be one voting day at all the regular polling places in all the interested zones. Absentee ballots would be permitted. For the initial zones, I would strongly suggest that the plan be put into effect only if the vote in favor of it were *four to one*, a fact that should be well publicized in advance of the voting.

If the vote for the plan in any zone reached this level of support, the plan would be put into place for a year. At the end of the year, another vote would take place and, if the plan were not re-endorsed by a four-to-one vote, it would be scrapped. If it were re-endorsed, a vote would be taken every three years. Any time it did not get a four-to-one majority it would be discontinued. If it were dropped, it could be reinstated after a waiting period of a year followed by another four-to-one vote. The reason for the four-to-one vote is that unless the plan were heavily supported, it would be seen as being forced on the community and would not be effective. Also, its constitutionality would be more likely to survive a challenge if it had heavy support.

OPERATING PROCEDURE

Using a foundation grant or federal money to fund a trial run, I suggest that the initial zones be in large cities like Los Angeles and New York. Any zone that endorsed the plan by a four-to-one vote should be established as a trial zone. Highly competent personnel could be recruited from the large pool of retired armed services members, many of whom would welcome a chance to serve in the NPF. (I have been told there is a bill before Congress now that would fund just such a group.) Many of these highly trained men and women live in the violent areas of our cities and are looking for meaningful post-service employment, so it should not be hard to recruit the small number needed to test the plan.

The NPF would be a private security force hired by a volunteer citizen board that would be elected to administer the plan in each zone. The NPF would be paid by a private, nonprofit corporation set up in each zone and administered by the same board. The sole mission of this corporation would be to make the streets safe for all members of the community.

To argue that the rights of zone residents would be violated by not being allowed to carry a weapon on the streets of the zone unless they had a permit issued by the zone board is the same as arguing that the right to free speech is abrogated by not allowing a person to cry "fire" in a crowded theater. The zone residents, by their vote, would be arguing that living in the zone makes them as vulnerable to violence as sitting in a crowded theater makes them vulnerable to fire.

A think tank like the RAND Corporation might be hired to study a typical zone in order to determine the number of NPF personnel and the training needed, but it is anticipated that around thirty-five NPF could do the job in any single zone. If several zones in an area were in the trial phase, all the NPF would be on call to each zone to assist in sweeps and other large, but temporary, operations.

Once they were settled into the community, the NPF would, with the assistance of student volunteers, begin a six-month process of community education meetings in churches and schools. In these meetings the NPF would stress that they are not police, that they have no arrest powers but only the power to confiscate weapons, drugs, and illegally driven cars. This would give the community a chance to meet the NPF and to see that they were obviously dedicated and competent individuals whom they could trust. They would always be very visible, none would work undercover, and it would be important that they always wear a spotless, distinctive uniform.

As they educated the community, in concert with student volunteers, the NPF would post signs at every street and sidewalk that was an entrance to the zone, as well as inside it. The signs would state (in all the major languages spoken in the community) that after the six-month information period all *nonresidents* of the zone would be subject to random search and the seizure of all weapons, drugs, and illegally driven cars that were discovered. Community members who could not prove through an ID card, issued by the board to all who wanted one, that they were residents of the zone would also be subject to search.

In addition to the signs and to the education meetings that preceded the initiation of the plan, it would be explained that a hotline to the NPF would be available to anyone, both in and out of the zone, to report that a resident or a nonresident of the zone was carrying a weapon, an illegal drug, or driving an illegal car in the zone. The NPF hotline would have a voice distortion device so that the voices of the callers could not be identified. All of these calls would be recorded and would serve as a probable cause for the search and seizure, thus satisfying the constitutionality of this vital part of the plan.

After this six-month sign-posting and education period, the NPF would begin the process of stopping any car or individual walking or driving in a public place (or in private places like malls or stores where this service was requested by the owners). Anyone who could not identify himself or herself as a resident of the zone would be searched for illegal weapons, drugs, and vehicles. In addition, all unlicensed drivers who were not residents of the zone would be removed from the driver's seats of any car they stopped. The NPF would also stop and search all people, residents or not, who were reported to them on the hotline.

After one year and another four-to-one supportive vote (which would give all the residents of the zone ample chance to move from the zone if they did not want to be subject to a random search), the nonresident restriction would be lifted and all people in the zone, residents or not, would be subject to the same random search and seizure. The two overwhelming votes (initially and a year later) in support of the plan would make it clear that what is at stake in these violence-plagued zones is the common welfare guaranteed by the Constitution in its preamble:

We the people of the United States, in order to form a more perfect Union, establish justice, insure domestic tranquility, provide for the common defense, promote the general welfare, and secure the blessings of liberty to ourselves and our posterity do ordain and establish this Constitution for the United States of America.

Basically, the vast majority of the voters residing in the zones who vote to support the plan would be saying that they consider life in the zone to be far from tranquil, and that what they are trying to do is to promote their general welfare. Since personal safety is the core of the general welfare, this plan should pass the test of constitutionality.

As they grew more skilled and the community more aware of what they were able to do and not do, the NPF would develop a variety of ways besides the hotline to find out who to stop and would not be required to reveal their sources. I believe, however, that after a few months of operation, most of the time when they stopped people they would be acting on an informant's information. Since no one could be arrested, the innocent would be protected; there would be no incentives for informants to make false accusations. The NPF would be trained to treat all citizens with utmost courtesy, and there would be no harassment.

THE KEY TO THE PLAN

To many civil libertarians, what I have suggested might seem unconstitutional—but there is good precedent for this approach. In two instances, looking for drunk drivers and airport security, it is legal, based on the general welfare, to invade an individual's right to privacy as long as ample notification is given and the individual has the right not to drive or not to fly commercially from the posted areas. The rationale for the constitutionality of these actions is that, in certain designated areas, the public welfare takes precedence over individual privacy. Drunk drivers and armed or drunken airline passengers are considered by the law to be enough of a threat to public safety that they can be arrested in designated places with no need for reasonable cause. Under the community safety zone plan, no arrests would be permitted, so it would not go as far in infringing on the right to freedom as what is now permitted.

People living in the zones who believe that their rights will be violated would have plenty of time, during the education period and during the year before residents themselves could be randomly searched, to move out of the zone. If they wanted, they could go to court to try to get compensation for the expense of their move, but it would be up to them to prove that removing illegal guns, drugs, and cars and drivers from their zone violated their rights enough to deserve this compensation. If they were minors (and many of those affected might be minors) whose parents, who paid for their room and board, did not want to move, it is unlikely that they could raise a legal challenge. It is possible that some adults would win in court, but the money paid to them would not be enough even to begin to offset the huge savings generated by the crime reduction of the plan.

Since the NPF would not be a police force, they would be allowed to respond only to any nonweapon drug or auto crime they observed by calling the police, who would, as now, be completely in charge of law enforcement in the zones. Furthermore, if in the course of doing their authorized job the NPF, discovered what seemed to be stolen property, they would give the possessor a receipt for the property and then turn it over to the police. If the possessor could prove that the property was not stolen, he or she could regain it by presenting the receipt.

The NPF would not be allowed to identify the possessor or to give evidence against the possessor if he or she were arrested by the police after contact with the NPF. All they would be authorized to do would be to turn the property over to the police, who would then attempt to return it to the owners and, with no involvement from the NPF, catch the perpetrator. The NPF would not be allowed to enter private property or obtain search warrants. This would remain the sole province of the police.

The police and the NPF would work separately, and neither would be allowed to accompany the other as they performed their duty. If this separation were not strictly enforced, the citizens would not trust the NPF enough to give them the citizen cooperation that is the real key to the success of the plan. Nevertheless, a great deal of time and effort would be expended to get the NPF and the police to accept and support each other and to see that an effective NPF would make the work of the police much safer and more focused.

Only if members of the NPF were physically attacked, which would be a state or a federal crime, would they be empowered to defend themselves by turning the assailants over to the police, who would take them into custody. In these cases, NPF members would be allowed to testify against their assailants. The "no arrest" limitations of the NPF would be widely publicized in the six-month phase prior to the implementation of the plan, so that all who were stopped would know that all they could lose were possessions—not freedom.

The following examples show how the plan would work: In the zone, signs would say that all weapons found in the possession of anyone in any public place who did not have a legal permit to carry them would be confiscated and publicly destroyed. The weapons carrier would not be arrested or charged with any crime, so if the carrier were informed on, perhaps by a fearful mother, the mother would not have to worry that her child would be arrested or charged with any crime. The gun would simply be confiscated and the carrier sent on his or her way. If the police observed the work of the NPF and arrested someone who had just been stopped, they could not make the arrest stick because the contraband would no longer be in the carrier's possession, and the NPF would be prohibited from testifying against anyone in any court who did not attack them.

The same could be said for illegal drugs. Aided by dogs, the NPF would search people for drugs, which, if found, would be confiscated and destroyed. There would be no arrests and no informing of the police or any agency. Possessors, especially buyers, would be relieved of their drugs and sent on their way. It is unlikely they would return to the zone to buy if this happened more than once. Also, this would provide a great incentive for families and friends to inform on both users and sellers whom they knew and cared for.

Situations involving cars would be a little more complicated. If a person were found to be driving a legal car but did not have a valid driver's license, the car would be impounded until the legal owner or a person designated by the legal owner who had a valid driver's license could come to the impound lot and drive it away. If the unlicensed drivers had no money, they would be driven home by the NPF or given a nominal sum to get home on their own.

For the impounded car, there would be no charge for up to a week and then a nominal charge by the day. It is inconceivable that someone would fail to pick up a legal car in a few days. If an illegal car were discovered, such as a stolen one, the car would be confiscated and turned over to the police—but only the car, not the driver. Drivers could go on their way. This would again encourage informants, for there would be no legal consequences for the illegal drivers.

Since the NPF would not arrest anyone, they would not pose a serious threat to the people they dealt with, and their safety on the job would be increased. Of course, their job would still be dangerous, and they would be made well aware of what they were getting into when they took the job. I suggest that each member of the NPF be insured against death or serious physical (not mental or emotional) injury on the job. They would still have to be cautious, for people might fight to keep guns and drugs, but they would be trained to deal with these eventualities and would get very good at protecting themselves as they gained experience.

BENEFITS OF THE PLAN

The police—although I am sure they would resent the NPF initially—would find their work easier because of the NPF and, with fewer guns and drugs on the street, much safer. They would be free to spend more time on seriously planned crime and less on the random "turf" violence or drug busts that take up so much of their time now.

The good citizens, who are actually a huge majority in the most violent communities, would be much safer and, by being able to inform on violators without getting them arrested, would have a way to protect themselves and their loved ones without subjecting them to the criminal justice system. Huge amounts of money now spent in arresting and prosecuting offenders would be saved, for there would be fewer offenders, which is the real purpose of law and order.

Our tax dollars would be conserved because the NPF would lessen the immediate need for more police, and, since the NPF would eventually be funded by federal crime protection funds, its cost would not be a drain on the community. The largest operational problem would be how to keep the NPF free from corruption, for it, like the police, would be vulnerable to bribes from drug dealers. I do not believe that there is enough money in illegal guns and cars to make bribes a problem. My guess is that the police would be jealous enough of their "turf" that they would keep a close watch for any irregularities on the part of the NPF.

If the police caught any NPF member taking a bribe, he or she would be arrested and charged with a serious crime. The NPF, on the other hand, would not be authorized to intervene in any police corruption they observed, except to confiscate any illegal drugs, guns, and cars. NPF members would also not be allowed to testify against any police from whom they confiscated contraband. This would help them to get along with the police, since even corrupt police would have little reason to fear them.

Since I envision the NPF to be made up mostly of discharged members of our armed forces, many of whom would be among the finest of our minority citizens, they could serve as a much-needed role model for the young people in the zone. In cooperation with these young people, the NPF, once their search-and-seizure work was lessened, as eventually it would be, could either be reduced and the surplus members sent to newly organized zones, or kept as a proactive force that would get involved in community recreation or education. If the plan did not work as the zone expected, the community after the first year could vote it away. To exist, it would have to be voluntary and have the continued support of a huge majority.

People reading this might say, "Well, all the bad guys will just leave that zone and move next door." These doubters are probably right. In fact, I would hope that, if this happened, it would prod that neighboring community into voting for the plan—tangible proof that the plan was working. Unlike laws, such as federal gun control legislation, that affect the whole country and that, in the minds of many citizens, penalize the law-abiding more than the criminal, any community that felt itself safe would have no need, and therefore no way, to muster the four-to-one vote needed to put this plan into effect.

The plan would need legislative support, for there is no precedent for seizure of illegal material without arrest. The argument to the legislature would be that there is no downside risk; the police and the criminal justice system not only remain intact, but also are greatly augmented by the plan. If there were overwhelming support for the plan in the most affected areas, it would take a strong legislator to vote against removing weapons, drugs, and illegal cars from any community that wanted them out.

The plan would not affect anyone's constitutional rights to buy guns to keep in their homes or to carry them legally, even in the safety zones. A person who wanted to buy a gun for his or her home in any zone would have to have it delivered to his or her home by the NPF and sign a paper stating that he or she knows that it cannot be carried on the street and that, if taken from the home without notifying the NPF, it would be subject to seizure.

People who lived in the zones who wanted to fire their weapons would be encouraged to keep them at a legal firing range, as many gun owners do now. To take them back and forth would require the assistance of the NPF as the gun owners entered or left the designated zone. This would be inconvenient, but this inconvenience would be the price of safety in these voluntary zones where safety is nonexistent now.

Occasionally, during the necessary initial sweeps, there would be traffic tie-ups but, in the education program that preceded the plan, the citizens would be told that this is a small price to pay for the increased safety the plan could provide. Law-abiding people would again own the streets, businesses would not be afraid to relocate back to the zones, and jobs close to home would once again become a reality in neighborhoods.

As guns disappeared from the zones, the huge hospital bills, sometimes over $1 billion per gunshot wound, that are common to these areas would be drastically reduced (the average cost of a gunshot wound is $14,000), and the reduction in human suffering from less violence, less fear, and less use of drugs would be dramatic. With reduced crime, law enforcement costs would be substantially reduced, freeing money for proactive services such as more police officers, better education opportunities, increased recreational opportunities, and expanded social services. I believe that many fine and well-trained retired military personnel would welcome a chance to volunteer to help their own families and friends. If our country is to be safe and strong, Bosnia, Somalia, and Haiti are no more important than Los Angeles, Detroit, and New York.

EDITOR'S NOTE

A recurrent theme in this book is that a school cannot be "safe" unless it has the continuing support and involvement of a safe community. Yet there seem to be persistent roadblocks to effective intervention in that larger community. These range from real legal constraints to a more general civic inertia—especially when a majority culture has fled to the suburbs and left various and fragmented minority communities to fend for themselves.

William Glasser offers a startling new model for intervention to achieve safe communities. It has a utopian flavor in that he optimistically as well as quite explicitly proposes measures that may seem impossibly unorthodox in today's political climate, which is oriented toward preserving individual rights and limiting police powers. Glasser asks us to take a very hard look at what must really be done and to suspend our instinctive hesitations about taking truly radical action. In today's argot, his chapter is very much "in your face." Glasser is saying, in fact, that today's most critical community safety problems are so severe that the collective "you" had better stop whining and start doing something that has heavy impact—something that makes a real difference.

Glasser sweeps aside objections to giving a private neighborhood security force—his proposed NPF—what are essentially police powers of search and seizure, citing the examples of airport traveler screening and drunk driving checkpoints in which personal rights of privacy yield to the larger issue of public safety.

Glasser's proposal for community safety zones will bring many questions to the minds of libertarians (of whatever persuasion); for example, why replace one tyranny with another? What Glasser is saying to these critics, however, is that it is time to mobilize and empower an incensed community majority. For better or worse, this is a concrete, outcome-oriented plan.

(Questions on the community safety zone program can be directed to Dr. William Glasser, The Institute for Control Theory, Reality Therapy, and Quality Management, 22024 Lassem Street, Suite 102, Chatsworth, California 91311, [808] 899- 0688.)

Selected Bibliography

Akbar, N. "Homicide among Black Males: Casual Factors." *Public Health Reports* 95, No. 6 (1980): 549.

Albini, J. L. *The American Mafia: Genesis of a Legend.* New York: Appleton-Century-Crofts, 1971.

Allen-Hagen, B. and M. Sickmund. *Juveniles and Violence: Juvenile Offending and Victimization.* Washington, D.C.: U. S. Department of Justice, 1993.

Alschuler, A. *School Discipline: A Socially Literate Solution.* New York: McGraw-Hill, 1980.

American Psychological Association. *Summary Report of the American Psychological Association Commission on Violence and Youth.* Vol. 1. Washington, D.C.: American Psychological Association, 1993.

Anderson, E. *Streetwise: Race, Class, and Change in an Urban Community.* Chicago: University of Chicago Press, 1990.

Bandura, A. *Social Learning Theory.* Englewood Cliffs, N. J.: John Wiley, 1972.

Bastian, L. D. and M. Taylor. *School Crime: A National Crime Victimization Survey Report.* Washington, D. C.: U. S. Department of Justice, 1991.

Bell, J. C. *Famous Black Quotations.* Chicago: SABAYT Publications, 1986.

Belson, W. A. *Television Violence and the Adolescent Boy.* Westmead, England: Saxon House, Teakfield Ltd., 1978.

Bodinger-deUriarte, C. *Hate-Crime: Sourcebook for Schools.* Los Alamitos, Calif.: Southwest Regional Laboratory, 1991.

Bonn, R. L. *Criminology.* New York: McGraw-Hill Book Co., 1984.

Bowlby, J. *Attachment and Loss.* Vol. I. *Attachment.* New York: Basic Books, 1969.

Brion-Meisels, S., G. Lowenheim, and E. Rendeiro. *Adolescent Decisions.* Boston: Judge Baker Children's Center, 1982.

Butterfield, G., and B. Turner. *Weapons in Schools: NSSC Resource Paper.* Malibu, Calif.: National School Safety Center, 1989.

Camras, L. A., and S. Rappaport. "Conflict Behaviors of Maltreated and Nonmaltreated Children." *Child Abuse and Neglect* 17 (1993): 455–64.

Carlson, N. R. *Physiology of Behavior.* 4th ed. Boston: Allyn and Bacon, 1991.

Centers for Disease Control. "Violence-Related Attitudes and Behaviors of High School Students—New York City, 1992." *Morbidity and Mortality Weekly Reviews* 42 (1993): 773–77.

Charren, P., and M. W. Sandler. *Changing Channels.* Reading, Mass.: Addison-Wesley Publishing Co., 1983.

Cloward, R. A., and L. E. Ohlin. *Delinquency and Opportunity.* New York: Free Press, 1960.

Comer, J. P. "Is 'Parenting' Essential to Good Teaching?" *NEA Today* 6 (1988): 34–40.

Conly, C., et al. *Street Gangs: Current Knowledge and Strategies, Isues and Practices in Criminal Justice.* Washington, D.C.: National Institute of Justice, 1993.

Crenshaw, D. *Bereavement, Counseling the Grieving Throughout the Life Cycle.* New York: Continuum Publishing Co., 1990.

Curwin, R. L., and A. N. Mendler. *Discipline with Dignity.* Alexandria, Va.: Association of Supervision and Curriculum Development, 1988.

Dejong, W. *Preventing Interpersonal Violence among Youth.* Washington, D.C.: National Institute of Justice, 1994.

Dutrey, Janet, and Linda Lantieri. *Peacing Our Schools.* Boston: Beacon Press, (forthcoming) 1996.

Edwards, E. "Campaign Beats Up on Violence." *Washington Post,* December 8, 1993, p. C1.

Erickson, E. *Identity, Youth and Crisis.* New York: W. W. Norton, 1968.

Eron, L. R. *The Problem of Media Violence and Children's Behavior.* New York: Henry Frank Guggenheim Foundation, 1993.

Etzioni, A. *The Spirit of Community: The Reinvention of American Society.* New York: Simon and Schuster, 1993.

Federal Bureau of Investigation. *Uniform Crime Report: Crime in the United States.* Washington, D.C.: U.S. Department of Justice, 1981, 1992.

Fisher, R., and W. Ury. *Getting to Yes: Negotiating Agreement Without Giving In.* Boston: Houghton Mifflin, 1981.

Freire, P. *The Pedagogy of the Oppressed.* New York: Continuum Press, 1970.

Frisby, D., and J. Beckham. "Dealing with Violence and Threats of Violence in the School." *NASSP Bulletin* 77, No. 552 (1993): 10–15.

Fry, D. P. "The Intergenerational Transmission of Disciplinary Practices and Approaches to Conflict." *Human Organization* 52 (1993): 176–85.

Funk, J. "Reevaluating the Impact of Video Games." *Clinical Pediatrics* 32 (1993): 86–90.

Garbarino, J., et al. *Children in Danger, Coping with the Consequences of Community Violence.* San Francisco: Jossey-Bass, 1992.

Gilligan, C. *In a Different Voice.* Cambridge, Mass.: Harvard University Press, 1982.

Goodwillie, S., ed. *Voices from the Future: Our Children Tell Us about Violence in America.* New York: Crown Publishers, 1993.

Hagedorn, J. M. and P. Macon. *People and Folks: Gangs, Crime, and the Underclass in a Rustbelt City.* Chicago: Lakeview Press, 1988.

Haugaard, J. J., and N. D. Reppucci. *The Sexual Abuse of Children.* San Francisco: Jossey-Bass, 1988.

Harris, L. *A Survey of the American People on Guns as a Children's Health Issue.* Boston: Harvard School of Public Health, 1993.

Harris, L., and Associates. *Violence in America's Public Schools.* Metropolitan Life Survey of the American Teacher, 1993.

Heath, L., et al. "Effects of Media Violence on Children." *Archives of General Psychiatry* 46 (1989): 376–79.

Huff, C. R. "Gangs in the United States." In *The Gang Intervention Handbook.* Eds. A. P. Goldstein and C. R. Huff. Champaign, Ill.: Research Press, 1993.

Klein, M. W. *Street Gangs and Street Workers.* Englewood Cliffs, N. J.: Prentice-Hall, 1971.

Knowles, J. *A Separate Peace.* New York: Boston Books, 1975.

Knox, G. W. *An Introduction to Gangs.* Berrien Springs, Mich.: Vande Vere Publishing, 1991.

Kozol, J. *Savage Inequalities: Children in America's Schools.* New York: Crown Publishers, 1991.

Krauss, C. "Urban Crime Rate Falling This Year." *New York Times,* November 8, 1994, p. A14.

Mansfield, W., D. Alexander, and E. Farris. *Teacher Survey on Safe, Disciplined, and Drug-Free Schools.* Washington, D.C.: U.S. Department of Education, 1991.

McCart, L., ed. *Kids and Violence.* Washington, D. C.: National Governor's Association, 1994.

Mead, G. H. *Mind, Self, and Society.* Chicago: University of Chicago Press, 1936.

Metropolitan Life Insurance Company. *Violence in America's Public Schools.* New York: Metropolitan Life Survey of the American Teacher, 1993.

Miller, A. *For Your Own Good.* Trans. by Hildegard and Hunter Hannun. New York: Farrar, Straus and Giroux, 1983.

Mullen, B. *Advanced Basic Meta-Analysis.* Hillsdale, N.J.: Lawrence Erlbaum, 1989.

National Crime Prevention Council. *Working Together to Stop the Violence.* Washington, D.C.: Presstar, 1994.

National School Boards Association. *Violence in Our Schools: How America's School Boards Are Safeguarding Our Children.* Alexandria, Va.: NSBA, 1993.

National School Safety Center. *School Safety Check Book.* Malibu, Calif.: Pepperdine University Press, 1990.

Nielson Media Research. *AC Nielson Company: 1992–1993 Report on Television.* New York: Nielson Media Research, 1993.

Noddings, N. *Caring: A Feminine Approach to Ethics and Moral Education.* Berkeley: University of California Press, 1984.

————. *The Challenge to Care in Schools*. New York: Teachers College Press, 1992.

Piaget, J. *The Moral Judgment of the Child*. New York: Free Press, 1965.

Power, F. C., A. Higgins, and L. Kohlberg. *Lawrence Kohlberg's Approach to Moral Education*. New York: Columbia University Press, 1989.

Prothrow-Stith, D., and M. Weissman. *Deadly Consequences: How Violence Is Destroying Our Teenage Population and a Plan to Begin Solving the Problem*. New York: HarperCollins, 1991.

Provenzo, E. F. *Video Kids: Making Sense of Nintendo*. Cambridge, Mass.: Harvard University Press, 1991.

Quinney, R. *Class State and Crime*. New York: David McKay Co., 1977.

Quint, S. *Schooling Homeless Children*. New York: Teachers College Press, 1994.

Rando, T. A. *Grief, Dying and Death*. Champaign, Ill.: Research Press, Co., 1984.

Ruddick, S. *Maternal Thinking: Towards a Politics of Peace*. Boston: Beacon Press, 1989.

Selman, R. L. *The Growth of Interpersonal Understanding*. New York: Academic Press, 1990.

Selman, R. L., and L. H. Schultz. *Making a Friend in Youth*. Chicago: University of Chicago Press, 1990.

Sheley, J. F., Z. T. McGee, and J. D. Wright. "Gun-Related Violence in and around Inner-City Schools." *American Journal of Diseases of Children* 146 (1992): 677–82.

Sheley, J. F., and J. D. Wright. *Gun Acquisition and Possession in Selected Juvenile Samples*. Washington, D.C.: National Institute of Justice, 1993.

Smith, M., ed. *Youth Mediation Resources Guide*. Tulsa, Okla.: National Resources Center for Youth Services, 1994.

Spivack, P., and M. Shure. *The Social Adjustment of Young Children*. San Francisco: Jossey-Bass, 1974.

Stark, E. "The Battering Syndrome: Social Knowledge, Social Therapy and the Abuse of Women." Ph.D. diss., Binghamton, N.Y., State University of New York, 1984.

Strasburger, V. C. "Children, Adolescents, and the Media: Five Crucial Issues." *Adolescent Medicine* 4 (1993): 479–93.

Sullivan, M. *Getting Paid: Youth and Crime and Work in the Inner City*. Ithaca, N. Y.: Cornell University Press, 1989.

Taylor, B. M. *A National Crime Victimization Survey Report*. Washington, D.C.: U. S. Department of Justice, 1991.

Taylor, C. S. *Dangerous Society*. East Lansing: Michigan State University Press, 1990.

Thrasher, F. M. *The Gang: A Study of 1,313 Gangs in Chicago*. Abridged edition. Chicago: University of Chicago Press, 1963.

Toby, J. "Violence in Schools." In *School Discipline: Order and Autonomy*. New York: Praeger, 1994.

U.S. Department of Education. *Goals 2000: Educate America Act.* Washington, D.C.: Government Printing Office, 1993.

————.*The National Education Goals Report for 1993: Building a Nation of Learners.* Washington, D.C.: Government Printing Office, 1993.

U.S. Department of Justice. *School Crime: A National Crime Victimization Survey Report.* Washington, D.C.: Government Printing Office, 1991.

Vestermark, S. D., Jr., and F. D. Blauvelt. *Controlling Crime in the School: A Complete Security Handbook for Administrators.* West Nyack, N.Y.: Parker Publishing, 1978.

Williams, J. W. "Discipline in the Public Schools: A Problem of Perception?" *Phi Delta Kappan* 60, No. 5 (January 1979): 385–87.

Williams, T. M., ed. *The Impact of Television: A Natural Experiment in Three Communities.* New York: Academic Press, 1985.

Wilson, W. J. *The Truly Disadvantaged: The Inner City, The Underclass, and Public Policy.* Chicago: University of Chicago Press, 1987.

Wyatt, G. E., and S. D. Peters. "Issues in the Definition of Child Abuse Research." *Child Abuse and Neglect* 10 (1984): 231–40.

Yablonski, L. *The Violent Gang.* New York: Macmillan Publishers, 1962.

Name Index

Subject Index

About the Contributors

DR. CHRISTIE BOURGEOIS served as Director of Research for Texas Governor Ann Richards from 1991 to 1995; in this capacity, she published numerous documents, reports, and position papers. Dr. Bourgeois has taught at the University of Texas at Austin and at Southwestern University in Georgetown, Texas. She holds a B.A. from the University of Hawaii and a master's degree and Ph.D. from the University of Texas at Austin.

DR. STEVEN BRION-MEISELS is manager of the Hooking Kids on School Program at the Cambridge Public Schools in Cambridge, Massachusetts. He is a member of the Peaceable Schools Group at Lesley College, which advises schools on violence prevention, and also teaches modules and supervises practicum students working on violence prevention at Harvard's Risk and Prevention Program. Dr. Brion-Meisels serves on local and national boards of Peace Action, the nation's largest grassroots peace and justice organization. He has been a classroom teacher, counselor for adolescents, school administrator, consultant, curriculum writer, and adjunct faculty member at various universities. Dr. Brion-Meisels holds an M.Ed. from the Harvard Graduate School of Education and a Ph.D. from the University of Utah.

DR. MELBA F. COLEMAN is Assistant Vice President for University and Government Relations at California State University, Dominguez Hills. She also holds the rank of Associate Professor in the Graduate Education Department of the School of Education at Dominguez Hills. Dr. Coleman came to higher education in 1991 after twenty-seven years of service in the Los Angeles Unified School District as a principal, project manager, and teacher. Her specialty is developing innovative solutions to critical urban school problems. One of her most successful programs, *Children Grieve, Too,* was profiled on *60 Minutes* and in *Newsweek,* the *Los Angeles Times,* and *The Detroit Free Press.*

DR. GWENDOLYN J. COOKE is Director of the Urban Services Office of the National Association of Secondary School Principals. She previously served as a teacher, a college administrator, coordinator of Gifted and Talented Programs for the Baltimore Public Schools, and principal of an elementary and a middle school. Dr. Cooke is a member of several associations and organizations, including The Education Excellence Network, National Black Child Development Institute, and the National Alliance of Black School Educators. She has received several awards, and is widely recognized for her recent work on violence. Dr. Cooke holds a B.A. from Alabama State College, an M.A. from Morgan State College, and a Ph.D. from the University of Connecticut.

RAMON C. CORTINES is Chancellor of the Board of Education of the City of New York, the nation's largest school system. He had been a member of the Clinton administration's transition team and left a position as Assistant Secretary for Intergovernmental Affairs in the U.S. Department of Education to accept the chancellorship. In an education career of more than thirty years, Mr. Cortines taught and held administrative positions at virtually all levels in the school systems in which he served, including several stints as superintendent of large school districts. Before joing the Clinton administration, Mr. Cortines was a consultant professor at Stanford University, serving as Associate Director of the Pew Charitable Trust Forum on School Reform. Mr. Cortines currently serves as a consultant to the Secretary of Education and is a Visiting Scholar at Stanford University.

DR. WILLIAM DeJONG, a social psychologist, is a lecturer in the Department of Health and Social Behavior at the Harvard School of Public Health, where he teaches graduate-level classes on the use of mass communications in health promotion. He is the author of over one thousand monographs, book chapters, and academic papers in the diverse fields of health promotion, criminal justice, and social psychology.

DR. DANIEL JOHN DERKSEN is an associate professor in the Department of Family and Community Medicine at the University of New Mexico Health Sciences Center in Albuquerque, New Mexico. Dr. Derksen is also the medical director of the Family Practice Center. He has worked in school-based adolescent clinics in inner-city Albuquerque. Dr. Derksen received his B.S. from the University of Arizona and his M.D. from the University of Arizona School of Medicine.

JANET DUTREY is Senior Program Associate for the Resolving Conflict Creatively Program (RCCP) and a leading national trainer in the program. She is a former bilingual teacher, counselor, and assistant principal, with over twenty years' experience in the field of education. Ms. Dutrey is an Ed.D. candidate in education leadership at the University of Northern Arizona.

MARGARET M. FEERICK is a doctoral student in the Department of Human

Development and Family Studies at Cornell University. Her current research includes the effects of child sexual abuse on gender development and on adult attachment. Ms. Feerick has been a junior high school teacher and a research assistant in a study of dually diagnosed patients. She received her B.A. in English and her M.A. in developmental psychology from Columbia University.

DR. JENNIFER C. FRIDAY, an (adjunct) assistant professor in the Department of Psychology at Morris Brown College, is a behavioral scientist at the National Center for Injury Prevention and Control, Centers for Disease Control, in Atlanta, Georgia. Dr. Friday also serves on the board of directors of the Rosalyn Carter Institute; as president-elect of the Southeastern Psychological Association; on the National Quality Caregiving Council; and on the Black Alumni Board of the University of Tennessee. She holds a B.A. from Millikin University and an M.A. and Ph.D. from the University of Tennessee.

DR. MARY HATWOOD FUTRELL is an associate professor and director of the Institute for Curriculum, Standards, and Technology in the School of Education and Human Development at George Washington University. She also serves as senior consultant and project director for the Quality Education for Minorities Network Teacher Leadership Corps, and as interim president of Education International—an organization that represents 20 million educators in approximately 150 countries. Dr. Futrell has received many awards—including seventeen honorary doctoral degrees—and has written and spoken extensively on a variety of educational issues. Dr. Futrell holds a bachelor's degree from Virginia State College and master's and doctoral degrees from George Washington University.

KEITH GEIGER, a high school mathematics and science teacher, is president of the National Education Association (NEA)—the nation's largest professional organization and labor union. He also co-chairs the Martin Luther King, Jr. National Education Committee; serves on the executive committees of Education International and the National Council for the Accreditation of Teacher Education; and serves on the National Board for Professional Teaching Standards. He earned his B.A. from Asbury College and his M.A. from Peabody College.

DR. WILLIAM GLASSER is a board-certified psychiatrist who is best known for his book *Reality Therapy*, a method of psychotherapy that can be applied to all human problems that is now taught all over the world. Early in his career, Dr. Glasser began to work in public schools; his thesis was that school failure was very destructive to the mental health of the child, as documented in his book *Schools Without Failure* (1969). Midway though his career, Dr. Glasser became involved with control theory and published a book on this topic in the early 1980s. In his subsequent books, *Control Theory in the Classroom*, *The Quality School: Managing Students Without Coercion*, *The Quality School Teacher*, and *The Control Theory*

Manager, Dr. Glasser emphasizes the importance of having a sound knowledge of control theory if we are to make meaningful changes not only in schools, but also in all other institutions.

IVAN B. GLUCKMAN is Director of Legal Services for the National Association of Secondary School Principals. As such, he provides information on legal matters of professional concern to NASSP members; legal advice to members on school law matters; and limited assistance to individuals on specific problems. Mr. Gluckman often writes and lectures on school law and related issues. He received his A.B. in philosophy from the University of Michigan and his LL.B. from Harvard Law School.

DR. JEFFREY J. HAUGAARD is assistant professor of Human Development and Family in the College of Human Ecology at Cornell University. His current research includes the development of families that adopt school-age children, and children's abilities as witnesses in legal proceedings; he teaches child, adolescent, and family psychopathology. Dr. Haugaard received his B.A. from the University of California, Santa Cruz; his M.A. in marriage, family, and child therapy from the Santa Clara University; and his Ph.D. in psychology from the University of Virginia.

DR. ALLAN M. HOFFMAN, an experienced administrator in education and health care, is Dean of the School of Health at California State University, Dominguez Hills. He has held academic appointments at several universities, as well as an executive-level leadership position at a large teaching hospital associated with the University of Southern California School of Medicine, where he currently holds the rank of Clinical Professor of Family Medicine. Dr. Hoffman has published numerous articles, been the editor of several books, and served on the editorial board of the *Journal of Allied Health.* He also served as a resource person on the Presidential Task Force on Healthcare Reform. He received his Ed.D. from Teachers College, Columbia University where he was named a Kellog Fellow. He holds national board certification as a health education specialist (CHES).

LINDA LANTIERI is a nationally known conflict-resolution educator, intergroup relations specialist, and a Fulbright Scholar. Currently, she serves as National Director of the Resolving Conflicts Creatively Program (RCCP) for Educators for Social Responsibility (ESR). RCCP is the largest school-based conflict resolution program in the country, serving over 120,000 students in three hundred schools. Ms. Lantieri cofounded and coordinated RCCP for the New York City Public Schools during 1985–93. She is a former teacher, assistant principal, and director of an alternative middle school in East Harlem.

DR. NEL NODDINGS is a Lee L. Jacks Professor of Child Education and Acting Dean of Education at Stanford University. Her areas of special interest are feminist ethics, moral education, and mathematical problem-solving. Dr. Noddings is past president of the national Philosophy of Education Society and president of the John Dewey Society. She was a Phi Beta Kappa Visiting Scholar for the year 1989-90. In addition to seven books—among them *Caring: A Feminine Approach to Ethics and Moral Education, Women and Evil, The Challenge to Care in Schools,* and *Educating for Intelligent Belief or Unbelief*—she is the author of more than one hundred articles and chapters on various topics. Dr. Noddings received her B.A. in math from Montclair State College, her M.A. in math from Rutgers University, and her Ph.D. in education from Stanford University.

DR. DEBORAH PROTHROW-STITH, a nationally recognized public health leader, is Assistant Dean for Government and Community Programs at the Harvard School of Public Health. She has applied and academic experience ranging from work in neighborhood clinics and inner-city hospitals to serving as a state commissioner of health. Dr. Prothrow-Stith trained in internal medicine at Boston City Hospital and is board certified in Massachusetts. She developed and wrote the first violence prevention curriculum for schools and co-wrote *Deadly Consequences*, the first book to present the public health perspective on violence to a mass audience. Dr. Prothrow-Stith has received numerous awards, including the Secretary of Health and Human Services Award in 1989. She holds a B.A. from Spelman College and an M.D. from Harvard Medical School.

SHER QUADAY is Director of Violence Prevention Programs at the Harvard School of Public Health, Office of Government and Community Programs. Her current research projects include the development of a model community violence-prevention program, *Peace by Piece*, and development and evaluation of a multimedia, community-based anti-handgun campaign. Ms. Quaday previously worked with the Harvard Injury Control Center; was staff assistant to U.S. Senator Kent Conrad of North Dakota; and worked as an outreach worker, program planner, and manager in community action agencies. She received her B.A. in journalism from the University of North Dakota.

ANN W. RICHARDS served as Governor of Texas from 1991 to 1995, during which time she made the fight against crime a priority. She also introduced site-based management to Texas schools, allowing parents, teachers, students, and principals to decide how best to make their schools succeed. Under her leadership, the dropout rate was cut in half, standardized test scores went up, and SAT scores reached their highest level in fourteen years. Governor Richards has had a lifetime of public service—as a teacher, a civil rights activist, Travis County (Texas) Commissioner, and Texas State Treasurer. She holds a bachelor's degree from Baylor University and a teaching certificate from the University of Texas.

DR. ROBERT L. SELMAN is professor of Education at the Harvard Graduate School of Education and professor in the Department of Psychiatry at the Harvard Medical School. At the Harvard Graduate School of Education, he is director of the Risk and Prevention Program for Human Development and Psychology. At the Harvard Medical School, Dr. Selman is co-chair of the Steering Committee of the Manville School of the Judge Baker Children's Center; the Manville School provides special educational and clinical services for children and academic training opportunities. He is the author of *The Growth of Interpersonal Understanding* and co-author of *Making a Friend in Youth*, as well as scores of articles on social development.

MELINDA SMITH is Executive Director of the New Mexico Center for Dispute Resolution; in that capacity, she has developed and implemented a range of youth mediation programs. She currently serves as co-chair of the board of the National Association for Community Mediation and is a former member of the Victim Offender Mediation Association. She has also served on the Community Justice Task Force for the National Institute for Dispute Resolution, during which time she received the 1993 Mary Parker Follett Award from the Society for Professionals in Dispute Resolution. She has written numerous articles, including the recent "Youth Mediation Guide for Youth Service and Community Mediation Practitioners." Ms. Smith holds an M.A. from the University of Michigan, Ann Arbor.

DR. VICTOR C. STRASBURGER is an associate professor in the Department of Pediatrics at the University of New Mexico Health Sciences Center in Albuquerque, New Mexico. He also serves as chief of the Division of Adolescent Medicine. Dr. Strasburger has written and lectured extensively on the effects of the media on American children and adolescents.

DR. RANDAL W. SUMMERS is an adjunct senior professor in the Schools of Business Administration and Health Care Administration at the University of La Verne, Burbank Center, California. He is also curriculum development specialist in the training and development department in the Business Services Division of Office Depot. Dr. Summers is a member of the American Society for Training and Development (Orange County, California) and a licensed psychologist in Alberta, Canada. He is a contributing author to *Violence in the Workplace* and *Total Quality Management in Higher Education*. Dr. Summers holds an M.S. degree in psychology and counseling from North Dakota State University and a doctoral degree in educational psychology from the University of Alberta (Canada).

YVONNE V. THAYER is Assistant Superintendent for Instructional Services in the Gloucester County Schools. Prior to joining the school system, Ms. Thayer worked for the Virginia Department of Education, where she directed leadership programs for school administrators and helped local schools learn about and implement total quality. Her recent publications include chapters in books on total quality for higher education and guidance counselors. Ms. Thayer is a doctoral candidate in adult education at Teachers College, Columbia University.

KENNETH S. TRUMP is Director of Safety and Security for the Parma (Ohio) City School District and Assistant Director of the Tri-City Task Force Comprehensive Gang Initiative. He is also an Adjunct Assistant Professor of Criminal Justice at Ashland University. Mr. Trump served over seven years with the Division of Safety and Security of the Cleveland Public Schools, where he designed and supervised the division's Youth Gang Unit. He writes for numerous publications and lectures nationally on school safety and gangs. He received his B.A. and M.P.A. from Cleveland State University.

S. D. VESTERMARK, JR. is a trained social scientist with a special interest in public policy. He helped establish the nationally recognized school security program in the Prince Georges County (Maryland) Public Schools, and served as Special Assistant for Security Policy for that system's superintendent. Mr. Vestermark has also served as a consultant to other public school systems; the U.S. Departments of Justice and Health, Education, and Welfare; and the International Association of Chiefs of Police. He is co-author of the only published text on school security: *Controlling Crime in the School: A Complete Security Handbook for Administrators*. He holds a B.A. from Swarthmore College and an M.A. from Harvard University.